DATE DUE

NOV 29 '72			
NOV 13 '96			

CONFLICT OR CONSENSUS
IN EARLY AMERICAN HISTORY

CONFLICT OR CONSENSUS

IN EARLY AMERICAN HISTORY

Edited with Introductions by

ALLEN F. DAVIS

HAROLD D. WOODMAN

UNIVERSITY OF MISSOURI

D. C. HEATH AND COMPANY

For Gregory and Paul

and Allan and David

PREFACE

The perceptive student quickly discovers that the names and dates, facts and figures which he learns from his textbook are subject to varying interpretations. Two historians dealing with the same period and with the same general material often come to very different conclusions about the meaning of the period. It is the controversy over differing interpretations of the past which helps to lend excitement to the study of history. This collection of readings has been designed to introduce the beginning student of American history to this controversial literature of interpretation.

One theme unites all the selections in the book: Has there been real conflict in American history between classes, sections, and interest groups, or has the story of the American past been primarily one of general agreement or consensus? This theme, expressed either explicitly or implicitly, may be found in virtually all major interpretations of our country's past. The problem—conflict or consensus—then is real and meaningful in any attempt to understand the American past and, indeed, in efforts to evaluate the contemporary American scene.

We have attempted to avoid presenting only two extreme positions on each problem raised. Such an either/or approach tends to force the student to see things as either black or white, or else to conclude that truth always lies somewhere in between. To avoid this we have in every case included more than two selections dealing with each problem and have attempted to illustrate subtle disagreements as well as extreme differences of opinion.

Our main concern has not been with historiography. The beginning student is not (and should not be) especially interested in the shifting interpretations of history, with revisions and re-revisions. He should rather be interested in learning what happened and why it happened, in learning how it is possible to examine the same evidence and then arrive at different conclusions. In this volume, therefore, we have concentrated not on the evolution of historical writing but on historical problems. We hope to leave the student with a heightened understanding of the problems of interpretation of the various periods in American history and also to provide the ammunition for thoughtful and spirited discussions. For those who wish to pursue any matter further, we have provided a brief, annotated bibliography at the end of each problem, and a more general bibliography at the end of the book.

The present two-volume edition of this book is an expanded version of the volume published in 1966 and is designed primarily for the two-semester college survey courses in American history. We have added seven new problems, but have maintained the same basic pattern of the one-volume edition. More advanced students, already familiar with the basic chronology of events in the American past, will find the book a useful introduction to one of the main controversies in present day historical writing.

Columbia, Missouri   Allen F. Davis
                                       Harold D. Woodman

ACKNOWLEDGMENTS

The editing of this book has put us in the debt of many. We wish to thank the various publishers and authors for permission to reprint copyrighted material. Former instructors in our introductory American history course at the University of Missouri will recognize many of the ideas in the book; we are grateful for their aid and recognize that in a real sense they have been collaborators. We would also like to thank the many teachers and students who have made useful comments on the one volume edition. Several of our colleagues at the University of Missouri have made useful suggestions from which we benefited: Richard S. Kirkendall, John Lankford, Stanley Johannesen, and Walter V. Scholes. We have also received invaluable aid from Thomas C. Barrow (Clark University), Robert L. Branyan and Lawrence H. Larsen (University of Missouri, Kansas City), Lyle W. Dorsett (University of Southern California), James F. Watts (City College of New York), Alonzo Hamby (Ohio University), John Burnham (Ohio State University), Stanley Lemons (Rhode Island State College) and James Chase (University of Texas). Needless to say, we alone are responsible for the finished product.

Finally, we want to express a special debt to our wives, Roberta Davis and Leonora Woodman, who offered aid and encouragement at every step in the preparation of this book.

CONTENTS

CONFLICT OR CONSENSUS
IN EARLY AMERICAN HISTORY

INTRODUCTION

"Everything is in a state of metamorphosis," observed the Roman philosopher-statesman, Marcus Aurelius, about eighteen hundred years ago. And historians before and since have attempted to chronicle and to explain the everlasting change in human lives and institutions.

Nowhere does the historian find change more manifest than when he studies the United States. In a twinkling of an eye a vast, scarcely populated continent was transformed into a major industrial power of phenomenal complexity. Overnight, virgin forests became fertile farms, Indian trails became roads, highways, and railroads, and empty spaces became bustling cities. Matching this transformation of the physical face of the continent were equally momentous changes in politics, social relations, ideas, and attitudes. For most Americans change was inevitable simply because it was so obvious. "Ten years in America are like a century in Spain," wrote the German immigrant Francis Lieber soon after his arrival in the United States early in the nineteenth century. "The United States really change in some respects more within ten years than a country like Spain has within a hundred."

Yet if change seemed faster and more continuous in America than it did in Europe, only the ignorant and the naive would find the Old World to be stable and unchanging. Indeed, time after time, Americans watched Europe swept by rebellion and war as one group after another sought to revolutionize their lives and institutions.

Generations of American historians have tried to describe and explain the vast alterations which have taken place on the North American continent. As they have done so, many have kept one eye on the changes in European institutions and have sought to compare and contrast the nature and quality of changes in the Old World with those in the New.

As a result, despite all the complexities and variations among historians, two rather distinct traditions have emerged in American historical writing. Both are based on an acceptance of change, and both seek an explanation for it. For one tradition, change is the result of relatively smooth and orderly progression—rapid, perhaps, but always evolutionary. For the other, change is the result of sharp, bitter, and often violent conflict—at times so rapid as to be revolutionary.

The first tradition stresses a uniqueness in the American experience by emphasizing a basic continuity in American history. While there were changes of great significance, they were gradual, exhibiting no sharp breaks with the past. Nor were there sharp differences within American society at any time. According to this tradition, all Americans of whatever class or station shared what was essentially a common outlook. To be sure, Americans did not all live alike nor did they always agree with one another. But their disagreements, especially when compared with the dissensions which divided European society, were not fundamental. Americans had achieved a consensus on fundamentals; if they disagreed, their disagreements were minor differences within this basic consensus.

The second tradition does not ignore the unique features of American history, but by emphasizing abrupt changes and sharp differences, it finds the American experience to be more consonant with European history than does the first tradition. This tradition speaks in terms of revolution and of class and sectional conflict. It stresses differences among Americans—class differences, social differences, political differences. Change was the result of conflict among different groups and classes in American society. And changes, when they came, were fundamental. Not consensus and continuity, but conflict and discontinuity comprise the central theme of this tradition.

In the selections which follow, the reader is introduced to these two traditions through the words of their most able exponents. The selections are not designed simply to give alternative explanations for events, but rather to present two very different ways of looking at American history. Were the remarkable changes in American history the result of orderly development—of evolution—or were these changes the result of bitter disputes and of momentous and abrupt breaks with the past—of revolution?

Is the story of the American past the story of CONSENSUS OR CONFLICT?

I ★
VIRGINIA ★
IN THE ★
SEVENTEENTH ★
CENTURY ★

In the spring of 1607, three small ships, the *Susan Constant,* the *Godspeed,* and the *Discovery,* sailed up Chesapeake Bay. In May, a small group of travel-weary colonists disembarked at what they thought was a suitable site and founded Jamestown, which was to be the first permanent English settlement in the New World. The venture was financed by the London Company, a joint stock enterprise backed by a group of London merchants. For the investors the goal was simple enough. They expected that their employees, the colonists, would earn for them a substantial return on their money. They envisioned profitable trade with the Indians, the discovery of precious metals, and the exploitation of rich natural resources. For other Englishmen and for the King who had granted the company its charter, there were other longer range goals as well. They spoke and wrote of enriching the kingdom, of breaking their dependence on other countries for necessary supplies and luxuries, of discovering a new and shorter passage to India, and of relieving population pressures at home.

But for the colonists, simple survival became the main concern. The Indians were a menace, not a market; precious metals were not to be found; and the climate and unfamiliar food brought disease and hardship. In an effort to save its investment, the company sent shipments of supplies and more food and instituted a harsh system of discipline among the colonists; but prosperity and profits did not result. The discovery in 1613 that tobacco grown in Virginia had a ready market in Europe held out the promise of prosperity but did not immediately solve the colony's problems. When it became apparent that the military-like rule would not accomplish its purpose, the company made a number of concessions in the hopes of stimulating incentive. It granted land to the colonists and gave them an opportunity to make some of the rules under which they lived and worked. In 1619 the Virginia settlers convened a popular assembly—the House of Burgesses—the first legislative assembly in the New World.

Despite concessions, profits remained elusive. Finally, in 1624, the Company was dissolved and Virginia became a royal colony. Although the Company had failed to achieve its main goal—profits for its investors—it had created a permanent colony and a set of institutions which would survive and prosper under royal domination. Private ownership of property, a legislative assembly, and a staple crop were all legacies of the Company rule, legacies which would profoundly influence the subsequent history of the colony.

The availability of land and the prospect of profits from tobacco growing drew many new colonists. By the middle of the seventeenth century Virginia boasted about 19,000 inhabitants; by the end of the century this number had swelled to over 58,000. Moderately wealthy men could buy large tracts of land relatively cheaply. Those who brought colonists, servants, and slaves to Virginia were granted headrights, warrants entitling them to land for each person imported. As a result, some colonists were able to acquire plantations of many hundreds or even thousands of acres. But it was not necessary to be rich to obtain land. The abundance of land made it inexpensive and in the early years grants were easily acquired. Profits from tobacco often made it possible for a small farmer to buy more land, expand his production, acquire servants or slaves, and join the ranks of the planters. Moreover, the House of Burgesses, which continued to meet after the Company lost its charter, provided a vehicle for self-government in the growing colony.

If the initial problems of survival had been overcome, other problems arose to plague the colonists. Success itself brought new difficulties. As tobacco production increased, prices on the world market tended to fall. At the same time, many planters found themselves facing rising costs of production. The rich land along the rivers on the coastal plain was soon taken up, and farmers settling land at a distance from the rivers and in the Piedmont area were forced to absorb additional transportation costs to get their tobacco to market. At the same time, the English government, eager to profit from the growth of its colony and intent on protecting its own merchants from competition, began to regulate the Virginia trade. Many Virginians felt that the Navigation Acts, which restricted the tobacco trade to England and forced planters to employ only English ships with English crews, imposed an added monopoly cost to the tobacco trade.

To these economic problems were added still other difficulties. Encroachment on Indian lands as farms were opened in the West posed the problem of adequate protection for the new settlers. This in turn was related to broader political differences within the colony. Westerners often complained that they were underrepresented in the assembly and that consequently their interests were not being protected by the colonial government. Easterners, they sometimes charged, were safe from the Indians and had adequate transportation facilities and therefore refused to support the needs of the Westerners. And, since the East dominated politically, the West was powerless.

Historians, viewing Virginia in the seventeenth century, often tend to emphasize one or another set of developments, thus coloring their overall assessment of the period. If stress is placed on widespread ownership of property and the development of popular government, the tendency is to depict a rather homogeneous population. Moreover, when to this emphasis is added the general opposition of Virginians to colonial restrictions, the resulting interpretation is one of unity and a consensus based on common experiences and common problems. On the other hand, when historians stress class differences based on the unequal distribution of land and political differences based on the unequal distribution of political power, the interpretation is one of conflict rather than consensus.

Samples of the varying approaches to seventeenth-century Virginia may be seen in the selections which follow. Each emphasizes a time of conflict, Bacon's

Rebellion, but interpretations are quite different despite superficial similarities. Thomas J. Wertenbaker, while recognizing East-West differences, gives major attention to the pernicious effects of the Navigation Acts which affected all Virginians. Curtis P. Nettels, however, finds the rebellion to be a class conflict arising from an unequal division of wealth in the colony. The Navigation Acts are important in his interpretation primarily because they emphasize class differences. Bernard Bailyn sees the period in a much different light. Conflicts and class differences are at the heart of his interpretation, but he sees them as essentially growing pains in the emergence of a new society. They mark the formation of an indigenous American society in the new world, a society marked by unique American configurations.

Obviously there were differences in wealth and power in seventeenth century Virginia. But the historian must decide how important these differences really were. Were conflicts merely minor differences within an essentially equalitarian society? Or were these conflicts more a reflection of profound class cleavages? Did fundamental differences with the mother country create unity in Virginia, a kind of united front which overrode minor internal differences? Or was the rhetoric of opposition to English restrictions merely a screen for conflict at home? Answers to these questions not only help in understanding Virginia in the seventeenth century, but, as will be seen, they provide a framework for viewing the Revolution in the eighteenth century.

The causes
of Bacon's
Rebellion

Thomas J. Wertenbaker

There were many who hailed the restoration of the monarchy as the dawn of an era of prosperity and happiness for Virginia. The colony, despite the efforts of some of its people, had remained loyal to the Crown until

From Thomas J. Wertenbaker, *Virginia Under the Stuarts*, 1607–1688, pp. 115-127, 130–140, 143–145. Reprinted by permission of Princeton University Press. Copyright, 1914, by Princeton University Press.

overpowered by force of arms. It might well expect especial favor and care from its prince, now that he was firmly established upon his throne. Of the ability and justice of the Governor Virginia had had ample experience during the ten years of his first administration.

Never was a people doomed to more bitter disappointment. The years which followed the Restoration were crowded with misfortunes greater than any that had befallen the colony since the ghastly days of the Great Sickness. Charles II, far from showing gratitude to his Old Dominion, overwhelmed it with injustice and oppression. The Virginians were crushed with tremendous duties on their tobacco and with ruinous restrictions upon their trade. The titles to their plantations were threatened by a grant of the entire colony to two unworthy favorites of the King. Governor Berkeley, embittered by the humiliation of the Commonwealth period, and growing avaricious and crabbed with advancing years, soon forfeited that respect and love which his former good conduct had gained him. His second administration was marred by partiality, oppression and inefficiency. The people were deprived of their right of suffrage by continued prorogation of the Assembly. Local government fell into the hands of small aristocratic cliques, while the poor were ground down with unequal and excessive taxes. Two wars with Holland added to the misfortunes of the colonists. Even the Heavens seemed to join with their enemies, for the country was visited by a terrific hurricane which swept over the plantations, destroying crops and wrecking houses. These accumulated misfortunes brought such deep suffering upon the colony that hundreds of families were reduced to poverty and many were forced into debt and ruin. No wonder that the commons, finally driven to desperation, should have risen in insurrection against the Governor and the King.

First among the causes of distress during this unhappy period must be placed the Navigation Acts. England, in the middle of the 17th century, was engaged in an unsuccessful contest with Holland for the carrying trade of the world. The merchantmen of Amsterdam and Flushing found their way even to Maryland and Virginia, where their low freight rates and the liberal prices they gave for tobacco, assured them a hearty welcome. The exports of the colonies to England itself were not infrequently carried in Dutch bottoms. This was a source of much anxiety and annoyance to the British government. It seemed unjust that the American colonies, which had been founded at such tremendous cost, should now prove as great a source of wealth to Holland as to the mother country. And it could not but anger the English shippers to find themselves elbowed by these foreigners in the ports of the Bermudas or the rivers of Virginia.

In 1651, the British Parliament, thinking it necessary to give their merchants some protection from this lively competition, passed the first of the Navigation Acts. Under its provisions no goods of the growth or manufacture of Asia, America or Africa should be introduced into England in any but English ships, of which the owner, master and three-fourths of the sailors were English subjects; and all foreign commodities imported to England should be conveyed directly thither from the place of growth or manufacture. This law injured the Virginians by excluding the Dutch carriers from the tobacco trade with England and thus causing a sharp rise in freight rates. During the early years of the Commonwealth period it was frequently avoided, but before 1660 the English government began to enforce it more strictly.

Nor did the people get relief with the restoration of the monarchy. Charles II proved more solicitous than Parliament for the welfare of the English merchants; even more indifferent to the complaints of the colonists. A new Navigation Act was passed in 1660 which struck a deadly blow at the prosperity of Virginia. Under its provisions all goods sent to the colonies, even though of foreign growth or manufacture, were to be exported from England, and all tobacco, sugar, wool, etc., produced in the colonies, must be shipped only to England or to her dominions.

Thus were the colonies sacrificed upon the altar of greed. The new act injured the Virginia planters in several ways. Since all their tobacco must now be brought to English ports, they could no longer seek the most advantageous markets. Had the demand for the commodity in England been more elastic, the consequences of this provision might not have been disastrous. Declining prices would have so stimulated the demand that the English could have consumed the entire crop. But the King's customs kept up the price to the consumer, and made it impossible for the merchants to dispose of the vast quantities of the leaf that had formerly gone to Holland and other countries. Moreover, the varieties sold to the Dutch were not popular in England, and could not be disposed of at any price. Soon the market became so glutted that the merchants refused to take more than half the crop, leaving the remainder to rot upon the hands of the planters.

There followed in Virginia a sharp decline in prices. The Dutch had given the colonists three pence a pound for their tobacco. A few years after the Restoration the planters considered themselves fortunate if they could dispose of their crops at a half penny a pound. Much was sold at a farthing. Now since tobacco was the staple product of Virginia and the main support of the people, this rapid decline in its value was disastrous. Frequent complaints were sent to England that the colonists could not maintain themselves and their families upon the meagre returns from their tobacco. "Twelve hundred pounds is the medium of men's yearly crops," wrote Secretary Ludwell in 1667, "and a half penny per pound is certainly the full medium of the price given for it." This made an average income for each planter of but fifty shillings. When the poor man had paid his taxes for the necessary support of the government, very little remained to him to clothe his wife and children. "So much too little," he adds, "that I can attribute it to nothing but the mercy of God, that he has not fallen into mutiny and confusion." In 1673 the Governor and the Council declared that the colony was full of indigent persons, who could barely support themselves with their utmost exertions.

Not only did the act of 1660 depress the price of tobacco, but it increased the already excessive freight rates. Since the bulk of the colonial exports had now to be brought directly to England, in English ships, the masters of Plymouth or London could double or triple their charges. Simultaneously there occurred a pronounced rise in the cost of manufactured goods. The far-famed skill of the Dutch workmen had made it possible for them to produce many articles more cheaply than the English, and to underbid them in their own colonies. But now that all foreign goods were excluded, the planters were forced to purchase the more expensive product of the English workshops.

Thus were the Virginians cut with a two-edged sword. At the very time that their incomes were being diminished, they were confronted by an increase in the cost of living. Nor could they, as Lord Baltimore declared they might, alleviate these evils by industry and thrift. For the more strenuous were their efforts to increase the tobacco crop, the greater would be the glut in the English market and the more disastrous the drop in prices.

The poor colonists found an able, but an unsuccessful advocate, in a London merchant named John Bland. "If the Hollanders," he wrote in a paper addressed to the King, "must not trade to Virginia how shall the Planters dispose of their Tobacco? The English will not buy it, for what the Hollander carried thence was a sort of Tobacco, not desired by any other people, . . . the Tobacco will not vend in England, the Hollanders will not fetch it from England; what must become thereof?" But Charles II, who knew little of economic matters, and cared nothing for the welfare of the colonists, ignored Bland's convincing appeal. No alleviation was given Virginia, and she was allowed to drift on through poverty and desperation to rebellion.

In a vain attempt to make the colony independent of the English manufacturers and to turn the people from the excessive planting of tobacco, the Assembly passed a series of acts designed to encourage local industrial establishments. It was especially desired that Virginia should make her own cloth, for the cost of the English fabrics was excessive. To stimulate the art of spinning and weaving the Assembly offered rewards for the best pieces of linen and woollen goods produced in the country. A bounty was placed on the manufacture of silk. In 1666, the establishment of cloth works in each county was made compulsory by act of Assembly. "Whereas," it was declared, "the present obstruction of trade and the nakedness of the country doe suffitiently evidence the necessity of provideing supply of our wants by improveing all meanes of raysing and promoteing manufactures amonge ourselves, . . . Be it enacted . . . that within two yeares at furthest . . . the commissioners of each county court shall provide and sett up a loome and weaver in each of the respective counties." Nor were other industries neglected. Tanhouses were erected in various places "to tanne, curry and make the hides of the country into leather and shoes." Bounties were offered for the construction of vessels, in the hope that Virginia might rival the prosperous ship-builders of New England.

These experiments added a heavy burden to the poor taxpayer, while they accomplished little for the relief of the colony. Virginia, with its scattered plantations and its lack of skilled artisans, could not hope to compete with the workshops of England. The commissioners, whether from corruption or from lack of ability, proved poor business managers, and their ill success occasioned loud and bitter complaints.

In May, 1661, Governor Berkeley sailed for England to combat a new design to revive the Virginia Company. It is quite probable that he took occasion during his stay at court to protest against the Navigation Acts. But he found it impossible to turn the King and Parliament from what had become their settled colonial policy. Ten years later, when the Lords of Trade and Plantations asked him what impediments there were to the improvement of trade in the colony, the Governor blurted out the truth with his accustomed vigor. "Mighty and destructive by that severe act of Parliament which excludes us from haveing any Commerce with any Nacon in Europe but our owne, Soe that wee cannot add to our plantacon any Comodity that growes out of itt . . . ffor it is not lawfull for us to carry a pipe-staff or a Bushel of Corne to any place in Europe out of the King's dominions. If this were for his Majesty's Service or the good of his Subjects wee should not repine what ever our Sufferings are for it. But on my Soule it is the Contrary for both."

In seeking relief from the evil consequences of the Navigation Acts the Virginians turned to their cousins of New England. And the hardy sailors of Massachusetts and Connecticut, tempted by the high prices of manu- factured goods in the southern colonies, brought their wares into the James, the York and the Potomac, where they entered into lively compe- tition with the English merchants. Nor did they hesitate, when occasion offered, to defy the law by transporting the Virginia tobacco to foreign markets. But England was unwilling to leave the colonists even this small loophole. Parliament decided, in 1672, to place a duty of one penny a pound upon tobacco shipped from one colony to another, and the pay- ment of this duty did not give liberty to the owners to transport it to a foreign country. This act completely crippled the intercolonial trade. A few years later, after Bacon's Rebellion, when the Virginia counties were presenting their grievances to the King's commissioners, the people of Lower Norfolk requested that the act of 1672 might be repealed. The only notice taken of their petition was the contemptuous comment of the commissioners that it was wholly mutinous for them "to desire a thing contrary to his Majesty's Royall pleasure & benefitt and also against an Act of Parliament."

It had been suggested, when the price of tobacco began to fall, that the evil might be remedied by governmental restraint upon the annual crop. The diminution of the demand for the leaf, brought about by the loss of the foreign market, was to be met by a corresponding limitation upon the supply. Prices would thus be restored and the planter would receive a greater return for a much smaller output. But for this remedy to be effective, it would be necessary to secure the coöperation of Maryland and perhaps North Carolina, as a cessation in Virginia would accomplish little, if no restraint were put upon the planters of the other colonies. Moreover, since the proposed step might diminish the revenue from the customs, it would be necessary to obtain the consent of the King.

In 1662 many of the planters and merchants petitioned Charles II to forbid the planting of tobacco in Maryland and Virginia for one year. At first this appeal was rejected and the colonists were commanded to refrain from presenting similar petitions in the future. Later, however, the Privy Council secured a reversal of this decision and an order was issued authorizing the Assembly to appoint commissioners to confer with the Marylanders upon the best means of lessening the excessive crops. Accordingly a meeting was held at Wiccocomico, May 12, 1664, which recommended that the planting of tobacco after the twentieth of June each year should be prohibited. The report met with the approval of the Virginians and was promptly ratified by the Assembly, but the Marylanders believed that a partial cessation would be detrimental to their interests and their legislature refused to give its consent.

But as prices sank lower and lower, and poverty became more general, the Virginians once more appealed to Maryland, this time for a total cessation for one year. Numerous letters were exchanged upon the subject, but at first nothing was accomplished. After many months had been consumed in useless negotiations Governor Berkeley, in the dead of winter, himself journeyed to Maryland and at last succeeded in convincing the leading men of that colony of the necessity of the measure. As a result, the Maryland Assembly passed an act prohibiting all tobacco planting in their province from February 1666 to February 1667, provided Virginia and North Carolina should do likewise. The Assembly at Jamestown promptly passed a similar law, but the North Carolinians, owing to Indian troubles, delayed their action so long that the Marylanders repudiated the entire agreement.

Somewhat discouraged the colonists again sent commissioners, this time to Saint Mary's, to resume the broken thread of negotiations. Here at last success seemed to crown their efforts, for all differences were adjusted, and the cessation was agreed upon by the three colonies. But the joy of

Virginia at this happy outcome was soon turned to grief and indignation, for the Marylanders received a letter from Lord Baltimore, "in absolute and princely terms prohibiting the execution of the . . . articles of cessation."

"This overtook us," wrote Governor Berkeley, "like a storm and enforced us like distressed marriners to throw our dear bought commodities into the sea, when we were in sight of our harbour, & with them so drown'd not only our present reliefs but all future hopes of being able to do ourselves good, whilst we are thus divided and enforced to steere by anothers compasse, whose needle is too often touched with particular interest. This unlimited and independent power . . . of the Lord Baltimore doth like an impetuous wind blow from us all those seasonable showers of your Majesty's Royall cares and favours, and leaves us, and his own province withering and decaying in distress and poverty. . . . This unreasonable and unfortunate prohibition . . . hath not only increased the discontent of many of the inhabitants of his province, but hath raised the grief and anger of allmost all your . . . subjects of this colony to such a height as required great care to prevent those disturbances which were like to arise from their eluded hopes and vain expences."

Can there be any doubt that the Navigation Acts and the futility of all attempts to escape their baleful effects, were largely instrumental in bringing on Bacon's Rebellion? As prosperity and contentment are the greatest safeguards of the public peace, so poverty, nakedness and distress are breeders of sedition. Philip Ludwell spoke of Bacon's army as "a Rabble of the basest sort of People; whose Condicion was such as by a chaunge could not admitt of worse." Had England been less selfish in her treatment of Virginia, there would not have been so many indigent men in the colony eager to join in this wild uprising against the government. Berkeley himself admitted, in 1673, that at least one third of the freemen had been rendered so desperate by poverty and debt that in times of foreign war their loyalty to England could not be relied upon.

But Charles II was indifferent to the welfare of these distant subjects and blind to their growing dissatisfaction. Just when the situation was most critical, he aroused their anger and grief to the highest pitch, by making a gift of the entire colony to Lord Culpeper and the Earl of Arlington. Previously he had granted that portion of Virginia which lies between the Potomac and the Rappahannock rivers, known as the Northern Neck, to Lord Hopton and several other noblemen. These patentees were to receive fees, remainders, reversions and escheats, and were given power to grant patents for all land that had not been taken up. This had caused the people of Virginia, and especially those residing in the Northern Neck, great uneasiness, and had proved a serious hindrance to the settling of that region. The Assembly, dreading the clash of jurisdiction which this grant made almost inevitable, had sent agents to England to persuade the King to annul the patent, or permit the purchase of the tract by the colony. While they were working to this end, there came the unexpected news that Arlington and Culpeper had received a grant of the entire colony. Without consulting in the least the desires of the people, Charles had given them over to two unscrupulous favorites, with the indifference he might have shown in presenting a necklace to his mistress. The colonists, "to their unspeakable griefe and Astonishment," felt now that they were "reduced to a far worse condition than that wherein they had adventured their lives and fortunes for the planting that Country under the Company."

The privileges and powers granted in this patent, had they ever been exercised by Arlington and Culpeper, would have rendered the government at Jamestown almost a nullity. The two lords were to receive all escheats, quit-rents, duties and reservations belonging to the Crown; they were given power to divide the territory into counties, hundreds and parishes; to erect churches and present ministers to them; to make manors, fairs, and markets; to appoint sheriffs, surveyors, and other important officers; to issue patents for land; to appropriate to their own use all arrears of "rents and other profits," accruing since the year 1669.

In great alarm the Virginia Assembly directed the agents in England to use their utmost endeavors to have this grant recalled. At the same time they drew up a statement of their objections to the patent, showing how unjust and ruinous were its provisions. It was in direct conflict with numerous royal concessions and patents, given them from time to time under the Great Seal. There was good reason to fear that the lords, by their deputies, might impose upon them new rents and services. They might demand new surveys and new patents for land which had long been occupied. They might, in fact, completely devastate the government of all its "just powers and authorities."

The agents, upon receiving these instructions, went to the Lords Patentees to request them to resign the most obnoxious of their new powers. In case they refused, the agents threatened to appeal at once to the King. Arlington and Culpeper received them courteously, and, after numerous delays, consented to relinquish the patent, provided Virginia would offer no objection to the passing of a new grant, assuring them the quit-rents and escheated property. The agents were well satisfied with this settlement, for it would relieve the colony of its fear of proprietary government, while the grant of the rents and escheats would impose little additional burden.

In order, however, to prevent the giving away of such disturbing powers in the future, they petitioned the King to grant "Letters Pattents for the incorporacon" of the colony. In this new charter they desired first that permission be given Virginia to purchase the Northern Neck. They next requested the King to promise that Virginia should have no other dependence than upon the Crown of England, "nor in the future be cantonized into parcells by grants made to particular persons." "And for the prevention of surreptitious grants" they desired his Majesty to promise in the charter that nothing should again pass concerning Virginia until a hearing had been given to some person impowered by the colony to represent their interests. Of even greater importance was their desire, "That there shall bee no Tax or Imposition layd on the people of Virginia, but by their owne Consente, and that Express'd by the Representatives in Assembly."

The whole matter came before the King in Council, June 23, 1675, and was referred to the judgment of Attorney-General William Jones and Solicitor-General Francis Winnington. In October these officers reported that in their opinion the patent of incorporation would be beneficial both to the colony and the King's service, and ought to be granted. Charles thereupon gave directions that the papers be drawn up for his signature. But here, for some unknown reason, the matter came to a halt. Several months passed and the patent had not been issued. At last, April 19, 1676, at the urgent request of the agents, his Majesty directed that the Lord Chancellor cause the papers to pass the Great Seal at once. But before this could be done, news came to England of Bacon's Rebellion, and the King immediately reversed his order. Later, other Letters Patent were granted, but they were very different from those sought by the agents, and contained little more than a bare declaration of the colony's direct dependence upon the Crown of England.

This unsatisfactory business caused great irritation among the colonists. The heavy expense of carrying on the negotiations in England "made them desperately uneasie, especially when, after a whole Year's Patience . . . they had no Encouragement from their Agents." A tax of fifty pounds of tobacco per poll, imposed for the purchase of the Northern Neck, aroused widespread dissatisfaction. In April, 1676, Governor Berkeley, fully conscious of the mutterings of revolution, was awaiting with anxiety the arrival of favorable news from the agents. "There are divers," he wrote, "that would fain persuade the people that al their high taxes will bring them no benefit, so that if the most advantageous terms had been proposed to us it would have been impossible to have persuaded the people to have parted with more tobacco til a more certain demonstration had been given them of what is already done. I appeased two mutinies this last year raysed by some secret villaines that whispered amongst the people that there was nothing intended by the fifty pounds levy but the enriching of some few people." In 1677, after Bacon's Rebellion, the King's commissioners heard from all sides that the imposition of this tax was one of the main causes of discontent.

The wars of 1664 and 1672 with Holland added much to the distress in Virginia. The bold Dutch mariners, angered at the injury done them by the Navigation Acts, preyed upon the English merchantmen in every sea. Woe to the tobacco ship that encountered a hostile privateer, in its journey across the Atlantic! The English vessels were not safe even in the Virginia rivers, under the guns of their forts. Twice the daring Dutch came through the capes and into the James River itself, where they wrought great damage to the shipping.

Great as was the distress caused by the depredations of the Dutch, the planters suffered even more during these wars by the stagnation of trade. The great risk incurred in crossing the ocean necessarily brought an increase both in freight rates and in the cost of manufactured goods. In 1667 the Governor and Council declared that the planters were "inforced to pay 12 pounds to £17 per ton freight" on their tobacco, "which usually was but at seven pounds." Conditions were even worse during the second war. 1673 Berkeley complained that the number of vessels that dared come to Virginia was so small, that they had "not brought goods and tools enough for one part of five of the people to go on with their necessary labor." "And those few goods that are brought," he added "have Soe few (and these hard Dealing) Sellers and Soe many Indigent and necessitous buyors that the Poore Planter gets not the fourth part . . . for his tobacco which he usually has had in other times."

In this period, so full of suffering and misfortune, the year 1667 was especially noteworthy for its long series of disasters. In November Secretary Thomas Ludwell wrote Lord Berkeley, "This poore Country . . . is now reduced to a very miserable Condicon by a continuall course of misfortune. In Aprill . . . we had a most prodigeous Storme of haile, many of them as bigg as Turkey Eggs, which destroyed most of our younge Mast and Cattell. On the fifth of June following came the Dutch upon us, and did soe much mischiefe that we shall never recover our reputations. . . . They were not gone before it fell to raineing and continued for 40 dayes together, which Spoiled much of what the haile had left of our English Graine. But on the 27th of August followed the most Dreadful Hurry Cane that ever the colony groaned under. It lasted 24 hours, began at North East and went round northerly till it came to west and soe on till it came to South East where it ceased. It was accompanied with a most violent raine, but no Thunder. The night of it was the most Dismall tyme that ever I knew or heard off, for the wind and rain raised soe Confused a noise, mixt with the continuall Cracks of falling houses. . . . The waves (were) impetuously beaten against the Shoares and by that violence forced and as it were crowded up into all Creeks, Rivers, and bayes to that prodigeous height that it hazarded the drownding many people who lived not in sight of the Rivers, yet were then forced to climbe to the topp of their houses to keep them selves above water. (The waves) carried all the foundation of the fort at point Comfort into the River and most of our Timber which was very chargably brought thither to perfect it. Had it been finished and a garison in it, they had been Stormed by such an enemy as noe power but Gods can restraine. . . . Had the Lightning accompanied it we could have beleeved nothing else from such a confusion but that all the elements were at Strife, which of them should doe most towards the reduction of the creation into a Second Chaos. It was wonderful to consider the contrary effects of that Storme, for it blew some shipps from their Anchors and carryed them safe over shelves of Sand where a wherry could Difficultly passe, and yet knockt out the bottome of a ship . . . in eight foot water more than she drew. But when the morning came and the Sun risen it would have comforted us after such a night had it not lighted us to ye Ruines of our plantations, of which I thinke not one escaped. The nearest computation is at least 10,000 houses blowne downe, all the Indian Graine laid flatt upon the ground, all the Tobacco in the fields torne to pieces and most of that which was in the houses perished with them. The fences about the Corne fields (were) either blown down or beaten to the ground by trees which fell upon them & before the owners could repair them the hoggs & Cattell gott in and in most places devoured much of what the Storme had left."

In the midst of the second Dutch war came another scourge no less distressing than the great hurricane. Throughout the 17th century cattle raising was one of the most important industries of the small Virginia proprietors. No planter, however insignificant his holdings, was without his cow and his calf. They constituted a most important portion of his wealth, and an indispensable source of support. In the winter of 1672-3 occurred an epidemic which destroyed more than half the cattle of Virginia. The mortality was increased by the cold, which was unusually severe. Many men, in an effort to preserve the poor beasts, gave them all their corn and thus brought hunger upon themselves. Before relief came with the spring, fifty thousand cattle had perished.

Perhaps the people of Virginia might have borne patiently all these misfortunes, had their Governor ruled them with wisdom and justice. Certain it is they would never have turned in wild anger to strike down his government, had that government not done much to make their condition intolerable. Sir William Berkeley was accused of destroying the representative character of the Assembly, of initiating a notorious spoils system, of intimidating Burgesses, of winking at embezzlement of public funds. And, although most of these charges were brought by the Governor's bitter enemies, some of them were undoubtedly true.

In Virginia, during this period, the commons could guard their interests only by means of the House of Burgesses. All other organs of government were controlled by Berkeley and his friends. The people had no voice in the selection of vestrymen, or sheriffs, or justices of the peace, and no control over their actions. The Council was entirely submissive to the Governor's will. Its members not only held their seats at Sir

William's pleasure, but were the recipients of numerous other favors that bound them closely to his interest. Thus in the executive, in all branches of the judiciary, and in the upper house of Assembly the Governor was all-powerful.

If then he could control the Burgesses and make them subservient to his desires, he would remove the only obstacle to almost complete despotism. Nor was it a matter of very great difficulty for him to gain a mastery of the House. In every county he could nominate government candidates, and exert tremendous pressure to secure their election. If necessary, they might be seated by fraud at the polls or false returns by the sheriff. "It is true," Bacon declared, "that the people's hopes of redemption did ly in the Assembly, as their Trusts, and Sanctuary to fly to, but I would have all men consider first how poore people are debarred of their fair election, the great men in many places haveing the Country in their debte and consequently in their aw. Secondly how meanly we are provided of men of Learning, ability and courage, nay indeed of honesty, to stand up in the people's behalf and oppose the oppressing party."

And if ever, despite these difficulties, the candidates of the people were elected, the Governor might still win their support in the House, by a judicious use of the patronage. He controlled enough offices of honor and profit to reward richly his friends in the Assembly. If the Burgess was careful never to thwart the wishes of the Governor, or to vote against his measures, he might reasonably expect a collectorship, a sheriff's place, a commission in the militia, or possibly a seat in the Council. A large percentage of the members of the House were office-holders.

If half the charges brought against Berkeley are to be believed, he was guilty of instituting a system of political corruption as effective as that maintained in France by Guizot during the reign of Louis Philippe. He has assumed to himself, it was declared, "the sole nominating, appointing and commissionating of all . . . officers both civil and military amongst us . . . (they) being . . . (the better to increase . . . his party) multiplied to a greate number. . . . All which offices he bestowed on such persons (how unfitt or unskillfull soever) as he conceived would be most for his designs. And that the more firmly to binde and oblige them thereunto and allure others to his party, he . . . permitted or connived at the persons soe commissionated by him . . . unwarrantably . . . to lay and impose what levies and imposicons upon us they should or did please, which they would often extort from us by force and violence, and which for the most part they converted to their owne private lucre and gaine. And . . . Sir William Berkeley, haveing by these wayes and meanes, and by takeing upon him contrary to law the granting collectors places, sherifs, and other offices of profitt to whome he best pleased, he soe gained uppon and obliged all the greatest number of the men of parts and estates in the whole country (out of which it was necessary our representatives and

Burgesses should be elected) hath there by soe fortifyed his power over us, as of himselfe without respect to our laws, to doe what soever he best pleased, and from time to time . . . to gaine and procure great quantities of Tobacco and mony from us to his proper use over and besides the Thousand pounds yearly salary . . . and over and besides the fees, profitts and per quisites to the place of Governour belonging."

Bacon himself declared, in justification of his rebellion, that oppression and injustice were rife in the colony, and that it was useless to appeal to the Assembly for redress. "The poverty of the Country is such," he said, "that all the power and sway is got into the hands of the rich, who by extortious advantages, having the common people in their debt, have always curbed and oppressed them in all manner of wayes." The poor, he declared, were kept in such perpetual bondage that it was not possible for labor or industry to extricate them. The great men of the colony had brought misery and ruin upon the common people by perverting all equity and right. The perpetual breach of laws, remiss prosecutions, excuses and evasions, but too plainly attested that things were carried by the men at the helm, "as if it were but to play a booty, game or divide a spoile." "Now consider," he adds, "what hope there is of redress in appealing to the very persons our complaints do accuse."

And when once the Governor had obtained a House that was subservient to his will, he might, by his power of prorogation, continue it indefinitely. During the years from the Restoration to Bacon's Rebellion, there were not more than two general elections, and probably only one—that of 1661. Under these circumstances the Assembly could no longer be said to represent the voters of the colony. The Burgesses might defy or betray the people as they chose, they could not be made to answer at the polls for their misconduct. And there is ample proof that this Long Assembly attended more to the commands of the Governor than to the wishes of electors that could no longer elect. Even Sir William's best friends admitted that his authority in Virginia was almost despotic. Secretary Thomas Ludwell, writing in 1666, declared that the Governor was "the sole author of the most substantial part" of the government, "either for Lawes or other inferior institutions." "Our representatives," complained the Charles City commons eleven years later "(of which for this county in nine yeares time last past there hath been a verry doubtful election as we conceive) have been overswayed by the power and prevalency of . . . Sir Wm. Berkeley and his councell, divers instances of which wee conceive might be given, and have neglected our grievances made knowne to them."

That this overthrow of representative government in the colony and the substitution of the Governor's despotic sway contributed greatly to the anger and desperation of the people, there can be no doubt. The evidence comes not only from the rebels and from the county grievances, but from disinterested persons, and even Berkeley's friends. "Whatever palliations," wrote Governor Thomas Notley, of Maryland, in 1677, "the grate men of Virginia may use at the Councell board in England, . . . yett you may be sure . . . much . . . if not every tittle" of the accusations against them are true. "If the ould Course be taken and Coll: Jeoffreys build his proceedings upon the ould ffoundation, its neither him nor all his Majesties Souldiers in Virginia, will either satisfye or Rule those people. They have been strangely dealt with by their former Magistracy." William Sherwood, if we may believe his own statement, forfeited Sir William's favor by reporting in England that "the general cry of the country was against ye Governour." And "it is most true," he added, "that the great oppressions & abuse of ye people by ye Governours arbitrary will hath been ye cause of the late troubles here."

The illegitimate influence of Berkeley over the Assembly was the more galling to the people inasmuch as they had no voice in local government. The justices of the peace, who exercised the most important powers in the counties, received their commissions, not by popular election, but by executive appointment. And the Governor, although often influenced in his selections by the advice of the Council, gave little heed to the wishes of the commons. His appointees were invariably men of means and influence, and could be relied upon to uphold the interests of the aristocracy and the Governor.

The justices were members of the county courts, and as such exercised judicial, executive and legislative functions in local affairs. The courts met every second month, and were empowered to settle cases involving not more than ten pounds sterling. Individual justices could "try and determine any cause to the value of twenty shillings or two hundred pounds of tobacco." Far more important was the power of the courts to impose direct taxes. The county levy was usually very heavy. In fact, during the Restoration period, it often exceeded the public levy voted by the Assembly. In Lower Norfolk county, during the years from 1666 to 1683, the local assessment amounted to 188,809 pounds of tobacco. This sum seems to us now almost insignificant, but it proved a very real burden to the indigent freemen of that unhappy period. Yet perhaps the people would not have complained had the assessments been voted by a body elected by themselves or representative of their interests. They were bitterly angered, however, that they should be taxed without their own consent and against their wishes, by appointees of the Governor; and the sense of wrong was aggravated by the fact that the taxes were often voted by the courts in secret session, not without grave suspicions of abuses and fraud. "It has been the custome," it was declared in the Surry grievances, "of the County Courts att the laying of the levy to withdraw into a private Roome by which the poor people not knowing for what they paid their levy did allways admire how their taxes could be so high." "Wee desire," declared the people of the Isle of Wight, "to know for what wee doe pay our Leavies everie year and that it may noe more be layd in private." From Charles City came the most startling charges of fraud and oppression. "The Commisoners or Justices of peace of this county," it was declared, "heretofore have illegally and unwarrantably taken upon them without our consent from time to time to impose, rayse, assess and levy what taxes, levies and imposicons upon us they have at any time thought good or best liked, great part of which they have converted to theire own use, as in bearing their expense at the ordinary, allowing themselves wages for severall businesses which ex officio they ought to do, and other wayes, as by account of the same on the booke for levies may appeare."

The people were even deprived, during Berkeley's second administration, of the right of electing the vestries. These bodies had always been composed of the foremost men in each parish. At this period they succeeded in shaking off entirely the control of the commons by themselves filling all vacancies in their ranks. Since they exercised the power of imposing a tax to pay the ministers' salaries and meet other obligations of the parishes, this attempt to make themselves self-perpetuating was a matter of no little importance. The people expressed their disapproval in the most emphatic terms, and after Bacon's Rebellion requests came from many counties that the vestrymen might be chosen, as formerly, by the whole body of parishioners.

The unjust poll-tax, which was then used in the public, county and parish levies, was an unending source of discontent. There can be no doubt that it bore with too great weight upon the poor people. "They complain," wrote Gyles Bland, on the eve of the Rebellion, "that great Taxes are imposed upon them every yeare, by wayes very unequall. Laying them very heavily, by the Poll, whereby the Poorer sort are in the hardest Condition." It must be remembered, however, that many of the servants and slaves were listed as tithables, or persons subject to the poll tax. This of course tended to increase the share of the wealthy. Yet the inequality was very real and the burden upon the poor very heavy. The number of tithables assessed of a man was by no means an accurate gage of his wealth. Later in the century, with the great influx of negro slaves, the burden upon the rich planters increased and became more nearly proportionate to their ability to pay.

Bland suggested that all inequality might be eliminated by adopting a land-tax. "Which," he said, "seems to be the most equal imposition and will generally take off the complaint of the people, although perhaps some of the richest sort will not like it, who hold greater proportions of land than they actually plant." The King's commissioners also thought the land tax just, but considered it "impracticable there." When the people of Warwick county asked, "That all persons may be rated and taxed according to their Estates," the commissioners reported that this was "a thing to be wish'd but never to be granted them." If the King should command it, they knew not how it would be relished by the landed men, since the common usage had been always taxing by poll.

The universal discontent was still further increased by the wasteful and lax use of public funds. The money which was wrung from the poor people by these unequal taxes, was seldom wisely or economically expended. Much was squandered upon foolish projects, costly in the extreme, and impossible of accomplishment. . . .

It would not be just to give credence to all the accusations made against Berkeley. The King's commissioners who conducted the investigation into his conduct, were his enemies; while many of the charges were brought by those who had taken part in the Rebellion. Thus the testimony against him is in most cases distinctly partisan. Moreover those that were closely associated with Sir William often expressed extravagant admiration for his ability and energy, and love for his character. "He hath," wrote the Council in 1673, "for neare 30 years governed this colony with that prudence and justice which hath gained him both love and reverence from all the Inhabitants here."

Singularly enough Berkeley seems to have prided himself upon his ability as a ruler. He never forgot the compliment paid him by the people in 1660, when they insisted, even against his will, upon making him their Governor. And long after he had forfeited their confidence and esteem he imagined himself as popular as in his first administration. It was a bitter blow to his pride when the commons rose against his government in 1676. His proclamations bear testimony to his pain that the youthful Bacon should have usurped his place in the affections of the people. His letter to the King asking to be recalled from his government was undoubtedly dictated by wounded pride. Upon the eve of his final departure for England he did not scruple to write Colonel Jeffreys, "I will confesse to you that I beleeve that the Inhabitants of this Colony will quickly find a difference between your management and mine."

It would be difficult to reconcile this attitude of mind with Berkeley's oppressive administration, did we not know his views upon governmental matters. He had never been in sympathy with republican institutions. It was the height of folly, he thought, to allow the people to participate either in administrative or legislative affairs. The King alone should rule; the people's duty was to obey. It was but five years before the Rebellion that he wrote to the Lords of Trade and Plantations, "I thanke God there is noe ffree schooles nor printing (in Virginia) and I hope wee shall not have these hundred yeares, for learning has brought disobedience & heresaye and sects into the world and printing has divulged them, and libells against the best Government: God keepe us from both." A man that could utter such sentiments as these would not scruple to throttle, if he could, all representative institutions in his government. If he intimidated voters and corrupted the Burgesses, it was perhaps because he thought himself justified in any measures that would render the Governor, the King's substitute, supreme in the government.

But whatever is the verdict of posterity upon the conduct and motives of Sir William Berkeley, the causes of the Rebellion stand out with great clearness:—England's selfish commercial policy, the Culpeper-Arlington grant, the Dutch wars, storms and pestilence, inefficient if not corrupt government, excessive taxes. The only wonder is that the insurrection did not occur earlier. In fact two mutinies did break out in 1674, when the excessively heavy taxes of that year were announced, but the rebels lacked leaders and were suppressed without great difficulty. As early as 1673 the defection of the planters was so great that it was feared many might attempt to deliver the colony into the hands of the Dutch. Berkeley wrote that a large part of the people were so desperately poor that they might reasonably be expected upon any small advantage of the enemy to "revolt to them in hopes of bettering their Condition by Shareing the Plunder of the Country with them." A certain John Knight reported "that the planters there doe generally desire a trade with the Dutch and all other nations and would not be singly bound to the trade of England, and speake openly there that they are in the nature of slaves, soe that the hearts of the greatest part of them are taken away from his Majesty." Thus the down-trodden planters, alienated from England, angered at the Governor, even distrusting their own Assembly, waited but an occasion and a leader to rise in open rebellion. A new Indian war offered the occasion, and they found their leader in young Nathaniel Bacon.

Social conflicts in the seventeenth century

Curtis P. Nettels

Despite the diversity and fluidity of early colonial society two dominant classes emerged during the seventeenth century—the aristocracy of wealthy landowners and merchants and the democracy of the small

From: *The Roots of American Civilization, A History of American Colonial Life* by Curtis P. Nettels. Copyright, 1938, by F. S. Crofts & Co., Inc.; Reprinted by permission of Appleton-Century-Crofts.

yeoman farmers. And in spite of the ideals of individual improvement entertained by members of the latter class they were not averse to united action in their struggle for social betterment. At many points, however, the democracy found the way to advancement blocked by the influence of the upper class. In consequence there ensued a series of social conflicts between the hostile forces—conflicts common to all the colonies because the underlying causes were present throughout the whole settled area. Assuming various forms of expression and flaring up intermittently in different localities, these conflicts exhibited one major issue: who should control the land and the products it yielded to the labor of the settlers?

With the growth of settlement along most of the seacoast there appeared a uniform tendency for a small group of wealthy men to acquire large landholdings worked by servants, tenants, or slaves. The temporary efficiency of larger producing units gradually forced the smaller farmers in the oldest areas to fall behind in the competitive struggle. If they sold their farms to the landed magnates or lost them through foreclosure proceedings, the trend toward larger holdings was accelerated. In the interior, however, lay vast stretches of virgin land to which the dispossessed farmers or the propertyless freedmen might repair for a new start. But even here they did not escape the influence of the magnates. The property and enterprise of men of wealth in the seaboard areas yielded increasing profits which demanded fresh fields of investment—and one such outlet was found in the financing of settlers in new areas.

Due to the cheapness of land it was usually easy for the poor freedman to acquire fifty acres of back country, but he generally lacked tools, seed, and livestock, and these he was obliged to purchase on credit. Two kinds of loans were available. The wealthy planters engaged in lending money on fairly long terms, while the merchants of the seacoast supplied imported goods on short-term credit. Now, one peculiar characteristic of the early land system in the colonies was the freedom with which land might be transferred—sold, bequeathed, divided, or taken in payment of every species of debt. Hence the colonial creditors, both merchants and planters, could safely give credit on land security, knowing that the improvements made by the farmer would augment its value and thus provide an increasingly ample guarantee to creditors, should it be necessary for them to foreclose in order to collect existing debts.

In this situation the farmer often found himself at a disadvantage. His debts, which were registered at a fixed sum in pounds, shillings, and pence, had to be paid in farm produce, which was valued at its current market price whenever payments were made. Thus if the price of such produce declined abruptly the farmer might have to deliver all his surplus to his creditor in order to discharge his debts. When this occurred in his dealings with a merchant, the farmer would be obliged to seek a new loan for the purchase of the year's supply of store goods and depend upon the next crop to pay the obligation. This meant that he again had to deliver his surplus produce to his creditor—a circumstance which placed him at a further disadvantage in that he had only one marketing outlet: his creditor was not forced to bid against competitive buyers; hence the complaint of low prices of farm products that were delivered to creditors. And when the farmer became hopelessly involved in debt he might lose his land by foreclosure, thus adding to the holdings of the wealthy class and extending into new areas the trend toward concentrated ownership. In this manner the farmer came to feel that the wealthy merchants and planters were his enemies in a contest for land titles and in a struggle over the prices of farm produce and laws affecting currency and debts.

A second series of social conflicts involved the colonial aristocracy in controversies with groups in England. Just as the colonial merchants became competitors of English merchants, so also the landed aristocracy opposed both the English laws which regulated trade and the claims of the proprietors of Maryland, Pennsylvania, and the Carolinas who held the immediate title to lands desired by the colonial magnates. Since the English merchants and the great proprietors generally had the support of the English government, the colonial aristocracy was impelled to resist imperial control. In the ensuing strife the planters could count upon the aid of the small farmers, who also opposed England's trade regulations, who also disliked to pay quit-rents to the proprietors, and who also desired to acquire proprietary lands. On the other hand, in their conflicts with the small farmers as debtors, the planters and merchants received the support of the English government, always a staunch defender of creditor rights. The strategy of the colonial aristocracy, therefore, was to use the yeoman farmers in opposition to English merchants and proprietors and to depend upon the English government for protection against measures demanded by the yeomen for their relief as a debtor class.

Cleavage in Virginia

Of all the early conflicts between the small farmers and the upper class the most critical contest occurred in Virginia in 1675–76, by which time the social stratification of the colony had become well marked. The planter class had evolved in response to many circumstances. During the Civil War and the Puritan regime in England many moderately well-to-do partisans of Charles I had migrated to Virginia. Although they were called Cavaliers they were not aristocrats but, rather, substantial members of the English middle class. They invested their money chiefly in tobacco lands and in the fur trade—and at an auspicious time. During the years 1640–60 Virginia enjoyed the benefit of free trade with foreign countries and prospered through relatively high prices of tobacco and furs. Such prosperity prompted the Dutch merchants to extend credit to the planters whereby they might purchase additional lands and servants. Two results followed. The most successful planters enlarged their land-holdings in the tidewater area while at the same time a large host of workers completed their terms of servitude and became freedmen. From the profits of tobacco and the fur trade the planters were able to make loans to such freedmen when they acquired small farms on the frontiers.

As a result of the Navigation Acts of 1660 and 1663 and the forcible exclusion of Dutch merchants from the tobacco trade an acute depression fell upon Virginia after 1660, when the planters were required to ship their products directly to England and to depend solely upon English shipping, which was not yet sufficient for their needs. One critic of England's policy wrote: "If the Hollanders must not trade to Virginia how shall the planters dispose of their tobacco? The English will not buy it, for what the Hollander carried thence was a sort of tobacco, not desired by any other people. . . . The tobacco will not vend in England, the Hollanders will not fetch it from England; what must become thereof?" Moreover, the Second Anglo-Dutch War dealt a severe blow to Virginia's trade: in 1667 Dutch warships in Chesapeake Bay captured twenty vessels of the English tobacco fleet. Reduced shipping and wartime risks boosted freight rates from the normal figure of £7 a ton of tobacco to charges ranging from £12 to £17 a ton—and this added cost had to be paid indirectly from the planters' profits. As markets contracted, the price of tobacco in the colony fell to a half-penny a pound—a return that did not yield the cost of production to the interior farmers. The secretary of the province in 1667 estimated the yearly income from the crop of the average settler as only fifty shillings—"which, when the taxes . . . shall be deducted, is very little to a poor man who hath perhaps a wife and children to clothe and other necessities to buy." Everywhere the shortage of imported goods was so extreme that the observers spoke hyperbolically of "the nakedness of the country."

A brief respite followed the Second Dutch War, only to be succeeded by another spell of hard times during the Third Dutch War of 1672–74. In the winter of 1672–73 an epidemic carried off half the cattle of Virginia —a loss of fifty thousand head before the spring brought relief. Once more the Dutch attacked the English tobacco fleet in the Chesapeake and in 1673 captured nine ships at the mouth of the James River. Vessels coming from England were so few that they brought goods and tools sufficient for only one planter in five; tobacco prices fell to a quarter of what they had been in "normal" times; and the colony seemed filled with "indigent persons who could barely support themselves with their utmost exertions."

This protracted depression further strengthened the wealthy planters at the expense of the poor farmers. As it became necessary to cut the cost of production the planter who had large landholdings and ample credit in England could buy additional servants or slaves, enlarge the scale of his business and reduce the unit cost of production. Menaced by the competition of the larger plantations (which enjoyed another advantage in their superior location for trade), the poor farmer found himself relentlessly squeezed by the necessity of paying fixed debts from sadly depleted income. "The poverty of the country," said Nathaniel Bacon in 1675, "is such that all the power and sway is got into the hands of the rich, who by extortious advantages, having the common people in their debt, have always curbed and oppressed them in all manner of ways."

The desperation of the small farmers led them to demand relief. But the peaceable channels of political action were closed, since the government of Virginia was completely in control of the upper class. The governor, Sir William Berkeley—an inflexible aristocrat, irascible, imperious, and arbitrary—was determined to rule the "rabble" with a firm hand, convinced that toil, ignorance, and subservience were the proper attributes of the common people. The large planters and merchants, allied with Berkeley, held all the offices in his executive council, which they used to secure personal land grants and to exempt themselves from taxes. Even the House of Burgesses, supposed to represent all the freemen, had become a satellite of the aristocracy. It is probable that between 1661 and 1676 no election of members of the lower house had been held, and it is certain that there was not more than one election, so that the burgesses serving in 1676 were ten or fifteen years removed from a popular mandate. A majority of them had become mere henchmen of the governor, who had secured their compliance by virtue of his power to grant land and to appoint revenue collectors, sheriffs, and officers of the county militia. Accordingly, all agencies of local government, both executive and judicial, were completely dominated by the governor's party. In 1670 the aristocracy enacted a law which denied the ballot to every resident who was not a freeholder.

Similarly the financial system of the colony was honeycombed with favoritism and privilege. Since 1619 the principal revenues for the support of government had been derived from poll taxes levied upon freemen, servants, and slaves. Although the large planters had to pay the taxes for their servants and slaves, the small farmers considered the poll levy unjust and preferred instead a land tax, since the inequalities in land ownership were much more marked than differences in tax payments determined on the poll basis. Moreover, land taxes would have prevented the engrossing of large estates by the planters for speculative purposes and would therefore have opened such holdings to the poor settlers—a consideration which induced the aristocracy to support the poll tax at all costs. Another grievance of the small farmers grew out of the power of the justices of the peace (representatives of the aristocracy) to impose direct levies without any semblance of the consent of the taxpayers.

Moreover, the justices, meeting every second month, composed the county courts, which decided all cases involving less than £10 sterling; hence the poor farmers felt that in disputes with the aristocracy the county courts were merely its champions. Finally, the yeomen charged that the governor's party used public funds to line the pockets of its members and sycophants, so that the colony derived little benefit from taxes levied for fortifications, the construction of buildings at Jamestown, and the encouragement of domestic manufactures.

When to the other woes of the interior farmers was added the distress of a destructive Indian war their plight became unbearable. In 1675 a raid of the Senecas from the north drove into western Virginia a band of Susquehannocks, who upset the existing balance between settler and Indian on the frontier. Preliminary quarrels and skirmishes in the summer of 1675 finally evoked a general massacre which cost the lives of more settlers than any Indian outbreak of the preceding fifty years. When the farmers appealed to the governor for aid they met a disappointing response. Berkeley and his friends at the time had a virtual monopoly of the western fur trade which they were loath to endanger by harsh measures against the Indians, while their practice of equipping the red men with powder, guns, and shot had been responsible for much of the bloodshed of the frontier war. In January 1676 Berkeley did assemble a military force, only to disband it when he feared that disaffected farmers, once armed, might turn upon the government. Thereafter he favored defensive measures, particularly the building of forts at the falls of the main rivers. This policy did not appease the harassed frontiersmen, who favored vigorous offensive raids into the Indian country and charged that the forts "were a design of the grandees to engross all their [the settlers'] tobacco in their own hands." Meanwhile the governor even refused to issue to frontier officers commissions authorizing them to wage, independently, an offensive war.

Such was the setting when Nathaniel Bacon, a young Englishman who had lived in the colony less than two years, assumed the leadership of the disaffected farmers. As a member of the governor's council Bacon had become contemptuous of Berkeley's defense policy, particularly after the Indians had attacked Bacon's own frontier plantation in Henrico County and killed its overseer. His independent spirit prompted him to organize a force of volunteer frontiersmen and to lead them in vigorous attacks upon the Indians. Berkeley declined to grant him a military commission and proclaimed him a rebel when he refused to disband his men. His followers were described by one of the Virginia aristocrats as "a rabble of the basest sort of people, whose condition was such as by a change could not admit of worse."

Bacon's successful exploits on the frontier made him such a power among the small farmers that Berkeley was obliged to yield concessions, and at last he ordered a new election of burgesses. The freeholders of Bacon's county sent him to Jamestown as their representative. There, however, he failed to obtain his desired commission, nor could he persuade the governor to reverse his frontier policy. Thoroughly exasperated, he finally used force to terrorize the council and to extract a commission from Berkeley. Then, when the insurrectionists had been called away to the frontier by new Indian raids, the governor raised a counter-revolutionary army, whereupon Bacon returned posthaste to Jamestown. Berkeley fled to the eastern shore as Bacon took charge of the government (styling himself "general by the consent of the people") and prepared to resist some royal troops which were presumably on the way to Virginia from England in response to Berkeley's hurried call for aid.

While in control of Jamestown the insurrectionists burned the town, Bacon himself setting fire to the Anglican church. Then in October he died, a victim of fever, and his leaderless following (which now included many runaway servants and slaves) became a disorganized, plundering mob. Berkeley returned from Accomac, rallied the eastern planters, suppressed the revolt, and exacted a terrible vengeance by hanging a score of insurrectionists and decreeing the confiscation of many estates. While this liquidation of the rebels was in progress three commissioners arrived from England with eleven hundred troops. Sent by Charles II to suppress the revolt and to examine into its causes these commissioners were soon at odds with Berkeley, who treated them with the utmost contempt and opposed them in every possible way. Their condemnation of his proceedings finally compelled him to return to England, where he encountered icy reproaches from the Lords of Trade and the displeasure of the king. He died in July 1677, a discredited and broken man. Of his tyranny Charles II is supposed to have said: "That old fool has hanged more men in that naked country than I have for the murder of my father."

Two gains for the yeomanry issued from the rebellion—the dismissal of Berkeley and the negotiation of a treaty with the Indians which restored peace to the frontiers. Otherwise the fundamental institutions of the colony remained intact. There was no change in the personnel and power of the council nor in the privileged status of the aristocracy with respect to landholdings, taxation, credit relations, and local government. The bitter experience of the planters may have antagonized them toward indentured servants and freedmen, may have caused them to depend increasingly upon Negro slaves; at any rate the progress of slavery after 1680 deepened the gulf between rich and poor. Meanwhile the English government did not champion the cause of the "underdog"; instead it insisted that the right to vote be limited to freeholders and attempted, unsuccessfully, to deny to the House of Burgesses the privilege of initiating legislative measures. Nor did England relax the trade and navigation laws which had contributed so materially to the colony's distress.

Continued dissatisfaction and agitation among the small farmers during the 1680's plainly indicated that the causes of popular discontent had not been removed. Three unsatisfactory governors served after Berkeley—Sir Henry Chicheley, old, infirm, and "superannuated"; Lord Culpeper, a spoilsman who used his office to enhance his private fortune; and Lord Howard of Effingham, a petty autocrat who mirrored the conceptions of absolute power held by his royal master, James II. The attempt of England to assert her authority over the colony resulted in a government not much more satisfactory than that of Berkeley and his clique. Disaffected groups, however, had been so thoroughly defeated in Bacon's Rebellion that no uprising in Virginia accompanied the Revolution of 1688 in England, although the news of the accession of William and Mary was received with "unfeigned joy and exaltation."

Politics and social structure in Virginia

Bernard Bailyn

By the end of the seventeenth century the American colonists faced an array of disturbing problems in the conduct of public affairs. Settlers from England and Holland, reconstructing familiar institutions on American shores, had become participants in what would appear to have been a wave of civil disobedience. Constituted authority was confronted with repeated challenges. Indeed, a veritable anarchy seems to have prevailed at the center of colonial society, erupting in a series of insurrections that began as early as 1635 with the "thrusting out" of Governor Harvey in Virginia. Culpeper's Rebellion in Carolina, the Protestant Association in Maryland, Bacon's Rebellion in Virginia, Leisler's seizure of power in New York, the resistance to and finally the overthrow of Andros in New England—every colony was affected.

These outbursts were not merely isolated local affairs. Although their immediate causes were rooted in the particular circumstances of the separate colonies, they nevertheless had common characteristics. They were, in fact, symptomatic of a profound disorganization of European society in its American setting. Seen in a broad view, they reveal a new

From Bernard Bailyn "Politics and Social Structure in Virginia" in *Seventeenth-Century America: Essays in Colonial History*, ed. James Morton Smith (1959), pp. 90–115. Reprinted by permission of the University of North Carolina Press.

configuration of forces which shaped the origins of American politics.

In a letter written from Virginia in 1623, George Sandys, the resident treasurer, reported despondently on the character and condition of the leading settlers. Some of the councilors were "no more then Ciphers," he wrote; others were "miserablie poore"; and the few substantial planters lived apart, taking no responsibility for public concerns. There was, in fact, among all those "worthie the mencioninge" only one person deserving of full approval. Lieutenant William Peirce "refuses no labour, nor sticks at anie expences that may aduantage the publique." Indeed, Sandys added, Peirce was "of a Capacitie that is not to bee expected in a man of his breedinge."

The afterthought was penetrating. It cut below the usual complaints of the time that many of the settlers were lazy malcontents hardly to be preferred to the Italian glassworkers, than whom, Sandys wrote, "a more damned crew hell never vomited." What lay behind Sandys' remark was not so much that wretched specimens were arriving in the shipments of servants nor even that the quality of public leadership was declining but that the social foundations of political power were being strangely altered.

All of the settlers in whatever colony presumed a fundamental relationship between social structure and political authority. Drawing on a common medieval heritage, continuing to conceive of society as a hierarchical unit, its parts justly and naturally separated into inferior and superior levels, they assumed that superiority was indivisible; there was not one hierarchy for political matters, another for social purposes. John Winthrop's famous explanation of God's intent that "in all times some must be rich some poore, some highe and eminent in power and dignitie; others meane and in subieccion" could not have been more carefully worded. Riches, dignity, and power were properly placed in apposition; they pertained to the same individuals.

So closely related were social leadership and political leadership that experience if not theory justified an identification between state and society. To the average English colonist the state was not an abstraction existing above men's lives, justifying itself in its own terms, taking occasional human embodiment. However glorified in monarchy, the state in ordinary form was indistinguishable from a more general social authority; it was woven into the texture of everyday life. It was the same squire or manorial lord who in his various capacities collated to the benefice, set the rents, and enforced the statutes of Parliament and the royal decrees. Nothing could have been more alien to the settlers than the idea that competition for political leadership should be open to all levels of society or that obscure social origins or technical skills should be considered valuable qualifications for office. The proper response to new technical demands on public servants was not to give power to the skilled but to give skills to the powerful. The English gentry and landed aristocracy remained politically adaptable and hence politically competent, assuming when necessary new public functions, eliminating the need for a professional state bureaucracy. By their amateur competence they made possible a continuing identification between political and social authority.

In the first years of settlement no one had reason to expect that this characteristic of public life would fail to transfer itself to the colonies. For at least a decade and a half after its founding there had been in the Jamestown settlement a small group of leaders drawn from the higher echelons of English society. Besides well-born soldiers of fortune like George Percy, son of the Earl of Northumberland, there were among them four sons of the West family—children of Lord de la Warr and his wife, a second cousin of Queen Elizabeth. In Virginia the West brothers held appropriately high positions; three of them served as governors. Christopher Davison, the colony's secretary, was the son of Queen Elizabeth's secretary, William Davison, M.P. and Privy Councilor. The troublesome John Martin, of Martin's Brandon, was the son of Sir Richard Martin, twice Lord Mayor of London, and also the brother-in-law of Sir Julius Caesar, Master of the Rolls and Privy Councilor. Sir Francis and Haute Wyatt were sons of substantial Kent gentry and grandsons of the Sir Thomas Wyatt who led the rebellion of 1554 against Queen Mary. George Sandys' father was the Archbishop of York; of his three older brothers, all knights and M.P.'s, two were eminent country gentlemen, and the third, Edwin, of Virginia Company fame, was a man of great influence in the city. George Thorpe was a former M.P. and Gentleman of the Privy Chamber.

More impressive than such positions and relationships was the cultural level represented. For until the very end of the Company period, Virginia remained to the literary and scientific an exotic attraction, its settlement an important moment in Christian history. Its original magnetism for those in touch with intellectual currents affected the early immigration. Of the twenty councilors of 1621, eight had been educated at Oxford, Cambridge, or the Inns of Court. Davison, like Martin trained in the law, was a poet in a family of poets. Thorpe was a "student of Indian views on religion and astronomy." Francis Wyatt wrote verses and was something of a student of political theory. Alexander Whitaker, M.A., author of *Good Newes from Virginia*, was the worthy heir "of a good part of the learning of his renowned father," the master of St. John's College and Regius Professor of Divinity at Cambridge. John Pory, known to history mainly as the speaker of the first representative assembly in America, was a Master of Arts, "protege and disciple of Hakluyt," diplomat, scholar, and traveler, whose writings from and about America have a rightful place in literary history. Above all there was George Sandys, "poet, traveller, and scholar," a member of Lord Falkland's literary circle; while in Jamestown he continued as a matter of course to work on his notable translation of Ovid's *Metamorphoses.*

There was, in other words, during the first years of settlement a direct transference to Virginia of the upper levels of the English social hierarchy as well as of the lower. If the great majority of the settlers were recruited from the yeoman class and below, there was nevertheless a reasonable representation from those upper groups acknowledged to be the rightful rulers of society.

It is a fact of some importance, however, that this governing elite did not survive a single generation, at least in its original form. By the thirties their number had declined to insignificance. Percy, for example, left in 1612. Whitaker drowned in 1617. Sandys and Francis Wyatt arrived only in 1621, but their enthusiasm cooled quickly; they were both gone by 1626. Of the Wests, only John was alive and resident in the colony a decade after the collapse of the Company. Davison, who returned to England in 1622 after only a year's stay, was sent back in 1623 but died within a year of his return. Thorpe was one of the six councilors slain in the massacre of 1622. Pory left for England in 1622; his return as investigating commissioner in 1624 was temporary, lasting only a few months. And the cantankerous Martin graced the Virginia scene by his absence after 1625; he is last heard from in the early 1630's petitioning for release from a London debtor's prison.

To be sure, a few representatives of important English families, like John West and Edmund Scarborough, remained. There were also one or two additions from the same social level. But there were few indeed of such individuals, and the basis of their authority had changed. The group of gentlemen and illuminati that had dominated the scene during the Company era had been dispersed. Their disappearance created a political void which was filled soon enough, but from a different area of recruitment, from below, from the toughest and most fortunate of the surviving planters whose eminence by the end of the thirties had very little to do with the transplantation of social status.

The position of the new leaders rested on their ability to wring material gain from the wilderness. Some, like Samuel Mathews, started with large initial advantages, but more typical were George Menefie and John Utie, who began as independent landowners by right of transporting themselves and only one or two servants. Abraham Wood, famous for his explorations and like Menefie and Utie the future possessor of large estates and important offices, appears first as a servant boy on Mathews' plantation. Adam Thoroughgood, the son of a country vicar, also started in Virginia as a servant, aged fourteen. William Spencer is first recorded as a yeoman farmer without servants.

Such men as these—Spencer, Wood, Menefie, Utie, Mathews—were the most important figures in Virginia politics up to the Restoration, engrossing large tracts of land, dominating the Council, unseating Sir John

Harvey from the governorship. But in no traditional sense were they a ruling class. They lacked the attributes of social authority, and their political dominance was a continuous achievement. Only with the greatest difficulty, if at all, could distinction be expressed in a genteel style of life, for existence in this generation was necessarily crude. Mathews may have created a flourishing estate and Menefie had splendid fruit gardens, but the great tracts of land such men claimed were almost entirely raw wilderness. They had risen to their positions, with few exceptions, by brute labor and shrewd manipulation; they had personally shared the burdens of settlement. They succeeded not because of, but despite, whatever gentility they may have had. William Claiborne may have been educated at the Middle Temple; Peirce could not sign his name; but what counted was their common capacity to survive and flourish in frontier settlements. They were tough, unsentimental, quick-tempered, crudely ambitious men concerned with profits and increased landholdings, not the grace of life. They roared curses, drank exuberantly, and gambled (at least according to deVries) for their servants when other commodities were lacking. If the worst of Governor Harvey's offenses had been to knock out the teeth of an offending councilor with a cudgel, as he did on one occasion, no one would have questioned his right to the governorship. Rank had its privileges, and these men were the first to claim them, but rank itself was unstable and the lines of class or status were fluid. There was no insulation for even the most elevated from the rude impact of frontier life.

As in style of life so in politics, these leaders of the first permanently settled generation did not re-create the characteristics of a stable gentry. They had had little opportunity to acquire the sense of public responsibility that rests on deep identification with the land and its people. They performed in some manner the duties expected of leaders, but often public office was found simply burdensome. Reports such as Sandys' that Yeardley, the councilor and former governor, was wholly absorbed in his private affairs and scarcely glanced at public matters and that Mathews "will rather hazard the payment of fforfeitures then performe our Injunctions" were echoed by Harvey throughout his tenure of office. Charles Harmar, justice of the peace on the Eastern Shore, attended the court once in eight years, and Claiborne's record was only slightly better. Attendance to public duties had to be specifically enjoined, and privileges were of necessity accorded provincial officeholders. The members of the Council were particularly favored by the gift of tax exemption.

The private interests of this group, which had assumed control of public office by virtue not of inherited status but of newly achieved and strenuously maintained economic eminence, were pursued with little interference from the traditional restraints imposed on a responsible ruling class. Engaged in an effort to establish themselves in the land, they sought as specific ends: autonomous local jurisdiction, an aggressive expansion of settlement and trading enterprises, unrestricted access to land, and, at every stage, the legal endorsement of acquisitions. Most of the major public events for thirty years after the dissolution of the Company—and especially the overthrow of Harvey—were incidents in the pursuit of these goals.

From his first appearance in Virginia, Sir John Harvey threatened the interests of this emerging planter group. While still in England he had identified himself with the faction that had successfully sought the collapse of the Company, and thus his mere presence in Virginia was a threat to the legal basis of land grants made under the Company's charter. His demands for the return as public property of goods that had once belonged to the Company specifically jeopardized the planters' holdings. His insistence that the governorship was more than a mere chairmanship of the Council tended to undermine local autonomy. His conservative Indian policy not only weakened the settlers' hand in what already seemed an irreconcilable enmity with the natives but also restricted the expansion of settlement. His opposition to Claiborne's claim to Kent Island threatened to kill off the lucrative Chesapeake Bay trade, and his attempt to ban the Dutch ships from the colony endangered commerce more generally. His support of the official policy of economic diversification, together with his endorsement of the English schemes of tobacco monopoly, alienated him finally and completely from the Council group.

Within a few months of his assuming the governorship, Harvey wrote home with indignation of the "waywardnes and oppositions" of the councilors and condemned them for factiously seeking "rather for their owne endes then either seekinge the generall good or doinge right to particuler men." Before a year was out the antagonisms had become so intense that a formal peace treaty had to be drawn up between Harvey and the Council. But both sides were adamant, and conflict was inescapable. It exploded in 1635 amid comic opera scenes of "extreame coller and passion" complete with dark references to Richard the Third and musketeers "running with their peices presented." The conclusion was Harvey's enraged arrest of George Menefie "of suspicion of Treason to his Majestie"; Utie's response, "And wee the like to you sir"; and the governor's forced return to England.

Behind these richly heroic "passings and repassings to and fro" lies not a victory of democracy or representative institutions or anything of the sort. Democracy, in fact, was identified in the Virginians' minds with the "popular and tumultuary government" that had prevailed in the old Company's quarter courts, and they wanted none of it; the Assembly as a representative institution was neither greatly sought after nor hotly resisted. The victory of 1635 was that of resolute leaders of settlement stubbornly fighting for individual establishment. With the reappointment of Sir Francis Wyatt as governor, their victory was assured and in the Commonwealth period it was completely realized. By 1658, when Mathews was elected governor, effective interference from outside had disappeared and the supreme authority had been assumed by an Assembly which was in effect a league of local magnates secure in their control of county institutions.

One might at that point have projected the situation forward into a picture of dominant county families dating from the 1620's and 1630's, growing in identification with the land and people, ruling with increasing responsibility from increasingly eminent positions. But such a projection would be false. The fact is that with a few notable exceptions like the Scarboroughs and the Wormeleys, these struggling planters of the first generation failed to perpetuate their leadership into the second generation. Such families as the Woods, the Uties, the Mathews, and the Peirces faded from dominant positions of authority after the deaths of their founders. To some extent this was the result of the general insecurity of life that created odds against the physical survival in the male line of any given family. But even if male heirs had remained in these families after the death of the first generation, undisputed eminence would not. For a new emigration had begun in the forties, continuing for close to thirty years, from which was drawn a new ruling group that had greater possibilities for permanent dominance than Harvey's opponents had had. These newcomers absorbed and subordinated the older group, forming the basis of the most celebrated oligarchy in American history.

Most of Virginia's great eighteenth-century names, such as Bland, Burwell, Byrd, Carter, Digges, Ludwell, and Mason, appear in the colony for the first time within ten years either side of 1655. These progenitors of the eighteenth-century aristocracy arrived in remarkably similar circumstances. The most important of these immigrants were younger sons of substantial families well connected in London business and governmental circles and long associated with Virginia; family claims to land in the colony or inherited shares of the original Company stock were now brought forward as a basis for establishment in the New World.

Thus the Bland family interests in Virginia date from a 1618 investment in the Virginia Company by the London merchant John Bland, supplemented in 1622 by another in Martin's Hundred. The merchant never touched foot in America, but three of his sons did come to Virginia in the forties and fifties to exploit these investments. The Burwell fortunes derive from the early subscription to the Company of Edward Burwell, which was inherited in the late forties by his son, Lewis I. The first William Byrd arrived about 1670 to assume the Virginia properties of his mother's family, the Steggs, which dated back to the early days of the Company. The Digges's interests in Virginia stem from the original investments of Sir Dudley Digges and two of his sons in the Company, but it was a third son, Edward, who emigrated in 1650 and established the American branch of the family. Similarly, the Masons had been financially interested in Virginia thirty-two years before 1652, when the first immigrant of that family appeared in the colony. The Culpeper clan, whose private affairs enclose much of the history of the South in the second half of the seventeenth century, was first represented in Virginia by Thomas Culpeper, who arrived in 1649; but the family interests in Virginia had been established a full generation earlier: Thomas' father, uncle, and cousin had all been members of the original Virginia Company and their shares had descended in the family. Even Governor Berkeley fits the pattern. There is no mystery about his sudden exchange in 1642 of the life of a dilettante courtier for that of a colonial administrator and estate manager. He was a younger son without prospects, and his family's interests in Virginia, dating from investments in the Company made twenty years earlier, as well as his appointment held out the promise of an independent establishment in America.

Claims on the colony such as these were only one, though the most important, of a variety of forms of capital that might provide the basis for secure family fortunes. One might simply bring over enough of a merchant family's resources to begin immediately building up an imposing estate, as, presumably, did that ambitious draper's son, William Fitzhugh. The benefits that accrued from such advantages were quickly translated into landholdings in the development of which these settlers were favored by the chronology of their arrival. For though they extended the area of cultivation in developing their landholdings, they were not obliged to initiate settlement. They fell heirs to large areas of the tidewater region that had already been brought under cultivation. "Westover" was not the creation of William Byrd; it had originally been part of the De la Warr estate, passing, with improvements, to Captain Thomas Pawlett, thence to Theodorick Bland, and finally to Byrd. Lewis Burwell inherited not only his father's land, but also the developed estate of his stepfather, Wingate. Some of the Carters' lands may be traced back through John Utie to a John Jefferson, who left Virginia as early as 1628. Abraham Wood's entire Fort Henry property ended in the hands of the Jones family. The Blands' estate in Charles City County, which later became the Harrisons' "Berkeley" plantation, was cleared for settlement in 1619 by servants of the "particular" plantation of Berkeley's Hundred.

Favored thus by circumstance, a small group within the second generation migration moved toward setting itself off in a permanent way as a ruling landed gentry. That they succeeded was due not only to their material advantages but also to the force of their motivation. For these individuals were in social origins just close enough to establishment in gentility to feel the pangs of deprivation most acutely. It is not the totally but the partially dispossessed who build up the most propulsive aspirations, and behind the zestful lunging at propriety and status of a William Fitzhugh lay not the narcotic yearnings of the disinherited but the pent-up ambitions of the gentleman *manqué*. These were neither hardhanded pioneers nor dilettante romantics, but ambitious younger sons of middle-class families who knew well enough what gentility was and sought it as a specific objective.

The establishment of this group was rapid. Within a decade of their arrival they could claim, together with a fortunate few of the first generation, a marked social eminence and full political authority at the county level. But their rise was not uniform. Indeed, by the seventies a new circumstance had introduced an effective principle of social differentiation among the colony's leaders. A hierarchy of position within the newly risen gentry was created by the Restoration government's efforts to extend its control more effectively over its mercantile empire. Demanding of its colonial executives and their advisors closer supervision over the external aspects of the economy, it offered a measure of patronage necessary for enforcement. Public offices dealing with matters that profoundly affected the basis of economic life—tax collection, customs regulation, and the bestowal of land grants—fell within the gift of the governor and tended to form an inner circle of privilege. One can note in Berkeley's administration the growing importance of this barrier of officialdom. Around its privileges there formed the "Green Spring" faction, named after Berkeley's plantation near Jamestown, a group bound to the governor not by royalist sympathies so much as by ties of kinship and patronage.

Thus Colonel Henry Norwood, related to Berkeley by a "near affinity in blood," was given the treasurership of the colony in 1650, which he held for more than two decades. During this time Thomas Ludwell, a cousin and Somerset neighbor of the governor, was secretary of state, in which post he was succeeded in 1678 by his brother Philip, who shortly thereafter married Berkeley's widow. This Lady Berkeley, it should be noted, was the daughter of Thomas Culpeper, the immigrant of 1649 and a cousin of Thomas Lord Culpeper who became governor in 1680. Immediately after her marriage to Berkeley, her brother Alexander requested and received from the governor the nomination to the surveyor-generalship of Virginia, a post he filled for twenty-three years while resident in England, appointing as successive deputies the brothers Ludwell, to whom by 1680 he was twice related by marriage. Lady Berkeley was also related through her mother to William Byrd's wife, a fact that explains much about Byrd's prolific office-holding.

The growing distinctiveness of provincial officialdom within the landed gentry may also be traced in the transformation of the Council. Originally, this body had been expected to comprise the entire effective government, central and local; councilors were to serve, individually or in committees, as local magistrates. But the spread of settlement upset this expectation, and at the same time as the local offices were falling into the hands of autonomous local powers representing leading county families, the Council, appointed by the governor and hence associated with official patronage, increasingly realized the separate, lucrative privileges available to it.

As the distinction between local and central authority became clear, the county magistrates sought their own distinct voice in the management of the colony, and they found it in developing the possibilities of burgess representation. In the beginning there was no House of Burgesses; representation from the burghs and hundreds was conceived of not as a branch of government separate from the Council but as a periodic supplement to it. Until the fifties the burgesses, meeting in the Assemblies with the councilors, felt little need to form themselves into a separate house, for until that decade there was little evidence of a conflict of interests between the two groups. But when, after the Restoration, the privileged status of the Council became unmistakable and the county magnates found control of the increasingly important provincial administration pre-empted by this body, the burgess part of the Assembly took on a new meaning in contrast to that of the Council. Burgess representation now became vital to the county leaders if they were to share in any consistent way in affairs larger than those of the counties. They looked to the franchise, hitherto broad not by design but by neglect, introducing qualifications that would ensure their control of the Assembly. Their interest in provincial government could no longer be expressed in the conglomerate Assembly, and at least by 1663 the House of Burgesses began to meet separately as a distinct body voicing interests potentially in conflict with those of the Council.

Thus by the eighth decade the ruling class in Virginia was broadly based on leading county families and dominated at the provincial level by a privileged officialdom. But this social and political structure was too new, too lacking in the sanctions of time and custom, its leaders too close to humbler origins and as yet too undistinguished in style of life, to be accepted without a struggle. A period of adjustment was necessary, of which Bacon's Rebellion was the climactic episode.

Bacon's Rebellion began as an unauthorized frontier war against the Indians and ended as an upheaval that threatened the entire basis of social and political authority. Its immediate causes have to do with race relations and settlement policy, but behind these issues lay deeper elements related to resistance against the maturing shape of a new social order. These elements explain the dimensions the conflict reached.

There was, first, resistance by substantial planters to the privileges and policies of the inner provincial clique led by Berkeley and composed of those directly dependent on his patronage. These dissidents, among whom were the leaders of the Rebellion, represented neither the downtrodden masses nor a principle of opposition to privilege as such. Their discontent stemmed to a large extent from their own exclusion from privileges they sought. Most often their grievances were based on personal rebuffs they had received as they reached for entry into provincial official-dom. Thus—to speak of the leaders of the Rebellion—Giles Bland arrived in Virginia in 1671 to take over the agency of his late uncle in the management of his father's extensive landholdings, assuming at the same time the lucrative position of customs collector which he had obtained in London. But, amid angry cries of *"pittyfull fellow, puppy* and *Sonn of a Whore,"* he fell out first with Berkeley's cousin and favorite, Thomas Ludwell, and finally with the governor himself; for his "Barbarous and Insolent Behaviors" Bland was fined, arrested, and finally removed from the collectorship. Of the two "chiefe Incendiarys," William Drummond and Richard Lawrence, the former had been quarreling with Berkeley since 1664, first over land claims in Carolina, then over a contract for building a fort near James City, and repeatedly over lesser issues in the General Court; Lawrence "some Years before . . . had been partially treated at Law, for a considerable Estate on behalfe of a Corrupt favorite." Giles Brent, for his depredations against the Indians in violation of official policy, had not only been severely fined but barred from public office. Bacon himself could not have appeared under more favorable circumstances. A cousin both of Lady Berkeley and of the councilor Nathaniel Bacon, Sr., and by general agreement "a Gent:man of a Liberall education" if of a somewhat tarnished reputation, he had quickly staked out land for himself and had been elevated, for reasons "best known to the Governour," to the Council. But being "of a most imperious and dangerous hidden Pride of heart . . . very ambitious and arrogant," he wanted more, and quickly. His alienation from and violent opposition to Berkeley were wound in among the animosities created by the Indian problem and were further complicated by his own unstable personality; they were related also to the fact that Berkeley finally turned down the secret offer Bacon and Byrd made in 1675 for the purchase from the governor of a monopoly of the Indian trade.

These specific disputes have a more general aspect. It was three decades since Berkeley had assumed the governorship and begun rallying a favored group, and it was over a decade since the Restoration had given this group unconfined sway over the provincial government. In those years much of the choice tidewater land as well as the choice offices had been spoken for, and the tendency of the highly placed was to hold firm. Berkeley's Indian policy—one of stabilizing the borders between Indians and whites and protecting the natives from depredation by land-hungry settlers—although a sincere attempt to deal with an extremely difficult problem, was also conservative, favoring the established. Newcomers like Bacon and Bland and particularly landholders on the frontiers felt victimized by a stabilization of the situation or by a controlled expansion that maintained on an extended basis the existing power structure. They were logically drawn to aggressive positions. In an atmosphere charged with violence, their interests constituted a challenge to provincial authority. Bacon's primary appeal in his "Manifesto" played up the threat of this challenge:

> Let us trace these men in Authority and Favour to whose hands the dispensation of the Countries wealth has been commited; let us observe the sudden Rise of their Estates [compared] with the Quality in wch they first entered this Country... And lett us see wither their extractions and Education have not bin vile, And by what pretence of learning and vertue they could [enter] soe soon into Imployments of so great Trust and consequence, let us ... see what spounges have suckt up the Publique Treasure and wither it hath not bin privately contrived away by unworthy Favourites and juggling Parasites whose tottering Fortunes have bin repaired and supported at the Publique chardg.

Such a threat to the basis of authority was not lost on Berkeley or his followers. Bacon's merits, a contemporary wrote, "thretned an eclips to there riseing gloryes. . . . (if he should continue in the Governours favour) of Seniours they might becom juniours, while there younger Brother . . . might steale away that blessing, which they accounted there owne by birthright."

But these challengers were themselves challenged, for another main element in the upheaval was the discontent among the ordinary settlers at the local privileges of the same newly risen county magnates who assailed the privileges of the Green Spring faction. The specific Charles City County grievances were directed as much at the locally dominant family, the Hills, as they were at Berkeley and his clique. Similarly, Surry County complained of its county court's highhanded and secretive manner of levying taxes on "the poore people" and of setting the sheriffs' and clerks' fees; they petitioned for the removal of these abuses and for the right to elect the vestry and to limit the tenure of the sheriffs. At all levels the Rebellion challenged the stability of newly secured authority.

It is this double aspect of discontent behind the violence of the Rebellion that explains the legislation passed in June, 1676, by the so-called "Bacon's Assembly." At first glance these laws seem difficult to interpret because they express disparate if not contradictory interests. But they yield readily to analysis if they are seen not as the reforms of a single group but as efforts to express the desires of two levels of discontent with the way the political and social hierarchy was becoming stabilized. On the one hand, the laws include measures designed by the numerically predominant ordinary settlers throughout the colony as protests against the recently acquired superiority of the leading county families. These were popular protests and they relate not to provincial affairs but to the situation within the local areas of jurisdiction. Thus the statute restricting the francise to freeholders was repealed; freemen were given the right to elect the parish vestrymen; and the county courts were supplemented by elected freemen to serve with the regularly appointed county magistrates.

On the other hand, there was a large number of measures expressing the dissatisfactions not so much of the ordinary planter but of the local leaders against the prerogatives recently acquired by the provincial elite, prerogatives linked to officialdom and centered in the Council. Thus the law barring office-holding to newcomers of less than three years' residence struck at the arbitrary elevation of the governor's favorites, including Bacon; and the acts forbidding councilors to join the county courts, outlawing the governor's appointment of sheriffs and tax collectors, and nullifying tax exemption for councilors all voiced objections of the local chieftains to privileges enjoyed by others. From both levels there was objection to profiteering in public office.

Thus the wave of rebellion broke and spread. But why did it subside? One might have expected that the momentary flood would have become a steady tide, its rhythms governed by a fixed political constellation. But in fact it did not; stable political alignments did not result. The conclusion to this controversy was characteristic of all the insurrections. The attempted purges and counterpurges by the leaders of the two sides were followed by a rapid submerging of factional identity. Occasional references were later made to the episode, and there were individuals who found an interest in keeping its memory alive. Also, the specific grievances behind certain of the attempted legal reforms of 1676 were later revived. But of stable parties or factions around these issues there were none.

It was not merely that in the late years of the century no more than in the early was there to be found a justification for permanently organized political opposition or party machinery, that persistent, organized dissent was still indistinguishable from sedition; more important was the fact that at the end of the century as in 1630 there was agreement that some must be "highe and eminent in power and dignitie; others meane and in subieccion." Protests and upheaval had resulted from the discomforts of discovering who was, in fact, which, and what the particular consequences of "power and dignitie" were.

But by the end of the century the most difficult period of adjustment had passed and there was an acceptance of the fact that certain families were distinguished from others in riches, in dignity, and in access to political authority. The establishment of these families marks the emergence of Virginia's colonial aristocracy.

It was a remarkable governing group. Its members were soberly responsible, alive to the implications of power; they performed their public obligations with notable skill. Indeed, the glare of their accomplishments is so bright as occasionally to blind us to the conditions that limited them. As a ruling class the Virginian aristocracy of the eighteenth century was unlike other contemporary nobilities or aristocracies, including the English. The differences, bound up with the special characteristics of the society it ruled, had become clear at the turn of the seventeenth century.

Certain of these characteristics are elusive, difficult to grasp and analyze. The leaders of early eighteenth-century Virginia were, for example, in a particular sense, cultural provincials. They were provincial not in the way of Polish *szlachta* isolated on their estates by poverty and impassable roads, nor in the way of sunken *seigneurs* grown rustic and old-fashioned in lonely Norman chateaux. The Virginians were far from uninformed or unaware of the greater world; they were in fact deeply and continuously involved in the cultural life of the Atlantic community. But they knew themselves to be provincials in the sense that their culture was not self-contained; its sources and superior expressions were to be found elsewhere than in their own land. They must seek it from afar; it must be acquired, and once acquired be maintained according to standards externally imposed, in the creation of which they had not participated. The most cultivated of them read much, purposefully, with a diligence the opposite of that essential requisite of aristocracy, uncontending ease. William Byrd's diary with its daily records of stints of study is a stolid testimonial to the virtues of regularity and effort in maintaining standards of civilization set abroad.

In more evident ways also the Virginia planters were denied an uncontending ease of life. They were not *rentiers*. Tenancy, when it appeared late in the colonial period, was useful to the landowners mainly as a cheap way of improving lands held in reserve for future development. The Virginia aristocrat was an active manager of his estate, drawn continuously into the most intimate contacts with the soil and its cultivation. This circumstance limited his ease, one might even say bound him to the soil, but it also strengthened his identity with the land and its problems and saved him from the temptation to create of his privileges an artificial world of self-indulgence.

But more important in distinguishing the emerging aristocracy of Virginia from other contemporary social and political elites were two very specific circumstances. The first concerns the relationship between the integrity of the family unit and the descent of real property. "The English political family," Sir Lewis Namier writes with particular reference to the eighteenth-century aristocracy,

is a compound of "blood," name, and estate, this last ... being the most important of the three. ... The name is a weighty symbol, but liable to variations. ... the estate ... is, in the long run, the most potent factor in securing continuity through identification. ... Primogeniture and entails psychically preserve the family in that they tend to fix its position through the successive generations, and thereby favour conscious identification.

The descent of landed estates in eighteenth-century England was controlled by the complicated device known as the strict settlement which provided that the heir at his marriage received the estate as a life tenant, entailing its descent to his unborn eldest son and specifying the limitations of the encumbrances upon the land that might be made in behalf of his daughters and younger sons.

It was the strict settlement, in which in the eighteenth century perhaps half the land of England was bound, that provided continuity over generations for the landed aristocracy. This permanent identification of the family with a specific estate and with the status and offices that pertained to it was achieved at the cost of sacrificing the younger sons. It was a single stem of the family only that retained its superiority; it alone controlled the material basis for political dominance.

This basic condition of aristocratic governance in England was never present in the American colonies, and not for lack of familiarity with legal forms. The economic necessity that had prompted the widespread adoption of the strict settlement in England was absent in the colonies. Land was cheap and easily available, the more so as one rose on the social and political ladder. There was no need to deprive the younger sons or even daughters of landed inheritances in order to keep the original family estate intact. Provision could be made for endowing each of them with plantations, and they in turn could provide similarly for their children. Moreover, to confine the stem family's fortune to a single plot of land, however extensive, was in the Virginia economy to condemn it to swift decline. Since the land was quickly worn out and since it was cheaper to acquire new land than to rejuvenate the worked soil by careful husbandry, geographical mobility, not stability, was the key to prosperity. Finally, since land was only as valuable as the labor available to work it, a great estate was worth passing intact from generation to generation only if it had annexed to it a sufficient population of slaves. Yet this condition imposed severe rigidities in a plantation's economy—for a labor force bound to a particular plot was immobilized—besides creating bewildering confusions in law.

The result, evident before the end of the seventeenth century, was a particular relationship between the family and the descent of property. There was in the beginning no intent on the part of the Virginians to alter the traditional forms; the continued vitality of the ancient statutes specifying primogeniture in certain cases was assumed. The first clear indication of a new trend came in the third quarter of the century, when the leading gentry, rapidly accumulating large estates, faced for the first time the problem of the transfer of property. The result was the subdivision of the great holdings and the multiplication of smaller plots while the net amount of land held by the leading families continued to rise.

This trend continued. Primogeniture neither at the end of the seventeenth century nor after prevailed in Virginia. It was never popular even among the most heavily endowed of the tidewater families. The most common form of bequest was a grant to the eldest son of the undivided home plantation and gifts of other tracts outside the home county to the younger sons and daughters. Thus by his will of 1686 Robert Beverley, Sr., bequeathed to his eldest son, Peter, all his land in Gloucester County lying between "Chiescake" and "Hoccadey's" creeks (an unspecified acreage); to Robert, the second son, another portion of the Gloucester lands amounting to 920 acres; to Harry, 1,600 acres in Rappahannock County; to John 3,000 acres in the same county; to William, two plantations in Middlesex County; to Thomas, 3,000 acres in Rappahannock and New Kent counties; to his wife, three plantations including those "whereon I now live" for use during her lifetime, after which they were to descend to his daughter Catherine, who was also to receive £200 sterling; to his daughter Mary, £150 sterling; to "the childe that my wife goeth with, be it male or female," all the rest of his real property; and the residue of his personal property was "to be divided and disposed in equall part & portion betwix my wife and children." Among the bequests of Ralph Wormeley, Jr., in 1700 was an estate of 1,500 acres to his daughter Judith as well as separate plantations to his two sons.

Entail proved no more popular than primogeniture. Only a small minority of estates, even in the tidewater region, were ever entailed. In fact, despite the extension of developed land in the course of the eighteenth century, more tidewater estates were docked of entails than were newly entailed.

Every indication points to continuous and increasing difficulty in reproducing even pale replicas of the strict settlement. In 1705 a law was passed requiring a special act of the Assembly to break an entail; the law stood, but between 1711 and 1776 no fewer than 125 such private acts were passed, and in 1734 estates of under £200 were exempted from the law altogether. The labor problem alone was an insuperable barrier to perpetuating the traditional forms. A statute of 1727, clarifying the confused legislation of earlier years, had attempted to ensure a labor force on entailed land by classifying slaves as real property and permitting them to be bound together with land into bequests. But by 1748 this stipulation had resulted in such bewildering "doubts, variety of opinions, and confusions" that it was repealed. The repeal was disallowed in London, and in the course of a defense of its action the Assembly made vividly clear the utter impracticality of entailment in Virginia's economy. Slaves, the Assembly explained, were essential to the success of a plantation, but "slaves could not be kept on the lands to which they were annexed without manifest prejudice to the tenant in tail. . . . often the tenant was the proprietor of fee simple land much fitter for cultivation than his intailed lands, where he could work his slaves to a much greater advantage." On the other hand, if a plantation owner did send entailed slaves where they might be employed most economically the result was equally disastrous:

the frequent removing and settling them on other lands in other counties and parts of the colony far distant from the county court where the deeds or wills which annexed them were recorded and the intail lands lay; the confusion occasioned by their mixture with fee simple slaves of the same name and sex and belonging to the same owner; the uncertainty of distinguishing one from another after several generations, no register of their genealogy being kept and none of them having surnames, were great mischiefs to purchasers, strangers, and creditors, who were often unavoidably deceived in their purchases and hindered in the recovery of their just debts. It also lessened the credit of the country; it being dangerous for the merchants of Great Britain to trust possessors of many slaves for fear the slaves might be intailed.

A mobile labor force free from legal entanglements and a rapid turn-over of lands, not a permanent hereditary estate, were prerequisites of family prosperity. This condition greatly influenced social and political life. Since younger sons and even daughters inherited extensive landed properties, equal often to those of the eldest son, concentration of authority in the stem family was precluded. Third generation collateral descendants of the original immigrant were as important in their own right as the eldest son's eldest son. Great clans like the Carters and the Lees, though they may have acknowledged a central family seat, were scattered throughout the province on estates of equal influence. The four male Carters of the third generation were identified by contemporaries by the names of their separate estates, and, indistinguishable in style of life, they had an equal access to political power.

Since material wealth was the basis of the status which made one eligible for public office, there was a notable diffusion of political influence throughout a broadening group of leading families. No one son was predestined to represent the family interest in politics, but as many as birth and temperament might provide. In the 1750's there were no fewer than seven Lees of the same generation sitting together in the Virginia Assembly; in the Burgesses they spoke for five separate counties. To the eldest, Philip Ludwell Lee, they conceded a certain social superiority that made it natural for him to sit in the Council. But he did not speak alone for the family; by virtue of inheritance he had no unique authority over his brothers and cousins.

The leveling at the top of the social and political hierarchy, creating an evenness of status and influence, was intensified by continuous inter-marriage within the group. The unpruned branches of these flourishing family trees, growing freely, met and intertwined until by the Revolution the aristocracy appeared to be one great tangled cousinry.

As political power became increasingly diffused throughout the upper stratum of society, the Council, still at the end of the seventeenth century a repository of unique privileges, lost its effective superiority. Increasingly through the successive decades its authority had to be exerted through alignments with the Burgesses—alignments made easier as well as more necessary by the criss-crossing network of kinship that united the two houses. Increasingly the Council's distinctions became social and ceremonial.

The contours of Virginia's political hierarchy were also affected by a second main conditioning element, besides the manner of descent of family property. Not only was the structure unusually level and broad at the top, but it was incomplete in itself. Its apex, the ultimate source of legal decision and control, lay in the quite different society of England, amid the distant embroilments of London, the court, and Parliament. The levers of control in that realm were for the most part hidden from the planters; yet the powers that ruled this remote region could impose an arbitrary authority directly into the midst of Virginia's affairs.

One consequence was the introduction of instabilities in the tenure and transfer of the highest offices. Tenure could be arbitrarily interrupted, and the transfer to kin of such positions at death or resignation—uncertain in any case because of the diffusion of family authority—could be quite difficult or even impossible. Thus William Byrd II returned from England at the death of his father in 1705 to take over the family properties, but though he was the sole heir he did not automatically or completely succeed to the elder Byrd's provincial offices. He did, indeed, become auditor of Virginia after his father, but only because he had carefully arranged for the succession while still in London; his father's Council seat went to someone else, and it took three years of patient maneuvering through his main London contact, Micajah Perry, to secure another; he never did take over the receivership. Even such a power as "King" Carter, the reputed owner at his death of 300,000 acres and 1,000 slaves, was rebuffed by the resident deputy governor and had to deploy forces in England in order to transfer a Virginia naval office post from one of his sons to another. There was family continuity in public office, but at the highest level it was uncertain, the result of place-hunting rather than of the absolute prerogative of birth.

Instability resulted not only from the difficulty of securing and transferring high appointive positions but also and more immediately from the presence in Virginia of total strangers to the scene, particularly governors and their deputies, armed with extensive jurisdiction and powers of enforcement. The dangers of this element in public life became clear only after Berkeley's return to England in 1677, for after thirty-five years of residence in the colony Sir William had become a leader in the land independent of his royal authority. But Howard, Andros, and Nicholson were governors with full legal powers but with at best only slight connections with local society. In them, social leadership and political leadership had ceased to be identical.

In the generation that followed Berkeley's departure, this separation between the two spheres created the bitterest of political controversies.

Firmly entrenched behind their control of the colony's government, the leading families battled with every weapon available to reduce the power of the executives and thus to eliminate what appeared to be an external and arbitrary authority. Repeated complaints by the governors of the intractable opposition of a league of local oligarchs marked the Virginians' success. Efforts by the executives to discipline the indigenous leaders could only be mildly successful. Patronage was a useful weapon, but its effectiveness diminished steadily, ground down between a resistant Assembly and an office-hungry bureaucracy in England. The possibility of exploiting divisions among the resident powers also declined as kinship lines bound the leading families closer together and as group interests become clearer with the passage of time. No faction built around the gubernatorial power could survive independently; ultimately its adherents would fall away and it would weaken. It was a clear logic of the situation that led the same individuals who had promoted Nicholson as a replacement for Andros to work against him once he assumed office.

Stability could be reached only by the complete identification of external and internal authority through permanent commitment by the appointees to local interests. Commissary Blair's extraordinary success in Virginia politics was based not only on his excellent connections in England but also on his marriage into the Harrison family, which gave him the support of an influential kinship faction. There was more than hurt pride and thwarted affection behind Nicholson's reported insane rage at being spurned by the highly marriageable Lucy Burwell; and later the astute Spotswood, for all his success in imposing official policy, fully quieted the controversies of his administration only by succumbing completely and joining as a resident Virginia landowner the powers aligned against him.

But there was more involved than instability and conflict in the discontinuity between social and political organization at the topmost level. The state itself had changed its meaning. To a Virginia planter of the early eighteenth century the highest public authority was no longer merely one expression of a general social authority. It had become something abstract, external to his life and society, an ultimate power whose purposes were obscure, whose direction could neither be consistently influenced nor accurately plotted, and whose human embodiments were alien and antagonistic.

The native gentry of the early eighteenth century had neither the need nor the ability to fashion a new political theory to comprehend their experience, but their successors would find in the writings of John Locke on state and society not merely a reasonable theoretical position but a statement of self-evident fact.

I have spoken exclusively of Virginia, but though the histories of each of the colonies in the seventeenth century are different, they exhibit common characteristics. These features one might least have expected to find present in Virginia, and their presence there is, consequently, most worth indicating.

In all of the colonies the original transference of an ordered European society was succeeded by the rise to authority of resident settlers whose influence was rooted in their ability to deal with the problems of life in wilderness settlements. These individuals attempted to stabilize their positions, but in each case they were challenged by others arriving after the initial settlements, seeking to exploit certain advantages of position, wealth, or influence. These newcomers, securing after the Restoration governmental appointments in the colonies and drawn together by personal ties, especially those of kinship and patronage, came to constitute colonial officialdom. This group introduced a new principle of social organization; it also gave rise to new instabilities in a society in which the traditional forms of authority were already being subjected to severe pressures. By the eighth decade of the seventeenth century the social basis of public life had become uncertain and insecure, its stability delicate and sensitive to disturbance. Indian warfare, personal quarrels, and particularly the temporary confusion in external control caused by the Glorious Revolution became the occasions for violent challenges to constituted authority.

By the end of the century a degree of harmony had been achieved, but the divergence between political and social leadership at the topmost level created an area of permanent conflict. The political and social structures that emerged were by European standards strangely shaped. Everywhere as the bonds of empire drew tighter the meaning of the state was changing. Herein lay the origins of a new political system.

SUGGESTIONS FOR FURTHER READING

A general scholarly survey of all of the Southern colonies in the seventeenth century is Wesley Frank Craven's *The Southern Colonies in the Seventeenth Century, 1607–1689* (Baton Rouge, 1949). Chapter X, "Bacon's Rebellion," shows how the conflict began over differences concerning Indian policy, But, he argues, what began from sectional differences developed into a general attack on political and economic abuses, making Bacon one of the many "who have shaped the long tradition of political liberalism in America." If Craven's emphasis is on conflict, it is not, however, conflict of class against class in the European sense. A similar approach on a much broader canvas is Leonard Woods Labaree, *Conservatism in Early American History* (Ithaca, N.Y., 1959).

Daniel J. Boorstin, *The Americans: The Colonial Experience* (New York, 1958) traces the efforts of Virginians to build a community based on the English example, an effort crowned by success not in transplanting England to America, but in creating a viable and unique community in America. Relevant also in this context is Sigmund Diamond, "From Organization to Society: Virginia in the Seventeenth Century," *American Journal of Sociology*, LXIII (March, 1958), 457–475. Emphasizing the general middle class, democratic unity, but for a later period than that covered in this chapter, is the recent study by Robert E. and Katheryn Brown, *Virginia, 1705–1786: Democracy or Aristocracy?* (East Lansing, 1964). Sharp class conflict is stressed by Herbert Aptheker, *The Colonial Era* (New York, 1959), a Marxist interpretation.

II
THE ★
GREAT ★
AWAKENING ★

Religious conviction played a large role in the early history of America. It provided the impetus that induced many men to face the terrors of the unknown wilderness and found a civilization in the New World. But religious conviction led to conflict and division in the American Colonies. Anglican disagreed with Puritan and Puritan with Baptist and Quaker. In Massachusetts, where followers of John Calvin attempted to build a religious zion in the wilderness, Puritan leaders used banishment and even the death penalty to enforce orthodoxy, but even these drastic measures failed to discourage the opposition. Religious orthodoxy proved impossible to enforce; those who disagreed could always leave and begin a new settlement elsewhere. Other factors including pressure from England and the decline of religious enthusiasm after the first generation, led to religious diversity in America, and eventually to a measure of tolerance.

By the early eighteenth century a kind of religious apathy had settled over the American colonies. Of course, many citizens maintained their orthodox faith, but much of the enthusiasm and the conviction of the early Puritan leaders were lacking. Some simply drifted away from the church, but others reacted sharply against the harsher aspects of Calvinism. A number accepted Arminianism, which projected a benevolent rather than a vindictive and angry God, and undermined the concept of original sin and predestination by suggesting that any who believed in Christ and did good deeds on earth could go to heaven. Other men, influenced by the Enlightenment, accepted Deism, which pictured God as a kind of great watchmaker who had constructed the world according to certain natural laws, but then allowed it to run without interference.

The decline of religious enthusiasm and the rise of rationalism prepared the way for the Great Awakening, a major religious revival which affected all of the American colonies and had its counterpart in Europe during the 1730's and 1740's. Theologically the Great Awakening was an attempt to revive orthodox Calvinism, to return to a belief in predestination, original sin, and a harsh and angry God who interfered constantly in the world. But the preachers of the Great Awakening put more emphasis on emotion than did the Puritan ministers of the seventeenth century. In part the revival was a protest against sophisticated and intellectual religion. Jonathan Edwards, the most important leader of the revival, pictured man dangling like a spider over a pit of eternal flame and in grave danger of falling in. He described the searing pain that men would have to endure through all eternity unless they repented; and they repented in droves. The Great Awakening spread throughout all the colonies, coming to a climax during the tour in 1740 of the great British evangelist George Whitefield.

Undeniably the Great Awakening led to conflict; it split most of the Protestant churches into "new light" and "old light" factions, and set off a bitter controversy between the revivalists and the religious establishment. It led to the founding of new colleges (Brown, Rutgers, Princeton, and Dartmouth), for even though the "new light" faction was suspicious of educated clergymen, and maintained that one did not have to be learned to believe, it did need institutions to train ministers. The Awakening also released a humanitarian impulse to help the disadvantaged—the Negro and Indian, the orphan and pauper

—for one tenet of the revival was that all men were equal in the sight of God. The religious turmoil also had a great influence on political, economic, and social trends. Some historians have even argued that the Great Awakening was a more significant event in the development of the American nation than was the American Revolution.

How should we evaluate the importance and influence of the Great Awakening? Some historians emphasize the class and regional conflict associated with the religious revival, arguing that the poorer citizens, especially the back-country farmers were most influenced. Religious differences, added to economic and political differences, widened the split between rich and poor and increased social and class conflict in America. Other historians suggest that the Great Awakening was great because it was general, that it affected equally all sections, regions, and classes in America, that its total impact was not divisive, but rather that it helped to develop a common heritage for all Americans.

The selections which follow present several ways of evaluating the Great Awakening. Winthrop Hudson introduces the problem and sets the religious revival in a theological and historical perspective. "Although the Awakening was productive of controversy and strife," he writes, "it was, paradoxically, at the same time a great unifying force . . . ." The other two selections view the problem from a different perspective. John Miller examines Massachusetts, and argues that the Great Awakening "cut a swath between rich and poor, stimulating the hostility that already divided them." Edwin Gaustad challenges Miller directly and maintains that far from being a class and regional matter, the religious upheaval in Massachusetts was a "great and general awakening."

The Great Awakening was an important event in the early history of the country, and it had ramifications for all aspects of American life. But was its real significance the conflict it sharpened, the divisions it created within the churches? Or is it rather to be found in the general atmosphere of religious tolerance and diversity which followed in its aftermath? In other words, in interpreting the Great Awakening, should we emphasize conflict or consensus?

Winthrop S. Hudson

The Great
Awakening
and national
consciousness

The Great Awakening, which was to exert a decisive and far-reaching influence upon the development of American religious life, was but one manifestation of a general spiritual quickening during the eighteenth century. There were scattered "awakenings" of new religious life in England, Scotland, and Wales, as well as in America, and the Pietist movement on the Continent was a parallel phenomenon. These several awakenings quickly reinforced each other and initiated the great tide of evangelical religion which swept through the English-speaking world, reaching a crest of influence in the latter half of the nineteenth century before it began to ebb away. Churches of all denominations were caught up in the surge of religious fervor and were profoundly affected by its impact. A new type of preaching dominated the pulpits, the structure of public worship was altered, and the "revival" became the most widely accepted means of introducing people to the Christian life.

Although the immediate effect of the Awakening was to arouse opposition, split congregations, set minister against minister, and divide most of the denominations, the opposition in the end was almost everywhere overwhelmed and the ultimate consequence was to mold the various denominations to a common pattern, to subordinate differences, and to make possible wide-ranging cooperative endeavors. Above all, this surging tide of evangelical religion supplied the dynamic which emboldened the Protestant churches of America to undertake the enormous task of Christianizing a continent, nerved those of the British Isles to assume a similar responsibility for an expanding population at home and overseas, and led both the British and the American churches to join forces in a vast mission to the entire non-Christian world.

Why the spark provided by any one of the local quickenings should suddenly have ignited a general conflagration is something of a mystery. The earlier drive and enthusiasm of the Puritan movement, which sprang from a transforming experience of God's grace and a consequent dedication to warfare against sin, had long since lost much of its force. For some the consciousness of entering the Christian life through a "new birth" had been replaced by an insistence upon mere assent to orthodox beliefs as the foundation of the Christian life. Others stressed the reasonable character of the "grand essentials" of all religion and emphasized moral behavior as the distinguishing mark of the Christian. At best the successors of the Puritans tended to appeal to the head without captivating the heart; at worst they promoted a spirit of rationalism (an attempt to validate the Christian faith by human reason) that frequently ended in indifference. There were, of course, exceptions to this general characterization. When Jonathan Edwards spoke of "the time of extraordinary dullness in religion" which preceded the outbreak of the revival in Northampton, Massachusetts, he was but echoing the lament that had been voiced by many of the New England clergy for the better part of a century. And from time to time there had been local awakenings—even in Northampton under the preaching of Solomon Stoddard—when consciences would be touched, faith awakened, and people brought into the churches in unusual numbers. But no general revival had occurred.

Nor is the suggestion that the revivals were the product of the unsettled conditions of frontier life an adequate explanation of a phenomenon that was equally widespread in both Britain and America. Furthermore, the communities along the Connecticut River and between New York and Philadelphia, where the revivals first appeared, were centers of an established agrarian economy rather than frontier settlements. Even after revivalism became an accepted feature of American religious life, revivals seldom occurred in an area until the frontier period was over; and they manifested themselves with equal power in many of the oldest communities.

It is true that the revivals were initially welcomed and later eagerly promoted as an answer to the problem posed by the fact that a large part of the population, in both England and America, stood outside the churches altogether. In England the parish system, which through custom and tradition provided the possibility of long-term nurture and instruction in the Christian faith, had broken down. And in America, with the possible exception of New England, the parish system had never been successfully established. Even in New England the loss of the charter in Massachusetts had made it clear that little confidence could be placed in external guarantees that were designed to ensure that at least the outward formalities of religion would continue to be observed. Thus the churches were confronted by a clear-cut summons to missionary endeavor. Given the circumstances that prevailed, the time was ripe for a type of preaching that would prick the conscience, convict men of sin, and lead them through the agony of repentance into a personally apprehended experience of the new life that was to be found in Christ. The mystery nonetheless remains, for such preaching had never completely disappeared. The novelty of the

Awakening was the widespread response it suddenly elicited, a response so unexpected that it surprised even those who sought it.

THE FIRST STIRRINGS OF REVIVAL

The Great Awakening in America had its antecedents in local revivals which developed among the Dutch Reformed churches of northern New Jersey under the leadership of Theodore J. Frelinghuysen (1691–1748?); among the Presbyterian churches of the same general area under the leadership of the Tennents, father and sons; and in Northampton and other communities of the Connecticut valley under the leadership of Jonathan Edwards. Although these local revivals were not to be consolidated into one great movement until George Whitefield (1714–70) arrived on the scene, they provided a foretaste of what was to come and did much to shape the subsequent outburst of religious fervor and activity.

Theodore J. Frelinghuysen. The "beginner of the great work" in America was a German born near the Dutch border, educated under Dutch auspices, ordained to the ministry of the Dutch Reformed church, and sent to America in 1719 to become the pastor of four Dutch Reformed churches in the Raritan valley of New Jersey. Although he has sometimes been described as a German Pietist, his real affinities and affiliation were with a group of Dutch Calvinists who had been deeply influenced by the experiential piety of the English Puritans.

When Frelinghuysen assumed his new responsibilities, he discovered, much to his dismay, that most of his parishioners were content with a perfunctory orthodoxy which had become for them more a symbol of their Dutch nationality than an expression of any deep-seated Christian conviction. He immediately embarked on a program of reform, seeking to rouse them from their lethargy by a strict enforcement of the provisions of the Reformed discipline with regard to admission to the Lord's Supper, by personal conferences in their homes, and above all by pointed evangelistic preaching which sought to induce the members of his congregations to take seriously the understanding of the Christian faith they ostensibly professed. Perhaps the emotional response he evoked was partially due to the vigor of the opposition he aroused. Many were scandalized by his bluntness, and his congregations were disrupted and thrown into turmoil. The cause of the disaffected was championed by the Dutch ministers of New York, one of whom visited them in their homes to encourage their opposition. Frelinghuysen, however, refused to be daunted and conversions became so frequent in the heated atmosphere that opposition within his own congregations was silenced. By 1726 the revival was at its height, had begun to spread to other Dutch communities, and within the next few years Frelinghuysen was to gain the support of the majority of the Dutch ministers. Nevertheless the rift between the two parties persisted and was not healed for several decades.

The Tennents. William Tennent (1673–1746) and his sons were the key figures in the outbreak of the revival among the Presbyterians. A graduate of the University of Edinburgh and an unusually able teacher and scholar, the father followed Irish precedent in giving his sons their theological training in his own home while he was a pastor at Bedford, New York, from 1720 to 1727. Gilbert Tennent (1703–64), his eldest son, received a Master's degree from Yale in 1725, perhaps in partial compensation for his father's disappointment in not being named to succeed Timothy Cutler as president of that institution. Two years later, the father moved to Neshaminy, Pennsylvania, where he established an embryo college of his own. Deeply indebted to the Puritan devotional classics for his own understanding of the Christian faith, the elder Tennent succeeded in transmitting his earnest concern for a vital inward faith both to his sons and to the graduates of his "log college" at Neshaminy.

The chronology of the awakening among the Presbyterians is somewhat obscure, for Gilbert Tennent reports that his brother John had the first actual revival. This must have been sometime in 1727 or 1728 when he was serving as a licentiate in the Presbytery of New Castle. Later, when John Tennent was pastor at Freehold, New Jersey (1730–32), another revival occurred which was carried forward after John's death by his brother William, Jr. Gilbert Tennent, however, was the most important of the brothers. He was the outstanding preacher and the natural leader of the men his father had trained.

In 1726 Gilbert Tennent had been called to the Presbyterian church at New Brunswick, New Jersey, where the revival among the Dutch Reformed was at its height. He and Frelinghuysen immediately recognized each other as kindred spirits, for the views of both men had been shaped by the characteristic emphases of evangelical Puritanism. Tennent's ministry, by his own account, was not conspicuously successful at first, but Frelinghuysen encouraged him and Frelinghuysen's success served both as a rebuke and as an inspiration. After a period of sickness, during which he was "exceedingly grieved" that he had "done so little for God" and had vowed to "promote his kingdom" with all his might if God would be pleased to spare him for this purpose, Tennent began to secure the response his father had taught him to seek.

The nub of the problem, as Tennent defined it, was what he called the "presumptuous security" of those who professed to be Christians. They had been baptized, catechized, and inducted into full membership in the church. They affirmed orthodox doctrines and were fully persuaded that one is saved by faith and not by works. But faith was interpreted as merely assent to orthodox ideas and was quite unrelated to most of the Christian graces. There was little of the inwardness and transforming power of the Christian faith to be found among them. To counter this smugness and complacency Tennent adopted the old Puritan technique of preaching for "conviction"—an acknowledgment or conviction of one's own sinful estate. He insisted that no one ever became a Christian without first being subjected to the terrifying realization that he is not a Christian. He must first know himself as a sinful creature, estranged from God, and rightfully subject to condemnation, before he can apprehend and receive God's forgiveness and acceptance.

Tennent's preaching had the desired effect and by 1729 scattered Presbyterian congregations from New Brunswick to Staten Island had begun to throb with new life under his leadership. Other products of his father's tuition, notably Samuel Blair (1712–51), were equally active. The participation of Presbyterian ministers of New England background, such as Jonathan Dickinson (1688–1747) at Elizabeth and Aaron Burr (1716–57) at Newark, was also enlisted. By the end of the 1730's there had been eight or ten local revivals of some degree of intensity. In the meantime Gilbert Tennent was gaining a wider hearing through the publication in 1735 of three of his sermons in New York and one in Boston. Earlier in the same year two sermons by John Tennent with an account of the revival at Freehold had also been published in Boston.

Jonathan Edwards. The third manifestation of religious excitement occurred in the Connecticut valley with Jonathan Edwards playing the central role. Edwards, one of the most brilliant and original minds America has produced, scarcely conforms to the popular image of the revivalist. His interests seem to have been wholly academic, and he spent long hours each day in his study. His sermons were tightly knit and closely reasoned expositions of theological doctrine which he read rather than speaking extemporaneously. But, however one may explain it, a revival of extraordinary power did spring from his preaching.

Edwards had been educated at Yale, graduating in 1720 at the age of seventeen. For some years he served there as a tutor, leaving in 1727 to assist his grandfather, Solomon Stoddard, who was pastor of the church at Northampton, Massachusetts, and succeeding him two years later when he died. Edwards was greatly distressed by the "licentiousness" which so generally prevailed among the youth of the town.

> Many of them [were] very much addicted to night walking, and frequenting the tavern, and lewd practices. . . . It was their manner very frequently to get together in conventions of both sexes for mirth and jollity, which they called frollics, and they would often spend the greater part of the night in them.

Furthermore, many of them were "indecent in their carriage at meeting." Edwards began to meet with the young people in their homes; they in turn responded to his pastoral concern; reformation in behavior set in; and by 1733 Edwards was able to report that they had grown "observably more decent in their attendance on public worship."

In the meantime he had been becoming increasingly alarmed by the complacency that was being engendered by the spread of "Arminian" principles. The doctrine of human ability, he was convinced, destroyed the very foundation of the Christian faith. To counter this threat, he preached a series of five sermons in 1734 on justification by faith alone. This, Edwards reported, proved to be "a word spoken in season" and was attended by "a very remarkable blessing of heaven to the souls of the people in this town." A young woman of questionable morals was converted, other young people were stirred by her example, the tempo of religious interest increased, and conversions multiplied.

> This work of God . . . made a glorious alteration in the town, so that in the spring and summer following (anno 1735) the town seemed to be full of the presence of God. It never was so full of love, nor so full of joy, and yet so full of distress, as it was then. There were remarkable tokens of God's presence in almost every house. It was a time of joy in families on the account of salvation being brought unto them; parents rejoicing over their children as new born, and husbands over their wives, and wives over their husbands.

There had been other revivals from time to time in the valley, most notably those which occurred under the ministry of Edwards' grandfather, Solomon Stoddard. None of them, however, had proved to be contagious. With the quickening of 1734 it was otherwise. News was carried to other communities, visitors came to Northampton, Edwards was invited to preach in neighboring churches, and by 1736 the revival had spread throughout the Connecticut valley. But by 1737 the revival in Northampton had come to a halt, ceasing almost as abruptly as it had begun. Even this, Edwards interpreted as further evidence of God's mercy, for by withdrawing his Spirit to other places he was but demonstrating "how entirely and immediately the great work lately wrought was his" and "how little we can do and how little effect great things have without him."

Edwards' fame as a revivalist was the product in part of his *Faithful Narrative of the Surprising Work of God in the Conversion of Many Hundred Souls in Northampton* which was published in London in 1737 and reprinted in Boston in 1738. John Wesley read it as he walked from London to Oxford, George Whitefield read it during his first brief visit to Georgia in 1738, and it had a decisive effect upon both men. Much more important than the stimulation and inspiration the book provided was the way in which it shaped subsequent revival efforts by the precise and detailed account it gave of how the revival at Northampton actually developed. The duplication of this pattern, of course, became a major objective of those who followed him. Even the conversion process itself tended to become stereotyped. Less influential but of greater inherent significance was the series of writings—*The Distinguishing Marks of a Work of the Spirit of God* (1741), *Some Thoughts concerning the Present Revival of Religion* (1742), and *A Treatise concerning Religious Affec-*

tions (1746)—in which he analyzed with amazing psychological insight and scientific detachment the twin phenomena of conversion and revival.

THE GREAT AWAKENING

It was not until 1740 that the local manifestations of intense religious interest and concern were transformed into a Great Awakening which was to spread throughout every colony from Nova Scotia to Georgia and to touch every area—urban and rural, tidewater and back-country—and every class—rich and poor, educated and uneducated—before its power was finally dissipated. There had been interconnections, to be sure, between the revival movements led by Frelinghuysen, the Tennents, and Edwards. Frelinghuysen and Gilbert Tennent actively supported one another. Edwards was at Yale when William Tennent was sufficiently well known there to think of himself as a possible choice for the presidency and when Gilbert Tennent received a degree. In his *Faithful Narrative* Edwards mentions an earlier revival "under the ministry of a very pious young gentleman, a Dutch minister, whose name as I remember was Frelinghuysen." But these were mostly tenuous connections and the revivals remained local in character until they were consolidated into a single movement by the itinerant activity of George Whitefield.

"The Grand Itinerant." A recent graduate of Oxford University, where he had been an intimate friend of the Wesleys and a member of the "Holy Club," Whitefield had spent a few months in Georgia in 1738. Upon his return to England he had adopted, much to the dismay of John Wesley, the expedient of preaching in the open air. Since both men had come to look upon "all the world" as their "parish" to the extent that they were convinced that wherever they chanced to be it was their "bounden duty to declare unto all that are willing to hear the glad tidings of salvation," Whitefield's expedient had the distinct advantage of making it unnecessary to secure an invitation from a local church in order to have an opportunity to preach. Moreover Whitefield's preaching in the open air met with such success that by the time he returned to America late in 1739 he had persuaded Wesley to "become more vile" and to preach in his stead to the great throngs he had assembled in the vicinity of Bristol.

Whitefield arrived in Philadelphia on November 2, 1739. He was a "slim slender youth," twenty-four years of age, with a strong but mellow voice, perfect enunciation, a keen sense of the dramatic, and an ability by subtle inflection to clothe almost any word with emotion. Later it was said that by merely pronouncing the word "Mesopotamia" he could bring tears to the eyes of his listeners. Although his intention had been to proceed immediately to Georgia to look after the affairs of his projected orphanage, Whitefield was prevailed upon to preach first in the Anglican church, then in other churches, and finally he spoke to great crowds each evening from the steps of the courthouse. The response was astonishing.

Even Benjamin Franklin was impressed, both with the young man himself and with the good moral effect of his preaching. William Tennent visited him and persuaded him to make a rapid evangelistic tour of the area between Philadelphia and New York, which had already been stirred by revivals. Conscious of the new opportunity that had opened before him, Whitefield determined to preach his way to Georgia, traveling by land instead of going by ship. After a brief period in Savannah, he was back in the Philadelphia area from the middle of April to the middle of May to collect funds for the building of his orphanage, announcing his intention to visit New England in the autumn on a similar mission.

Whitefield arrived at Newport, Rhode Island, on September 14, 1740, having sailed from Charleston three weeks before. His arrival had been well publicized, and the Boston newspapers carried advertisements of numerous books and tracts by and about Whitefield and even called attention to other writings which he approved. During the next seventy-three days he was to travel eight hundred miles and to preach one hundred and thirty sermons. He was met everywhere by great throngs. The ministers of Boston were enthusiastic in the welcome they extended (Charles Chauncy may have had some reservations), Harvard and Yale threw open their doors, the visit to Jonathan Edwards at Northampton was a triumphant pilgrimage, and by the time Whitefield had made his way through New York and New Jersey to Philadelphia he was convinced that America was to be his "chief scene of action." While this was not to be true, he did make three other tours of the colonies and had just embarked upon a fourth when he died at Newburyport, Massachusetts, on September 30, 1770.

If America was not the chief scene of his labors, Whitefield nonetheless did as much to shape the future of American religious life as anyone else. Previous to his coming the "quickening" sermons had been preached in churches and at stated hours of public worship. And when sermons were delivered to congregations other than one's own it was at the invitation of the pastor. But Whitefield knew no such restrictions. He preached whenever and wherever he could find anyone to listen; and in this, as well as in his extemporaneous preaching, he had many imitators. Through him also, with his incessant traveling and a catholicity of spirit that welcomed an opportunity to preach from any pulpit that was opened to him, the revival impulse permeated every denomination. America in turn did much to shape Whitefield. He was early indebted to Edwards, and Gilbert Tennent helped win him to a type of Calvinism that later cost him the friendship of the Wesleys. Henceforth he was to be firmly convinced that the doctrine of election was the only sure guard against the notion that one is saved by one's own choice and decision.

THE MOUNTING OPPOSITION. Although the early revivals among the Dutch Reformed and Presbyterians had provoked discord and strife and although Whitefield had encountered vigorous opposition among his fellow Anglican ministers, the Edwardsean revival and the subsequent visit of Whitefield to New England had been viewed with remarkable equanimity and approval. In 1741, however, the storm broke.

Among the Presbyterians the occasion for the violent rupture was Gilbert Tennent's sermon on *The Danger of an Unconverted Ministry*, delivered at Nottingham, Pennsylvania, on March 8, 1740, and published at Philadelphia before the end of the year. It was an intemperate discourse. Even though he had been goaded into a denunciation of "pharisee-teachers" by the persistent efforts of men who gave little evidence of any serious Christian concern to sabotage his father's "log college," Gilbert Tennent's response only served further to inflame them. "Is a blind man," he asked,

fit to be a guide in a very dangerous way? Is a dead man fit to bring others to life? . . . Is an ignorant rustic that has never been at sea in his life fit to be a pilot? . . . Isn't an unconverted minister like a man who would learn others to swim before he has learned it himself, and so is drowned in the act and dies like a fool?

And the sermon ended with an open invitation for people to forsake the ministry of "natural" men and to seek out instead a congregation where they would receive profitable instruction.

The result could have been predicted. The opposition was both consolidated and angered. At the meeting of the Synod of Philadelphia in 1741 the revivalist group was expelled, and later formed the rival Synod of New York. At the time of the expulsion the antirevivalist group was slightly stronger with twenty-seven ministers as against the twenty-two members of the Tennent party. Seventeen years later, in 1758, when the schism was finally healed with the formation of the Synod of New York and Philadelphia, the antirevivalist ministers in the old Synod of Philadelphia had dwindled in number to twenty-three while the ministers of the newer Synod of New York had more than tripled in number to seventy-three. The initial defeat was turned into an ultimate triumph by the withering of the antirevivalist party and by the subsequent conciliatory spirit displayed by Gilbert Tennent.

When Whitefield left New England on his way to Philadelphia he had met Gilbert Tennent and had insisted that Tennent must go to New England in order to carry forward the work Whitefield had begun. Tennent's tour, from December 13, 1740, to March 3, 1741, was marked by the same large crowds that had greeted Whitefield, and at New Haven many of the students were converted. There was, however, an undercurrent of opposition among some of the clergy. Charles Chauncy (1705–87) in particular had had second thoughts which caused him to regard Tennent's preaching as unlearned, confused, ill-prepared, and ill-delivered. Rumors had begun to circulate concerning Tennent's Nottingham sermon which, if the rumors were true, was clearly calculated to undermine and foster disrespect for ministerial authority.

After Tennent's departure a sizable portion of the New England clergy exploded in indignation. Not only were the rumors concerning Tennent's sermon confirmed, but printed copies of Whitefield's journal of his New England tour were found to contain disparaging comments concerning the caliber of many of the New England ministers. Whitefield, to be sure, had paid tribute to the general level of religious life in New England which he regarded as exceeding that of any other part of the world, but many of those who preached, he felt, did not "experimentally know Christ."

> The ministers' preaching almost universally by note is a certain mark they have in a great measure lost the old spirit of preaching. . . . It is a sad symptom of decay of vital religion when reading sermons becomes fashionable where extempore preaching did once almost universally prevail.

Whitefield even echoed Tennent's denunciation of unconverted ministers. The reason that congregations have been dead, he wrote, is that "dead men preach to them," and "how can dead men beget living children?" God may, if he chooses, "convert people by the Devil," and he may also "by unconverted ministers," but "he seldom or never makes use of either of them for this purpose." Nor could one look to the New England colleges, Harvard and Yale, to supply ministers of different caliber, said Whitefield, for "their light is become darkness, darkness that may be felt and is complained of by the most godly ministers."

Opposition was further aroused by the fanatical spirit and emotional extravagance of James Davenport (1716–57) who projected himself on the scene at this particular juncture. The revival preaching, to be sure, was highly emotional and on occasion people were known to cry out, to weep and sob, and even to faint and swoon. But the leaders of the revival were careful to restrain such public displays and to cast doubt upon them as evidence of conversion. Thomas Prince (1687–1758) reported that he did not "remember any crying out or falling down or fainting, either under Mr. Whitefield's or Mr. Tennent's ministry all the while they were here [in Boston]." It was otherwise with James Davenport who did so much to bring the revival into disrepute by encouraging all manner of excess.

The grandson of the founder of New Haven and a graduate of Yale, Davenport had been called to a pastorate on Long Island in 1738. Stirred by the revival excitement, he crossed to Connecticut in the summer of 1741 to follow the itinerant path blazed by Whitefield and Tennent. His sermons were marked by invective, incoherent ejaculations, and indiscriminate denunciations of ministers. He sang as he made his way through the streets to the place of worship. He claimed to be able to distinguish infallibly the elect from the damned, publicly greeting the former as "brethren" and the latter as "neighbors." He was obviously unbalanced mentally, and the leaders of the revival immediately sought to dissociate themselves from him. But the damage was done, and the revival cause was brought into further disrepute when Davenport invaded Massachusetts the following summer. He had been arrested in Connecticut and transported under guard out of the colony. In Massachusetts he was jailed, again adjudged insane, and sent back to Long Island. In the end his sanity seems to have been restored, and through the friendly counsel of Eleazar Wheelock and Solomon Williams he came to see the error of his ways. In 1744 he published his *Confessions and Retractions*, expressing the hope that this would remove the prejudices which his extravagant behavior had evoked. It was a vain hope, for those who had been affronted by Whitefield's ill-considered observations were only too happy to utilize Davenport's excesses as a weapon to discredit the revivalists as a whole.

Charles Chauncy led the attack and blasted the revival from the pulpit of the First Church of Boston in a sermon entitled *Enthusiasm Described and Cautioned Against*. This was followed in 1743 by a more extended denunciation, *Seasonable Thoughts on the State of Religion in New England*. The Harvard faculty was also incensed. When Whitefield had first visited Boston he had been entertained and commended by the president of the college, and the Overseers had set aside a day of thanksgiving for the beneficent effects of his labors. When he returned in 1744 the doors of the college were closed to him and the faculty issued a statement, later endorsed by the Yale faculty, blistering his message, his methods, and his character.

The situation was quite confused and the ministers were badly divided. The "Old Lights," under the leadership of Chauncy, embraced perhaps a third of the ministers of New England. They tended to move in the direction of "rationalism" in theology and constituted the group out of which Unitarianism was later to emerge. As many as another third were "New Lights" who favored the revival and participated wholeheartedly in it, while deploring the unfortunate excesses which the "Old Lights" so vigorously denounced. Only a handful were ready to insist upon emotional manifestations as evidence of conversion and to defend itinerancy and lay preaching. The others were uncommitted. This basic division among the Congregational ministers of New England between "Old Lights" and "New Lights," with certain subsequent refinements and shifts in alignments, was to persist until it was finally obliterated in the first quarter of the nineteenth century by the coming of the "Second Great Awakening" and by the withdrawal of the Unitarians from the Congregationalist fold. . . .

THE IMPACT OF THE AWAKENING

The Awakening was much more than the activity of a few conspicuous leaders. It was "Great" because it was general. People everywhere

were caught up in the movement, and its influence was spread by innumerable local pastors, passing itinerants, and lay exhorters. No one
could escape the excitement or avoid the necessity to declare himself as
friend or foe.

And because the Awakening was general, it played an important role
in forming a national consciousness among people of different colonies
whose primary ties were with Europe rather than with one another. As a
spontaneous movement which swept across all colonial boundaries, generated a common interest and a common loyalty, bound people together in a
common cause, and reinforced the conviction that God had a special
destiny in store for America, the Awakening contributed greatly to the
development of a sense of cohesiveness among the American people. It
was more influential in this respect than all the colonial wars the colonists
were called upon to fight, more influential in fact than many of the political squabbles they had had with the mother country since the latter as
often served to separate as to unite them. Whitefield, Tennent, and
Edwards were rallying names for Americans a full three decades before
Washington, Jefferson, Franklin, and Samuel Adams became familiar
household names. Perhaps it is significant that the Awakening did not
reach Nova Scotia until 1776, too late to create the intangible ties which
bound the other colonies together.

INSTITUTIONAL CONSEQUENCES. No exact estimate can be made of
members added to the churches by the Awakening, but the number in all
denominations was large. Interest in Indian missions was revived. A wide
variety of charitable projects, including schools for Indians, Negroes, and
the children of indentured servants, were initiated. The role of the laity in
the churches was enhanced. The setting of minister against minister
undermined ministerial authority at a time when a stress upon a self-
authenticating religious experience was freeing the individual from dependence upon clerical opinion. On the other hand, quite paradoxically,
the ministerial office was also given added luster by the fame of the
revivalists, and the number of young men drawn into the ranks of the
ministry rapidly mounted.

Apart from the multiplication of churches, the major institutional
survivals of the Awakening came from the impulse that was given to
higher education by the necessity to provide educational opportunities
for the swelling number of ministerial recruits. The Presbyterians were
especially active in this endeavor and many of their ministers established
classical academies, similar in character to William Tennent's "Log
College" and patterned after the small private Presbyterian academies of
Ireland and the Dissenting academies of England which at this time
enjoyed an educational reputation that was greater than that of the

ancient universities. Several colleges—Washington and Lee, Washington and Jefferson, and Dickinson—trace their ancestry back to these early academies. In 1746 the Synod of New York secured a charter for the College of New Jersey (Princeton) which was designed as the capstone of the Presbyterian educational structure, and in 1776 the Hanover Presbytery in Virginia established Hampden-Sydney College. The Baptists also organized several academies and in 1764 founded the College of Rhode Island (Brown University) as their major center for the training of the ministry. In 1766 the pro-revivalists among the Dutch Reformed obtained a charter for Queen's College (Rutgers University). Dartmouth, an outgrowth of an Indian charity school, was incorporated in 1769. Columbia University (originally King's College), of course, had no connection with the Awakening, nor did the University of Pennsylvania which became a degree-granting college in 1755. The latter, it is true, had its origin in the tabernacle which had been constructed in 1740 for George Whitefield to use when inclement weather made it impossible for him to speak in the open air.

Although the clergy of the English settlements along the seaboard did not have the opportunity to duplicate the work of the priests who accompanied the French traders and trappers on their far-ranging travels through the interior of the continent, the evangelization of those tribes with whom the English came into contact did not suffer neglect. The effect of the Awakening was to pour new enthusiasm into this task. Eleazar Wheelock, Samuel Kirkland, David Brainerd, and for a time Jonathan Edwards were among those who devoted themselves to Indians missions. The diary of David Brainerd, edited by Jonathan Edwards, is a moving testament of devotion which tells the story of his experiences among the Indians, and it inspired many others to give themselves to mission work.

THE THEOLOGICAL TEMPER GENERATED BY THE AWAKENING. Evangelicalism, to use the term by which the new surge of spiritual life is usually described, has often been interpreted as a revolt against Calvinism. While this may have been its ultimate consequence, it was far from that in the beginning. The understanding of the Christian faith as set forth in the great Reformed Confessions was taken for granted. John Wesley was an important exception but, in many respects, even Wesley stood firmly within the Genevan tradition. Evangelicalism, however, was much more a mood and an emphasis than a theological system. Its stress was upon the importance of personal religious experience. If it was a revolt against anything, it was a revolt against the notion that the Christian life involved little more than observing the outward formalities of religion. . . .

Although the Awakening was productive of controversy and strife, it was, paradoxically, at the same time a great unifying force which gave to "four-fifths" of the Christians in America "a common understanding of the Christian life and the Christian faith." Since the revival had penetrated many denominations quite indiscriminately, this common understanding tended to minimize the importance of denominational distinctions and to provide a basis for mutual respect, appreciation, and cooperation. Typical of the new spirit was John Wesley's emphatic declaration that he renounced and detested all distinctions among Christians, and refused to be distinguished from other men by anything but "the common principles of Christianity." From "real Christians" he had no desire to be distinguished at all. "Dost thou love and fear God? It is enough! I give thee the right hand of fellowship." This catholicity of spirit was even more conspicuously exhibited in George Whitefield. Whitefield spoke with equal readiness from Anglican, Presbyterian, Congregational, Baptist, and Dutch Reformed pulpits, and he counted men of all denominations among his converts. Preaching from the courthouse balcony in Philadelphia, he raised his eyes to the heavens and cried out:

Father Abraham, whom have you in heaven? Any Episcopalians? No! Any Presbyterians? No! Any Independents or Methodists? No, no, no! Whom have you there? We don't know those names here. All who are here are Christians. . . . Oh, is this the case? Then God help us to forget party names and to become Christians in deed and truth.

His attitude was echoed by Samuel Davies in Virginia.

My brethren, I would now warn you against this wretched, mischievous spirit of party. . . . A Christian! a Christian! Let that be your highest distinction; let that be the name which you labor to deserve. God forbid that my ministry should be the occasion of diverting your attention to anything else. . . . It has . . . been the great object of my zeal to inculcate upon you the grand essentials of our holy religion, and make you sincere practical Christians. Alas! . . . unless I succeed in this, I labor to very little purpose though I should presbyterianize the whole colony.

In addition to a common understanding of the Christian faith, a particular understanding of the nature of the Church underlay this broadminded spirit. It was what has been called the "denominational" concept of the Church, and it had been elaborated a century earlier by the Dissenting Brethren in the Westminster Assembly of Divines.

This concept of the Church was to be of decisive future importance in American religious life. Denominationalism, as these men used the term, was the opposite of sectarianism. A "sect" regards itself alone as the true Church. By definition a "sect" is exclusive. "Denomination," on the other hand, was adopted as a neutral and inclusive term. It implied that the group referred to is but one member, called or denominated by a particular name, of a larger group—the Church—to which other denominations belong. Gilbert Tennent stated the concept with clarity and incisiveness when he declared: "All societies who profess Christianity and retain the foundational principles thereof, notwithstanding their different denominations and diversity of sentiments in smaller things, are in reality but one Church of Christ, but several branches (more or less pure in minuter points) of one visible kingdom of the Messiah."

On the basis of this understanding of the Church which acknowledged the unity that existed within the diversity of outward ecclesiastical forms, the Protestant churches were able to develop a functional catholicity which was to find expression in the creation of a whole system of cooperative societies for the promotion of a host of worthy causes, including both home and foreign missionary activity. These were to be the instruments into which much of the evangelical fervor released by the Awakening was to be channeled when the Protestant churches subsequently addressed themselves to the overwhelming task of attempting to Christianize a whole continent.

Religion and class conflict in Massachusetts

John C. Miller

In comparison with the feverish changes of our own day, the eighteenth century in New England followed a singularly steady and quiet development during its first three quarters. But beneath this outward calm the stage was being set for revolution, and when the curtain rises for a moment, in 1740, we catch a glimpse of the social unrest and political tumult that marked Shays's Rebellion and the nineteenth-century populist revolts. As the curtain goes up on this period of New England's history, conservatives were getting the worst fright they received between Anne Hutchinson and Sam Adams. The rift between rich and poor was steadily widening; "Mutiny, Sedition, and Riots" seemed imminent; and the popular branch of the government was in the hands of a formidable party bent upon overthrowing the existing regime. Instead of damning the Devil for their misfortunes, New Englanders were damning the rich merchants and gentry of Boston and demanding sweeping changes in government and finance. But just as the factions appeared about to come to open blows in Massachusetts, a religious revival swept through the country, and the people were soon whooping hallelujahs and tumbling in Puritan meeting-houses. The political turmoil in Massachusetts was

From John C. Miller, "Religion, Finance, and Democracy in Massachusetts," *The New England Quarterly* (1933), Vol. VI, pp. 29–49, 55–58. Reprinted by permission of *The New England Quarterly*.

suddenly brought to an end and the threat of revolution in the state faded away. Yet the revolutionary spirit remained in New England, and after five years of religious turbulence the Congregational Church was shattered by the "mad Frolicks of the Rabble" and its ministers became a "hissing to the People."

What caused the Great Awakening to split up the Congregational Church and cut a swath between rich and poor, stimulating the hostility that already divided them? Because the Great Awakening burst upon New England at a time of social conflict, it is impossible to answer these questions satisfactorily without taking its environment into account. When social unrest and a religious revival are contemporary, they do not remain in water-tight compartments; the Great Awakening and the Land Bank ferment must be viewed together in order to explain the outburst of hatred and the uprising of democracy which brought Massachusetts close to insurrection.

In 1740 Massachusetts was nearing the crisis of a business depression caused primarily by the financial chaos in the colony. The scarcity of a stable currency made the burden of payment unbearable to debtors; the province was drained of its hard money, and its paper money was so debased as to be almost unfit for the purposes of trade. This jumble gave the poor a common grievance and rallying-cry, for both town artisans and farmers were in a "pretty Pickle" and many were desperately in debt. When the depression was at its worst, a scheme was set on foot in Massachusetts to form a Land Bank, which would issue enough paper money to satisfy the business needs of the province. The promoters of the Land Bank held out to the ignorant debtor class an easy way of escaping from poverty: cheap Land Bank money would bring back prosperity and at the same time break the Boston merchants' grip on the colony's finances. This mixture of rosy promises and hard times formed a leaven which puffed the Land Bank faction to portentous dimensions. The bulk of the party was composed of the lower classes: "the needy part of the Province," "the Mobility," "the Idle and Extravagant." Out of these materials the Land Bank leaders built a powerful political machine designed to "humble the proud Merchants" and bring the government within the grasp of the common people. Over a large part of Massachusetts elections were controlled by the "numerous swarm of the village" and by "gangs . . . at the beck of the Land Bank." Boston itself was under the thumb of the "Boston Chaps who rule the roast" and the Land Bankers piled up a large majority in the House of Representatives. It was very evident to the uneasy gentlemen of Boston that the question which lay at the root of the struggle was whether the common people or the wealthy families of the town should control the political life of the colony; the balance trembled between the "Idle and Extravagant who want to borrow money at any bad Lay" and "our considerable Foreign traders and rich Men."

The merchants fought the proposed Land Bank tooth and nail, for they saw in it nothing more than a scheme of "fraudulent Debtors" to cheat their creditors and overturn the existing political order. They were in a flutter of apprehension at the prospect of seeing Massachusetts flooded with "weak bottom'd" Land Bank currency and "desperate and fraudulent" debtors firmly seated in the political saddle. With these bugbears to spur them on, the merchants were not lax in attempting to throttle the plan, and Governor Belcher in particular "exerted himself to blast this fraudulent undertaking." In spite of these efforts, the Land Bank made steady headway, and the rising tide of radicalism in Massachusetts seemed more and more likely to swamp the aristocracy. Faced with this growing menace, the merchants and Crown officials looked to the British Parliament as the last remaining bulwark against the colonial radicals. The Land Bankers were gathering up the threads of power so rapidly in Massachusetts that parliamentary intervention seemed to be the only way of curbing them; "I question," wrote Governor Belcher, "whether anything less than an act of Parliament will be sufficient to stop the progress" of the Land Bank scheme and prevent the "ruin of government and people." But for the moment, the merchants' efforts to crush the Land Bank through parliamentary interference succeeded only in bringing the bad blood to a boiling point. The Land Bankers assumed the name of the "Patriot Party" and attacked the merchants in language similar to that later used by the "Sons of Liberty" against the tories. They were denounced as "griping and merciless usurers" who "heaped up vast Estates" and made themselves "Lord of Mannors" by bringing ruin and poverty upon the common people. They plunged the people into debt until "Hundreds of Thousands are due to them" and they made the paper money worthless by sending all the hard currency abroad to pay their debts. In a short time, it was said by the Land Bankers, one merchant would "swallow up thousands of Families;" if the merchants continued to dominate Massachusetts, yeomen would be forced into the degradation of "Husbandmen, Laborers and Tenants." Even a French invasion was pictured as preferable to remaining as the "Slaves and Vassals" of the mercantile overlords.

It was in this thick atmosphere of fear and rancor that George Whitefield attempted to revive Puritanic fervor. But in spite of the efforts made by his friends to put him in the spotlight as "an Angel sent from God," he became the object, even before he reached the country, of bitter attacks which reflected the prevailing uneasiness and distrust. Many feared that Whitefield was a sort of Jack Cade in a cassock. It was known in Massachusetts that his preaching in other colonies had "produc'd Disorder and Confusion among the People, and possess'd the Minds of many of the Populace with Notions dangerous to the well being of the Constitution both in Church and State." To allay this alarm, Benjamin Franklin published several articles in which he represented Whitefield as urging people "to submit themselves to all their Governors, Teachers, Spiritual Pastors, Masters, etc." Nevertheless, the more timid or conservative continued to look upon Whitefield with suspicion. Massachusetts offered such fertile soil for the growth of radicalism that the merchants had qualms whenever they considered what would happen if some ranting demagogue, such as Whitefield was thought to be, should come into the colony. "Vast Confusions" seemed to be in store for New England, and even the local brand of agitator was too much for the merchants to handle. If demagoguery and levellism got into the pulpits, the work of "knaves upon fools" would begin in earnest. The merchants were already in a cold sweat lest the Land Bankers ride into power on the crest of the wave of popular unrest and turn "this Province noted for Trade" into "a Habitation of Rude Rusticks." To let loose a religious fanatic in the colony would simply be throwing fuel on a fire that seemed only too likely to scorch both gentry and merchants.

This fear of the effects of Whitefield's pulpit-pounding was not altogether unfounded. But Whitefield was no leveler of distinctions in the State. He did not mix his revivalism with political democracy, nor did he attempt to set class against class. He preached a hot gospel, but it was not the gospel of discontent. Whitefield set out to destroy "all that Bigotry and Party Zeal that has divided Christians" and largely as a result of his efforts to unite rich and poor in the "Work of God." The Great Awakening momentarily salved the wounds which the Land Bank fracas had given to class relations in Massachusetts. Rich and poor left off wrangling to join in the exhilarating work of casting the Devil out of New England. Merchants regularly closed shop in order that they and their assistants might hear Whitefield preach. Rubbing shoulders in crowds and experiencing the emotions of a common religious exaltation, proved to be a good antidote for the exacerbating effects of the financial and political struggle that had set New Englanders by the ears. The clergy began to feel that Whitefield had succeeded in shelving the Land Bank question and that a new Puritan Age was just around the corner. "Old and Young, Parents and Children, Masters and Servants, High and Low, Rich and Poor together," said the Reverend Benjamin Colman, "gather in the Streets, and as Doves on the Wing in Flocks flying to the Doors and Windows of our Places of Worship; and hovering about the same, those that could not get in."

However earnest Whitefield may have been in urging New Englanders to erase old scores and unite in furthering the revival, he remained in New England for only a few weeks and he was able to give merely a temporary respite to the Land Bank furor. The man he selected to succeed him in "crowning Christ anew" in Boston was scarcely of the temperament necessary to bring about an era of good feeling. The Reverend Gilbert

Tennent had been educated in the Jersey backwoods at his father's "Log College," and his style of pulpit-thwacking and thundering earned him the name among the delighted yokels of the "Son of Thunder." It was said that Tennent's "beastly Brayings" seemed to have a "particular quarrel with Reason, Learning and Morality; he seldom finished a Sermon without saying something against them." Both Whitefield and Tennent emphasized the doctrine that the real danger to salvation lay not in ignorance but in learning. Education was liable to clog the spiritual passages with the rubbish of books; the soul must be free to soar, and education was so much ballast. They preached that the people should follow their "inward impressions" and "whisperings of the Spirit" for these were the voice of God. Consequently, from the beginning, the Great Awakening was spiced with a good deal of contempt for "worldly learning" and each successive leader of the revival threw in larger and larger quantities of this seasoning. This aspect of the awakening had not been evident while Whitefield was in New England, but Tennent's preaching soon made it apparent that beneath a superficial renewal of Puritan fervor, the Great Awakening carried a threat to the most enduring of Puritan traditions—that of an educated clergy.

The open hostility of the revivalists to education was one of the first causes which drew the upper classes away from the movement. The wealthy and educated could have little sympathy for men who made deprecating comparisons between the "carnal Colleges" of England and America and the New Jersey Log College which Whitefield thought to resemble "the Schools of the old Prophets." But Whitefield and Tennent did not let the matter rest here. By playing up this scorn of education they attempted to oust many of the Congregational clergy from their pulpits. When Whitefield was called upon to revive Puritanism in New England, he began by demanding first of all a "purification of the pulpits" —a weeding out of the ministers who had slipped into the error of spending their time in libraries. "I am fully persuaded," Whitefield wrote in his Journal, "the generality of Preachers (in New England) talk of an unknown, unfelt Christ. . . . How can dead Men beget living Children?" The only right course for New England was to rid itself of the "Formalists" that cluttered up the pulpits and put in preachers who "knew" Christ and were able to give the people some really "rousing" gospelling. When Tennent came to Boston, he proposed to "water the Seed sown by Mr. Whitefield"—which meant spattering the "unregenerate clergy" with the exceedingly muddy water that Tennent used in his pious gardening. In scurrility and bluster, the evangelists left the Land Bank rabble-rousers far behind: nothing would content them but "harrying" out the ministers who had sinned on the side of education. The people themselves were to be the ultimate judges of the spiritual state of their ministers; both Whitefield and Tennent taught that ordinary individuals might follow the "whisperings of the Spirit" that came to them in determining whether a preacher spoke of a "felt" or "unfelt" Christ. Making this "inner light" the primary test in affairs of Church and State opened wide the door to the spread of new-fangled notions. When the evangelists began haranguing crowds about the sanctity of whispers, the levellism of the Great Awakening was well on its way.

Many people listened to these "unjust and hard Speeches belch'd out against their own proper Pastors not only with Patience but with Pleasure." But a considerable number of those who had distrusted the Great Awakening from the beginning regarded these insults heaped by the revivalists upon the regular clergy as ominous proof of the necessity of stopping the revival before it got out of hand. The appearance of the "Opposers" or "Old Lights," led by Charles Chauncy and a group of conservative ministers, marks the end of New England's religious unity and the adding of sectarian bitterness to the financial and political struggle that was taking place in Massachusetts.

While Tennent was railing against the "unsanctified ministers and Opposers," and the first cracks were beginning to appear in the Congregational Church, economic conditions in Massachusetts were going from bad to worse. The widespread distress worked in favor of the Land Bank party and increased the fear of the upper classes that the leaders of the "Patriot Party" would get the upper hand. The winter was unusually severe and the colony seemed to be upon the brink of a serious food shortage; "there is at present," wrote Governor Belcher early in 1741, "a great scarcity of all kinds of grain, beyond what I can remember for forty years past." In Boston, the "quarrelsome, mobish Spirit and Impatience under Government that has so long been growing," gave rise to fears of mob-rule and outright insurrection. The House of Representatives reflected the popular unrest by going completely out of control and treating the Crown with "all possible rudeness and ill-Manners." It flatly ignored the royal instructions concerning the issuance of paper money and seemed inclined to pull the royal beard so lustily that Belcher doubted whether it would "leave Jupiter a hair upon his face, but will bid defyance to his imperial resentment." The Land Bankers' determination to put an end to the regime of merchants and gentry was strengthened by the huzzas of yokels and town laborers who believed that they could do as they pleased since the colony was "pretty much out of the reach of the government at home." Massachusetts was filled with "Clamours and Threatenings," and the friendship between social classes that the Great Awakening had ushered in was forgotten as the Land Bankers prepared to play their trump cards in a desperate effort to make the colony "ripe for a smarter sort of government."

In May, 1741, the Land Bank party reached the "height of its Malignity." The clergy were still dreaming of a new Puritan Age, but there was little in the temper of the people to remind one of the days of Cotton and Winthrop. "They are grown so brassy and hardy," wrote Governor Belcher, "as to be now combining in a body to raise a rebellion." For election day there was planned a march of thousands of farmers on Boston to join forces with the town laborers. The embattled farmers, assisted by their urban allies, would then "force the currency of the Land Bank Bills" and demand grain from the merchants; "if corn was there and the merchants would not let them have it they would throw them into the dock."

What might have gone down in history as the Great Massachusetts Rebellion, was nipped in the bud. Governor Belcher was too busy ferreting out radicals not to have learned of this plan of certain extremists among the Land Bankers to risk all at a single throw. He had been prophesying that such an outbreak would take place, and he and his agents were prepared to act if the "madness and infatuation of this great Province" should lead to open revolt. Belcher struck quickly and hard. The leading conspirators were rounded up and jailed. Election day came, and the province remained outwardly calm. But the vote was overwhelmingly in favor of the Land Bankers; so complete was their victory that they gained control of the Council, normally the bulwark of conservatism in the colony. Yet it proved to be a short-lived triumph. Just as the Land Bank party was taking the reins of government in Massachusetts, it was learned that Parliament had responded to the pleas of Belcher and the Boston merchants by extending the Bubble Act to the colonies. This was the death-warrant for the Land Bank; the disgruntled patriots were forced to dissolve their party and bring the political turmoil to an end. Parliament's belated action in clamping the lid on colonial radicalism saved Massachusetts from passing under the control of the common people, but it did not extinguish the democracy or ill-feeling between rich and poor that had flared up so luridly during the Land Bank crisis. The subsequent history of the Great Awakening shows how this pent-up discontent passed from secular to ecclesiastical affairs and at last succeeded in wrecking the Congregational Church.

Thus far the Great Awakening had lacked the kind of leadership that would make it an out-and-out crusade against the established order. Whitefield and Tennent had smoothed the way for a genuine demagogue to lead the revival, but it was not until the Reverend James Davenport appeared in New England that levellism and hatred between social classes became one of the "distinguishing Marks" of what Jonathan Edwards called "this Work of God." In the spring of 1742, Davenport's work in Connecticut began to send chills down the spines of conservative New Englanders; "we rejoice with Fear and Trembling," wrote the Reverend Benjamin Colman as he anxiously watched the storm brewing in the neighboring province. In his native Southold, Long Island, Davenport

had received a sudden impression that the "Glory of the Lord was about
to fill the whole World" and that he was to be an "eminent Instrument"
in the work of conversion. This impression was so overpowering that
Davenport set off in the middle of winter to bring Connecticut to glory.
When he began to whoop and sing in the fields and meeting-houses, the
common people responded in a manner which further disgusted the upper
classes with the antics of the "giddy-head'd Rabble." All the hysteria—
the tumbling, groaning and wailing—of backwoods hot-gospelling flared
up in the colony. At Groton over a thousand rustics assembled to quake,
shout, and pray with "sweet Mr. Davenport." The meeting was protracted
until two o'clock in the morning, when, after much spiritual wrestling
and devout tumbling, the worshippers fell asleep in the meeting-house
and yard. It was true that Davenport's preaching was "without form or
Comelyness . . . all meer confused Medley," but he had "a knack at
raising the Passions, by a violent straining of his Lungs." Davenport's
haranguing swept the people completely off their feet and Connecticut
began to taste true-blue revivalism.

Wherever Davenport preached, disorder broke out—as the people were
seized with paroxysms of devotion or were pricked by his oratory into
hatred of the upper classes. Davenport gave his audiences a mixture of
brimstone pulpit-pounding and social levellism. He condemned ministers
as "unsanctified" at a glance and urged a virtual mobilization of the
countryside against those who had fallen under his strictures. Magistrates
fared no better at his hands, for Davenport damned both magistrates and
ministers in the same breath. He preached that all laws of government
which restrained the revival "ought to be disregarded and were against
the laws of God." This was too much for the land of steady habits; even
some of the New Lights urged that "all who fear God should rise up and
labour to crush the enthusiastical Cockatrice in the Egg." Davenport was
accused of inciting the people into "indecencies" and haled before the
Connecticut Assembly, where he was found guilty on the grounds that
his doctrines and preaching had "a natural tendency to disturb and destroy the peace and order of this government." Leniency was recommended, however, because it was apparent that he was mentally deranged
and "therefore to be pittied and compassionated, and not to be treated
as otherwise he might be." He was ordered to be transported to Southold
to his own congregation, and all precautions were taken lest this sentence
should lead to an uprising of his adherents. The evangelist was marched
down to the Connecticut river between "two files of musketiers" and put
aboard a sloop. The crowds that lined the way were restive but they were
overawed by the militia, and no attempt was made to free Davenport.
In this summary manner, Connecticut wiped her hands of Davenport
and his levellism. Conservatives saw the end of Davenport's "mad Career"
in this action taken by the Assembly; in Boston in particular there was

a general feeling of relief when it became known that the self-appointed Apostle to New England was safely stowed away and on his way to Long Island. But while the upper classes were beginning to breathe more easily after the fright Davenport's activities had given them, it was learned that instead of sailing home, the revivalist was on his way to Boston to bring "many Sons and Daughters to Glory there."

Surrounded by a "Rabble of Men, Women, and Children," Davenport landed at New Boston "near the Causeway" on June 22, 1742. Immediately the evangelist and his followers began to sing praises of King Jesus and set off through the streets bawling for sinners to take heart because Davenport would convert them and save them from hell-fire. Davenport himself was a lusty singer and usually led the street-singing; he saw no reason to boggle over such a slight breach of the proprieties, for he was convinced that his arrival in New England marked the beginning of the new Apostolic Age. Davenport's purpose was to prepare New England for the impending visit of Christ; in the meanwhile, whooping and singing about Christ was sanctioned, for "since King Jesus is now riding in Triumph over his Enemies in a Glorious Manner, we may well sing Hosannas to him even in the Streets, as they did of Old."

The Boston clergy banged their pulpits shut and issued a public "Declaration" in which Davenport was pronounced to be "deeply tinctur'd with the Spirit of Enthusiasm" and his preaching "big with Errors, Irregularities, and Mischief." The declaration urged that the people stand behind their ministers and have nothing to do with the "Enthusiasts" who were making the Great Awakening a rough-and-tumble affair of shrieks and jerks. But much to the ministers' surprise, their declaration—"faithful and wise, soft and tender"—did little more than arouse the people's resentment against their own pastors. Instead of quashing Davenport, the clergy simply brought him into the limelight and his popularity among the common people skyrocketed. It was a certain sign that the leadership of the Great Awakening was slipping out of the regular clergy's hands when it became apparent that "many of the good People of Boston . . . were so much offended" at the declaration against Davenport. The Boston ministers had been holding a bridle upon the revival, and anything that savored of impropriety was ruled out as long as they held the reins. They had pictured the Great Awakening as a re-birth of Puritanism under their leadership, but on the first day that Davenport preached in Boston it was evident that they no longer controlled the revival. Ignoring the ministers' advice, the crowd swarmed to the Common several thousand strong. Many came out of curiosity, but a large part of the audience was composed of the "rabble," "those of the lowest Rank," "idle and ignorant Persons" who saw in Davenport a martyr persecuted by an oppressive Church and State. The Great Awakening had passed into their hands, and it was among them that Davenport began the work of bringing about the fall of the hated educated clergy.

Davenport's mannerisms in preaching were highly theatrical, "his Voice Tumultuous, his whole Speech and Behaviour discovering the Freaks of Madness, and Wilds of Enthusiasm;" "were you to see him in his most violent Agitations," said Thomas Fleet, "you would be apt to think, that he was a Madman just broke from his Chains." This was a new kind of brimstone spell-binding which had the effect of turning the meeting into an uproar of shrieks and moans; it seemed as if bedlam had broken loose when Davenport screamed that all were "damned, damned, damned— damned to Hell, damned to Hell," and then began to enact the sufferings of Christ upon the Cross. Finally he brought his harangue to an end and returned to his lodgings with a large mob singing and howling at his heels, looking "more like a Company of Bacchanalians after a mad Frolick, than sober Christians who had been worshipping God."

Davenport soon repaid with interest the rebuff the Boston ministers had given him by closing their pulpits and warning the people to beware of his fanaticism. Following in the footsteps of Whitefield, he began to purify the Congregational Church by damning the clergy. He set himself up as an inquisitor and made the rounds of the Boston ministers in order that he might scrutinize their souls and decide whether they were fit to preach. After this preliminary catechism, although most of the ministers had slammed their doors in Davenport's face, he fell to the task of weeding out the "unregenerate." By the number of clergymen he classified under that heading it was apparent that he would be satisfied with nothing less than the wholesale eviction of the Boston ministry. They were all damned, he exclaimed, and to hear them preach was as ruinous to the peoples' souls as "swallowing Rats-bane or Bowls of Poison was to their Bodies." These "carnal and unconverted Men" were "destroying and murdering Souls by thousands" and were leading their congregations down to hell by the shortest route. The only way for the people to escape this danger was to set up separatist meetings and even laymen would be preferable to the regular clergy. The Boston ministers, declared Davenport, "knew nothing of Jesus Christ" and so were to be shunned like the Devil. When he was not terrifying the people with threats of hell-fire, Davenport worked to bring them to a pitch of passion against their ministers. "Pull them down, turn them out, and put others in their Places," he screamed, and there was a surging among the crowd at his words which might well have disturbed the guardians of order and authority in the Church.

The result of Davenport's fulminations against the clergy was to divide social classes much as during the Land Bank furor. The Opposers were joined by more and more of the wealthy and educated as Davenport carried the Great Awakening down to a lower stratum and preached the gospel of discontent and levellism. Under such stimulation, to hate an Opposer became one of the tests of salvation; if Opposers were tolerated, one had no more chance of getting into heaven than if one were on friendly terms with "the Devil and his works." Davenport gave such emphasis to this idea that many people in Boston became uneasy at the ugly mood and "menacing Speech" of his followers; it was said that many of Davenport's converts would "make Nothing to kill Opposers, and in so doing, think they did God Service." If an Opposer was so hardy as to attempt to restrain the people, he was lucky to escape with a whole skin; no interference was permitted, for the Great Awakening was a "Work of God" and the lower classes had now come to regard themselves as its chosen guardians. This conviction among the common people that they had been singled out by God for salvation and that the Opposers—the upper classes—were for the most part damned gave class feeling a new twist in Massachusetts. Whereas during the Land Bank controversy, hatred had been justified upon economic grounds it now began to take on a religious tinge. The aristocracy that had lately quashed the Land Bankers and had been denounced as usurious blood-suckers became in 1742 "Carnal Wretches, Hypocrites, Fighters against God, Children of the Devil, cursed Pharisees." The Land Bank had fallen flat as a pancake. But what would be the outcome of this new crusade of town laborers and farmers that drew its strength not from economic grievances but from religious exaltation? "The Times are dangerous we live in," wrote Gilbert Tennent in a letter of repentance and self-condemnation, "perhaps the Revival of God's Work in diverse Places is but a prelude to a storm." . . .

Although the expedition against Louisbourg in 1745 gave a momentary respite to this disintegrating process within the Church by bringing together Protestants of all ranks in a crusade against the "Papists," the ground swell of discontent and class hostility never completely died down while Massachusetts remained a colony. In 1748, the cry of the common people against the mercantile aristocracy was still the familiar chant of "O wretched Members of Society, who shall deliver us from them?" Even though economic grievances might subside for the moment, there remained the undercurrent of ill-feeling which drew its source from differences in religious outlook. The Great Awakening gave these religious differences an institutional basis; as a consequence, Massachusetts was racked by the almost incessant wrangling of sects that were divided to a large extent upon class lines. In this manner, hostility between rich and poor took on a pungent religious flavoring, and the enmity that the Land Bank had stirred up was carried by the Great Awakening deep into the lives of the common people.

The patriot party that emerged from the Land Bank ferment had been crushed just as it was about to taste the sweets of political power. With the aid of Parliament the rise of democracy in Massachusetts was staved off for a generation. But it was impossible to overlook the fact that it was only the alliance of the colonial aristocracy with the British Parliament that saved Massachusetts from passing into the hands of the popular party. From the bitter experience of 1741, radical leaders in the colony learned that it was futile to kick against the pricks of the mercantile over-lords as long as Parliament stood ready to strike down the democrats whenever they seemed to menace the merchants' interests. Yet this alliance of merchants and Parliament—so effective in putting a bridle upon the radicals—proved to be merely a brief honeymoon. The Stamp and Sugar Acts wiped out the gratitude the merchants felt towards Parliament and drove many of them to join hands with the patriots. This put an entirely new complexion upon the popular party. Whereas the patriot party of 1740 had met with the determined opposition of the upper classes, that of 1765 was bolstered by a good measure of support from the aristocracy. Revolution was made possible by the leadership of men who had resisted the threatened uprising of workingmen and farmers in the days of the Land Bank. Religious excitement had momentarily brought rich and poor together during the Great Awakening; they again rubbed shoulders when Parliament's policy began to raise a sense of insecurity and alarm among the people. Patriotism was diverted into a new channel when Parliament entered colonial affairs with commercial and taxation schemes which seemed to spell ruin not simply for part of the population but for merchants, farmers, and artisans alike.

*   *   *

As the flood of religious enthusiasm of the Great Awakening receded, it left behind the wreckage of churches over a good part of the American colonies. The results of the Great Awakening in Massachusetts had their counterpart elsewhere: churches were split by the secession of New Lights and democratic tendencies were strengthened by being linked with religious fervor. In a sense, the Great Awakening was a nationwide movement before a nation had been formed and its contribution towards making the nation that later came into being is perhaps not the least of its influences. The eruption of New Light churches over the colonies produced hundreds of itinerants who worked to bring the common people into spiritual contact with the separatist congregations of other provinces. Persecution likewise helped the New Lights scattered along the Atlantic seaboard and backwoods to learn their common identity and to spur them into hatred of the ruling class. And arbitrary rule, whether from Parliament or from the local aristocracy, pressed heavily upon men who believed themselves singled out for salvation and who held the militant faith to which the Great Awakening had given rise.

The Great Awakening: a general religious revival

Edwin S. Gaustad

Contemporaries of the turbulent religious upheaval which took place in New England in the years 1740 to 1742 described it as a "great and general awakening." Later historians, less ready to admit either its greatness or its generality, have in concert described the revival as limited to this area or that, to this social class exclusive of that and as brought about by this or that socio-economic force. We have come a long way from "the economic interpretation of religion," when all felt obliged to excuse the obtrusion of churches and pious sentiments by explaining that this sheep's clothing of religion concealed an economic wolf within. Yet the phenomenon known as the Great Awakening is of such proportions as to lead to its interpretation as something other than a religious movement.

It would be folly to suggest that the Awakening was completely divorced from the culture of eighteenth-century New England, from the shortage of specie, from the growth of trade, from the greater leisure and less crudity of life, from the vigilant struggles for popular representation and the increasing degree of political independence. To admit its connection with these secular developments is, however, vastly different from cataloguing the revival as a "deep-rooted social movement," as a lower class uprising, or as "a revolt of the backcountry producers." John Chester Miller viewed the movement as riding on the wave of hostility between rich and poor created by the Land Bank uproar, and producing a full and permanent cleavage between the social classes. . . .

There is, on the contrary, abundant evidence that this religious turmoil was in fact "great and general," that it knew no boundaries, social or geographical, that it was both urban and rural, that it reached both lower and upper class. The geographical non-particularity of the Great Awakening is readily established, though it is necessary to distinguish it from the earlier series of revivals emanating from Northampton. Beginning in 1734 and continuing for two or three years, these revivals were largely a frontier phenomenon, concentrated along the banks of the Connecticut River from

From Edwin S. Gaustad, "Society and the Great Awakening in New England." *William and Mary Quarterly* (October, 1954), Third Series, Vol. XI, pp. 566–577. Reprinted by permission of the *William and Mary Quarterly*.

Northfield to Saybrook Point. They arose under the influence of Jonathan Edwards and the "surprising conversions" which took place in Northampton. To them, but only to them, the term "frontier revivalism" can with propriety be applied, and not to the Great Awakening, which began after the earlier revivals were "very much at a Stop" and the initial phase of which occurred rather in the coastal than in the inland area. Edwards regarded the two movements as quite distinct, speaking of the revivalism early in 1741 as "the beginning of that extraordinary religious commotion, through the land. . . . In the frontier revivals, no churches were split, no clergy were offended, no flagrant itineracy occurred, no elaborate apologetic was necessary, no legislation was provoked, and no vast array of abusive epithets came into use.

The Awakening itself began when, on September 14, 1740, the proud, portly, and pompous George Whitefield arrived at Newport to preach (he tells us) with "much Flame, Clearness and Power. . . . The People were exceedingly attentive. Tears trickled down their Cheeks. . . ." His arrogance passed for conviction, his sentiment for piety, his superficiality for simplicity, and his moving rhetoric for inspiration. And wherever the youthful Anglican went, so did the Awakening. It spread from Newport to Bristol to Boston, and northeast to Roxbury, Marblehead, Ipswich, Newbury, Hampton, Portsmouth, and York. It moved west of Boston into Concord, Sudbury, Worcester, Leicester, Brookfield, and Northampton; thence south, through Springfield, Suffield, Windsor, Hartford, and New Haven; and southwest, through Milford, Stratford, Fairfield, and Stamford. In less than two months, the tour of New England by "the Grand Itinerant" was over. From the many areas left shaking, tremors reached out to meet each other, and to move all that lay between.

At the small town of Harvard, about forty miles west of Boston, "God was pleased . . . to rouze and awaken sleepy Sinners," this being done without the intervention of any itinerants or "Strangers." On November 23, 1741, all heaven broke loose in Middleborough, Massachusetts. "I have written Accounts of seventy-six that Day struck, and bro't first to inquire what they should do to escape condemnation." Their joyful pastor, Peter Thacher, further notes that from that time on, there was "an uncommon Teachableness among my People." In Weathersfield, Connecticut, Eleazar Wheelock reported late in 1741 that "the Lord bowed the heavens and Came Down upon a Large assembly in one of the Parishes of the town the Whole assembly Seam'd alive with Distress. . . ." Gilbert Tennent, who followed Whitefield in a tour of New England, observed that at Charlestown "multitudes were awakened, and several had received great consolation, especially among the young people, children and Negroes." He recorded also a general "shaking among the dry bones" at Harvard College, while in New Haven the concern was considerable and "about thirty students came on foot ten miles to hear the word of God." In brief, it is simply not possible to draw any meaningful lines on a map of New England in order to distinguish where in 1741 the revival was and where it was not. It was a phenomenon not alone of the back country or exclusively of the cities, of the coast or of the frontier. From Stamford, Connecticut, to York, Maine, from Danbury to Northfield (the New England Dan to Beersheba), there had been a great and general awakening.

In 1742, six Boston ministers testified that these "uncommon religious Appearances" were found "among Persons of all Ages and Characters." Another Boston clergyman, the fiery Presbyterian John Moorhead, extolled "the wonderful things which God is adoing, and has already Manifested amongst Indians, Negroes, Papists and Protestants of all Denominations." Though somewhat extreme, Moorhead's observation points to the truly universal character of the Awakening. If it reached Indians, Negroes, and even Quakers, is it possible that it extended also to the upper classes?

It has never seemed urgently necessary to offer proof of lower-class participation in the revival, perhaps because of the finality of such a quotation as the following, which describes James Davenport and his Boston listeners:

> Were you to see him in his most violent agitations, you would be apt to think, that he was a Madman just broke from his Chains: But especially had you seen him returning from the Common after his first preaching, with a large Mob at his Heels, singing all the Way thro' the Streets . . . attended with so much Disorder, that they look'd more like a Company of Bacchanalians after a mad Frolick, than sober Christians who had been worshipping God. . . .

A strong image such as this lingers long in the imagination, causing Davenport and his large mob, in retrospect, to seem the epitome of the Awakening. Even in those surveys of New England's revival where Davenport is not regarded as its personification, he is given disproportionate emphasis. There was no Davenport party. By the ardent supporters of the revival he was judged, in the middle of 1742, to be "deeply tinctur'd with a Spirit of Enthusiasm," and unworthy to be invited "into our Places of public Worship"—this from the ministers who diligently worked in behalf of the "great and glorious work of God." Indeed, the friends of the Awakening feared him more than its foes, for they recognized in him the potential for discrediting the entire movement. Thomas Prince, joyfully describing the successes of the revival in Boston, tells of Davenport's coming in these words: "And then through the providence of the sovereign God, the wisdom of whose ways are past finding out, we unexpectedly came to an unhappy period, which it exceedingly grieves me now to write of. . . ." His fellow Presbyterian, Gilbert Tennent, himself repeatedly condemned for going to rash and intemperate extremes, denounced Davenport's technique as "enthusiastical, proud, and schismatical." Further, in the summer of 1742, a Connecticut court found Davenport "disturbed in the rational Faculties of his Mind," while a Massachusetts court declared him *non compos mentis*. To be sure, if Davenport represented anything at all, it would be of a lower order. The point is, however, that he was the spokesman for no class or party, and least of all is he a symbol of the Great Awakening as a whole.

When Whitefield departed from Boston on his first New England tour, the *Evening-Post* editorialized that "the Town is in a hopeful way of being restor'd to its former State of Order, Peace and Industry." Three days later, a letter, appearing in the *News-Letter*, deplored this attitude, affirming that "the Generality of sober and serious Persons, of all Denominations among us (who perhaps are as much for maintaining Order, Peace and Industry as Mr. Evening-Post and Company) have been greatly Affected with Mr. Whitefield's Plain, Powerful, and Awakening Preaching. . . ." Were the "sober and serious" actually reached by the revival? Benjamin Colman, of the Brattle Street Church, wrote Whitefield that after Tennent's visit to Boston "great Additions are made to our Churches. . . . Many of them among the Rich and Polite of our Sons and Daughters. This week the overseers of our Colleges have appointed a Day of Prayer and Humiliation with thanksgiving, for the Effusion of the Spirit of God. . . ." The phrase, "especially among young people," often occurs in contemporary accounts of the revival, suggesting a greater concentration of "concern" in that generation. But that the movement followed class lines, there is no indication.

With reference to the colleges, of which Colman spoke and of whose social standing there can be little question, their sympathies would have remained with the Awakening had not Whitefield heedlessly insulted them. Yale and Harvard both cheerfully heard the leading exponents of the movement, and some of the instructional staff left their posts to carry the word. An effective deterrent to their support was this remark, published in Whitefield's *Journal*: "As for the Universities, I believe it may be said, their Light is become Darkness, Darkness that may be felt, and is complained of by the most godly Ministers." Whitefield sought to mitigate the effect of this unwarranted affront by writing a letter in July, 1741, "To the Students, &c. under convictions at the colleges of Cambridge and New-Haven," declaring that "It was no small grief to me, that I was obliged to say of your college, that 'your light was become darkness;' yet are ye now become light in the Lord." The damage had already been done; nevertheless, not until 1744 did Harvard issue a formal testimony against Whitefield, Yale following suit in 1745. Even then, it must be noted, the testimony was "Against the Reverend Mr. George Whitefield, And his Conduct" and not against the revival in general. Yale and Harvard graduates alike continued to bear the main responsibility in furthering the "extraordinary Work of God."

Pro-revivalism was in no way the equivalent of social egalitarianism. One of the sins for which Jonathan Edwards reproved his young people was their spending much time in "frolicks," without having "any regard to order in the families they belonged to. . . ." There was a large measure of social consciousness in Edwards's Northampton parish, as later events even more clearly revealed; yet the church could hardly be regarded as outside the scope of the Awakening. Ebenezer Parkman of Westborough, a peerless social conservative, was fully sympathetic with the revival at the same time that he complained in horror that the young men of the lower classes had the presumption to adorn themselves with "Velvet Whoods." Gilbert Tennent, often represented as a leveller and "a Man of no great Parts or Learning," had in fact received from his father no mean education in Hebrew, the classics, and theology, and could move easily in any stratum of society.

In Boston, then if not now, the upper reaches of New England society were concentrated. And that city's support of the revival was an effective force in the entire movement. When Whitefield first came to town, he was "met on the Road and conducted to Town by several Gentlemen." Later in the week, he dined with the governor, Jonathan Belcher, with whom he enjoyed a most cordial relationship. Of Boston's four newspapers, three were either favorable to the Awakening or successfully maintained some degree of neutrality. Only Timothy Fleet's rather coarse *Evening-Post* was openly opposed to the revival, and even this paper did not dare to swim against the tide of public feeling until near the end of 1742, when the movement had already begun to ebb.

The established clergy of New England's capital were preponderantly pro-revivalist or New Light: the proportion was three to one. Of the three divines hostile to the Great Awakening, only Charles Chauncy was open and active in his opposition, and he did not begin a deliberate refutation of the revival until 1743. Throughout 1741, Chauncy allowed himself to be carried along in the main current of the movement, even to the point of telling sinners that they "hang, as it were, over the bottomless pit, by the slender thread of life, and the moment that snaps asunder, you sink down into perdition. . . ." As late as May of 1742, Chauncy declared, "There are, I doubt not, a number in this land, upon whom God has graciously shed the influence of his blessed Spirit. . . ." So that during the height of the Awakening, 1740 to 1742, its most able and prodigious opponent sounded much like Jonathan Edwards himself. The two remaining Old Lights or "Opposers" among Boston's established clergy, both of the Mather family, published nothing concerning the religious excitement, though they privately expressed their disdain of the affair. Samuel Mather, son of Cotton, was dismissed from Second Church in 1741 because, among other reasons, of his negative attitude toward the Awakening and his reluctance to participate in it. In a vain attempt at reconciliation, Mather promised "to beware of any thing in my sermons or conversation which may tend to discourage the work of conviction and conversion among us." Mather Byles, grandson of Increase and first pastor of the Hollis Street Church, succeeded in avoiding any public controversy over the revival. Though publishing a sermon in 1741 on *Repentance and Faith The Great Doctrine of the Gospel of Universal Concernment*, Byles' position—religious and political—was unalterably conservative, and his sympathies were thoroughly Old Light.

Except for three wavering neutrals, the other Boston ministers vigorously, tirelessly, promoted the revival. The city's senior pastor at this time was Benjamin Colman, of Brattle Street Church. A great friend to institutions of higher learning and widely respected abroad as well as at home for his erudition, Colman received the degree of Doctor of Divinity in 1731 from the University of Glasgow. Liberal and learned, he did not hesitate to "play the Artillery of Heaven against the hardy Sons of Vice," and in 1741 he happily reported that "The Work of God with us goes on greatly . . . our crowded serious Assemblies continue, and great Additions are made to our Churches." Following Whitefield's initial visit, Colman spoke at Boston's first evening lecture of the pleasure it gave the ministers to see "in the Weeks past, Old and Young, Parents and Children, Masters and Servants, high and low, rich and poor together, gathering . . . to the Doors and Windows of our Places of Worship. . . ." Benjamin Colman is certainly to be regarded as a constant friend of the Awakening—though, just as certainly, he is to be distinguished from such fanatics as James Davenport and Andrew Croswell. His position, however, was rather one of discrimination than of moderation. He had even shown great interest in the earlier Northampton revival, corresponding with Edwards and others connected with it, passing on to his friends abroad news of religious awakenings in the colonies, and urging Edwards to write the *Faithful Narrative of Surprising Conversions*. The first minister of New England to correspond with Whitefield, he was instrumental in bringing the latter to that area. With much zeal and sincere concern, he favored and furthered the revival to the very end, seeking, like Edwards, to discourage the excesses and abnormalities as no proper part of the true display of God's grace.

William Cooper, Colman's associate since 1715, joined with his colleague in praising "the remarkable Work of Grace begun, and I hope going on amongst us; the eminent Success which God has been pleas'd to give to his preached Gospel of late; the surprizing Effusion of the Holy Spirit, as a Spirit of Conversion to a blessed Number. . . ." At First Church, there was no such harmony. Chauncy's opposition was offset by the approbation of his associate, Thomas Foxcroft, of what he called the "Pauline Spirit and Doctrine remarkably exemplify'd among us." Thomas Prince and Joseph Sewall of Old South Church were eminently successful in making that church a vital center of revival activity. Prince, Boston's foremost reporter of the Awakening, was largely responsible for the creation of the disorganized but important *Christian History*, the first specifically religious magazine in the colonies, the purpose of which was to give accounts of the "surprizing and . . . extensive Revivals." Although it was ostensibly edited by Thomas Prince, Junior, the magazine's enemies were probably correct in declaring the elder Prince to be the power behind the pen. Joseph Sewall, who looked upon the revival as itself a means or channel of grace, inveighed against "every Thing that hath a Tendency to quench his [God's] Spirit, and obstruct the Progress and Success of his good Work." John Webb, senior minister at New North Church, vividly portrayed Christ entreating reluctant sinners in this time of concern to seek and receive the saving grace. His colleague, Andrew Eliot, in 1743 signed a testimony favoring the Great Awakening, noting only that itineracy had not been sufficiently protested against. Samuel Checkley of New South Church, who in 1741 preached on the topic "Little children brought to Christ," was among the same group of signers. And Joshua Gee of Second Church, having reproved the cool indifference of his associate, Samuel Mather, exploded with bitterness when in 1743 a group of ministers issued a testimony against errors and disorders in the Awakening without making "an open acknowledgement of the late remarkable Effects of a gracious Divine Influence in many of our Churches." Gee succeeded in calling a gathering of ninety New England ministers who were "persuaded there has of late been a happy Revival of Religion," and in issuing a favorable witness to the revival signed by sixty-eight divines and attested to by forty-three others unable to attend the meeting.

The division of Boston's Congregational clergy in this turbulent period is, therefore, as follows: nine New Light, three Old Light, three neutral. Five churches were pro-revivalist (Brattle Street, Old South, Second, New North, and New South); New Brick and West were neutral; Hollis Street was anti-revivalist; and First was divided. The city's one Presbyterian church, with John Moorhead as pastor, was as determined in its support of the Awakening as the one Baptist church was in its opposition. One segment of Boston society did hold aloof: namely, that which attended the city's three Anglican churches. But respectability, in eighteenth-century New England at least, was not wholly identified with Anglicanism. Even as it is impossible to fix any meaningful geographical boundaries to the sweep of the Awakening, so the attempt to limit its sway or ascribe its rise to any single social class proves misleading.

As the revival declined and the "distinguishing names of reproach" came to be employed more freely and less gently, theological and ecclesiastical factions hardened, sometimes producing divisions that were social —in Connecticut, even political. With the increase in animosities, reports of revivalism were dismissed as "stupid Bombast Stuff," and Ezra Stiles in 1760 described the period of the revival as a time when "Multitudes were seriously, soberly and solemnly out of their wits." A Connecticut divine summarized the effects of the movement as follows:

Antinomian Principles are advanc'd; preach'd up and printed;—Christian Brethren have their Affections widely alienated;—Unchristian Censoriousness and hard judging abounds, Love stands afar of, and Charity cannot enter; —Many Churches and Societies are broken and divided. . . . Numbers of illiterate Exhorters swarm about as Locusts from the Bottomless Pit. . . .

As such reports came to abound, it seemed plausible, if not desirable, to describe the revival as socially suspect from the beginning, as carried along by a disinherited, rural debtor class. It is, however, tendentious history that sees New England's religious upheaval of 1740 to 1742 as something less than "a great and general awakening."

SUGGESTIONS FOR FURTHER READINGS

A brief but perceptive introduction to religion in American history is Winthrop S. Hudson, *Religion in America* (New York, 1966), from which a portion is reprinted here. A general account which emphasizes the role of the frontier is William W. Sweet, *The Story of Religions in America* (New York, 1930). An interesting interpretation of the American religious heritage by a sociologist, which suggests a common consensus of the three major religious groups in the twentieth century, is Will Herberg, *Protestant-Catholic-Jew: An Essay in American Religious Sociology* (New York, 1955). A general and lively account of religious revivalism in America is Bernard Weisberger, *They Gathered at the River* (Boston, 1958).

Edwin Gaustad's thesis is spelled out in greater detail in *The Great Awakening in New England* (New York, 1957). For an account of the Awakening in another colony which supports Miller's contention of class and regional division see Wesley M. Gewehr, *The Great Awakening in Virginia, 1740–1790* (Durham, N.C., 1930). An intellectual biography of the most important leader in the Awakening is Perry Miller, *Jonathan Edwards* (New York, 1949). Alan Heimert, *Religion and The American Mind: From the Great Awakening to the Revolution* (Cambridge, 1966), is a fascinating and detailed account of the impact of religion on all aspects of American life and thought in the decades following the Great Awakening. Heimert recognizes the conflict created by the revival, but suggests that the Great Awakening promoted an American consensus more significant than that produced by the Revolution.

III

THE ★

AMERICAN ★

REVOLUTION ★

The basic question which must be asked about the American Revolution is, "What was it?" At first glance, the answer to this question seems obvious; a more important problem, it would appear, would deal with the causes of the Revolution. Yet, the question is not so easy to answer as it might seem, and the causes of the Revolution cannot be dealt with without first seeking its answer.

Writing in 1909, the historian Carl Becker argued that the American Revolution was really two revolutions in one —a dual revolution: "The American Revolution was the result of two general movements: The contests for home-rule and independence, and the democratization of American politics and society. Of these movements, the latter was fundamental." In addition to the antagonism toward the British, Becker saw conflicts within America during the Revolutionary period, conflicts arising from sharp class cleavages in American society. The Revolution, then, arose from the desire to reform the British empire—by separating from it—*and* the desire to reform society at home—by instituting democratic and libertarian reforms and by undermining the power of the local aristocracy. Conflict, not consensus, is the theme of this interpretation.

Not all historians accept Becker's answer to the question, "What was the American Revolution?" While granting that there were differences among Americans before and during the Revolutionary period, some historians maintain that to emphasize these differences is to distort the true picture of American society in the eighteenth century. Becker's stress on conflict, they argue, obscures the fact that there was a general agreement among Americans which was stronger and more significant than the differences which divided them. In a variety of ways the experience in the New World had created a new man with new ideas and the Revolution was simply the attempt to maintain what Americans had already rather uniformly accepted. The Revolution was not revolutionary at all, concludes historian Daniel J. Boorstin; it was merely a "conservative colonial rebellion." Obviously, the theme of this interpretation is consensus, not conflict.

The selections which follow illustrate the lack of agreement among historians concerning the nature of the American Revolution. Quoting John Adams, Clinton Rossiter maintains that the "real American Revolution" took place during the colonial period. The change was "in the minds and hearts of the people" and it occurred before the outbreak of hostilities. While Rossiter does not deny that there were differences among the colonial Americans, he finds that these very differences resulted in a general consensus in America.

Merrill Jensen also quotes John Adams and he too returns to the pre-Revolutionary period as a means of understanding the American Revolution. But Jensen sees conflict, not consensus, in the period. He argues that colonial society was marked by vigorous class conflict and that the agitation during the Revolutionary period allowed the democratic, radical elements in America to achieve ascendancy over the aristocratic classes which had ruled colonial society. For Jensen, the Declaration of Independence and the Articles of Confederation were the embodiments of the radical philosophy which had become dominant.

The selections by Robert R. Palmer and Louis Hartz deal with the same general problems in a wider context. Both view the American Revolution in terms of European revolutionary movements and ideas. Palmer finds that although the American Revolution had certain unique features it was, as was the French Revolution, a violent social upheaval. Hartz disagrees sharply with this interpretation. The American Revolution, he maintains, was not a social upheaval simply because there was no feudal aristocracy for it to overthrow. Thus while Palmer finds sharp class divisions which lead to internal conflict, Hartz finds a con-

sensus stemming from the absence of these class differences.

It is evident that the American Revolution was a colonial rebellion resulting in the independence of thirteen
of the English colonies in the New World. Had the colonial
experience resulted in the creation of an American consensus, making the Revolution merely the culmination of
generations of gradual change? If so, then perhaps the
greatest significance of the American Revolution was that
it was not revolutionary!

But such an interpretation may tell only half the story.
Was the American Revolution also a bitter social conflict
on the order of the French Revolution of 1789 or the Russian Revolution of 1917? Perhaps class conflict within the
colonies transformed the colonial rebellion into a revolutionary turning point in American history.

A revolution
to conserve

Clinton Rossiter

In the year 1765 there lived along the American seaboard 1,450,000 white and 400,000 Negro subjects of King George III of England. The area of settlement stretched from the Penobscot to the Altamaha and extended inland, by no means solidly, to the Appalachian barrier. Within this area flourished thirteen separate political communities, subject immediately or ultimately to the authority of the Crown, but enjoying in fact large powers of self-government. Life was predominantly rural, the economy agrarian, religion Protestant, descent English, and politics the concern of men of property.

To the best of the average man's knowledge, whether his point of observation was in the colonies or England, all but a handful of these Americans were contented subjects of George III. It was hard for them to be continually enthusiastic about a sovereign or mother country so far away, yet there were few signs that the imperial bonds were about to chafe so roughly. Occasionally statements appeared in print or official correspondence accusing the colonists of republicanism, democracy, and a hankering for independence, but these could be written off as the scoldings of overfastidious travelers or frustrated agents of the royal will. Among the ruling classes sentiments of loyalty to the Crown were strongly held and eloquently expressed, while the attitude of the mass of men was not much different from that of the plain people of England: a curious combination of indifference and obeisance. Benjamin Franklin, who had more firsthand information about the colonies than any other man, could later write in all sincerity, "I never had heard in any Conversation from any Person drunk or sober, the least Expression of a wish for a Separation, or Hint that such a Thing would be advantageous to America."

Yet in the summer and fall of this same year the colonists shook off their ancient habits of submission in the twinkling of an eye and stood revealed as almost an alien people. The passage of the Stamp Act was greeted by an overwhelming refusal to obey, especially among colonial leaders who saw ruin in its provisions—lawyers, merchants, planters, printers, and ministers. Although the flame of resistance was smothered by repeal of the obnoxious act, the next ten years were at best a smoldering truce. In 1775 the policies of Lord North forced a final appeal to

From *The First American Revolution*, © 1953, 1956 by Clinton Rossiter. Reprinted by permission of Harcourt, Brace & World, Inc.

arms, and enough Americans answered it to bring off a successful war of independence.

Dozens of able historians have inquired into the events and forces that drove this colonial people to armed rebellion. Except among extreme patriots and equally extreme economic determinists, fundamental agreement now prevails on the immediate causes of the American Revolution. Less attention has been devoted to the question: What made this people ripe for rebellion, or, more exactly, what was there about the continental colonies in 1765 that made them so willing to engage in open defiance of a major imperial policy?

One answer, perhaps the best and certainly the best-known, was volunteered in 1818 by John Adams, himself a cause of the American Revolution: "The Revolution was effected before the war commenced. The Revolution was in the minds and hearts of the people. . . . This radical change in the principles, opinions, sentiments, and affections of the people, was the real American Revolution." What Adams seems to have argued was that well before Lexington and Concord there existed a collective outlook called the American mind, a mind whose chief characteristics, so we learn in other parts of his writings, were self-reliance, patriotism, practicality, and love of liberty, with liberty defined as freedom from alien dictation. It was the alien dictation of North, Townshend, Grenville, and the other shortsighted ministers of a shortsighted king that forced the American mind to assert itself boldly for the first time.

Adams did not find it necessary to describe in detail the long-range forces that had produced this mind, perhaps because that extraordinary student of political realities, Edmund Burke, had already given so perceptive a description. In his magnificent speech on conciliation with the colonies March 22, 1775, Burke singled out "six capital sources" to account for the American "love of freedom," that "fierce spirit of liberty" which was "stronger in the English colonies probably than in any other people of the earth": their English descent; their popular forms of government; "religion in the northern provinces"; "manners in the southern"; education, especially in the law; and "the remoteness of the situation from the first mover of government." Implicit in Burke's praise of the American spirit of liberty, as in Adams's recollection of it, was a recognition that this liberty rested on firm and fertile ground, that the colonists enjoyed in fact as well as in spirit a measure of opportunity and self-direction almost unique in the annals of mankind.

The grand thesis of American history toward which Adams and Burke were groping, not altogether blindly, was rounded off by Alexis de Tocqueville a half-century after the Revolution. With one of his most brilliant flashes of insight De Tocqueville revealed the unique nature of the American Republic: "The great advantage of the Americans is that they have arrived at a state of democracy without having to endure a democratic revolution" or, to state the thesis in terms of 1776, the Americans, unlike most revolutionists in history, already enjoyed the liberty for which they were fighting. The "real American Revolution" was over and done with before the Revolution began. The first revolution alone made the second possible.

My purpose . . . is to provide an extended commentary in support of Adams, Burke, and De Tocqueville—not that this glorious threesome needs support from anyone. I accept with practically no reservations the notion that the American Revolution was wholly different in character and purpose from the French, Russian, and almost all other revolutions, and I ascribe this difference largely to the plain truth that the Americans had no need and thus no intention to "make the world over." By 1765 their world had already been made over as thoroughly as most sensible men—most sensible white men, to be sure—could imagine or expect. Americans had never known or had long since begun to abandon feudal tenures, a privilege-ridden economy, centralized and despotic government, religious intolerance, and hereditary stratification. Americans had achieved and were prepared to defend with their blood a society more open, an economy more fluid, a religion more tolerant, and a government more popular than anything Europeans would know for decades to come. The goal of the rebellious colonists was largely to consolidate, then expand by cautious stages, the large measure of liberty and prosperity that was already part of their way of life. . . .

I think it necessary to point to four all-pervading features of the colonial experience that were hastening the day of liberty, independence, and democracy. Over only one of these massive forces did the colonists or English authorities have the slightest degree of control, and the political wisdom that was needed to keep it in tight rein simply did not exist in empires of that time.

I

The first ingredient of American liberty was the heritage from England. Burke acknowledged this "capital source" in words that his countrymen could understand but apparently not act upon.

> The people of the colonies are descendants of Englishmen. England, Sir, is a nation which still I hope respects, and formerly adored, her freedom. The colonists emigrated from you when this part of your character was most predominant; and they took this bias and direction the moment they parted from your lands. They are therefore not only devoted to liberty, but to liberty according to English ideas, and on English principles.

"Wee humbly pray," wrote the General Assembly of Rhode Island to the Board of Trade in 1723, "that their Lordships will believe wee have a Tincture of the ancient British Blood in our veines." The colonists had considerably more than a tincture: at least seven in ten were English in blood, and virtually all their institutions, traditions, ideas, and laws were English in origin and inspiration. The first colonists had brought over both the good and evil of seventeenth-century England. The good had been toughened and in several instances improved; much of the bad had been jettisoned under frontier conditions. As a result of this interaction of heredity and environment, the eighteenth-century American was simply a special brand of Englishman. When it pleased him he could be more English than the English, and when it pleased him most was any occurrence in which questions of liberty and self-government were at issue. In a squabble over the question of a fixed salary between Governor Joseph Dudley and the Massachusetts Assembly, the latter could state without any sense of pretension:

> It hath been the Priviledge from Henry the third & confirmed by Edward the first, & in all Reigns unto this Day, granted, & is now allowed to be the just & unquestionable Right of the Subject, to raise when & dispose of how they see Cause, any Sums of money by Consent of Parliament, the which Priviledge We her Majesty's Loyal and Dutiful Subjects have lived in the Enjoym^t of, & do hope always to enjoy the same, under Our most gracious Queen Ann & Successors, & shall ever endeavour to discharge the Duty incumbent on us; But humbly conceive the Stating of perpetual Salaries not agreable to her Majesty's Interests in this Province, but prejudicial to her Majesty's good Subjects.

Southerners were, if anything, more insistent. In 1735 the South Carolina legislature resolved:

> That His Majesty's subjects in this province are entitled to all the liberties and privileges of Englishmen . . . [and] that the Commons House of Assembly in South Carolina, by the laws of England and South Carolina, and ancient usage and custom, have all the rights and privileges pertaining to Money bills that are enjoyed by the British House of Commons.

And the men of the frontier, who were having the same trouble with assemblies that assemblies were having with governors, made the echo ring.

> 1st. We apprehend, as Free-Men and English Subjects, we have an indisputable Title to the same Privileges and Immunities with his Majesty's other Subjects, who reside in the interior Counties of Philadelphia, Chester and Bucks, and therefore ought not to be excluded from an equal Share with them in the very important Privilege of Legislation.

These were the words of men who made much of the English tie, even when, as in the last of these instances, most of them were Scotch-Irish or German. Their traditions—representative government, supremacy of law, constitutionalism, liberty of the subject—belonged to them as Englishmen. Their institutions, especially the provincial assembly, were often looked upon as sound to the extent that they conformed to English models, or at least to colonial interpretations or recollections of those models. The rights for which they contended were not the natural rights of all men but the ancient rights of Englishmen. "It is no Little Blessing of God," said Cotton Mather to the Massachusetts Assembly in 1700, "that we are a part of the *English Nation.*"

Throughout the colonial period the English descent and attitudes of the great majority of Americans gave impetus to their struggles for liberty. It is a momentous fact of American history that until 1776 it was a chapter in English history as well. Just as England in 1765 was ahead of the Continent in the struggle for law and liberty, so America, this extraordinary part of England, was even further ahead, not least because most of its leading inhabitants thought of themselves as Englishmen. Such men would not easily be cheated or argued out of their heritage—a truth that Burke did his best to advertise:

The temper and character which prevail in our colonies are, I am afraid, unalterable by any human act. We cannot, I fear, falsify the pedigree of this fierce people, and persuade them that they are not sprung from a nation in whose veins the blood of freedom circulates. The language in which they would hear you tell them this tale would detect the imposition; your speech would betray you. An Englishman is the unfittest person on earth to argue another Englishman into slavery.

The clash of imperial policy and colonial self-reliance is almost always productive of the spirit of liberty. This is especially true if the policy of the parent state is conceived purely in its own interests, and if the colonists are men of high political aptitude and proud descent. Such was the pattern of Anglo-American relations in the colonial period. From the time of the earliest settlement, which like all the important settlements was the result of private initiative, English and American opinions on the political and economic status of the colonies were in sharp conflict.

The conduct of colonial affairs by the English government rested on these assumptions: The colonies were dependents of the parent state. Since their interests were subordinate to those of England, the welfare of the latter was to be the one concern of all agencies charged with governing them. They were therefore to serve, apparently forever, as a source of wealth and support for the land out of which their inhabitants had departed. If the English government had acted on these assumptions consistently throughout the colonial period, the contrasting ideas of the colonists would have had less chance to strike deep root. But confusion at the beginning, domestic troubles in the middle, and "salutary neglect" throughout most of this period permitted the colonists to build not only a theory but a condition of self-government. And it was this condition, of course, as some perceptive Englishmen were aware, that helped the colonies develop into prizes worth retaining by force of arms. The interests of England were, in this important sense, fatally self-contradictory.

The views of the colonists on their place in the imperial structure were somewhat mixed, ranging from the arrogant independence asserted by Massachusetts in the seventeenth century to the abject dependence argued by a handful of Tory apologists in the eighteenth. In general, the colonial attitude was one looking to near-equality in the present and some sort of full partnership in the future, all within the confines of a benevolent and protecting empire. The colonist acknowledged that for certain diplomatic and commercial purposes his destiny would rest for some time to come in the hands of men in London. But in all other matters, especially in that of political self-determination, he considered himself a "freeborn subject of the Crown of England." Theories of the origin and nature of the colonial assemblies are a good example of these divergent views. In English eyes the assemblies were founded by royal grant and existed at royal pleasure; in American eyes they existed as a matter of right. The Board of Trade looked upon them as inferior bodies enjoying rule-making powers under the terms of their charters; the men of Virginia and Massachusetts looked upon them as miniature Houses of Commons with power to make all laws they could get away with in practice. The struggle between these assemblies and the royal governors sent to control them was the focus of conflict of colonial and imperial interests.

Had Parliament not decided to intrude its authority into colonial affairs, the old-fashioned imperial views of the English authorities and the prophetic self-governing claims of the American colonists might have co-existed for decades without producing a violent break. The tardy policies of stern control initiated by the Grenville ministry brought this long-standing conflict fully into the open. In the years before 1765 the push-and-pull of imperialism and home rule had been a spur to the growth of liberty in the colonies. In the next decade it ignited a rebellion.

II

Let us hear again from the member for Bristol.

The last cause of this disobedient spirit in the colonies is hardly less powerful than the rest, as it is not merely moral, but laid deep in the natural constitution of things. Three thousand miles of ocean lie between you and them. No contrivance can prevent the effect of this distance in weakening government. Seas roll, and months pass, between the order and the execution; and the want of a speedy explanation of a single point is enough to defeat a whole system. . . . In large bodies, the circulation of power must be less vigorous at the extremities. Nature has said it. . . . This is the immutable condition, the eternal law, of extensive and detached empire.

This harsh fact of geography, the remoteness of the colonies, squared the difference between imperial purpose and colonial aspiration. The early colonists, thrown willy-nilly on their own devices, developed habits of self-government and passed them on to their descendants. The descendants, still just as far if not farther from London, fell naturally into an attitude of provincialism well suited to their condition but corrosive of empire. The lack of contact between one colony and another, the result of distance and unbelievably bad roads, allowed each to develop on its own. The diversity in character of the key colonies of Virginia, Massachusetts, New York, and Pennsylvania made a mockery of any notion of uniform imperial policy.

Worst of all from the imperial point of view, the ill effects of the inconsistency, inefficiency, corruption, stupidity, arrogance, and ignorance displayed to some degree at all times and to a perilous degree at some times by the English authorities were doubled and redoubled by the rolling seas and passing months. English laxity in enforcing the Navigation Acts and colonial habits of disobeying them were one instance of the extent to which three thousand miles of ocean could water down a policy of strict control. The technique of royal disallowance, which seemed so perfectly designed to keep the colonial assemblies in check, was likewise weakened by the mere fact of distance. For example, the disallowance in 1706 of two New Hampshire judiciary acts passed in 1699 and 1701 was never reported properly to the province, and the judiciary in that colony continued to function under these laws for a half century. And the royal governor, the linchpin of empire, was a far more accommodating fellow in Boston or Charleston than he appeared in his commissions and instructions issued from London. A governor like Sir Matthew Johnson of North Carolina, whose reports to the Board of Trade went astray four years in a row, could not have been much of a buffer against colonial urges to independence. When we realize that no regular mail-service of any kind existed until 1755, and that war disrupted communications more than one-third of the time between 1689 and 1763, we can understand how the ocean was at once a highway to freedom and a barrier to imperialism. Rarely in history have the laws of geopolitics worked so powerfully for liberty.

Had Burke ever lived in the colonies, he might have listed still another "capital source" to explain the rise of liberty in America, and thus have anticipated Frederick Jackson Turner and his celebrated thesis. We need not go all the way with Turner—"American democracy is fundamentally the outcome of the experiences of the American people in dealing with the West"—to acknowledge the significance of the frontier in early American history. Whatever the extent of that influence in the nineteenth century, in the seventeenth and eighteenth centuries—when America was one vast frontier and perhaps one in three Americans a frontiersman at some time in his life—it was clearly of the first importance. If we may take the word "frontier" to mean not only the line of farthest settlement to the west, but also the primitive conditions of life and thought which extended throughout the colonies in the seventeenth century and continued to prevail in many areas east of the Appalachians during most of the eighteenth, we may point to at least a half-dozen indications of the influence of the American environment.

First, the frontier impeded the transfer to America of outworn attitudes and institutions. The wilderness frustrated completely such attempts to plant feudalism in America as the schemes of Sir Ferdinando Gorges and the stillborn Fundamental Constitutio..s of Carolina, and everywhere archaic laws and customs were simplified, liberalized, or rudely abandoned. In the matter of church-state relations the frontier was especially influential as a decentralizing and democratizing force. The positive result of this process of sloughing off the old ways was an increase in mobility, experimentation, and self-reliance among the settlers.

The wilderness demanded of those who would conquer it that they spend their lives in unremitting toil. Unable to devote any sizable part of their energies to government, the settlers insisted that government let them alone and perform its severely limited tasks at the amateur level. The early American definition of liberty as freedom *from* government was given added popularity and meaning by frontier conditions. It was a new and invigorating experience for tens of thousands of Englishmen, Germans, and Scotch-Irish to be able to build a home where they would at last be "let alone."

The frontier produced, in ways that Turner and his followers have made clear, a new kind of individual and new doctrines of individualism. The wilderness did not of itself create democracy; indeed, it often encouraged the growth of ideas and institutions hostile to it. But it did help produce some of the raw materials of American democracy—self-reliance, social fluidity, simplicity, equality, dislike of privilege, optimism, and devotion to liberty. At the same time, it emphasized the importance of voluntary co-operation. The group, too, had its uses on the frontier, whether for defense or barn-raising or cornhusking. The phrases "free association," "mutual subjection," and "the consent of the governed" were given new content in the wilderness.

Next, the fact that wages were generally higher and working conditions better in the colonies than in England did much to advance the cause of liberty. The reason for this happy condition was a distinct shortage of labor, and a prime reason for the shortage was land for the asking. The frontier population was made up of thousands of men who had left the seaboard to toil for themselves in the great forest. The results of this constant migration were as important for the seaboard as they were for the wilderness.

From the beginning the frontier was an area of protest and thus a nursery of republican notions. Under-represented in assemblies that made a habit of overtaxing them, scornful of the privileges and leadership assumed by the tidewater aristocracy, resentful of attempts to saddle them with unwanted ministers and officials, the men of the back country were in fact if not in print the most determined radicals of the colonial period. If their quaint and strangely deferential protests contributed very little to the literature of a rising democracy, they nevertheless made more popular the arguments for liberty and self-government.

Finally, all these factors combined to give new force to the English heritage of law, liberty, and self-government. The over-refined and often archaic institutions that the settlers brought along as part of their intellectual baggage were thrust once again into the crucible of primitive conditions. If these institutions emerged in shapes that horrified royal governors, they were nevertheless more simple, workable, and popular than they had been for several centuries in England. The laws and institutions of early Rhode Island or North Carolina would not have worked in more civilized societies, but they had abandoned most of their outworn features and were ready to develop along American lines. The hardworking, long-suffering men and women of the frontier—"People a litle wilful Inclined to doe when and how they please or not at al"—were themselves a primary force in the rise of colonial self-government.

The English descent and heritage of the colonists, the conflict of imperial and colonial interests, the rolling ocean, the all-pervading frontier —these were the "forces-behind-the-forces" that shaped the history of the colonies and spurred the peaceful revolution that preceded the bloody one of 1776. . . .

III

The colonists were not completely at the mercy of their environment. Much of the environment was of their own making; and if circumstances were favorable to the rise of liberty, they did not relieve the colonists of the formidable task of winning it for themselves. The condition of liberty in 1765 was in large part the work of men determined to be free, and the questions thus arise: Who were these men who talked so much of their rights and privileges? Whence came they to America, and how did they fare? . . .

It is now generally agreed that almost all immigrants to the colonies came from the middle and lower classes. "The rich stay in Europe," wrote Crèvecoeur; "it is only the middling and the poor that emigrate." The myths of aristocratic lineage die hard, especially in Cavalier country, but diaries, shipping lists, and court minutes tell us in no uncertain terms of the simple origins of even the most haughty families of New York and Virginia. This does not mean that early America was a land of rogues and poor servant-girls. England and the Continent sent over thousands upon thousands of substantial, intelligent, propertied men and women. Yet fully half the people who came to the colonies could not pay their own passage, and gentleman immigrants, even in the seventeenth century, were amazingly few.

As a matter of fact, those twentieth-century Americans who like to go searching for an ancestor among the gentry of East Anglia may wind up with three or four among the riffraff of Old Bailey. Probably thirty to forty thousand convicts were shipped from England to the colonies in the eighteenth century, a fact that inspired Dr. Johnson's famous growl: "Sir, they are a race of convicts, and ought to be content with anything we allow them short of hanging." Their behavior in the colonies, especially in unhappy Virginia and Maryland, moved Franklin to offer America's rattlesnakes to England as the only appropriate return. Not only did transported convicts commit a large proportion of the crimes in eighteenth-century America, but their presence did much to degrade the servant class and make a callous society even more callous. The mother country's insistence on dumping "the dregs, the excrescence of England" in the colonies was a major item in the catalogue of American grievances, especially since the Privy Council vetoed repeatedly the acts through which the colonies sought to protect themselves.

Well before 1765 the colonies had begun to take on a pattern of national origins that was "characteristically American": They looked to one country for their language, institutions, and paramount culture, but to many for their population. Americans were predominantly English in origin, but they were also Scotch, Irish, German, French, Swiss, Dutch, Swedish, and African. It is impossible to fix precisely the proportions of each nationality in the total white population of 1765; the necessary statistics are simply not available. These general percentages are about as accurate as can be expected: English, 65 to 70 per cent; Scots and Scotch-Irish, 12 to 15 per cent; Germans, 6 to 9 per cent; Irish, 3 to 5 per cent; Dutch 3 per cent; all others 3 to 5 per cent. Out of a total population of 1,850,000, probably 400,000 were Negroes and mulattoes. . . .

What was the total effect on society, culture, and government of this influx of nationalities into the American settlement? . . .

First, the melting pot had only just begun to heat up in the latter part of the eighteenth century. Crèvecoeur's example of the English-French-Dutch family "whose present four sons have now four wives of four different nations" was a phenomenon more prophetic of the Republic than typical of the colonies. The great process of national fusion had made little progress by 1765. Assimilation into the English stock rather than the creation of a new people was the result of such intermarriage as took place in colonial times. Nor were all the ingredients yet in the pot; the essential racial (Teutonic-Celtic) and religious (Protestant) unity of the population must not be overlooked.

The arrival of non-English immigrants did much to weaken the hold of the mother country. The newcomer wanted to be as loyal as anyone else, but his allegiance to the Crown could have little real emotional content. The Germans were inclined to be conservatively neutral about English dominion; the Scots and Irish were, for all the loyal humility that oozed from their petitions, innately hostile to the Georges and their agents. They lacked, as one traveler put it, the "same filial attachment" to England "which her own immediate offspring have."

Next, the influx of aliens did much to strengthen the Protestant, dissenting, individualistic character of colonial religion. The Presbyterian, Lutheran, Baptist, and German Pietist churches were the chief beneficiaries of this immigration. The numbers and enthusiasm of these dissenting groups gave a tremendous lift to the cause of religious liberty in the colonies south of Pennsylvania.

The eighteenth-century immigrants helped democratize the political institutions that had been brought over from England and put to work in the wilderness. This was especially true of the Scotch-Irish, whose only quarrel with the representative governments of their adopted colonies was that they were not representative enough. The Germans were inclined to be politically passive; their major contribution to the coming democracy was the support they brought to the middle-class creed of industry, frugality, and self-reliance. The Scotch-Irish, on the other hand, were more politically conscious. If the controlling groups of the coastal counties refused to honor their legitimate claims to participation in public life, this rebuff served only to make their radicalism more insistent. They had little intention of altering the English-American scheme of government, but they did mean to show the world how democratic it could be. The sentiments of "leveling republicanism" were especially active on the Scotch-Irish frontier; here the "real American Revolution" went on apace.

Finally, the mere volume of immigration from Germany and Ireland had a pronounced effect on colonial life. The swarming of these industrious peoples made possible the remarkable expansion in territory and population that marked the eighteenth century in America. If the Scotch-Irishman was America's typical frontiersman, the German was its typical farmer; and between them they made it possible for cities like Philadelphia and towns like Lancaster to grow and flourish. Though they were men of different natures, both sought the same blessing. "And what but LIBERTY, charming LIBERTY, is the resistless Magnet that attracts so many different Nations into that flourishing Colony?" ...

THE SECOND AMERICAN REVOLUTION SUCCEEDS THE FIRST

On March 22, 1765, George III gave his royal assent to the Stamp Act, a stick of imperial dynamite so harmless in appearance that it had passed both houses of Parliament as effortlessly as "a common Turnpike Bill." Eleven years later, July 2, 1776, the Continental Congress resolved after "the greatest and most solemn debate":

That these United Colonies are, and, of right, ought to be, Free and Independent States; that they are absolved from all allegiance to the *British* crown, and that all political connexion between them, and the state of *Great Britain,* is, and ought to be totally dissolved.

In the tumultuous years between these two fateful acts the American colonists, at least a sufficient number of them, stumbled and haggled their way to a heroic decision: to found a new and independent nation upon political and social principles that were a standing reproach to almost every other nation in the world. Not for another seven years could they be certain that their decision had been sound as well as bold; only then would the mother country admit reluctantly that the new nation was a fact of life rather than an act of treason. The colonists were to learn at Brooklyn and Valley Forge that it was one thing to resolve for independence and another to achieve it.

Yet the resolution for independence, the decision to fight as a "separate and equal" people rather than as a loose association of remonstrating colonials, was as much the climax of a revolution as the formal beginning of one, and it is this revolution—the "real American Revolution"—that I have sought to describe. . . . By way of conclusion, I would think it useful to point briefly to those developments in the decade after 1765 that speeded up and brought to bloody conclusion "this radical change in the principles, opinions, sentiments, and affections" of the hitherto loyal American subjects of George III.

The progress of the colonies in these years was nothing short of astounding. Thanks to the fecundity of American mothers and the appeal of the American land, population increased from 1,850,000 in 1765 to more than 2,500,000 in 1776. America's troubles seemed only to make America more alluring; immigrants arrived in especially large numbers between 1770 and 1773. The westward pressure of 650,000 new colonists was, of course, enormous, and many new towns and settlements were planted in frontier lands east of the proclamation line of 1763. The sharp increase in population of the continental colonies lent support to arguments, especially popular after 1774, that Americans would some day outnumber Englishmen, and that there was "something absurd in supposing a continent to be perpetually governed by an island." Signs of increased wealth and well-being inspired other Americans to sing the glories of "a commerce out of all proportion to our numbers."

Far more significant than this material progress was the quickened influence of the "forces-behind-the-forces." . . . The English heritage, the ocean, the frontier, and imperial tension never worked so positively for political liberty as in this decade of ferment. Until the last days before independence the colonists continued to argue as Englishmen demanding English rights. The more they acted like Americans, the more they talked like Englishmen. Heirs of a tradition that glorified resistance to tyranny, they moved into political combat as English Whigs rather than American democrats, reminding the world that "it is the peculiar Right of Englishmen to complain when injured." The other basic forces were no less favorable to the swift advance of the spirit of liberty. In a situation that called desperately for accurate information, firm decisions, and resolute administration, the very distance between London and Boston frustrated the development of a viable imperial policy. In a situation that called no less desperately for colonial understanding of the imperial difficulties facing Crown and Parliament, the push to the frontier weakened the bonds of loyalty to an already too-distant land. And the Stamp Act and Townshend Acts forced most articulate colonists to reduce the old conflict of English and American interests to the simplest possible terms. Since some Englishmen proposed to consign other Englishmen to perpetual inferiority, was it not simply a question of liberty or slavery?

The forces that had long been working for political freedom underwent a sharp increase in influence. The ancient struggle between royal governor and popular assembly took on new vigor and meaning. The depths of ill feeling were plumbed in the maneuvers and exchanges of Governors Bernard and Hutchinson and the Massachusetts legislature. The colonial press engaged in more political reporting and speculation in the single year between June, 1765, and June, 1766, than in all the sixty-odd years since the founding of the *Boston News-Letter*. In early 1765 there were twenty-three newspapers in the colonies, only two or three of which were politically conscious; in early 1775 there were thirty-eight, only two or three of which were not. The spirit of constitutionalism and the demand for written constitutions also quickened in the course of the far-ranging dispute over the undetermined boundaries of imperial power and colonial rights. The word "unconstitutional," an essential adjunct of constitutionalism, became one of America's favorite words. Most important, the Stamp Act was a healthy spur to political awareness among all ranks of men. Wrote John Adams in 1766:

The people, even to the lowest ranks, have become more attentive to their liberties, more inquisitive about them, and more determined to defend them, than they were ever before known or had occasion to be; innumerable have been the monuments of wit, humor, sense, learning, spirit, patriotism, and heroism, erected in the several provinces in the course of this year. Their counties, towns, and even private clubs and sodalities have voted and determined; their merchants have agreed to sacrifice even their bread to the cause of liberty; their legislatures have resolved; the united colonies have remonstrated; the presses have everywhere groaned; and the pulpits have thundered.

The thundering pulpit, an old and faithful servant of American freedom, set out to demonstrate anew the affinity of religious and political liberty. Bumptious Protestantism vied with temperate rationalism as spurs to disestablishment and liberty of conscience. Conditions for the final triumph of unqualified religious liberty grew more favorable in this unsettled decade. So, too, did conditions of economic independence. The over-all state of the American economy lent impressive support to radical claims that the colonies would get along just as well, if not better, outside the protecting confines of British mercantilism. In wealth, resources, production, ingenuity, and energy the Americans were fast approaching the end of the colonial line. . . .

In every colony the middle class formed the nucleus of the patriot party, and in Boston it attained a position of commanding political influence. The aristocracy split into opposing camps, but the Lees of Virginia and Livingstons of New York are reminders that a decisive share of patriotic leadership fell to the American aristocrat. The political storms of the decade, which deposited power in new hands in almost every colony, did much to stimulate social mobility and class conflict. The career of the Sons of Liberty attests the growing fluidity of colonial society; the uprisings of the "Paxton Boys" in Pennsylvania and the Regulators in North Carolina attest the heightened tensions of class and section.

Finally, the colonial mind took rapid strides forward in this period, not alone in the field of political thought. Deism, rationalism, and the scientific spirit claimed increasing numbers of men in positions of leadership. The cult of virtue enjoyed a vogue even more intense than in the colonial period. The arts showed new signs of indigenous strength. The sharp increase in the number of newspapers was matched by an even sharper increase in the output of books and pamphlets. Three new colleges opened their doors to eager students, and King's and the Philadelphia Academy instituted the first American medical schools. Despite all the shouting about English rights and ways, the colonial mind was growing steadily less English and more American. By the standards of the old world, it was a mind not especially attractive, not least because it was setting out at last to find standards of its own.

The American colonies moved fast and far between 1765 and 1776. While the King fumed, the ministry blundered, assemblies protested, mobs rioted, and Samuel Adams plotted, the people of the colonies, however calm or convulsed the political situation, pushed steadily ahead in numbers, wealth, self-reliance, and devotion to liberty. The peaceful revolution that had been gathering momentum from the time of the first settlements moved irresistibly to conclusion, and the fighting revolution could now begin. It could begin, moreover, with high hopes for its success. Blessed by a way of life that knew much freedom and held the promise of much more, the Americans, like the Englishmen who unseated James II, could make their revolution "a parent to settlement, and not a nursery of future revolutions." This was one colonial people that went to war for liberty knowing in its bones what liberty was.

Merrill Jensen

Radicals vs. conservatives

The American Revolution was far more than a war between the colonies and Great Britain; it was also a struggle between those who enjoyed political privileges and those who did not. Yet the conclusions which may be drawn from the history of social conflict within the colonies and applied to such matters of mutual concern as the writing of a common constitution are seldom drawn and applied. Ordinarily the Revolution is treated as the end of one age and the beginning of another; a new country was born; political parties sprang into being; political leaders, full of wisdom learned during the Revolution, sought to save the new nation from the results of ignorance and inexperience. So runs the story.

But the story is true only in an external sense. The basic social forces in colonial life were not eliminated by the Declaration of Independence. There was no break in the underlying conflict between party and party representing fundamental divisions in American society. Those divisions had their roots in the very foundation of the colonies, and by the middle of the eighteenth century there had arisen broad social groupings based on economic and political conditions. More and more, wealth and political power were concentrated along the coast, in the hands of planters in the South and of merchants in the North. There were exceptions, of course, but by and large the colonial governments were in the hands of the economic upper classes. Exceedingly conscious of its local rights, the ruling aristocracy was willing to use democratic arguments to defeat the centralizing policies of Great Britain, but it had no intention of widening the base of political power within the colonies to accord with the conclusions which could be, and were, drawn from those arguments. On the contrary, it had kept itself in power through the use of a number of political weapons. As wealth accumulated and concentrated along the coast, as the frontier moved westward and became debtor and alien in character, and as the propertyless element in the colonial towns grew larger, the owners of property demanded "a political interpretation of their favored position"—that is, political supremacy—as a protection against the economic programs of debtor agrarians and the town poor. Encouraged by the British government, they gradually secured the political safeguards they demanded—property qualifications for participation in government and representation disproportionate to their numbers. The imposition of property qualifications for the suffrage and of even higher qualifications for office effectively quelled the political ambitions of the greater part of the town population, and the denial of proportional representation to the newly settled areas prevented the growing West from capturing control of colonial governments. Laws of entail and primogeniture insured the economic basis of colonial society, so much so that Thomas Jefferson believed that their abolition in Virginia would annul the privileges of an "aristocracy of wealth."

But the economic-political aristocracy which Jefferson hoped to abolish had not always been characteristic of the American colonies. In early Virginia and Maryland every free man, whether holding property or not, could vote. The first serious attempt to impose a property qualification for the suffrage came with the Restoration and it met with bitter opposition. One of the significant acts of Bacon's Assembly in 1676 was the abolition of the property qualification imposed by the Berkeley regime. But the victory of the poorer elements was short-lived at best, and in Virginia, as elsewhere in the colonies by the end of the seventeenth century, the property qualification was an integral part of the political system. During the eighteenth century the tendency was in the direction of ever higher qualifications, and colonial assemblies continued to refuse adequate representation to the expanding West. By the middle of the century a small minority of the colonial population wielded economic and political powers which could not be taken from them by any legal means. This political oligarchy was able to ignore most of the popular demands, and when smoldering discontent did occasionally flare up in a violent outburst, it was forcibly suppressed. Thus democracy was decreasingly a characteristic of constitutional development in the American colonies.

Opposition to the oligarchical rule of the planters and merchants came from the agrarian and proletarian elements which formed the vast majority of the colonial population. Probably most of them were politically inert, but from their ranks nevertheless came some of the effective leadership and much of the support for revolutionary activity after 1763. In the towns the poorer people, although a small part of the colonial population, far outnumbered the large property-owners. Most of them—laborers, artisans, and small tradesmen—were dependent on the wealthy merchants, who ruled them economically and socially. Agrarian discontent, too, was the product of local developments: of exploitation by land speculators, "taxation without representation," and the denial of political privileges, economic benefits, and military assistance. The farmer's desire for internal revolution had already been violently expressed in Bacon's Rebellion and in the Regulator Movement, events widely separated in time but similar in cause and consequence.

To a large extent, then, the party of colonial radicalism was composed of the masses in the towns and on the frontier. In Charleston, Philadelphia, New York, and Boston the radical parties were the foundation of the revolutionary movement in their towns and colonies.[1] It was they who provided the organization for uniting the dispersed farming population, which had not the means of organizing, but which was more than ready to act and which became the bulwark of the Revolution once it had started. Located at the center of things, the town radicals were able to seize upon issues as they arose and to spread propaganda by means of circular letters, committees of correspondence, and provincial congresses. They brought to a focus forces that would otherwise have spent themselves in sporadic outbursts easily suppressed by the established order.

Colonial radicalism did not become effective until after the French and Indian War. Then, fostered by economic depression and aided by the bungling policy of Great Britain and the desire of the local governing classes for independence within the empire, it became united in an effort to throw off its local and international bonds. The discontented were given an opportunity to express their discontent when the British government began to enforce restrictions upon the colonies after 1763. The colonial merchants used popular demonstrations to give point to their more orderly protests against such measures as the Stamp Act, and it was only a step from such riots, incited and controlled by the merchants, to the organization of radical parties bent on the redress of local grievances which were of far more concern to the masses than the more remote and less obvious effects of British policy. Furthermore, there arose, in each of the colonies, leaders of more than ordinary ability, men who were able to create issues when none were furnished by Great Britain, and who seized on British acts as heaven-sent opportunities to attack the local aristocracy—too strongly entrenched to be overthrown on purely local issues—under the guise of a patriotic defense of American liberties. Thus, used as tools at first, the masses were soon united under capable

---

[1]The terms "radical" and "conservative" in this discussion are not synonymous with "revolutionist" and "loyalist." That they are not interchangeable is obvious from the easily demonstrable fact that there were in internal colonial politics radicals who became loyalists, and conservatives who became revolutionists.

The interpretation of the Revolution is too often confused by the insistence that all revolutionists were radicals. Probably most radicals were revolutionists, but a large number of revolutionists were not radicals. The conservatives were those who —whether they desired independence or not—wanted to maintain the aristocratic order in the American colonies and states. The radicals were those who wanted changes in the existing order, changes which can be best described as democratic, though the term is necessarily relative.

By and large the majority of the colonial aristocracy was opposed to independence. This attitude was due partly to training, partly to self-interest, and partly—increasingly after 1774—to the fear that independence would result in an internal revolution. The radicals, on the other hand, shifted from mere opposition to British measures to a demand for independence as they came to realize that only independence would make possible the internal revolution which radicalism in the colonies had come more and more to demand.

leadership in what became as much a war against the colonial aristocracy as a war for independence.

The American Revolution thus marks the ascendancy of the radicals
of the colonies, for the first time effectively united. True, this radical ascendancy was of brief duration, but while it lasted an attempt was made
to write democratic ideals and theories of government into the laws and
constitutions of the American states. Fulfillment was not complete, for
the past was strong and in some states the conservatives retained their
power and even strengthened it. And once independence was won, the
conservatives soon united in undoing, so far as they could, such political
and economic democracy as had resulted from the war. Nevertheless it is
significant that the attempt at democratization was made and that it was
born of colonial conditions. The participation of the radicals in the creation of a common government is all-important, for they as well as the
conservatives believed that a centralized government was essential to the
maintenance of conservative rule. Naturally the radicals who exercised
so much power in 1776 refused to set up in the Articles of Confederation
a government which would guarantee the position of the conservative
interests they sought to remove from power.

The conservatives gradually became aware that internal revolution
might be the result of continued disputes between themselves and Great
Britain, but they were not agreed on the measures necessary to retain
both "home rule" and the power to "rule at home." Some of them, like
Joseph Galloway, sought to tighten the bonds between the colonies and
the mother country and thus to consolidate the power and bulwark the
position of the colonial aristocracy. Other conservatives, like John Dickinson, denied that Parliament had any authority over the colonies and
cared little for a close tie with the mother country; what they demanded
was a status that was in effect home rule within the British Empire.
Complete independence was to be avoided if possible, for it was fraught
with the danger of social revolution within the colonies. As these men became aware that conservative rule had as much or more to fear from the
people of the colonies as from British restrictions, they sought more and
more for reconciliation with the mother country, in spite of her obvious
intention to enforce her laws by means of arms. But they made the fatal
yet unavoidable error of uniting with the radicals in meeting force with
force. They made themselves believe that it was neither traitorous nor
illegal to resist with arms the British measures they disliked.

When independence could no longer be delayed, the conservatives
were forced to choose between England and the United States. Some became "Tories," or "Loyalists." Others, the victims of circumstances partly
of their own creation, fearfully and reluctantly became revolutionists.
But in so doing they did not throw away their ideals of government. They
were too cool, too well versed in checkmating radicalism and in adminis-

tering governments in their own interest, to be misled by the democratic propaganda of the radicals. Not even John Adams, one of the few conservatives who worked for independence, was willing to stomach the ideas of Tom Paine when it came to the task of forming governments within the American colonies.

The continued presence of groups of conservatives in all the states, weakened though they were by the Revolution, is of profound importance in the constitutional history of the United States. They appeared in strength in the first Continental Congress. In it their ideas and desires were expressed. They were still powerful at the beginning of the second Continental Congress, but gradually their hold was weakened by the growing revolutionary movement in the various states. They were strong enough, however, to obstruct the radical program during 1775 and to delay a declaration of independence in 1776 until long after the radicals believed that independence was an accomplished fact. In the bitter controversies which occurred the conservatives stated their ideas of government. In its simplest form their objection to independence was that it involved internal revolution. When forced to accept independence, they demanded the creation of a central government which would be a bulwark against internal revolution, which would aid the merchant classes, which would control Western lands, which would, in short, be a "national" government. In this they were opposed by the radicals, who created a "federal" government in the Articles of Confederation and who resisted the efforts of the conservatives to shape the character of those Articles while they were in process of writing and ratification.

It is against such a background of internal conflict that the Articles of Confederation must be considered. Naturally any statement of the issues or principles of the Revolution, however broad the terminology, is likely to be misleading, for, as John Adams wrote, "the principles of the American Revolution may be said to have been as various as the thirteen states that went through it, and in some sense almost as diversified as the individuals who acted in it." There are inconsistencies and contradictions that cannot be forced into a logical pattern. Generalizations must therefore be understood as statements of tendencies and of presumed predominance rather than as unexceptionable statements of fact. Thus when the Revolution is interpreted in the following pages as predominantly an internal revolution carried on by the masses of the people against the local aristocracy, it is not without recognition of the fact that there were aristocratic revolutionists and proletarian loyalists; that probably the majority of the people were more or less indifferent to what was taking place; and that British policy after 1763 drove many conservatives into a war for independence.

Any interpretation of the American Revolution is subject to such qualifications, discomforting as it is to those who want complexities reduced to simple formulas. Any collection of facts must, however, be grouped around a theme, and particularly is this true of a movement having so many aspects as the American Revolution. Such grouping is unavoidable if one seeks to understand how the course of events, how the course of social revolution within the several states, often played a far more important role in determining political attitudes than did the more remote dangers of British policy.

In spite of the paradoxes involved one may still maintain that the Revolution was essentially, though relatively, a democratic movement within the thirteen American colonies, and that its significance for the political and constitutional history of the United States lay in its tendency to elevate the political and economic status of the majority of the people. The Articles of Confederation were the constitutional expression of this movement and the embodiment in governmental form of the philosophy of the Declaration of Independence.

THE INTERNAL REVOLUTION

The Articles of Confederation were written by men many of whom rose to leadership as a result of the tempestuous local political battles fought in the years before the Revolution. Most of these new leaders gained power because they voiced the animosities and thus won the support of the discontented—the masses in the towns and the farmers of the back country—, who in most of the states won the right to express themselves politically, or were able to force concessions where the conservative element remained in control of the new governments created.

When it came to the formation of a common government for all the states, the radicals were guided by experience and by certain political ideas. Experience had taught them to dislike the colonial governing classes and to fear the concentration of wealth and political power. Their political philosophy taught that governments exercising power over wide areas were inherently undemocratic in action. This distrust of the concentration and centralization of unchecked political authority was deepened by the fact that most of the revolutionary leaders were essentially local leaders whom necessity had forced into an international movement for independence but who continued to be guided and controlled by the exigencies of local politics. It is necessary, therefore, to turn to the revolutionary history of the individual colonies for an explanation of the many exceptions one must make to any generalizations regarding the revolutionary movement as a whole and the constitution it produced.

*   *   *

Pennsylvania offers the clearest illustration of some of the basic issues upon which the course of the American Revolution turned. In no other colony were the racial-political-economic lines so sharply drawn, nowhere was the ruling class so opposed to change or to concession, and nowhere was the political revolution so complete in 1776.

As the colony had grown in wealth and population, political control had been retained by the three old counties of Philadelphia, Bucks, and Chester, and the city of Philadelphia. By the middle of the century an oligarchy of Quaker merchants and lawyers was dictating most of the policies of government. Their instrument was the colonial assembly, control of which they retained by denying representation to the ever-growing west. Even when new counties were created, they were made so vast in extent and were allotted so few representatives in the Assembly that the rule of the east was never endangered. In the east itself the masses were prevented from threatening oligarchical rule by suffrage laws which excluded all but a small minority of the population. The right to vote was contingent upon the possession of fifty pounds in personal property or a freehold. Neither was easy to secure, at least in the east. In Philadelphia in 1775 only 335 of 3,452 taxable males had estates large enough to give them the vote.

Opposition to the oligarchy was centered in the Susquehanna Valley and in the city of Philadelphia. The Susquehanna Valley, peopled largely by Scotch-Irish and Germans, was separated from the east by geography, by economic interest, by race, and by religion. Its natural market was the city of Baltimore, which very early improved roads to attract the trade of its northern neighbors, while the Pennsylvania Assembly refused to build roads or in any way to tie the west to the east.

Aside from racial and religious animosities, the grievances of the west against the east were very specific. It carried a burden of taxation without adequate representation, which in 1771, when an excise tax on hard liquor was instituted, was opposed in a manner prophetic of the later Whiskey Rebellion. The Presbyterian Scotch-Irish were driven to desperation by the refusal of the Quaker Assembly to aid them in their ever-continuing war with the Indians. The Proclamation line of 1763, which threatened to dispossess many westerners of lands already settled, was blamed on the Quakers. The pacifism of the Quaker merchants enraged frontiersmen, who suspected them of being moved more by a desire to maintain the fur trade than by humanitarian concern over the fate of the Indians.

The western farmer could meet the eastern merchant on terms of approximate equality only if he could secure adequate representation in the Assembly. This too was the demand of the populace of Philadelphia, where government was in the hands of the same wealthy class as controlled the colony. The sources of urban discontent were even more immediate than those of the west. All through the century the merchants had tried by various means to overthrow the system of markets and auctions in order to get a monopoly of the retail trade. Finally, in 1771, they devised a scheme which led to the most startling outburst of popular feeling that occurred before the Revolution. They agreed among themselves to buy from none but vendue masters who would agree to sell in large quantities. It was obvious that to continue in business the vendue masters would have to meet the demands of the big merchants. It was equally obvious that the poor could not afford to buy in large quantities and would thus be forced to buy from the merchants, who had long shown a disposition to take a more than "reasonable" profit in fixing retail prices. The merchants likewise tried to check the activity of wandering peddlers. Fishing rights in the navigable rivers were restricted, a measure which the poor felt to be aimed directly at them. In the face of such events it was natural that the lawyer-agents of the merchants should be bitterly attacked by the masses of the population.

The attempt of the Quaker element in the east to convert Pennsylvania from a proprietary into a crown colony was fought bitterly by the Presbyterians in both east and west. Though they had none too great a love for the Penn family, they knew full well that the creation of a crown colony would place them entirely at the mercy of the oligarchy. In this struggle John Dickinson led the proprietary party, which had the support of the west. Franklin, who, oddly enough, has since acquired a reputation as a democrat, was the agent of the oligarchy in England. A future loyalist, Joseph Galloway, led its forces in the Pennsylvania Assembly.

British policy was at once the occasion and the excuse for action in Pennsylvania. As in the other colonies, the propertied classes were strongly opposed to any acts of Parliament infringing upon their local independence or interfering with the profits of trade. But the arguments they advanced in support of their rights were a double-edged weapon that cut in favor of the unrepresented classes as well as colonial self-government. By 1775 the oligarchy began to realize that it was caught between the hammer and the anvil. This became increasingly clear as a revolutionary organization was developed wherein the old restrictions on the franchise and county representation no longer held. The creation of a provincial congress gave the west a dominance in the colony and deprived the three old counties of the hold they had had over the majority of the others. Yet the old Assembly continued to meet and to refuse concessions that would have weakened the radical program and enabled the Assembly to assume the leadership itself. By thus refusing either to lead or to guide, the conservative party was thrown from power in June, 1776. The radical party, temporarily unhampered, was able to write the most democratic constitution any American state has ever had.

The conservatives, led by James Wilson, Robert Morris, John Dickinson, and others, opposed the new order so bitterly that they very nearly wrecked the government of the state and did in fact render it largely ineffective in fighting the Revolution. The unicameral legislature, which they had considered satisfactory so long as it had been in their own control, they now criticized as the worst of all possible forms of government. Their proposal of a system of "checks and balances" as the remedy for all political ills was a thin disguise for their desire to regain control of the state. By 1779 they had made some political gains, but since they were a minority their control of a democratic government was bound to be precarious. Recognizing this to be so, they turned more and more to "nationalism" in the hope of gaining power and protection in another political sphere. They became more and more insistent upon the creation of a "national" government. Their program involved strengthening the Articles of Confederation, but when this failed they participated in a conservative political revolution which ignored the legal methods of constitutional change and created a government in harmony with conservative ideas and experiences. . . .

*   *   *

The calling of the first Continental Congress wrought a fundamental change in the growing revolutionary movement. No longer were the scattered revolutionary forces, feeding upon the vacillations of British policy and the exigencies of local politics, the center of the movement. When Congress outlined general policies which achieved the status of law as a result of popular support, it took the lead in the Revolution, although its effectiveness as a revolutionary organization was determined ultimately by the political character of the state organizations sending delegates to it. As the local radical parties gained power and sent radicals to Congress, it changed its policies. The history of those changing policies is the history of the outbreak of the American Revolution.

An ambivalent revolution

Robert R. Palmer

THE REVOLUTION: WAS THERE ANY?

It is paradoxical . . . to have to begin by asking whether there was any American Revolution at all. There may have been only a war of independence against Great Britain. The British lid may have been removed from the American box, with the contents of the box remaining as before. Or there may have been a mechanical separation from England, without chemical change in America itself. Perhaps it was all a conservative and defensive movement, to secure liberties that America had long enjoyed, a revolt of America against Great Britain, carried through without fundamental conflict among Americans, by an "American consensus," in the words of Clinton Rossiter, or, as George Bancroft said a century ago, a revolution "achieved with such benign tranquillity that even conservatism hesitated to censure."

A populous country, much given to historical studies, has produced an enormous literature on the circumstances of its independence. Occupied more with European than with American history, I have been able only to sample this literature. It is apparent, however, that there is no agreement on what the American Revolution was. Differences reflect a different understanding of historical fact, a difference of attitude toward the concept of revolution, or a difference of feeling on the uniqueness, if it be unique, of the United States.

The old patriotic historians, like Bancroft, who fumed against British tyranny, had no doubt that there had been a real revolution in America, even if "benignly tranquil." Writers of a liberal orientation in a twentieth-century sense, admitting that all revolutions are carried through by minorities and by violence, have said that the American Revolution was no exception. Some have seen a kind of bourgeois revolution in America, in which merchants and planters made a few concessions to the lower classes, but then, at the Philadelphia convention of 1787, rallied to the defense of property in a kind of Thermidor. Still others, of conservative temperament, sympathizing with the American loyalists, have found the ruthlessness of a true revolution in the American upheaval. It must be admitted that, for the purposes of the present book, it would be convenient to present the American part of the story in this way, on the analogy of revolutions in Europe.

But there is the contrary school that minimizes the revolutionary character of the American Revolution. Some in this school hold that there was no "democratic revolution" in America because America was already democratic in the colonial period. Thus, it has recently been shown that, contrary to a common impression, as many as ninety-five per cent of adult males had the right to vote in many parts of colonial Massachusetts. Others find the Revolution not very revolutionary because the country was still far from democratic when it became independent. They point to the maintenance of property qualifications for voting and office-holding, or the fact that estates confiscated from loyalists found their way into the hands of speculators or well-to-do people, not of poor farmers. Those who discount the revolutionary character of the American Revolution seem to be gaining ground. For example, thirty years ago, J. F. Jameson in his little book, *The American Revolution Considered as a Social Movement,* suggested a variety of social changes that he said took place, in landholding and land law, in the disestablishment of churches and the democratizing tendencies in an aristocratic society. The book won followers and inspired research. F. B. Tolles described the aristocratic *ancien régime* of colonial Philadelphia, dominated by Quaker grandees whose social ascendancy, he said, came to an end in the American Revolution. But in 1954 the same Professor Tolles, reviewing the Jameson thesis and summarizing the research of recent decades, concluded that, while Jameson's ideas were important and fruitful, the degree of internal or social or revolutionary change within America, during the break with Britain, should not be unduly stressed.

Whether one thinks there was really a revolution in America depends on what one thinks a revolution is. It depends, that is to say, not so much on specialized knowledge or on factual discovery, or even on hard thinking about a particular time and place, as on the use made of an abstract concept. "Revolution" is a concept whose connotation and overtones change with changing events. It conveyed a different feeling in the 1790's from the 1770's, and in the 1950's from the 1930's.

No one in 1776, whether for it or against it, doubted that a revolution was being attempted in America. A little later the French Revolution gave a new dimension to the concept of revolution. It was the French Revolution that caused some to argue that the American Revolution had been no revolution at all. In 1800 Friedrich Gentz, in his *Historisches Journal* published at Berlin, wrote an essay comparing the French and American revolutions. He was an acute observer, whose account of the French Revolution did not suit all conservatives of the time, and would not suit them today; still, he made his living by writing against the French Revolution, and later became secretary to Metternich. He considered the French Revolution a bad thing, all the worse when compared to the American. He thought the American Revolution only a conservative defense of established rights against British encroachment. John Quincy Adams, then in Berlin, read Gentz's essay, liked it, translated it, and published it in Philadelphia in 1800. It served as a piece of high-toned campaign literature in the presidential election of that year, in which the elder Adams and the Federalist party were challenged by Jefferson and the somewhat Francophile democrats. The merit of Gentz's essay, said the younger Adams in his preface, was that "it rescues that revolution [the American] from the disgraceful imputation of having proceeded from the same principles as the French." In 1955 Adams' translation of Gentz was reprinted in America as a paper-back for mass distribution, with a foreword by Russell Kirk, known as a publicist of the "new conservatism." There was something in the atmosphere of 1955, as of 1800, which made it important, for some, to dissociate the American Revolution from other revolutions by which other peoples have been afflicted.

My own view is that there was a real revolution in America, and that it was a painful conflict, in which many were injured. I would suggest two quantitative and objective measures: how many refugees were there from the American Revolution, and how much property did they lose, in comparison to the French Revolution? It is possible to obtain rough but enlightening answers to these questions. The number of émigré loyalists who went to Canada or England during the American Revolution is set as high as 100,000; let us say only 60,000. The number of émigrés from the French Revolution is quite accurately known; it was 129,000, of whom 25,000 were clergy, deportees rather than fugitives, but let us take the whole figure, 129,000. There were about 2,500,000 people in America in 1776, of whom a fifth were slaves; let us count the whole 2,500,000. There were about 25,000,000 people in France at the time of the French Revolution. There were, therefore, 24 émigrés per thousand of population in the American Revolution, and only 5 émigrés per thousand of population in the French Revolution.

In both cases the revolutionary governments confiscated the property of counterrevolutionaries who emigrated. Its value cannot be known, but the sums paid in compensation lend themselves to tentative comparison. The British government granted £3,300,000 to loyalists as indemnity for property lost in the United States. The French émigrés, or their heirs, received a "billion franc indemnity" in 1825 during the Bourbon restoration. A sum of £3,300,000 is the equivalent of 82,000,000 francs. Revolutionary France, ten times as large as revolutionary America, confiscated only twelve times as much property from its émigrés, as measured by subsequent compensations, which in each case fell short of actual losses. The difference, even allowing for margins of error, is less great than is commonly supposed. The French, to be sure, confiscated properties of the church and other public bodies in addition; but the present comparison suggests the losses of private persons.

It is my belief also, John Quincy Adams notwithstanding, that the American and the French revolutions "proceeded from the same principles." The difference is that these principles were much more deeply rooted in America, and that contrary or competing principles, monarchist or aristocratic or feudal or ecclesiastical, though not absent from America, were, in comparison to Europe, very weak. Assertion of the same principles therefore provoked less conflict in America than in France. It was, in truth, less revolutionary. The American Revolution was, indeed, a movement to conserve what already existed. It was hardly, however, a "conservative" movement, and it can give limited comfort to the theorists of conservatism, for it was the weakness of conservative forces in eighteenth-century America, not their strength, that made the American Revolution as moderate as it was. John Adams was not much like Edmund Burke, even after he became alarmed by the French Revolution; and Alexander Hamilton never hoped to perpetuate an existing state of society, or to change it by gradual, cautious, and piously respectful methods. America was different from Europe, but it was not unique. The difference lay in the fact that certain ideas of the Age of Enlightenment, found on both sides of the Atlantic—ideas of constitutionalism, individual liberty, or legal equality—were more fully incorporated and less disputed in America than in Europe. There was enough of a common civilization to make America very pointedly significant to Europeans. For a century after the American Revolution, as is well known, partisans of the revolutionary or liberal movements in Europe looked upon the United States generally with approval, and European conservatives viewed it with hostility or downright contempt.

It must always be remembered, also, that an important nucleus of conservatism was permanently lost to the United States. The French émigrés returned to France. The émigrés from the American Revolution did not return; they peopled the Canadian wilderness; only individuals, without political influence, drifted back to the United States. Anyone who knows the significance for France of the return of the émigrés will ponder the importance, for the United States, of this fact which is so easily overlooked, because negative and invisible except in a comparative view. Americans have really forgotten the loyalists. Princeton University, for example, which invokes the memory of John Witherspoon and James Madison on all possible occasions, has been chided for burying in oblivion the name of Jonathan Odell, of the class of 1759, prominent as a physician, clergyman, and loyalist satirical writer during the Revolution, who died in New Brunswick, Canada, in 1818. The sense in which there was no conflict in the American Revolution is the sense in which the loyalists are forgotten. The "American consensus" rests in some degree on the elimination from the national consciousness, as well as from the country, of a once important and relatively numerous element of dissent.

ANGLO-AMERICA BEFORE THE REVOLUTION

The American Revolution may be seen as a conflict of forces some of which were old, others brought into being by the event itself.

The oldest of these forces was a tradition of liberty, which went back to the first settlement of the colonies. It is true that half of all immigrants into the colonies south of New England, and two-thirds of those settling in Pennsylvania, arrived as indentured servants; but indentured servitude was not a permanent status, still less a hereditary one; the indentures expired after a few years, and all white persons soon merged into a free population.

Politically, the oldest colonies had originated in a kind of *de facto* independence from the British government. Even after the British made their colonial system more systematic, toward the close of the seventeenth century, the colonies continued to enjoy much local self-determination. Only five per cent of the laws passed by colonial assemblies were disallowed in Great Britain, and, while these often concerned the most important subjects, the infrequency of the British veto was enough to make it the exception. The elected assemblies, as already noted, were the most democratically recruited of all such constituted bodies in the Western World. In general, it was necessary to own land in order to have the right to vote for a member of the assembly, but small owner-farmers were numerous, most of all in New England; and recent studies all tend to raise the estimates of the proportion of those enjoying the franchise before the Revolution. It seems to have been above eighty per cent of adult white males in Massachusetts, half or more in New Jersey, perhaps a little under half in Virginia. Many who had the right to vote did not often use it, and this was in part because the procedure of elections was not made convenient for the ordinary hard-working man; but non-voting also suggests an absence of grievances, or perhaps only that the common man neither expected much nor feared much from government. The elected assemblies enjoyed what in Europe would be thought a dangerously popular mandate. By 1760, decades of rivalry for power between the assemblies and the governors had been resolved, in most of the colonies, in favor of the assemblies. The idea of government by consent was for Americans a mere statement of fact, not a bold doctrine to be flung in the teeth of government, as in Europe. Contrariwise, the growing assertiveness of the assemblies made many in England, and some in America, on the eve of the Revolution, believe that the time had come to stop this drift toward democracy—or, as they would say, restore the balance of the constitution. In sum, an old sense of liberty in America was the obstacle on which the first British empire met its doom. Here the most sophisticated latest researches seem to return to the old-fashioned American patriotic historical school.

From the beginnings of British America there had also been a certain rough kind of equality. Except for slaves, the poor were less poor than in Europe, and the rich were not so wealthy. Almost a quarter of the population of England were classified as paupers in 1688; almost a tenth in 1801. There was no pauperism in America, accepted and institutionalized as such; anyone not hopelessly shiftless, or the victim of personal misfortune, could make a living. At the other extreme, on the eve of the Revolution, there were men who owned hundreds of thousands of acres, mostly vacant, the main values being speculative and in the future. It is hard to say how wealthy a wealthy colonial was. A fortune of £30,000 was thought very large in Massachusetts; Joseph Galloway of Pennsylvania was said to possess £70,000. In England in 1801 there were probably 10,000 families with an average income of £1,500 a year or more, of which the capital value would be about £30,000. There is ground for believing that in England at this time, as in the United States in 1929, five per cent of the population received over thirty-five per cent of the income. The distribution of wealth in colonial America was far more equal.

There were recognized inequalities of social rank. But rank somehow lacked the magic it enjoyed in Europe. In the migration from England and Europe, the well-situated and the high-born had been notably absent. There were Americans of aristocratic pretensions, but the most ambitious genealogy led only to some middling English gentleman's manor house; most Americans were conscious of no lineage at all, American genealogy being largely a nineteenth-century science. No American could truthfully trace his ancestry to the mists of time or the ages of chivalry— nor, indeed, could many British peers or French noblemen. It was the complaint of Lord Stirling, as the New Jersey revolutionary, William Alexander, was called, that he was *not* recognized as a lord in England. A Swedish clergyman arriving in New Jersey in 1770, to take over the old Swedish congregation on the Delaware, found that well-to-do farmers were like lesser gentry in Sweden, in their use of fine linen and fondness for good horses. The significant thing for America was that people of this style of life did not, as in Sweden, consider themselves nobles. Everyone worked, and to the Swedish newcomer it seemed that "all people are generally thought equally good."

Whether religion acted as a force in the conflict of the American Revolution is disputed. Since the Worship of Reason at Notre-Dame de Paris in November 1793, there have always been those who have stressed the religious principles of the founders of the United States. It is a way of showing how different they were from Jacobins or Communists. The truth is that the age was not notably religious, and that the sentiments that burst out violently in Paris in 1793 were, as sentiments, not uncommon. We read, for example, of an Anglican rector in England who, about 1777, so admired the writings of Catherine Macaulay that "he actually placed her statue, adorned as the Goddess of Liberty, within the altar railing" of his parish church. "It will never be pretended," wrote John Adams in 1786, that the men who set up the new governments in America "had interviews with the gods, or were in any degree under the inspiration of Heaven, more than those at work on ships or houses, or laboring in merchandise or agriculture; it will forever be acknowledged that these governments were contrived by reason and the senses, as Copley painted Chatham . . . [or] as Paine exposed the mistakes of Raynal. . . ." John Adams, while differing with him in detail, had not yet broken with Thomas Paine.

Aggressive anti-Christianity did not develop in America, to the great good fortune of the future United States. It failed to develop, however, not because American revolutionary leaders were warmly religious, but because no religious body seriously stood in their way. Here again it was the weakness of conservative forces, not their strength, that made the Revolution "conservative." No church seriously opposed the political aims of the Revolution. No church figured as a first estate in colonial America, none had its dignitaries sitting in the highest councils of government, and none lost vast tracts of material property, since none possessed any. The Anglican clergy generally opposed the Revolution, because of their close connection with British authority. Revolutionaries drove them out of their churches, for the same reason; worse would have happened to them had they not been so easily dislodged. In any case, even where the Anglican church was established, in New York and the South, Anglicans were not a majority of the population. At the opposite end of the religious spectrum the Quakers, because of their doctrine of non-resistance to established authority, were in effect a force to be reckoned on the British side. But they were unimportant politically outside of Pennsylvania. Over half the colonial Americans, and probably ninety per cent of New Englanders, were, vaguely or exactly, some species of Calvinists. No allegation was more common, from the British or the American loyalists, than that the whole Revolution had been stirred up by old Presbyterian disaffection. It is true that New England Congregationalists and Scotch-Irish Presbyterians did not admire some of the contemporary institutions of England, and that their ministers, when the time came, generally supported the Revolution. They probably infused, in a way hard to define, a certain religious atmosphere into the American patriot program.

A great many Americans, however, before and during the Revolution, belonged to no church at all. In conditions of constant movement, uprooting, settlement, and resettlement, probably a larger proportion of Americans were unchurched than in any European country. What aroused horror, when violently pursued as dechristianization in France a few years later, had gone pretty far, without violence, in America. As for the leaders of the American Revolution, it should be unnecessary to demonstrate that most of them were deists. They were strongly on the side of the best human virtues, or at least of those which were not ascetic; but they saw no connection between such virtues and religious practice. Like Jefferson in the Declaration of Independence, they appealed to the laws of Nature's God. They seem not to have felt, however, like Burke, that these laws placed serious limits upon their freedom of political action.

The simplicities in which British America had originated gave way to more complex forms of society in the eighteenth century. A liberty almost like that of the "state of nature," a liberty defined by the remoteness of government, gradually changed, especially after the British revolution of 1688, into the more organized and channelized liberty of British subjects under the British constitution. There was a bias toward equality in the foundations. The superstructure, as it was raised, exhibited palpable inequalities. As America became more civilized it began to have, like all civilized countries, a differentiation of social classes. Even the once unmanageable Quakers took on new social refinements. The Philadelphia Yearly Meeting of 1722 officially declared its "decent respect" for "ranks and dignities of men," and called for honor and obedience "from subjects to their princes, inferiors to superiors, from children to parents, and servants to masters." Increasingly there was a kind of native American aristocracy. No question was of more importance for the future than the way in which this new aristocracy would develop.

The colonial aristocracy, as it took form in the eighteenth century, owed a good deal to close association with government. From New Hampshire to the far South . . . there were intermarried families which monopolized seats in the governors' councils, in some cases, now, to the third and fourth generation. There were Americans, close to the British authorities, who regarded themselves as the natural rulers of the country. Sometimes, like Englishmen of the class to which they would compare themselves, they expected to draw a living from public offices, to which they need devote only part of their time. This practice has been most closely studied for Maryland, where there were a number of offices in which a man could live like a gentleman, with a good deal of leisure, for £150 a year.

More generally, the wealth of the growing American upper class came from early land grants, or from inheritance of land in a country where land values were always rising, or from mercantile wealth in the half-dozen seaboard cities, all of which except Charleston lay from Philadelphia to the North, or from the ownership of plantations and Negro slaves in the South. New York and the Southern provinces, because of their systems of landholding, were the most favorable to the growth of aristocratic institutions, but an upper class existed everywhere in the settled regions. In places where landed and mercantile wealth came together, as at New York and Charleston, people mixed easily with mutual regard; there was no standoffishness between "trade" and "gentry."

Without the rise of such a colonial aristocracy there could have been no successful movement against England. There had to be small groups of people who knew each other, who could trust each other in hazardous undertakings, who had some power and influence of their own, who could win attention and rally followers, and who, from an enlarged point of view, felt a concern for the welfare of the provinces as a whole. "While there are no noble or great and ancient families . . . they cannot rebel," as an observer of New England remarked in 1732. A generation later such "great" families, if not noble or very ancient, could be found everywhere in the colonies.

On the other hand, the rise of such an aristocracy brought class friction and internal tension. "In many a colony in 1764," according to Professor Rossiter (whose view of an "American consensus" I do not wish to misrepresent), "civil war seemed more likely than war with Britain." There was everlasting bickering over land titles, quitrents, debts, and paper money. There was complaint, in the western part of several provinces, at under-representation in the elected assemblies, or at the long distances it was necessary to go to cast a vote or to be present in a court of law. Rich and poor were not so far apart as in Europe, but they were far enough apart to cause trouble. Western Massachusetts, suspicious of Boston, was not hostile to Britain until 1774. There was a great rent riot in the Hudson valley in 1766, directed against the manorial system on which the Van Rensselaers and the Livingstons grew wealthy. A thousand angry western Pennsylvania farmers marched on Philadelphia in 1764, enraged that the over-represented East, and its opulent and pacifistic Quaker aristocracy, begrudged them military protection at the time of Pontiac's Indian war. The best example was afforded by the Regulators of North Carolina.

This province, though scarcely a century old, had developed a fine system of decayed boroughs on the British model. The five oldest coastal counties, thinly inhabited, enjoyed a dozen times as much representation in the assembly, per capita, as the newer uplands, so that the bulk of the people, while having the vote, could get little accomplished. Political life was most active at the county level, and in each county a few families named the judges and sheriffs, who are estimated to have embezzled over half the public funds. The governing elite, if one may so term it, unabashedly made a living off the legal business that small farmers could not avoid. A group of these farmers founded an "association" for "regulating public grievances," and these Regulators began to refuse to pay taxes. The governor finally called out the militia against them, chiefly a mounted troop of Gentlemen Volunteer Light Dragoons, in which 8 "generals" and 14 "colonels" led less than 1,300 enlisted men. The Regulators were routed in the Battle of Alamance in 1771. Seven of them were hanged. Later, when the gentry led the province into the Revolution, the British found many loyalist strongholds in the back country of Carolina.

Conflicting forces were therefore at work in America, when the Stamp Act added the conflict between America and Great Britain. Americans all but universally opposed the Stamp Act. Most of those who eventually became loyalists disapproved of British policy in the ten years before the Revolution. The doctrine of parliamentary supremacy was an innovation, accepted in England itself only since the revolution of 1689; the trend toward centralization of the empire under parliamentary authority, with attendant plans for reordering the colonial governments, was a modern development, a new force, much less old than the American liberties. On this Americans could agree. They began to disagree on the means used to uphold the American position. It was one thing to sit in meetings or submit petitions to Parliament; it was another to persist stubbornly in defiance, to insult or intimidate the King's officers, stop the proceedings of law courts, and condone the violence of mobs. Whether the British constitution really assured no taxation without representation was, after all, uncertain. It was far more certain that the British constitution secured a man against physical violence, against his having his house plundered and wrecked by political adversaries, or against being tarred and feathered for refusing to join a non-import agreement decided on by some unauthorized assembly which had no right to use force. As events unfolded, men took sides, and Americans found themselves disputing with each other on a new subject, the attitude to be taken to British law.

What happened to Plymouth Rock offers a parable. The stone on which the Pilgrims of 1620 had supposedly first set foot already enjoyed a local fame, as a symbol of what was most ancient and natively American in the New World. In 1774 a party of patriots decided to use it as the base for a liberty pole. They tried to haul it, with twenty oxen, from the shore to the town square. Under the strain, it broke in two.

THE REVOLUTION: DEMOCRACY AND ARISTOCRACY

Fighting between the King's troops and the people of Massachusetts began at Lexington and Concord in April 1775. In the following December the British government put the insurgent colonists outside the protection of the British crown. The Americans were now in what they would call a state of nature, and what was in fact a condition of anarchy. Lawful authority melted away. Governors, unable to control their assemblies, undertook to disband them, only to see most of the members continue to meet as unauthorized congresses or associations; or conventions of counties, unknown to the law, chose delegates to such congresses for provinces as a whole; or local people forcibly prevented the sitting of law courts, or the enforcement of legal judgments by the sheriffs. Violence spread, militias formed, and the Continental Congress called into existence a Continental army, placing General George Washington in command.

In whose name were these armed men to act? To what civilian authority were they to be subordinated? How could the courts be kept open, or normal court decisions and police protection be carried out? If American ships, breaking the old navigation system, should enter the ports of Europe, in whose name should they appear? If diplomatic agents were sent to Versailles or the Hague, whom were they to say that they represented? If aid was to be sought from France, would the French give it for any purpose except to break up the British empire, and undo the British victory of 1763? These practical needs, together with the inflaming of feeling against England by war and bloodshed, and the extraordinary success of Thomas Paine's pamphlet, *Common Sense,* induced the Congress, more than a year after the battle of Lexington, to announce the arrival of the United States of America "among the powers of the earth," able to do "all acts and things which independent states may of right do."

With the Declaration of Independence, and the new constitutions which most of the states gave themselves in 1776 and 1777, the revolutionary colonials began to emerge from the anarchy that followed the collapse or withdrawal of British power. They sought liberty, it need hardly be said; but they also sought authority, or a new basis of order. A revolution, it has been wisely observed, is an unlawful change in the conditions of lawfulness. It repudiates the old definitions of rightful authority, and drives away the men who have exercised it; but it creates new definitions of the authority which it is a duty to obey, and puts new men in a position to issue legitimate commands. The new lawfulness in America was embodied in the new constitutions, which will be considered shortly. Meanwhile, what happened in America was against the law.

The Revolution could be carried out, against British and loyal American opposition, only by the use of force. Its success "was impossible without a revolutionary government which could enforce its will." Let us look simply at the case of New Jersey. Late in 1776 the danger to the patriots became very pressing, as the British pursued Washington's army across the state. One of the New Jersey signers of the Declaration of Independence was forced to recant; the man who had presided over the convention which had proclaimed independence of the state went over to the British. The state was full of open and hidden enemies of the new regime. Taxes were neither levied nor collected with any regularity; the paper money which financed the Revolution flooded the state, swollen by counterfeits that poured from loyalist presses in New York. Prices soared; price controls were imposed, but were generally ineffective. The new government had no means of enforcing its authority except the thirteen county courts carried over from colonial times. These proved ineffectual under conditions of civil war. Revolutionary leaders thereupon created a Council of Safety as a temporary executive. Its twelve members were chosen by the state legislature. They toured the state to arouse local patriots and speed up action of the courts. They took the law into their own hands wherever they wished, hunted out suspects, ordered arrests, exacted oaths of allegiance, punished evasion of militia service, and instituted proceedings to confiscate the property of those who openly joined the British. One member of this Council of Safety was William Paterson, born in Ireland, son of a storekeeper. His career had been made by the Revolution, during which he became attorney-general to the state. He became a heated revolutionary, detesting more than all others, as he once said, that "pernicious class of men called moderates." His position allowed him to buy confiscated lands on advantageous terms; he became a well-to-do man. He lived to be a justice of the United States Supreme Court, and a terror to democrats in the days of the Alien and Sedition laws.

Revolutionary government as a step toward constitutional government, committees of public safety, representatives on mission to carry revolution to the local authorities, paper money, false paper money, price controls, oaths, detention, confiscation, aversion to "moderatism," and Jacobins who wind up as sober guardians of the law—how much it all suggests what was to happen in France a few years later! With allowance for differences of scale and intensity, there was foreshadowed in the America of 1776 something of the *gouvernement révolutionnaire* and even the Terror of France in 1793—except for the death sentences and the horrors that went with them, and except for the fact that the victims of these arbitrary proceedings never returned to political life as an organized force, to keep alive for all time an inveterate hatred of the Revolution.

It is not easy to say why some Americans warmly embraced the Revolution, or why others opposed it, or how many there were on each side. Independence made it in principle necessary to choose between loyalty and rebellion. But there were many who by isolation managed to avoid commitment, or whose inclinations swayed with the course of battle, or who, torn in their beliefs, prepared passively to accept whichever authority in the end should establish itself. Numbers therefore cannot be given. It has often been repeated, as a remark of John Adams, that a third of the American people were patriot, a third loyalist, and a third neutral; but this neat summary has gone into the attic of historical fallacies; what Adams meant, when he offered it in 1815, was that a third of the Americans in the 1790's had favored the *French* Revolution, a third had opposed it, and a third had not cared. The bulk of American opinion, after July 1776, seems to have been actively or potentially for independence. Positive and committed loyalists were a minority, but not therefore unimportant. They had the strength of the British empire on their side, and much also in the American tradition to support them. They believed in liberties for the colonies, and in old and historic rights under the British constitution, which, however, they felt to be less threatened by Parliament than by unruly new forces in America itself.

It is not possible to explain the division between patriot and loyalist by other or supposedly more fundamental divisions. The line coincided only locally or occasionally with the lines of conflict that had appeared before the war. Families divided, brothers often went different ways. Doubtless many a man marked himself for a lifetime by the impulsive decision of a moment. Economic and class motivations are unclear. The most firmly established merchants and lawyers tended to loyalism, but there were respected merchants and lawyers who embraced the revolution. New York and Virginia were both full of great landowners, but New York was the most loyalist province, Virginia one of the most revolutionary. Ironmasters, who had reason to object to British controls on the American iron industry, wound up in both camps. Debtors had reason to object to British attempts, over the previous half century, to limit paper money in America and stop inflation; but people do not always act from reason, and indebtedness in any case was scarcely a class phenomenon, since it was characteristic of the free-spending southern aristocracy, the businessmen in the towns, and farmers whose land was mortgaged, as well as of such actually poor people as may have been able to borrow any money. Religion of the Calvinist type was a force working against England, but the Presbyterians of the Carolina frontier, not eager to be governed by their own gentry, supplied many soldiers to the King. National origin had no general influence, for the Middle Colonies, the least English in origin, were stronger centers of loyalism than New England or the South. The young men, if we may judge by the infinitesimal proportion who were in the colleges, were ardently patriot. The colleges, from Harvard to William and Mary, were denounced by loyalists as hotbeds of sedition.

An obvious explanation, quite on the surface, is as good as any: that the patriots were those who saw an enlargement of opportunity in the break with Britain, and the loyalists were in large measure those who had benefited from the British connection, or who had organized their careers, and their sense of duty and usefulness, around service to the King and empire. These would include the American-born governors, Thomas Hutchinson in Massachusetts and William Franklin in New Jersey. There were also the families that customarily sat on the governors' councils or held honorific or lucrative offices under the crown. There were some in the rising American upper class who admired the way of life of the aristocracy in England, and who would imitate it as best they could. Such was surely their right as British subjects, but it might alienate them from Americans generally, even many of the upper class, who were willing to have social distinctions in America develop in a new way.

It is estimated that from half to two-thirds of those who had sat on the governors' councils became loyalists. For New Jersey we know exactly what happened. Of the twelve members of the provincial council in 1775, five became active and zealous loyalists, two became cautious or neutral loyalists, one went into retirement for age, and four became revolutionaries, one of whom made his peace with the British when he thought they were going to win. Massachusetts had as few loyalists as any province, but when the British troops evacuated Boston in 1776 they took over 1,100 civilians with them. Of these, 102 had been councillors or officials and 18 were clergymen, mainly Anglican; but 382 were farmers, 213 were merchants "and others," and 105 came from country towns. The rest were probably women and children. Like the émigrés from the French Revolution, the émigrés from America came from all classes. But those connected with the English government or English church, and identifying themselves with English society and the values of the British governing class, were more numerous among loyalists than in the general population. On the other hand, lest any one thesis be carried too far, it should be pointed out that Virginia, a very English province in some ways, was so solidly patriotic that only thirteen natives of the Old Dominion ever applied to Britain for compensation for loyalist losses.

The war itself polarized the issues. Each side needed strength, and the revolutionary leaders looked for it in the mass of the population, the loyalists among the ruling circles of Great Britain. In legal form, the struggle was between the sovereignty of the former colonies and the sovereignty of the British King-in-Parliament. Rebellious leaders, however, clothed themselves in the sovereignty of the "people," both in form and to a large degree in content. The social content of Parliament in the eighteenth century needs no further elaboration. The struggle, whatever men said, and whatever has been said since, was inseparable from a struggle between democratic and aristocratic forces. If the rebellion was successful, democracy in America would be favored. If it failed, if Parliament and the loyal Americans had their way, development in America would move in an aristocratic direction. In this respect the American Revolution resembled the revolutions in Europe.

That the war favored democracy in America is apparent in many ways. In some places, notably Massachusetts, the suffrage was nearly universal before the Revolution; in others, notably Virginia, the Revolution did not extend it. But in Pennsylvania the pro-British leanings of the Quaker patriciate brought them into disrepute after hostilities began; and their aversion to military solutions, at a time when any solution was bound to be military, threw power into the hands of the western farmers, who by becoming soldiers made themselves indispensable to the infant state, so that Pennsylvania developed the most democratically organized government in the new union. In New Jersey the provincial congress, enjoying no legality and in rebellion against the legal authorities, sought to broaden its mandate by extending the voting franchise. In fact, petitions streamed into the Congress, urging that all householders or taxpayers should have the vote, the better to oppose enemies of the "American cause." The provincial congress in February 1776, five months before independence, granted the vote to all males at least twenty-one years old, resident in the state a year, and possessing goods worth £50 "proclamation money." With wartime depreciation of proclamation money, virtual universal manhood suffrage ensued. Voters also, after July 1776, were re-

quired to take an oath abjuring allegiance to George III, and some pur-
ists, pained by revolutionary illiberalism, have deprecated such restriction of political rights, as if the only feasible alternative would have been
more democratic, and as if oaths did not exist in Britain itself, where
men could still be obliged to abjure the House of Stuart.

An experience of Colonel Thomas Randolph of Virginia well illustrates
the same spread of democracy. Randolph, one of the many Virginia aristocrats who fought for the Revolution, was entertaining a captured British officer in his home. Three farmers came in, sat down, took off their
boots, did a little spitting, and talked business with the colonel. After they
left, Randolph commented to his guest on how "the spirit of independ-
ency was converted into equality, and everyone who bore arms esteemed
himself on a footing with his neighbor." He added, with distaste: "No
doubt, each of these men conceives himself, in every respect, my equal."
War, and a citizen army, had somewhat the same effects as in France after 1792. Leaders who did not fight for equality accepted it in order to
win.

On the other hand, the American loyalists, who were in any case the
Americans most inclined to favor hierarchic ideas, were made more so by
the necessities of their position. William Eddis of Maryland, as early as
1770, thought that noblemen and bishops should be established in America as soon as possible. The commonest of all loyalist ideas was that the
democratic branch, under the mixed British constitution in America,
had gotten out of control. Their commonest allegation, during the war,
was that the Revolution was the work of their social inferiors—"mechanics and country clowns," who had no right to dispute "what Kings, Lords,
and Commons had done," as a South Carolina clergyman expressed it.
He was driven out by his congregation.

The loyalists fully expected the British army to put down the rebellion
very soon. They believed that the whole disturbance had been caused by
a few troublemakers, from whom the bulk of the people in America were
patiently awaiting liberation. Hence, they had plans ready for the government of America after the restoration of order. These plans paral-
lelled some of the British ideas mentioned in the last chapter. Like them,
they called for the setting up in the colonies of something like a nobility.
They expressed the idea that I have tried to show was so common in the
eighteenth century, the idea of Blackstone and Gibbon and Montesquieu
and the French parlements and many others, that some sort of nobility
was a prerequisite to political liberty. There must be, in this view, an in-
termediate order of men having the personal right to take part in government, neither elected and hence under the influence of constituents, nor
yet too amenable to influence by a king, so that they should be hereditary
if possible, and at least hold office for life.

Loyal Americans congregated in New York, which was occupied by the

British during most of the war. Here, as they talked over the sad state of their country, they found much on which they could agree. David Ogden of New Jersey was typical. He had served for twenty-one years on the New Jersey governor's council. After he fled to New York in January 1777, the revolutionary government in New Jersey confiscated from him twenty-three pieces of real estate, which he himself later valued at £15,231. He was one of the more prominent of the fugitives in New York, becoming a member of the Board of Refugees established there in 1779. He proposed that, after suppression of the rebellion, an American parliament be set up for all the colonies, subordinate to that of Great Britain, to consist of three branches, as in Britain: namely, a lord lieutenant, certain "barons" created for the purpose, and a house of commons chosen by the several colonial assemblies. The new parliament, incidentally, was to supervise the colleges, those "grand nurseries of the late rebellion."

The case of Joseph Galloway is more fully known. In 1774 he had tried to restrain the First Continental Congress by submitting a plan of American union, which that body had rejected as too favorable to parliamentary claims. During the war, after spending some time in New York, where he convinced himself that all Americans of any standing agreed with him, Galloway proceeded in 1778 to England, where for ten years he submitted a series of plans on colonial government to various persons in authority in London. These plans built on the plan of 1774, retaining its proposal for an autonomous inter-colonial parliament subordinate to the Parliament of Great Britain; but they added new ideas of structural reform.

The revolutionary states in America, according to Galloway, would be dissolved by the coming British victory, and the old forms of government would be forfeited by rebellion. There would therefore be a "state of nature without a civil constitution," or what he also called a Chart Blanche, "a perfect blank upon which a new policy shall be established." Opportunity would thus be afforded for certain long-needed changes. Temporarily, because of the war, there were two parties in America, the party of independence, "actuated by views of ambition and private interest," and the party favoring perpetual union with Great Britain. The former was "a mere republican party firmly attached to democratical government"; it had "vested the powers of all their new states originally and ultimately in the People." The other party, favoring union with England, preferred a "mixed form of government," to guard against abuse of power by either the sovereign or the people. Most Americans, Galloway was persuaded, were tired of being pushed about by revolutionary cliques. Most of the colonists, and certainly most men of property, would therefore welcome his plan of reorganization.

In this reorganization, the old governments of the charter provinces

(Connecticut and Rhode Island) and of the proprietary provinces (Pennsylvania and Maryland) were to be abolished, and all the provinces made to conform to the same model, the balanced government of the British constitution. If Britain and America were to remain long together, it was imperative that they should have "the same customs, manners, prejudices and habits." These would then give "the same spirit to the laws." There should be an American union with a lord lieutenant or governor general representing the crown, an upper house appointed for life and with "some degree of rank or dignity above the Commons," and a lower house chosen by the various colonial assemblies. The "weight and influence" of the crown would be assured by making all offices, "civil and military, honorable and lucrative," depend on royal appointment. Thus a group of Americans would be built up, hostile to pure democracy and with an interest in mixed government and the British connection. The Americans also, declared Galloway, recurring to the almost forgotten origin of the whole controversy, would willingly pay an agreed-upon share toward military and imperial expenses, by taxing themselves through such a parliament as he outlined.

As among Americans themselves, it is clear that the Revolution involved a contest between men committed either to a more popular or a more aristocratic trend in government and society. Had the loyalists returned, received back their property, and resumed the positions of prestige and public influence which many of them had once enjoyed, it seems unlikely that the subsequent history of the United States would have been like the history that we know. . . .

Ambivalence of the American Revolution

In conclusion, the American Revolution was really a revolution, in that certain Americans subverted their legitimate government, ousted the contrary-minded and confiscated their property, and set the example of a revolutionary program, through mechanisms by which the people was deemed to act as the constituent power. This much being said, it must be admitted that the Americans, when they constituted their new states, tended to reconstitute much of what they already had. They were as fortunate and satisfied a people as any the world has known. They thus offered both the best and the worst example, the most successful and the least pertinent precedent, for less fortunate or more dissatisfied peoples who in other parts of the world might hope to realize the same principles.

Pennsylvania and Georgia gave themselves one-chamber legislatures, but both had had one-chamber legislatures before the Revolution. All states set up weak governors; they had been undermining the authority of royal governors for generations. South Carolina remained a planter oligarchy before and after independence, but even in South Carolina

fifty-acre freeholders had a vote. New York set up one of the most conservative of the state constitutions, but this was the first constitution
under which Jews received equality of civil rights—not a very revolutionary departure, since Jews had been prospering in New York since
1654. The Anglican Church was disestablished, but it had had few
roots in the colonies anyway. In New England the sects obtained a little
more recognition, but Congregationalism remained favored by law. The
American revolutionaries made no change in the laws of indentured
servitude. They deplored, but avoided, the matter of Negro slavery. Quit-
rents were generally abolished, but they had been nominal anyway, and
a kind of manorial system remained long after the Revolution in New
York. Laws favoring primogeniture and entail were done away with, but
apparently they had been little used by landowners in any case. No general or statistical estimate is yet possible on the disposition of loyalist
property. Some of the confiscated estates went to strengthen a new propertied class, some passed through the hands of speculators, and some
either immediately or eventually came into the possession of small owners. There was enough change of ownership to create a material interest
in the Revolution, but obviously no such upheaval in property relations
as in France after 1789.

Even the apparently simple question of how many people received the
right to vote because of the Revolution cannot be satisfactorily answered.
There was some extension of democracy in this sense, but the more we
examine colonial voting practices the smaller the change appears. The
Virginia constitution of 1776 simply gave the vote to those "at present"
qualified. By one estimate the number of persons voting in Virginia actually declined from 1741 to 1843, and those casting a vote in the 1780's
were about a quarter of the free male population over twenty-one years of
age. The advance of political democracy, at the time of the Revolution,
was most evident in the range of officers for whom voters could vote. In
the South the voters generally voted only for members of the state legislatures; in Pennsylvania and New England they voted also for local officials, and in New England for governors as well.

In 1796, at the time of the revolution in Europe, and when the movement of Jeffersonian democracy was gathering strength in America,
seven of the sixteen states then in the union had no property qualification for voters in the choice of the lower legislative house, and half of
them provided for popular election of governors, only the seaboard South,
and New Jersey, persisting in legislative designation of the executive.
The best European historians underestimate the extent of political democracy in America at this time. They stress the restrictions on voting
rights in America, as in the French constitution of 1791. They do so because they have read the best American historians on the subject and
have in particular followed the school of Charles Beard and others. The

truth seems to be that America was a good deal more democratic than Europe in the 1790's. It had been so, within limits, long before the revolutionary era began.

Nor in broad political philosophy did the American Revolution require a violent break with customary ideas. For Englishmen it was impossible to maintain, in the eighteenth century or after, that the British constitution placed any limits on the powers of Parliament. Not so for Americans; they constantly appealed, to block the authority of Parliament or other agencies of the British government, to their rights as Englishmen under the British constitution. The idea of limited government, the habit of thinking in terms of two levels of law, of an ordinary law checked by a higher constitutional law, thus came out of the realities of colonial experience. The colonial Americans believed also, like Blackstone for that matter, that the rights of Englishmen were somehow the rights of all mankind. When the highest English authorities disagreed on what Americans claimed as English rights, and when the Americans ceased to be English by abjuring their King, they were obliged to find another and less ethnocentric or merely historical principle of justification. They now called their rights the rights of man. Apart from abstract assertions of natural liberty and equality, which were not so much new and alarming as conceptual statements as in the use to which they were applied, the rights claimed by Americans were the old rights of Englishmen—trial by jury, *habeas corpus*, freedom of the press, freedom of religion, freedom of elections, no taxation without representation. The content of rights was broadened, but the content changed less than the form, for the form now became universal. Rights were demanded for human beings as such. It was not necessary to be English, or even American, to have an ethical claim to them. The form also became more concrete, less speculative and metaphysical, more positive and merely legal. Natural rights were numbered, listed, written down, and embodied in or annexed to constitutions, in the foundations of the state itself.

So the American Revolution remains ambivalent. If it was conservative, it was also revolutionary, and vice versa. It was conservative because colonial Americans had long been radical by general standards of Western Civilization. It was, or appeared, conservative because the deepest conservatives, those most attached to King and empire, conveniently left the scene. It was conservative because the colonies had never known oppression, excepting always for slavery—because, as human institutions go, America had always been free. It was revolutionary because the colonists took the risks of rebellion, because they could not avoid a conflict among themselves, and because they checkmated those Americans who, as the country developed, most admired the aristocratic society of England and Europe. Henceforth the United States, in Louis Hartz's phrase, would be the land of the frustrated aristocrat, not of the frustrated democrat; for to be an aristocrat it is not enough to think of one-self as such, it is necessary to be thought so by others; and never again would deference for social rank be a characteristic American attitude. Elites, for better or for worse, would henceforth be on the defensive against popular values. Moreover the Americans in the 1770's, not content merely to throw off an outside authority, insisted on transmuting the theory of their political institutions. Their revolution was revolutionary because it showed how certain abstract doctrines, such as the rights of man and the sovereignty of the people, could be "reduced to practice," as Adams put it, by assemblages of fairly levelheaded gentlemen exercising constituent power in the name of the people. And, quite apart from its more distant repercussions, it was certainly revolutionary in its impact on the contemporary world across the Atlantic.

Democracy without a democratic revolution

Louis Hartz

I

"The great advantage of the American," Tocqueville once wrote, "is that he has arrived at a state of democracy without having to endure a democratic revolution. . . ." Fundamental as this insight is, we have not remembered Tocqueville for it, and the reason is rather difficult to explain. Perhaps it is because, fearing revolution in the present, we like to think of it in the past, and we are reluctant to concede that its romance has been missing from our lives. Perhaps it is because the plain evidence of the American revolution of 1776, especially the evidence of its social impact that our newer historians have collected, has made the comment of Tocqueville seem thoroughly enigmatic. But in the last analysis, of course, the question of its validity is a question of perspective. Tocqueville was writing with the great revolutions of Europe in mind, and from that point of view the outstanding thing about the American effort of 1776 was bound to be, not the freedom to which it led, but the established feudal structure it did not have to destroy. He was writing too, as no French liberal of the nineteenth century could fail to write,

From *American Political Science Review* (Washington, D.C., June, 1952), Vol. XLVI, pp. 321–342. Reprinted by permission of the American Political Science Association.

with the shattered hopes of the Enlightenment in mind. The American revolution had been one of the greatest of them all, a precedent constantly appealed to in 1793. In the age of Tocqueville there was ground enough for reconsidering the American image that the Jacobins had cherished.

Even in the glorious days of the eighteenth century, when America suddenly became the revolutionary symbol of Western liberalism, it had not been easy to hide the free society with which it started. As a matter of fact, the liberals of Europe had themselves romanticized its social freedom, which put them in a rather odd position; for if Reynal was right in 1772, how could Condorcet be right in 1776? If America was from the beginning a kind of idyllic state of nature, how could it suddenly become a brilliant example of social emancipation? Two consolations were being extracted from a situation which could at best yield only one. But the mood of the Americans themselves, as they watched the excitement of Condorcet seize the Old World, is also very revealing. They did not respond in kind. They did not try to shatter the social structure of Europe in order to usher in a Tenth and Final Epoch in the history of man. Delighted as they were with the support that they received, they remained, with the exception of a few men like Paine and Barlow, curiously untouched by the crusading intensity we find in the French and the Russians at a later time. Warren G. Harding, arguing against the League of Nations, was able to point back at them and say, "Mark you, they were not reforming the world." And James Fenimore Cooper, a keener mind than Harding, generalized their behavior into a comment about America that America is only now beginning to understand: "We are not a nation much addicted to the desire of proselytizing."

There were, no doubt, several reasons for this. But clearly one of the most significant is the sense that the Americans had themselves of the liberal history out of which they came. In the midst of the Stamp Act struggle, young John Adams congratulated his colonial ancestors for turning their backs on Europe's class-ridden corporate society, for rejecting the "canon and feudal law." The pervasiveness of Adams' sentiment in American thought has often been discussed, but what is easily overlooked is the subtle way in which it corroded the spirit of the world crusader. For this was a pride of inheritance, not a pride of achievement; and instead of being a message of hope for Europe, it came close to being a damning indictment of it. It saturated the American sense of mission, not with a Christian universalism, but with a curiously Hebraic kind of separatism. The two themes fought one another in the cosmopolitan mind of Jefferson, dividing him between a love of Europe and fear of its "contamination"; but in the case of men like Adams and Gouverneur Morris, the second theme easily triumphed over the first. By the time the crusty Adams had gotten through talking to politicians abroad, he had

buried the Enlightenment concept of an oppressed humanity so completely beneath the national concept of a New World that he was ready
to predict a great and ultimate struggle between America's youth and
Europe's decadence. As for Morris, our official ambassador to France in
1789, he simply inverted the task of the Comintern agent. Instead of
urging the French on to duplicate the American experience, he badgered
them by pointing out that they could never succeed in doing so. "They
want an American constitution," he wrote contemptuously, "without real-
izing they have no Americans to uphold it."

Thus the fact that the Americans did not have to endure a "democratic
revolution" deeply conditioned their outlook on people elsewhere who
did; and by helping to thwart the crusading spirit in them, it gave to the
wild enthusiasms of Europe an appearance not only of analytic error but
of unrequited love. Symbols of a world revolution, the Americans were
not in truth world revolutionaries. There is no use complaining about the
confusions implicit in this position, as Woodrow Wilson used to complain when he said that we had "no business" permitting the French to
get the wrong impression about the American revolution. On both sides
the reactions that arose were well-nigh inevitable. But one cannot help
wondering about something else: the satisfying use to which our folklore
has been able to put the incongruity of America's revolutionary role. For
if the "contamination" that Jefferson feared, and that found its classic
expression in Washington's Farewell Address, has been a part of the
American myth, so has the "round the world" significance of the shots
that were fired at Concord. We have been able to dream of ourselves as
emancipators of the world at the very moment that we have withdrawn
from it. We have been able to see ourselves as saviours at the very moment that we have been isolationists. Here, surely, is one of the great
American luxuries that the twentieth century has destroyed.

II

When the Americans celebrated the uniqueness of their own society, they were on the track of a personal insight of the profoundest importance. For the nonfeudal world in which they lived shaped every aspect of their social thought: it gave them a frame of mind that cannot be
found anywhere else in the eighteenth century, or in the wider history of
modern revolutions.

One of the first things it did was to breed a set of revolutionary thinkers in America who were human beings like Otis and Adams rather than
secular prophets like Robespierre and Lenin. Despite the European flavor
of a Jefferson or a Franklin, the Americans refused to join in the great
Enlightenment enterprise of shattering the Christian concept of sin, re-
placing it with an unlimited humanism, and then emerging with an
earthly paradise as glittering as the heavenly one that had been de-

stroyed. The fact that the Americans did not share the crusading spirit of the French and the Russians, as we have seen, is already some sort of confirmation of this, for that spirit was directly related to the "civil religion" of Europe and is quite unthinkable without it. Nor is it hard to see why the liberal good fortune of the Americans should have been at work in the position they held. Europe's brilliant dream of an impending millennium, like the mirage of a thirst-ridden man, was inspired in large part by the agonies it experienced. When men have already inherited the freest society in the world, and are grateful for it, their thinking is bound to be of a solider type. America has been a sober nation, but it has also been a comfortable one, and the two points are by no means unrelated.

Sam Adams, for example, rejects the hope of changing human nature: in a mood of Calvinist gloom, he traces the tyranny of England back to "passions of Men" that are fixed and timeless. But surely it would be unreasonable to congratulate him for this approach without observing that he implicitly confines those passions to the political sphere—the sphere of Parliaments, ministers, and Stampmasters—and thus leaves a social side to man which can be invoked to hold him in check. The problem was a different one for Rousseau and Marx, who started from the view that the corruption of man was complete, as wide as the culture in which he lived, with the result that revolutions became meaningless unless they were based on the hope of changing him. Here, obviously, is a place where the conclusions of political thought breathe a different spirit from the assumptions on which they rest. Behind the shining optimism of Europe, there are a set of anguished grievances; behind the sad resignation of America, a set of implicit satisfactions.

One of these satisfactions, moreover, was crucially important in developing the sober temper of the American revolutionary outlook. It was the high degree of religious diversity that prevailed in colonial life. This meant that the revolution would be led in part by fierce Dissenting ministers, and their leadership destroyed the chance for a conflict to arise between the worldly pessimism of Christianity and the worldly ambitions of revolutionary thought. In Europe, especially on the Continent, where reactionary church establishments had made the Christian concept of sin and salvation into an explicit pillar of the *status quo,* liberals were forced to develop a political religion, as Rousseau saw, if only in answer to it. The Americans not only avoided this compulsion; they came close, indeed, to reversing it. Here, above all in New England, the clergy was so militant that it was Tories like Daniel Leonard who were reduced to blasting it as a dangerous "political engine," a situation whose irony John Adams caught when he reminded Leonard that "in all ages and countries" the church is "disposed enough" to be on the side of conservatism. Thus the American liberals, instead of being forced to pull the Christian heaven down to earth, were glad to let it remain where it was.

They did not need to make a religion out of the revolution because religion was already revolutionary.

Consider the case of Rev. William Gordon of Roxbury. In 1774, when all of Boston was seething with resentment over the Port Bill, Gordon opened one of his sermons by explicitly reminding his congregation that there were "more important purposes than the fate of kingdoms" or the "civil rights of human nature," to wit, the emancipation of men from the "slavery of sin and Satan" and their preparation "for an eternal blessedness." But the Sons of Liberty did not rise up against him; they accepted his remarks as perfectly reasonable. For instead of trying to drug Bostonians with a religious opiate, Gordon proceeded to urge them to prepare for open war, delivering a blast against the British that the Tories later described as a plea for "sedition, rebellion, carnage, and blood." When Christianity is so explosive, why should even the most ardent revolutionary complain if heaven is beyond his grasp?

Of course, the Gordons and the Mayhews of America were quite unaware that their work had this significance—the indirect significance of keeping political thought down to earth. If anything impressed them in their role as religious figures, it was undoubtedly the crusade they were carrying forward against the "popery" of the Anglican Tories—in other words, what mattered to them was not that they were helping America to avoid the eighteenth century, but that they were helping it to duplicate the seventeenth. However, their achievement on the first count was actually far more important than their achievement on the second. The revolutionary attack on Anglicanism, with its bogy of a Bishop coming to America and its hysterical interpretation of the Quebec Act of 1774, was half trumped up and half obsolete; but the alliance of Christian pessimism with liberal thought had a deep and lasting meaning. Indeed, the very failure of the Americans to become seventeenth-century prophets like the English Presbyterians enhances this point considerably. For when we add to it the fact that they did not become latter-day prophets like the Jacobins and the Marxists, they emerge, if we wish to rank them with the great revolutionaries of modern history, as in a curious sense the most secular of them all.

Perhaps it was this secular quality that Joel Barlow was trying to describe when he declared, in a Fourth of July oration in Boston in 1778, that the "peculiar glory" of the American revolution lay in the fact that "sober reason and reflection have done the work of enthusiasm and performed the miracles of Gods." In any case, there was something fateful about it. For if the messianic spirit does not arise in the course of a country's national revolution, when is it ever going to arise? The post-revolutionary age, as the experience of England, France, and even in some sense Russia shows, is usually spent trying to recuperate from its effects. The fact that the Americans remained politically sober in 1776 was, in other words, a fairly good sign that they were going to remain that way during the modern age which followed; and if we except the religiosity of the Civil War, that is exactly what happened. There have been dreamers enough in American history, a whole procession of "millennial Christians," as George Fitzhugh used to call them; but the central course of our political thought has betrayed an unconquerable pragmatism.

Sir William Ashley, discussing the origins of the "American spirit," once remarked that "as feudalism was not transplanted to the New World, there was no need for the strong arm of a central power to destroy it." This is a simple statement, but, like many of Ashley's simple statements, it contains a neglected truth. For Americans usually assume that their attack on political power in 1776 was determined entirely by the issues of the revolution, when as a matter of fact it was precisely because of the things they were not revolting against that they were able to carry it through. The action of England inspired the American colonists with a hatred of centralized authority; but had that action been a transplanted American feudalism, rich in the chaos of ages, then they would surely have had to dream of centralizing authority themselves.

They would, in other words, have shared the familiar agony of European liberalism—hating power and loving it too. The liberals of Europe in the eighteenth century wanted, of course, to limit power; but confronted with the heritage of an ancient corporate society, they were forever devising sharp and sovereign instruments that might be used to put it down. Thus while the Americans were attacking Dr. Johnson's theory of sovereignty, one of the most popular liberal doctrines in Europe, cherished alike by Bentham and Voltaire, was the doctrine of the enlightened despot, a kind of political deism in which a single force would rationalize the social world. While the Americans were praising the "illustrious Montesquieu" for his idea of checks and balances, that worthy was under heavy attack in France itself because he compromised the unity of power on which so many liberals relied. Even the English Whigs, men who were by no means believers in monarchical absolutism, found it impossible to go along with their eager young friends across the Atlantic. When the Americans, closing their eyes to 1688, began to lay the axe to the concept of parliamentary sovereignty, most of the Whigs fled their company at once.

A philosopher, it is true, might look askance at the theory of power the Americans developed. It was not a model of lucid exposition. The trouble lay with their treatment of sovereignty. Instead of boldly rejecting the concept, as Franklin was once on the verge of doing when he said that it made him "quite sick," they accepted the concept and tried to qualify it out of existence. The result was a chaotic series of forays and retreats in which a sovereign Parliament was limited, first by the distinction between external and internal taxation, then by the distinction between rev-

enue and regulation, and finally by the remarkable contention that colonial legislatures were as sovereign as Parliament was. But there is a
limit to how much we can criticize the Americans for shifting their
ground. They were obviously feeling their way; and they could hardly be
expected to know at the time of the Stamp Act what their position would
be at the time of the first Continental Congress. Moreover, if they clung
to the concept of sovereignty, they battered it beyond belief, and no one
would confuse their version of it with the one advanced by Turgot or
even by Blackstone in Europe. The meekness of the American sovereign
testifies to the beating he had received. Instead of putting up a fierce and
embarrassing battle against the limits of natural law and the separation
of powers, as he usually did in the theories of Europe, he accepted those
limits with a vast docility.

If we look at what happened to America's famous idea of judicial control when the physiocrats advanced it in France, we will get an insight
into this whole matter. Who studies now the theory of legal guardianship
with which La Rivière tried to bind down his rational and absolute sovereign? Who indeed remembers it? American students of the judicial
power rarely go to Cartesian France to discover a brother of James Otis—
and the reason is evident enough. When the physiocrats appealed to the
courts, they were caught at once in a vise of criticism: either they were
attacked for reviving the feudal idea of the *parlements* or they were
blasted as insincere because they had originally advanced a despot to
deal with the feudal problem. They had to give the idea up. But in America, where the social questions of France did not exist and the absolutism
they engendered was quite unthinkable, the claim of Otis in the Writs of
Assistance Case, that laws against reason and the Constitution were
"void" and that the "Courts must pass them into disuse," met an entirely
different fate. It took root, was carried forward by a series of thinkers,
and blossomed ultimately into one of the most remarkable institutions in
modern politics.

The question, again, was largely a question of the free society in which
the Americans lived. Nor ought we to assume that its impact on their
view of political power disappeared when war and domestic upheaval
finally came. Of course, there was scattered talk of the need for a "dictator," as Jefferson angrily reported in 1782; and until new assemblies
appeared in most places, Committees of Public Safety had authoritarian
power. But none of this went deep enough to shape the philosophic mood
of the nation. A hero is missing from the revolutionary literature of
America. He is the Legislator, the classical giant who almost invariably
turns up at revolutionary moments to be given authority to lay the foundations of the free society. He is not missing because the Americans were
unfamiliar with images of ancient history, or because they had not read
the Harringtons or the Machiavellis and Rousseaus of the modern pe-

riod. Harrington, as a matter of fact, was one of their favorite writers. The Legislator is missing because, in truth, the Americans had no need for his services. Much as they liked Harrington's republicanism, they did not require a Cromwell, as Harrington thought he did, to erect the foundations for it. Those foundations had already been laid by history.

The issue of history itself is deeply involved here. On this score, inevitably, the fact that the revolutionaries of 1776 had inherited the freest society in the world shaped their thinking in a most intricate way. It gave them, in the first place, an appearance of outright conservatism. We know, of course, that most liberals of the eighteenth century, from Bentham to Quesnay, were bitter opponents of history, posing a sharp antithesis between nature and tradition. And it is an equally familiar fact that their adversaries, including Burke and Blackstone, sought to break down this antithesis by identifying natural law with the slow evolution of the past. The militant Americans, confronted with these two positions, actually took the second. Until Jefferson raised the banner of independence, and even in many cases after that time, they based their claims on a philosophic synthesis of Anglo-American legal history and the reason of natural law. Blackstone, the very Blackstone whom Bentham so bitterly attacked in the very year 1776, was a rock on which they relied.

The explanation is not hard to find. The past had been good to the Americans, and they knew it. Instead of inspiring them to the fury of Bentham and Voltaire, it often produced a mystical sense of Providential guidance akin to that of Maistre—as when Rev. Samuel West, surveying the growth of America's population, anticipated victory in the revolution because "we have been prospered in a most wonderful manner." The troubles they had with England did not alter this outlook. Even these, as they pointed out again and again, were of recent origin, coming after more than a century of that "salutary neglect" which Burke defended so vigorously. And in a specific sense, of course, the record of English history in the seventeenth century and the record of colonial charters from the time of the Virginia settlement provided excellent ammunition for the battle they were waging in defense of colonial rights. A series of circumstances had conspired to saturate even the revolutionary position of the Americans with the quality of traditionalism—to give them, indeed, the appearance of outraged reactionaries. "This I call an innovation," thundered John Dickinson, in his attack on the Stamp Act, "a most dangerous innovation."

Now here was a frame of mind that would surely have troubled many of the illuminated liberals in Europe, were it not for an ironic fact. America piled on top of this paradox another one of an opposite kind, and thus as it were, by misleading them twice, gave them a deceptive sense of understanding.

Actually, the form of America's traditionalism was one thing, its content quite another. Colonial history had not been the slow and glacial record of development that Bonald and Maistre loved to talk about. On the contrary, since the first sailing of the *Mayflower*, it had been a story of new beginnings, daring enterprises, and explicitly stated principles— it breathed, in other words, the spirit of Bentham himself. The result was that the traditionalism of the Americans, like a pure freak of logic, often bore amazing marks of anti-historical rationalism. The clearest case of this undoubtedly is to be found in the revolutionary constitutions of 1776, which evoked, as Franklin reported, the "rapture" of European liberals everywhere. In America, of course, the concept of a written constitution, including many of the mechanical devices it embodied, was the end-product of a chain of historical experience that went back to the Mayflower Compact and the Plantation Covenants of the New England towns: it was the essence of political traditionalism. But in Europe just the reverse was true. The concept was the darling of the rationalists—a symbol of the emancipated mind at work.

Thus Condorcet was untroubled. Instead of bemoaning the fact that the Americans were Blackstonian historicists, he proudly welcomed them into the fraternity of the illuminated. "American constitutionalism," he said, "had not grown, but was planned"; it "took no force from the weight of centuries but was put together mechanically in a few years." When John Adams read this comment, he spouted two words on the margin of the page: "Fool! Fool!" But surely the judgment was harsh. After all, when Burke clothes himself in the garments of Sieyès, who can blame the loyal rationalist who fraternally grasps his hand? The reactionaries of Europe, moreover, were often no keener in their judgment. They made the same mistake in reverse. Maistre gloomily predicted that the American Constitution would not last because it was created out of the whole cloth of reason.

But how then are we to describe these baffling Americans? Were they rationalists or were they traditionalists? The truth is, they were neither, which is perhaps another way of saying that they were both. For the war between Burke and Bentham on the score of tradition, which made a great deal of sense in a society where men had lived in the shadow of feudal institutions, made comparatively little sense in a society where for years they had been creating new states, planning new settlements, and, as Jefferson said, literally building new lives. In such a society a strange dialectic was fated to appear, which would somehow unite the antagonistic components of the European mind; the past became a continuous future, and the God of the traditionalists sanctioned the very arrogance of the men who defied Him.

This shattering of the time categories of Europe, this Hegelian-like revolution in historic perspective, goes far to explain one of the enduring secrets of the American character: a capacity to combine rock-ribbed traditionalism with high inventiveness, ancestor worship with ardent optimism. Most critics have seized upon one or the other of these aspects of the American mind, finding it impossible to conceive how both can go together. That is why the insight of Gunnar Myrdal is a very distinguished one when he writes: "America is . . . conservative. . . . But the principles conserved are liberal and some, indeed, are radical." Radicalism and conservatism have been twisted entirely out of shape by the liberal flow of American history.

III

What I have been doing here is fairly evident: I have been interpreting the social thought of the American revolution in terms of the social goals *it did not need to achieve.* Given the usual approach, this may seem like a perverse inversion of the reasonable course of things; but in a world where the "canon and feudal law" are missing, how else are we to understand the philosophy of a liberal revolution? The remarkable thing about the "spirit of 1776," as we have seen, is not that it sought emancipation but that it sought it in a sober temper; not that it opposed power but that it opposed it ruthlessly and continuously; not that it looked forward to the future but that it worshipped the past as well. Even these perspectives, however, are only part of the story, misleading in themselves. The "free air" of American life, as John Jay once happily put it, penetrated to deeper levels of the American mind, twisting it in strange ways, producing a set of results fundamental to everything else in American thought. The clue to these results lies in the following fact: the Americans, though models to all the world of the middle class way of life, lacked the passionate middle class consciousness which saturated the liberal thought of Europe.

There was nothing mysterious about this lack. It takes the contemptuous challenge of an aristocratic feudalism to elicit such a consciousness; and when Richard Price glorified the Americans because they were men of the "middle state," men who managed to escape being "savage" without becoming "refined," he explained implicitly why they themselves would never have it. Franklin, of course, was a great American bourgeois thinker; but it is a commonplace that he had a wider vogue on this score in Paris and London than he did in Philadelphia; and indeed there is some question as to whether the Europeans did not worship him more because he seemed to exemplify Poor Richard than because he had created the philosophy by which Poor Richard lived. The Americans, a kind of national embodiment of the concept of the bourgeoisie, have, as Mr. Brinkmann points out, rarely used that concept in their social thought, and this is an entirely natural state of affairs. Frustration produces the social passion, ease does not. A triumphant middle class, unassailed by the agonies that Beaumarchais described, can take itself for granted. This point, curiously enough, is practically never discussed, though the failure of the American working class to become class conscious has been a theme of endless interest. And yet the relationship between the two suggests itself at once. Marx himself used to say that the bourgeoisie was the great teacher of the proletariat.

There can, it is true, be quite an argument over whether the challenge of an American aristocracy did not in fact exist in the eighteenth century. One can point to the great estates of New York where the Patroons lived in something resembling feudal splendor. One can point to the society of the South where life was extraordinarily stratified, with slaves at the bottom and a set of genteel planters at the top. One can even point to the glittering social groups that gathered about the royal governors in the North. But after all of this has been said, the American "aristocracy" could not, as Tocqueville pointed out, inspire either the "love" or the "hatred" that surrounded the ancient titled aristocracies of Europe. Indeed, in America it was actually the "aristocrats" who were frustrated, not the members of the middle class, for they were forced almost everywhere, even in George Washington's Virginia, to rely for survival upon shrewd activity in the capitalist race. This compulsion produced a psychic split that has always tormented the American "aristocracy"; and even when wealth was taken for granted, there was still, especially in the North, the withering impact of a colonial "character" that Sombart himself once described as classically bourgeois. In Massachusetts Governor Hutchinson used to lament that a "gentleman" did not meet even with "common civility" from his inferiors. Of course, the radicals of America blasted their betters as "aristocrats," but that this was actually a subtle compliment is betrayed in the quality of the blast itself. Who could confuse the anger of Daniel Shays with the bitterness of Francis Place even in the England of the nineteenth century?

Thus it happened that fundamental aspects of Europe's bourgeois code of political thought met an ironic fate in the most bourgeois country in the world. They were not so much rejected as they were ignored, treated indifferently, because the need for their passionate affirmation did not exist. Physiocratic economics is an important case in point. Where economic parasites are few, why should men embark on a passionate search for the productive laborer? Where guild restrictions are comparatively slight and continental tariffs unknown, why should they embrace the ruthless atomism of Turgot? America's attack on the English Acts of Trade was couched in terms of Locke, not in terms of Quesnay; and though Franklin and Jefferson were much taken by the "modern economics," they did not, here as in certain other places, voice the dominant preoccupation of American thought. It had often been said, of course, that the Americans were passionately "laissez faire" in their thinking, but this is to confuse either bourgeois ease with bourgeois frustration or a hatred of absolute power with the very economic atomism which, in physiocratic terms, was allied to it. Turgot himself saw that the Americans did not long to smash a feudal world into economic atoms any more than they longed for a unified sovereign to accomplish this feat. A lover of the Americans who, like most European liberals, could not quite imagine life outside the *ancien regime,* he complained bitterly on both counts. His complaint on the count of sovereignty is legendary, but his complaint on the count of laissez faire has, alas, been entirely forgotten. This is because John Adams replied to the one in his *Defence of the Constitutions* but did not mention the other. And yet it appears in the same place, in Turgot's famous letter to Richard Price: *On suppose partout le droit de regler le commerce . . . tant on est loin d'avoir senti que la loi de la liberté entière de tout commerce est un corrollaire du droit de proprieté.*

The lament of Turgot reveals that America's indifference to the bourgeois fixations of Europe had in itself a positive meaning: the failure to develop a physiocratic conscience led to a quiet and pragmatic outlook on the question of business controls. This is the outlook that characterizes a whole mass of early economic legislation that American historians are now beginning to unearth in what should have been, reputedly, the most "laissez faire" country in the world. But it is in connection with materialism and idealism, utilitarianism and natural law, that the inverted position of the Americans comes out most clearly. There was no Bentham, no Helvetius among the superlatively middle-class American thinkers. On the contrary, they stuck with Puritan passion to the dogma of natural law, as if an outright hedonism were far too crass for consideration. In a purely political sense this may be interesting, for the Americans, at least during the Stamp Act phase of their struggle, were fighting that corrupt system of parliamentary representation which in England Benthamism later rose to assail. But it is in terms of the wider significance of utility as an attack on feudal norms, as an effort to make of "business a noble life," as Crane Brinton has put it, that America's indifference to it takes on its deepest meaning. Benjamin Franklins in fact, the Americans did not have to become Jeremy Benthams in theory. Unchallenged men of business, they did not have to equate morality with it. And this has been a lasting paradox in the history of American thought. The American tradition of natural law still flourishes after a century and a half of the most reckless material exploitation that the modern world has seen. A persistent idealism of mind, reflected in Emerson's remark that utilitarianism is a "stinking philosophy," has been one of the luxuries of a middle class that has never been forced to become class conscious.

But this is not all. If the position of the colonial Americans saved them from many of the class obsessions of Europe, it did something else as well: it inspired them with a peculiar sense of community that Europe had never known. For centuries Europe had lived by the spirit of solidarity that Aquinas, Bossuet, and Burke romanticized: an organic sense of structured differences, an essentially Platonic experience. Amid the "free air" of American life, something new appeared: men began to be held together, not by the knowledge that they were different parts of a corporate whole, but by the knowledge that they were similar participants in a uniform way of life—by that "pleasing uniformity of decent competence" which Crèvecoeur loved so much. The Americans themselves were not unaware of this. When Peter Thacher proudly announced that "simplicity of manners" was the mark of the revolutionary colonists, what was he saying if not that the norms of a single class in Europe were enough to sustain virtually a whole society in America? Richard Hildreth, writing after the levelling impact of the Jacksonian revolution had made this point far more obvious, put his finger directly on it. He denounced feudal Europe, where "half a dozen different codes of morals," often in flagrant contradiction with each other, flourished "in the same community," and celebrated the fact that America was producing "one code, one moral standard, by which the actions of all are to be judged. . . ." Hildreth knew that America was a marvellous mixture of many peoples and many regions, but he also knew that it was characterized by something more marvellous even than that: the power of the liberal norm to penetrate them all.

Now a sense of community based on a sense of uniformity is a deceptive thing. It looks individualistic, and in part it actually is. It cannot tolerate internal relationships of disparity, and hence can easily inspire the kind of advice that Professor Nettels once imagined a colonial farmer giving his son: "Remember that you are as good as any man— and also that you are no better." But in another sense it is profoundly anti-individualistic, because the common standard is its very essence, and deviations from that standard inspire it with an irrational fright. The man who is as good as his neighbors is in a tough spot when he confronts all of his neighbors combined. Thus William Graham Sumner looked at the other side of Professor Nettels's colonial coin and did not like what he saw: "public opinion" was an "impervious mistress. . . . Mrs. Grundy held powerful sway and Gossip was her prime minister."

Here we have the "tyranny of the majority" that Tocqueville later described in American life; here too we have the deeper paradox out of which it was destined to appear. Freedom in the fullest sense implies both variety and equality; but history, for reasons of its own, chose to separate these two principles, leaving the one with the old society of Burke and giving the other to the new society of Paine. America, as a kind of natural fulfillment of Paine, has been saddled throughout its history with the defect which this fulfillment involves, so that a country like England, in the very midst of its ramshackle class-ridden atmosphere, seems to contain an indefinable germ of liberty, a respect for the privacies of life, that America cannot duplicate. At the bottom of the American experience of freedom, not in antagonism to it but as a constituent element of it, there has always lain the inarticulate premise of conformity, which critics from the time of Cooper to the time of Lewis have sensed and furiously attacked. "Even what is best in America is compulsory," Santayana once wrote, "—the idealism, the zeal, the beautiful happy unison of its great moments." Thus while millions of Europeans have fled to America to discover the freedom of Paine, there have been a few Americans, only a few of course, who have fled to Europe to discover the freedom of Burke. The ironic flaw in American liberalism lies in the fact that we have never had a real conservative tradition.

One thing, we might suppose, would shatter the unprecedented sense of uniform values by which the colonial American was beginning to live: the revolution itself. But remarkably enough, even the revolution did not produce this result; John Adams did not confront Filmer, as Locke did, or Maistre, as the followers of Rousseau did. He confronted the Englishmen of the eighteenth century; and most of these men, insofar as the imperial struggle went, themselves accepted the Lockean assumptions that Adams advanced. Nor did the American Tories, with the fantastic exception of Boucher, who stuck to his thesis that Filmer was still "unrefuted," confront him with a vision of life completely different from his own. Samuel Seabury and Joseph Galloway accepted the Lockean principles, even sympathized with the American case, insisting only that peaceful means be used to advance it. Among their opponents, indeed, there were few who would fundamentally deny the "self-evident" truths the Americans advanced in 1776. The liberals of Europe always had a problem on their hands, which they usually neglected, to be sure, of explaining how principles could be "self-evident" when there were obviously so many people who did not believe them. Circumstance nearly solved this problem for the Americans, giving them, as it were, a national exemption from Hume's attack on natural law—which may be one of the reasons why they almost invariably ignored it. When one's ultimate values are accepted wherever one turns, the absolute language of self-evidence comes easily enough.

This then is the mood of America's absolutism: the sober faith that its norms are self-evident. It is one of the most powerful absolutisms in the world, more powerful even than the messianic spirit of the Continental liberals which, as we saw, the Americans were able to reject. That spirit arose out of contact with an opposing way of life, and its very intensity betrayed an inescapable element of doubt. But the American absolutism, flowing from an honest experience with universality, lacked even the passion that doubt might give. It was so sure of itself that it hardly needed to become articulate, so secure that it could actually support a pragmatism which seemed on the surface to belie it. American pragmatism has always been deceptive because, glacier-like, it has rested on miles of submerged conviction, and the conformitarian ethos which that conviction generates has always been infuriating because it has refused to pay its critics the compliment of an argument. Here is where the joy of a Dewey meets the anguish of a Fenimore Cooper; for if the American deals with concrete cases because he never doubts his general principles, this is also the reason he is able to dismiss his critics with a fine and crushing ease. But this does not mean that America's General Will always lives an easy life. It has its own violent moments—rare, to be sure, but violent enough. These are the familiar American moments of national fright and national hysteria when it suddenly rises to the surface with a vengeance, when civil liberties begin to collapse, and when Cooper is actually in danger of going to jail as a result of the Rousseauian tide. Anyone who watches it then can hardly fail to have a healthy respect for the dynamite which normally lies concealed beneath the free and easy atmosphere of the American liberal community.

When we study national variations in political theory, we are led to semantic considerations of a delicate kind, and it is to these, finally, that we must turn if we wish to get at the basic assumption of American thought. We have to consider the peculiar meaning that American life gave to the words of Locke.

There are two sides to the Lockean argument: a defense of the state that is implicit, and a limitation of the state that is explicit. The first is to be found in Locke's basic social norm, the concept of free individuals in a state of nature. This idea untangled men from the myriad associations of class, church, guild, and place, in terms of which feudal society defined their lives; and by doing so, it automatically gave to the state a much higher rank in relation to them than ever before. The state became the only association that might legitimately coerce them at all. That is why the liberals of France in the eighteenth century were able to substitute the concept of absolutism for Locke's conclusions of limited government and to believe that they were still his disciples in the deepest sense. When Locke came to America, however, a change appeared. Because the basic feudal oppressions of Europe had not taken root, the fundamental social norm of Locke ceased in large part to look like a norm and began, of all things, to look like a sober description of fact. The effect was significant enough. When the Americans moved from that concept to the contractual idea of organizing the state, they were not conscious of having already done anything to fortify the state, but were conscious only that they were about to limit it. One side of Locke became virtually the whole of him. Turgot ceased to be a modification of Locke, and became, as he was for John Adams, the destruction of his very essence.

It was a remarkable thing—this inversion of perspectives that made the social norms of Europe the factual premises of America. History was on a lark, out to tease men, not by shattering their dreams, but by fulfilling them with a sort of satiric accuracy. In America one not only found a society sufficiently fluid to give a touch of meaning to the individualist norms of Locke, but one also found letter-perfect replicas of the very images he used. There was a frontier that was a veritable state of nature. There were agreements, such as the Mayflower Compact, that were veritable social contracts. There were new communities springing up *in vacuis locis,* clear evidence that men were using their Lockean right of emigration, which Jefferson soberly appealed to as "universal" in his defense of colonial land claims in 1774. A purist could argue, of course, that even these phenomena were not enough to make a reality out of the pre-social men that liberalism dreamt of in theory. But surely they came as close to doing so as anything history has ever seen. Locke and Rousseau themselves could not help lapsing into the empirical mood when they looked across the Atlantic. "Thus, in the beginning," Locke once wrote, "all the world was America. . . ."

In such a setting, how could the tremendous, revolutionary social impact that liberalism had in Europe be preserved? The impact was not, of course, missing entirely; for the attack on the vestiges of corporate society in America that began in 1776, the disestablishment of the Anglican church, the abolition of quitrents and primogeniture, the breaking up of the Tory estates, tinged American liberalism with its own peculiar fire. Nor must we therefore assume that the Americans had wider political objectives than the Europeans, since even their new governmental forms were, as Becker once said, little more than the "colonial institutions with the Parliament and king left out." But after these cautions have been taken, the central point is clear. In America the first half of Locke's argument was bound to become less a call to arms than a set of preliminary remarks essential to establishing a final conclusion: that the power of the state must be limited. Observe how it is treated by the Americans in their great debate with England, even by original thinkers like Otis and Wilson. They do not lavish upon it the fascinated inquiry that we find in Rousseau or Priestley. They advance it mechanically, hurry through it, anxious to get on to what is really bothering them: the limits of the British Parliament, the power of taxation. In Europe the idea of social liberty is loaded with dynamite; but in America it becomes, to a remarkable degree, the working base from which argument begins.

Here, then, is the master assumption of American political thought, the assumption from which all of the American attitudes discussed in this essay flow: the reality of atomistic social freedom. It is instinctive to the American mind, as in a sense the concept of the polis was instinctive to Platonic Athens or the concept of the church to the mind of the middle ages. Catastrophes have not been able to destroy it, proletariats have refused to give it up, and even our Progressive tradition, in its agonized clinging to a Jeffersonian world, has helped to keep it alive. There has been only one major group of American thinkers who have dared to challenge it frontally: the Fitzhughs and Holmeses of the pre-Civil War South who, identifying slavery with feudalism, tried to follow the path of the European reaction and of Comte. But American life rode roughshod over them—for the "prejudice" of Burke in America was liberal and the positive reality of Locke in America transformed them into the very metaphysicians they assailed. They were soon forgotten, massive victims of the absolute temper of the American mind, shoved off the scene by Horatio Alger, who gave to the Lockean premise a brilliance that lasted until the crash of 1929. And even the crash, though it led to a revision of the premise, did not really shatter it.

It might be appropriate to summarize with a single word, or even with a single sentence, the political outlook that this premise has produced. But where is the word and where is the sentence one might use? American political thought, as we have seen, is a veritable maze of polar contradictions, winding in and out of each other hopelessly: pragmatism and absolutism, historicism and rationalism, optimism and pessimism, materialism and idealism, individualism and conformism. But, after all, the human mind works by polar contradictions; and when we have evolved an interpretation of it which leads cleanly in a single direction, we may be sure that we have missed a lot. The task of the cultural analyst is not to discover simplicity, or even to discover unity, for simplicity and unity do not exist, but to drive a wedge of rationality through the pathetic indecisions of social thought. In the American case that wedge is not hard to find. It is not hidden in an obscure place. We find it in what the West as a whole has always recognized to be the distinctive element in American civilization: its social freedom, its social equality. And yet it is true, for all of our Jeffersonian nationalism, that the interpretation of American political thought has not been built around this idea. On the contrary, instead of interpreting the American revolution in terms of American freedom, we have interpreted it in terms of American oppression, and instead of studying the nineteenth century in terms of American equality, we have studied it in terms of a series of cosmic Beardian and Parringtonian struggles against class exploitation. We have missed what the rest of the world has seen and what we ourselves have seen whenever we have contrasted the New World with the Old. But this is a large issue, which brings us not only to the Progressive historians but to the peculiar subjectivism of the American mind that they reflect, and it is beyond the scope of our discussion here.

IV

The liberals of Europe in 1776 were obviously worshipping a very peculiar hero. If the average American had been suddenly thrust in their midst, he would have been embarrassed by the millennial enthusiasms that many of them had, would have found their talk of classes vastly overdone, and would have reacted to the Enlightenment synthesis of absolutism and liberty as if it were little short of dishonest doubletalk. Bred in a freer world, he had a different set of perspectives, was animated by a different set of passions, and looked forward to different goals. He was, as Crèvecoeur put it, a "new man" in Western politics.

But, someone will ask, where did the liberal heritage of the Americans come from in the first place? Didn't they have to create it? And if they did, were they not at one time or another in much the same position as the Europeans?

These questions drive us back to the ultimate nature of the American experience, and, doing so, confront us with a queer twist in the problem of revolution. No one can deny that conscious purpose went into the making of the colonial world, and that the men of the seventeenth century who fled to America from Europe were keenly aware of the oppressions of European life. But they were revolutionaries with a difference, and the fact of their fleeing is no minor fact: for it is one thing to stay at home and fight the "canon and feudal law," and it is another to leave it far behind. It is one thing to try to establish liberalism in the Old World, and it is another to establish it in the New. Revolution, to borrow the words of T. S. Eliot, means to murder and create, but the American experience has been projected strangely in the realm of creation alone. The destruction of forests and Indian tribes—heroic, bloody, legendary as it was—cannot be compared with the destruction of a social order to which one belongs oneself. The first experience is wholly external and, being external, can actually be completed; the second experience is an inner struggle as well as an outer struggle, like the slaying of a Freudian father, and goes on in a sense forever. Moreover, even the matter of creation is not in the American case a simple one. The New World, as Lord Baltimore's ill-fated experiment with feudalism in the seventeenth century illustrates, did not merely offer the Americans a virgin ground for the building of a liberal system: it conspired itself to help that system along. The abundance of land in America, as well as the need for a lure to settlers, entered so subtly into the shaping of America's liberal tradition, touched it so completely at every point, that Sumner was actually ready to say, "We have not made America, America has made us."

It is this business of destruction and creation which goes to the heart of the problem. For the point of departure of great revolutionary thought everywhere else in the world has been the effort to build a new society on the ruins of an old society, and this is an experience America has never had. Tocqueville saw the issue clearly, and it is time now to complete the sentence of his with which we began this essay: "The great advantage of the American is that he has arrived at a state of democracy without having to endure a democratic revolution; *and that he is born free without having to become so.*"

Born free without having to become so: this idea, especially in light of the strange relationship which the revolutionary Americans had with their admirers abroad, raises an obvious question. Can a people that is born free ever understand peoples elsewhere that have to become so? Can it ever lead them? Or to turn the issue around, can peoples struggling for a goal understand those who have inherited it? This is not a problem of antitheses such, for example, as we find in Locke and Filmer. It is a problem of different perspectives on the same ideal. But we must not for that reason assume that it is any less difficult of solution; it may in the end be more difficult, since antitheses define each other and hence can understand each other, but different perspectives on a single value may, ironically enough, lack this common ground of definition. Condorcet might make sense out of Burke's traditionalism, for it was the reverse of his own activism, but what could he say about Otis, who combined both concepts in a synthesis that neither had seen? America's experience of being born free has put it in a strange relationship to the rest of the world.

SUGGESTIONS FOR FURTHER READING

Carl Becker's argument that the American Revolution was a conflict within the colonies as well as a struggle against England may be found in his *History of Political Parties in the Province of New York, 1760–1776* (Madison, 1909). Arthur M. Schlesinger, *Colonial Merchants and the American Revolution* (New York, 1918) gives support to Becker's position by showing how merchants sought to protect their interests against both England and other groups in colonial society. A classic little study showing the social upheaval resulting from the revolutionary struggle is J. Franklin Jameson, *The American Revolution Considered as a Social Movement* (Princeton, N.J., 1926). These views are generally upheld in a more recent study by Elisha P. Douglass, *Rebels and Democrats* (Chapel Hill, 1955).

Edmund S. Morgan, *The Birth of the Republic, 1763–89* (Chicago, 1956) disputes the contention that there were sharp divisions among the colonists and instead finds a basic consensus among the revolutionaries. Robert E. Brown,

* Books in paperback editions will be indicated with an asterisk.

Middle-Class Democracy and the Revolution in Massachu-setts, 1691–1780 (Ithaca, N.Y., 1955) supports Clinton Ros-siter's argument that most Americans felt they had what they wanted and were only fighting to preserve it. In Chapter III of his *Genius of American Politics* (Chicago, 1953) Daniel J. Boorstin uses very different evidence to come to conclusions similar to those of Louis Hartz.

Useful bibliographical articles surveying the litera-ture on the Revolution are Edmund S. Morgan, "The Ameri-can Revolution: Revisions in Need of Revising," *William and Mary Quarterly*, XIV (January, 1957) and Frederick B. Tolles, "The American Revolution Considered as a Social Movement: A Re-Evaluation," *American Historical Review*, LX (October, 1954).

IV
THE ★
CONSTITUTION ★

There was widespread unrest and dissatisfaction with government under the Articles of Confederation. With thirteen states often going thirteen different ways, many feared for the future of the new nation. Men of property lamented the inability of Congress to collect taxes, to regulate interstate commerce, and to negotiate a favorable trade treaty with England. Widespread depression following the end of the war compounded the difficulties. In the summer of 1786 a group of farmers in western Massachusetts, hard hit by depression and angered by the state legislature's failure to heed their demands for a paper money issue and debtors' stay laws, took matters into their own hands. Led by Daniel Shays, they organized an army, marched on several courthouses, and threatened to take over the government. The governor called out the militia which easily crushed the uprising, but the spectre of rebellion remained and had a significant influence on those who wanted a stronger, more centralized national government.

Even as rebellion raged in Massachusetts, a small group of delegates met at Annapolis to discuss the conflicting regulations regarding interstate commerce. The Annapolis Convention went beyond problems of trade, however, and issued a call for another convention to meet the following year in Philadelphia to consider remedies for the defects in the Articles of Confederation. Delegates to the Philadelphia convention quickly scrapped the idea of revising the Articles and instead drafted a new Constitution of the United States.

The American people have come to venerate, indeed,

almost to worship their constitution. For many, the founding fathers are god-like and their handiwork, almost divine. The student of history, however, quickly discovers that the Constitution was very controversial at the time it was drafted, and that its ratification was hotly contested. He also discovers that there has been a lively controversy among historians regarding the meaning and significance of the Constitution.

Some scholars have argued that the Constitution was the work of a political and economic minority striving to create a government which would limit the power of the majority. Opposed to this wealthy aristocracy of large property owners were the small farmers and artisans, men such as those who had followed Daniel Shays in Massachusetts. The struggle over the Constitution therefore was essentially a class struggle, exhibiting a basic conflict in American society.

Others have strongly contested this interpretation of the Constitution. Disputes over the ratification of the Constitution, they maintain, did not represent basic differences based on property and class. On fundamentals most Americans agreed. They knew why they had fought the Revolution and what kind of government they wanted. But they had no precedents to follow; they were feeling their way, searching for the best means to institutionalize the goals for which they had fought. Differences over means rested on the solid foundation of a basic consensus on ends.

These two interpretations are illustrated in the selections which follow. Carl Van Doren describes some of the compromises which produced the Constitution, and by emphasizing compromise, he minimizes the existence of fundamental conflict. Charles Beard and Robert Brown clash over the economic meaning of the Constitution. In a path-breaking study Beard argues that the Constitution was written by men of property who did not believe in democracy and who wanted to promote their own economic interests. Brown attacks Beard at every point and argues that it is wrong to assume that the new nation was marked by sharply delineated economic classes. In fact, Brown maintains, the country was largely middle class, and the overall aim of the framers of the Constitution was a middle-class democracy.

The last two selections view the problem from another

perspective. Richard Hofstadter depicts the founding fathers as realists who wanted a strong central government because they had little faith in human nature and democracy. They were anxious to protect property, yet they were not aristocratic tyrants. Stanley Elkins and Eric McKitrick, although they would agree that the founding fathers were realists with little faith in human nature, picture them as young men who came to power and prominence during the Revolution. In drafting a constitution they were working out some of the implications of their experiences, not reacting against the ideas of the Revolution. Elkins and McKitrick see few ideological differences dividing those who favored and those who opposed the Constitution. Once the debate over ratification was over, the opponents quickly accepted the new Constitution, illustrating that a basic consensus united both groups.

Few historians would deny that many of the founding fathers were brilliant men; the Philadelphia convention brought together perhaps the most remarkable group of men ever assembled. Yet when they probe further, historians begin to disagree. Whom did these men represent and what were they trying to accomplish? Were the men who gathered in Philadelphia in the summer of 1787 a representative cross section of the American people, or did they represent particular classes or property interests? Did the Constitutional Convention and the contest over ratification reveal fundamental conflict in America or fundamental agreement?

Carl Van Doren

The federal
compromise

Early in the morning of July 3 Washington began sitting for his portrait by Charles Willson Peale, who wished to make the mezzotint soon to appear with the title lettered round the margin: "His Excel: G: Washington Esq: LLD. Late Commander in Chief of the Armies of the U.S. of America & President of the Convention of 1787." Washington was painted in a close-fitting wig and his famous uniform of blue and buff (taken over from the First Virginia Regiment which he had commanded when he was a soldier of the Crown) with three gold stars on his epaulets. That day, and perhaps other days, he went to the State House in uniform, general as well as president. Although this day's session was only a meeting of the grand committee of the states, of which Washington was not a member, he attended along with other delegates who were there as observers not debaters.

With Gerry as chairman, the committee took up the problem of conciliating the opposed views which were the same in the committee as they had been in the Convention. The majority favored proportional representation in both houses of the legislature of the United States; the minority favored equal representation in both. Sherman had earlier proposed that the states have proportional representation in the popular branch, but equal votes in the Senate. Franklin had proposed that the states be equally represented in the Senate, but that in money matters the Senate votes be based on the amount of contributions from the separate states. Now in the committee Sherman, who had taken the place of Ellsworth, offered a new compromise: that the states should have an equal vote in the Senate but that no decision could be final unless the states voting for it should comprise a majority of the inhabitants of the United States. None of these compromises suited the committee. At last, after debates of which there is no record, Franklin made the motion which, with "some modifications," was agreed to. As modified, it proposed that in the first branch each state be allowed one member for every 40,000 of its inhabitants (counting three-fifths of the slaves) and that any state with less than that number of inhabitants have one member; that all bills for raising or apportioning money and for paying salaries to federal officers originate in the first branch, without alteration or amendment by the Senate; and that in the Senate each state have an equal vote.

From *The Great Rehearsal* by Carl Van Doren. Copyright 1948 by Carl Van Doren. Reprinted by permission of The Viking Press, Inc.

This compromise combined and redefined Sherman's proposed compromise on different modes of representation in the two houses, and Franklin's on a special mode for allowing more votes to the states which paid more money for federal expenses. It was satisfactory to a majority of the members of the grand committee, though the large states were now in dissent because of the equal vote granted to all states in the Senate. The committee agreed to report their compromise to the Convention, with the condition that the provisions relating to both houses must be "generally adopted" together.

On Thursday July 5 Gerry reported for the committee to the Convention. Madison vigorously opposed the concession to the small states of equality in the Senate. It was, he thought, the surrender of a fundamental principle on the mere ground of expediency. It was conciliating a minority, by doing an injustice to the majority of the people of the United States. "It was in vain to purchase concord in the Convention on terms which would perpetuate discord among their constituents." He did not believe that Delaware "would brave the consequences of seeking her fortunes apart from the other States" or "pursue the rash policy of courting foreign support"; or that New Jersey "would choose rather to stand on its own legs, and bid defiance to events," than to accept a government which was absolutely necessary to protect the state from its overshadowing neighbors. "Harmony in the Convention was no doubt much to be desired. Satisfaction to all the States" from the first would be still more desirable. "But if the principal States comprehending a majority of the people of the United States should concur in a just & judicious plan, he had the firmest hopes that all the other States would by degrees accede to it."

Gouverneur Morris was rhetorical. "He came here as a Representative of America; he flattered himself he came here in some degree as a Representative of the whole human race; for the whole human race will be affected by the proceedings of this Convention." But it seemed to him, from some things he had heard, "that we were assembled to truck and bargain for our particular States." He believed that "this Country must be united. If persuasion does not unite it, the sword will." He spoke of the horrors of civil war. "The stronger party will then make traytors of the weaker; and the Gallows & Halter will finish the work of the sword." In the compromise report from the grand committee he saw prospects of confusion and conflict. "State attachments, and State importance have been the bane of this Country. We cannot annihilate; but we can perhaps take out the teeth of the serpents"—the jealousies of the states.

Bedford, who had let slip the unfortunate hint that the smaller states might turn to foreign alliances, again protested that he had not meant what he had said; that he had been speaking as a lawyer, for whom "warmth was natural & sometimes necessary." But no man could foresee "to what extremities the small States may be driven by oppression." Paterson thought the talk about the sword and the gallows was "little calculated to produce conviction." Both he and Bedford resented the treatment the small states had endured from the large in the Convention. Paterson was not entirely satisfied with the grand committee's compromise plan, but he agreed with Bedford that something must be done for the United States. "Better that a defective plan should be adopted," Bedford said, "than that none should be recommended." Defects might be remedied by later meetings.

Gerry had objections to the new plan, but he insisted that the United States were "in a peculiar situation. We were neither the same Nation nor different Nations. We ought not therefore to pursue the one or the other of these ideas too closely." If that were done, some of the states might secede from the Convention, and from the union. "If we do not come to some agreement among ourselves some foreign sword will probably do the work for us." Mason thought there must be an accommodation between the opposing sides in the conflict. "It could not be more inconvenient to any gentleman to remain absent from his private affairs, than it was for him; but he would bury his bones in this city rather than expose his Country to the Consequences of a dissolution of the Convention without anything being done."

Both Gouverneur Morris and Rutledge objected to basing representation in the lower house purely on numbers, one member for each 40,000 inhabitants. Life and liberty might be the first considerations of savages, Morris said, but in civilized conditions "property was the main object of Society." Property, Rutledge agreed, "was certainly the principal object of Society." Here Rutledge was speaking for the slave-owners of South Carolina and Morris for the large land-owners of New York. Moreover, they were both thinking of the new states in the Western territory which might in time be admitted to the union. Any one of these, according to the grand committee's plan, might be entitled to one member even though it had less than 40,000 inhabitants. Some arrangement must be made to protect the rich maritime states from the lean voters of the backwoods.

Nothing was decided that day, and the debate went over to Friday the 6th. On Friday the Convention readily agreed that the proposal of one member in the lower house for each 40,000 inhabitants called for further detailed study. The matter was referred to a smaller committee made up of Gouverneur Morris, Gorham, Randolph, Rutledge, and King. Then the debate continued on the clause providing that all money bills should originate in the popular branch of the federal legislature.

The delegates from the small states were silent. They had won what they wanted in the proposal that the states be equally represented in the

Senate, and were willing to let the larger states, with more votes in the lower house, have some advantage in raising revenues and fixing apportionments. The delegates from the large states failed to see that the small had made any real concession. What was the difference, Wilson asked, which house had the right to originate bills, since the other must concur? Mason explained that the committee had desired to put the voting of money as directly as possible into the hands of the people. If the members of the Senate should have "the power of giving away the people's money, they might soon forget the Source from whence they received it. We might soon have an aristocracy." He had been disturbed by certain aristocratic principles advanced in the Convention, but he was glad to find they did not prevail among the members.

Gouverneur Morris, to whom Mason had obviously referred, declared that he was sure "there never was, nor ever will be a civilized society without an Aristocracy. His endeavour was to keep it as much as possible from doing mischief." He assumed that the American aristocracy would dominate the Senate. If the sole right to originate money bills lay in the popular house, the country would lose the benefit of the superior abilities of the Senate in devising such bills; and the Senate, having no responsibility, would fall into disputes with the originating house, as in the British Parliament. Morris believed that the proposed restriction would be "either useless or pernicious."

Franklin summed up the argument with a clarity which enabled Madison, taking down the slow words, to make them sound almost like one of Franklin's written speeches. "It had been asked," the philosopher said, "what would be the use of restraining the second branch from medling with money bills. He could not but remark that it was always of importance that the people should know who had disposed of their money, & how it had been disposed of. It was a maxim that those who feel, can best judge." (It was a maxim of Franklin's own. He had used it as far back as February 1766 in his examination before the House of Commons, when he said: "Those that feel can judge best.") "This end would, he thought, be best attained, if money affairs were to be confined to the immediate representatives of the people. This was his inducement to concur in the report. As to the danger or difficulty that might arise from a negative in the second [branch] where the people would not be proportionally represented, it might easily be got over by declaring that there should be no such Negative; or if that will not do, by declaring that there shall be no such branch at all"—which was what Franklin preferred in any case.

In the vote which followed, the Convention agreed by a narrow margin to let the clause relating to money bills stand for the present in the report. Connecticut, New Jersey, Delaware, Maryland, and North Carolina were now in the affirmative, with only Pennsylvania, Virginia, and South Carolina in the negative; and Massachusetts, New York, and Georgia divided.

If the popular branch of the legislature was to have the sole right to originate money bills, then the representation in that branch was bound to be of the greatest importance. On Saturday the 7th the Convention agreed that each state should "have an equal vote" in the Senate. There was some lively discussion, but the vote was not too close. Several of the delegates voted aye because they realized that this was only a part of the grand committee's report, and that another vote would later be taken on the whole of it. Before that could be done, there must be some settlement as to the actual number of representatives the people of the respective states would have to speak for them in the disposition of their money.

II

Gouverneur Morris, for the smaller committee, reported on Monday the 9th. His committee had been handicapped by lack of knowledge as to what the population of the states was. For want of better information, they had gone back to the estimates of 1774 with some guesses as to changes since then. They now proposed that at the first meeting of the lower house it should consist of fifty-six members, divided as follows: New Hampshire 2, Massachusetts 7, Rhode Island 1, Connecticut 4, New York 5, New Jersey 3, Pennsylvania 8, Delaware 1, Maryland 4, Virginia 9, North Carolina 5, South Carolina 5, Georgia 2. These figures were to be temporary. The legislature of the United States should be authorized "from time to time" to augment the number of representatives. "In case any of the States shall hereafter be divided, or any two or more States united, or any new State created within the limits of the United States," the legislature should have authority to regulate the number of the representatives of the new states "upon the principles of their wealth and number of inhabitants."

There had been talk in the Convention of the possible division of some of the larger states and the possible union of some of the smaller. The committee had provided for either possibility. But the proposal that new states should be granted representation according to their wealth as well as to their population roused fresh debate. Gorham, a member of the committee, explained the report. One member of the popular house to every 40,000 inhabitants, the committee thought, would make the house unworkably large as the population increased. Moreover, there was danger that new Western states, if admitted on those terms, might soon "out-vote the Atlantic." But if the Atlantic states kept the "Government in their own hands," they could take care of their own interest "by dealing out the right of Representation in safe proportions to the Western States. These were the views of the Committee."

Those were the views of several of the delegates who thought wealth no less than numbers should be represented in all the states. Butler of South Carolina "urged warmly the justice & necessity" of taking wealth into account. King of Massachusetts said that, as the Southern states were the richest, they must naturally hesitate to "league themselves with the Northern unless some respect were paid to their superior wealth." But the Northern states, which looked for commercial advantages from the union, had already consented to the representation of Southern wealth, which was slaves, by agreeing that three-fifths of them might be reckoned as inhabitants.

Nine states now agreed (New York and New Jersey dissenting) that the legislature of the United States should have authority in the future to regulate the representation of all the states "upon the principles of their wealth and number of inhabitants." As to the number of representatives for the present, that matter was referred to another committee of the states. The members were King, Sherman, Yates, Brearley, Gouverneur Morris, Read, Daniel Carroll (who had just taken his seat for Maryland), Madison, Williamson, Rutledge, and Houstoun.

They came in on July 10 with a proposal that the lower house begin with sixty-five members: New Hampshire 3, Massachusetts 8, Rhode Island 1, Connecticut 5, New York 6, New Jersey 4, Pennsylvania 8, Delaware 1, Maryland 6, Virginia 10, North Carolina 5, South Carolina 5, Georgia 3.

At once there was a scuffle of arguments over these figures. Butler and General Pinckney of South Carolina moved that New Hampshire be reduced from three representatives to two. "Her numbers did not entitle her to 3 and it was a poor State." King of Massachusetts, supporting the claim of New Hampshire to three members, made it plain that he was thinking less of New Hampshire in particular than of the Northern states in general. He had been willing to yield something to the Southern states for their security, but "no principle would justify giving them a majority." General Pinckney replied that the Southern states did not expect to have a majority, but he wished them "to have something like an equality." Otherwise, they would be "nothing more than overseers for the Northern states," since the regulation of trade would be in the hands of the central government. He was glad that one member had been added to Virginia, "as he considered her a Southern state. He was glad also that the members of Georgia were increased"—and he did not object to her being given a larger number than her population then entitled her to.

The motion to reduce New Hampshire from three to two members was lost by a vote of eight to two. Motions made by Southern delegates to increase the number of members for the Carolinas and Georgia by one each were lost by decisive votes.

Madison moved that the number of members be doubled, "A *majority* of a *Quorum of* 65 members was too small a number to represent the whole inhabitants of the United States." Ellsworth and Sherman of Connecticut objected on the grounds of expense. Read of Delaware approved because the change would give Delaware two votes. Rutledge thought the state legislatures were at present too numerous, and the national legislature should not follow that bad example. The members would be forced by the interests of their states to attend regularly. He supposed "the General Legislature would not sit more than 6 or 8 weeks in the year."

Only two states, Delaware and Virginia, favored doubling the number of members. The number as fixed by the report of the committee of the states was approved by a vote of nine to two: only South Carolina and Georgia opposed.

Washington in the Chair, entertaining motions, putting questions, announcing votes, was troubled by the persistent conflicts. They were, he wrote that day to Hamilton in New York, worse than ever. "I *almost* despair of seeing a favourable issue to the proceedings of our Convention, and do therefore repent having had any agency in the business. The Men who oppose a strong and energetic government are, in my opinion, narrow minded politicians, or are under the influence of local views. The apprehension expressed by them that the *people* will not accede to the form proposed is the *ostensible*, not the *real* cause of the opposition. . . . I am sorry you went away. I wish you were back. The crisis is equally important and alarming, and no opposition under such circumstances should discourage exertions till the signature is fixed." Hamilton returned to the Convention three days later. His colleagues Yates and Lansing left it on the day Washington wrote.

The conflicts which troubled Washington went on for a week in a tangle of motions and motives. Randolph on the 10th moved that "in order to ascertain alterations in the population & wealth of the States the Legislature of the United States be required to cause a proper census and estimate to be taken" at regular intervals which were to be agreed on. Williamson of North Carolina on the 11th proposed an amendment to the effect that in the census enumeration the "free white inhabitants" be counted and three-fifths of "those of other descriptions"—that is, slaves. Butler and Charles Cotesworth Pinckney of South Carolina at once insisted that "blacks be included . . . equally with the Whites," and made a motion to that effect. The labor of a slave in South Carolina, Butler said, was as productive and valuable as that of a free man in Massachusetts. Wealth was the "great means of defence and utility to the Nation." Consequently wealth ought to be considered equal to numbers of free men "in a Government which was instituted principally for the protection of property, and was itself to be supported by property."

Mason of Virginia said that this principle of representation, however favorable it might be to Virginia, was unjust, and he could not vote for it. But since slaves by their labor raised the value of land, increased imports and exports and therefore revenues, "would supply the means of feeding & supporting an army, and might in cases of emergency become themselves soldiers," he believed they should not be wholly excluded from the estimates of population. He would be satisfied if three-fifths of them were counted. Like other Virginia delegates, Mason was opposed to slavery on principle, regretted the existence of it in their state, and desired to see slavery abolished if this could be done without destroying the economy of a society which had inherited its slaves as it had inherited its land and its laws.

Only three states, South Carolina, Georgia, and (for some reason) Delaware, voted to count slaves and free citizens equally in representation. The strength of the vote led the Convention to reconsider its earlier decision to reckon three-fifths of the slaves as inhabitants. Wilson did not see on what principle they could be so counted. "Are they admitted as Citizens? Then why are they not admitted on an equality with White Citizens? Are they admitted as property? Then why is not other property admitted into the computation?" Nevertheless he was willing to see them included as a necessary compromise. Gouverneur Morris said he found himself in the "dilemma of doing injustice to the Southern States or to human nature," and must decide in favor of human nature. To count slaves, in any ratio, as part of the population must encourage the slave trade, since the importing of slaves would increase not only the wealth but also the representation of the slave-holding states. He could not concur in that, even if the Southern states should refuse to "confederate" without it. On the question, six states voted against counting slaves at all in the estimate of population.

But on the 12th Morris made another motion to the effect that taxation should be proportioned according to representation. This naturally changed the position of the Southern states. South Carolina and Georgia were still willing to pay taxes on all their slaves if all of them could be counted as inhabitants. But the other states with large numbers of slaves were unwilling. Davie of North Carolina demanded, in the name of his state, merely that three-fifths of the slaves be included. Randolph of Virginia urged the same ratio. "He lamented that such a species of property existed. But as it did the holders of it would require this security." On another motion six states now favored the ratio of five to three, with Massachusetts and South Carolina divided, and only New Jersey and Delaware opposed.

On the 13th Randolph moved to alter the vote of July 9 which had said that representation should be based on wealth and population, by striking out wealth altogether. Gouverneur Morris objected. Suppose the population of the South should increase as it was expected to, and the South should make common cause with the Western states. Then between them they would have a majority which would overwhelm the Northern and Middle states. Butler replied that the South did not expect a majority, only an increase in relation to the other states, since "the people & strength of America are evidently bearing Southwardly & Southwestwardly." But the Southern states did want to feel sure that "their negroes may not be taken from them, which some gentlemen within or without doors have a very good mind to do."

Wilson in one of his ablest speeches carried the house with him. "Conceiving," he said, "that all men wherever placed have equal rights and are equally entitled to confidence, he viewed without apprehension the period when a few States should contain the superior number of people. The majority of the people wherever found ought in all questions to govern the minority." Nor was he troubled by the fear that the "interior Country" might some time contain the majority of the population. If they became the majority, they would have a majority's rights, "whether we will or no." Did the delegates not remember that Great Britain had been jealous and apprehensive over the growth of the American colonies? That had led to rebellion and independence. The Atlantic states must avoid behaving toward the interior as Great Britain had once unwisely behaved toward them. The numbers of people had to be regarded as the proper rule of representation, since no better could be found. Congress in 1783, after long discussion, had been satisfied that "the rule of numbers does not differ much from the combined rule of numbers & wealth. Again he could not agree that property was the sole or the primary object of Government & Society. The cultivation & improvement of the human mind was the most noble object. With respect to this object, as well as to other *personal* rights, numbers were surely the natural & precise measure of Representation. And with respect to property, they could not vary much from the precise measure."

On the question of striking "wealth" out of the clause relating to representation in the popular house, all the states on July 13 voted aye except Delaware, which was divided. One of the most important decisions which ever came here to a vote found the Convention nearly unanimous in agreement.

By a memorable coincidence this decision was made on the very day when Congress in New York at last adopted the Ordinance of 1787 for the government of the Northwest Territory. The Ordinance provided that five new states (eventually named Ohio, Indiana, Illinois, Wisconsin, Michigan) from this Territory might be admitted to the union as soon as any of them should have 60,000 inhabitants, which was about the population of Delaware. Slavery was prohibited, thanks to an earlier suggestion of Jefferson, a bill of rights and freedom of religious worship guaranteed, and laws forbidden which might impair the obligations of private contracts. This was federal legislation over separate states-to-be of the sort contemplated by the constitution which the Convention was now trying to make.

The old Congress and the new Convention were in accord on a matter which was fundamental to the future. While Congress was arranging to admit Western states to the United States, the Convention was arranging that this should be on an equality in law with the original Thirteen. The states themselves had long shown partiality to the cities and counties on the seaboard. The "back counties" of Pennsylvania were now in resentful conflict with Philadelphia and the counties nearest it. In South Carolina the "up country," rebelling against the dominance of the "low country," had in 1786 voted the removal of the capital of the state from Charleston to Columbia, still almost in the primeval forest—though this had not yet been carried out. The seaboard shipowners, merchants, and planters all along the Atlantic had made every effort to protect themselves and their property against the rising demands of the frontier. Various delegates to the Convention, notably Gorham of Massachusetts, Gouverneur Morris of Pennsylvania, and Rutledge of South Carolina, had insisted that the Atlantic states must keep control of the government.

Gerry thought on July 14 that the Convention ought to limit the number of Western states to be admitted, so that there should never be more of them than of the Atlantic states. "There was a rage for emigration from the Eastern States to the Western Country," he said, "and he did not wish those remaining behind to be at the mercy of the Emigrants" once they had established themselves in new states. Sherman, with an odd mixture of shortsightedness and enlightenment, thought there was no probability that the Western states would ever outnumber the Eastern. "If the event should ever happen, it was too remote to be taken into consideration at this time." For the present, he said, "We are providing for our posterity, for our children & our grand Children, who would be as likely to be citizens of new Western States, as of the old States." They should not be discriminated against as Gerry proposed.

While deciding that wealth (except for three-fifths of the slaves) should not be represented in the legislature of the United States, the Convention decided also that the legislature must not be left free to regulate changes in representation at its own will. "From the nature of man," Mason said on July 11, "we may be sure, that those who have power in their hands will not give it up while they can retain it." He agreed with Randolph that alterations must be according to a regular census called for by a constitutional provision. Sherman, who was at first disposed to leave alterations to the discretion of the legislature of the United States, was convinced, he said, "by the observations of Mr. Randolph & Mr. Mason that the *periods* & the *rule* of revising the Representation ought to be fixt by the Constitution." After much discussion and numerous amendments proposed, it was decided on July 12 that representation ought to be "proportioned according to direct Taxation," and that the necessary revisions should be based on a census to be taken within six years after the first meeting of the legislature of the United States and again every ten years thereafter.

III

On the morning of July 14 Martin of Maryland called for the question on the whole report brought in by the grand committee of the states on the 5th. The Convention had now gone piecemeal through the compromise proposal and had accepted, or amended, its various clauses. Instead of one member in the legislature of the United States for every 40,000 inhabitants of a given state, as proposed, the Convention preferred for the present a fixed number of members for each state, subject to revision according to a decennial census as the population might change in the future. But money bills were to originate in the popular branch, and each state should have an equal vote in the Senate, as the committee had recommended. Since the committee had stipulated that the parts of their proposal were not to be adopted separately, the Convention must now either accept or reject it as a whole.

Some of the delegates were not yet ready to put the matter to a vote. Gerry moved that the new states to be admitted should never be allowed more representatives than the original members of the Confederation. Four states (Massachusetts, Connecticut, Delaware, and Maryland) voted aye, all the others no except Pennsylvania, which was divided. Charles Pinckney moved that instead of equal votes in the Senate the states have fixed numbers of representatives in that branch: New Hampshire 2, Massachusetts 4, Rhode Island 1, Connecticut 3, New York 3, New Jersey 2, Pennsylvania 3, Delaware 1, Maryland 3, Virginia 5, North Carolina 3, South Carolina 3, Georgia 2. Wilson seconded the motion. King approved, because he could see no better reason for equality of representation in one branch of the legislature than in the other. What they proposed to create was "a General and National Government over the people of America. There never will be a case," he said, "in which it will act as a federal Government on the States and not on the individual Citizens." Therefore the citizens through their representatives, and not the states as states, ought to influence the operations of the central authority. He thought that to consent to equality of votes in the Senate would be injustice, and worse than doing nothing. Better "a little more confusion & convulsion" than to submit to such an evil. Strong of Massachusetts believed that unless some accommodation could be agreed on, "the Union itself must soon be dissolved." If, as had been suggested, the principal states were to form and recommend a scheme of government without the others, there was no certainty that the smaller would ever be more likely than now to accede to it, or even that the people of the larger would "embrace and ratify it." Wilson thought nothing "so pernicious as bad first principles." If equality in the Senate were merely "an error that time would correct," he might accept it, being aware "that perfection was unattainable in any plan." But this was "a fundamental and a perpetual error." An evil in representation, like poison in a first potion, "must be followed by disease, convulsions, and finally death itself."

Charles Pinckney's motion for proportional votes in the Senate "passed in the negative," in the language of the time, with six states opposed. Massachusetts was among them, because Gorham was absent that day, and King was outvoted by Gerry and Strong.

On Monday the 16th the Convention voted on the compromise proposal as a whole. The vote was nearly as close as it could be, and as it had regularly been during all the recent deliberations. Connecticut, New Jersey, Delaware, Maryland, and North Carolina approved; Pennsylvania, Virginia, South Carolina, and Georgia opposed; Massachusetts was divided. Even if Massachusetts had voted with the larger states, the result would have been merely a tie. The Convention was at a standstill.

Randolph, original proposer of the Virginia plan over which they had been working for six weeks, said that the vote had "embarrassed the business extremely." He had come this morning with a series of suggestions which he thought might conciliate the smaller states. His suggestions provided for an enumeration of special cases in which the states might have equal votes in the Senate, proportional votes in all others. But since he now saw that the smaller states persisted in demanding equal votes in every case, he "could not but think we were unprepared to discuss this subject further. It will probably be in vain to come to any final decision with a bare majority on either side. For these reasons he wished the Convention might adjourn, that the large States might consider the steps proper to be taken in the present solemn crisis of the business, and that the small States might also deliberate on the means of conciliation."

Paterson thought it was high time to adjourn. The rule of secrecy ought to be rescinded, and the delegates ought to be free to consult their constituents. But the smaller states, he assured the Convention, would in no circumstances yield their absolute demand for equality in the Senate. If Randolph were willing to move that the Convention adjourn sine die, Paterson would second it "with all his heart." Whether or not Paterson was actually in favor of a permanent adjournment, he seized on this troubled moment to make a suggestion that amounted to a threat.

Randolph "had never entertained the idea of an adjournment sine die; & was sorry that his meaning had been so readily & strangely interpreted." He had meant merely to adjourn till the next day "in order that some conciliatory experiment might if possible be devised." If the smaller States should continue to hold back, then the larger might take "such measures, he would not say what, as might be necessary." Here Randolph too was hinting a threat.

Paterson seconded the adjournment for a day, since the larger states seemed to wish, as he reversed Randolph's terms to put it, "to deliberate further on conciliatory expedients."

In the following discussion nobody favored an adjournment sine die. Gerry said that Massachusetts was opposed to adjournment even for a day, since there appeared to be no "new ground of compromise," but the state could concur with the majority. Rutledge also thought there was no chance of a compromise, and no need of an adjournment. "The little states were fixt. They had repeatedly & solemnly declared themselves to be so. All that the large States then had to do, was to decide whether they would yield or not. For his part he conceiv'd that altho' we could not do what we thought best, in itself, we ought to do something. Had we not better keep the Government up a little longer, hoping that another Convention will supply our omissions, than abandon everything to hazard? Our Constituents will be very little satisfied with us if we take the latter course."

In such words, on the careful level of parliamentary courtesy, the delegates were saying that the Convention despaired of finding any just design for a government which the two parties could agree on, and doubted whether anything was to be gained by debating further. They had got nowhere in their plans for a new constitution. Perhaps the United States would never have a better constitution than the ineffectual old one. Perhaps there would not long be any United States.

The occasion might seem to call for the dramatic interchange of burning speeches, with angry and unhappy men on both sides, such as were in the Convention. There was more fire in the speeches than appears in Madison's quiet notes, which are the sole record of this crucial episode. But there is no missing, in his record, the essential drama of an immense decision being made by men who did not know how immense the decision was.

Nor is there less drama in his brief account of what happened on the morning of July 17. A number of delegates from the larger states, all unnamed in the record like heroes in masks, met "before the hour of the Convention." They believed that the smaller states were inflexible in their demand for equal representation in the Senate. That was what the delegates from the smaller states had said. Some of them were present at this meeting, and their faces today confirmed their words of yesterday.

The delegates from the larger states talked together. Nobody had a specific proposal. There was no agreement on any general principle. An equal vote in the Senate was anathema to some, to others an injustice, a mistake, or only an inconvenience. Some were willing to break off the Convention rather than yield to the smaller states' demand, but more were by no means sure it worth opposing further. Several insisted that the larger states, which meant a majority of the people of the United States, should make a constitution of their own, recommend it to Congress and any states that would accept it, and let the smaller states go their own way. Others were inclined to yield to the smaller states and to concur in some general plan or other. If there was none on which a large majority could agree, then continue, as lately, with a bare majority of the states and even now and then with only a minority of the people represented in the decisions.

The delegates from the smaller states, listening to this inconclusive discussion, were gradually reassured. There was no danger, they perceived, that their opponents would unite in any roughshod resistance to equal votes in the Senate. This was enough for the smaller states. They talked no more of withdrawing from the Convention. From the time of this morning caucus, this clash of drama without remembered words, they were active in support of the general plan for the new government which was to succeed the Confederation without abolishing the states as entities in one branch of the future legislature.

The Great Compromise, as this settlement is commonly called, or the Connecticut Compromise, was a federal compromise. The small states, by giving up their claim to equal representation in the popular branch of the legislature of the United States, had given up their attachment to a mere confederation. The large states, by giving up their claim to proportional representation in the Senate, had given up any hopes they may have had for a consolidated government. The states would now survive as states in a federal system to which they conceded the right to make, execute, and interpret federal laws, while themselves retaining the right to govern themselves within their own borders. The federal compromise was what Hamilton called a "motley measure," what Madison called a "novelty & a compound." Perhaps not a single delegate in the Convention was fully satisfied with the compromise. It was the creation of the corporate mind of the assemblage, reconciling differences, coming to such general agreement as was possible.

Naturally the desires of the conflicting parties in the Convention, or of the states they represented, were affected by their interests. The Southern states desired to be represented in part by their wealth, which was slaves, neither quite property nor quite population. They had been permitted to count three-fifths of the slaves in the estimate of their numbers. This gave them an anomalous advantage in the lower house of the legislature of the United States. The Northern states, averse to letting slaves be counted, nevertheless could realize that slaves would not be represented in the Senate if the votes of the states were there equal. As there were more Northern states than Southern, the North would have a majority in the Senate, and might look to it for security against the Southern votes in the lower house. These were compromises of interest which went with the compromises of political structure in the proposed government, entirely favorable neither to the several states nor to the United States. The individual states had special interests, as the individual delegates had. But the primary concern of all of them was for preservation of the union, defense against foreign aggression and domestic dissension, and the general prosperity of the American people. With these indispensable things provided for, the delegates believed, by the government they were devising, they could hope according to their interests for the particular blessings they might enjoy in the society which could develop under the guarantee of the new government.

At the end of these wrangling days which saw the federal compromise agreed on, a note appeared in the *Pennsylvania Packet* for July 19 which said: "So great is the unanimity, we hear, that prevails in the Convention, upon all great federal subjects, that it has been proposed to call the room in which they assemble—Unanimity Hall." It has been guessed, on no evidence, that this was deliberately given out by some delegate or delegates for the purpose of contradicting any rumors which might reach the public. The note was widely reprinted in newspapers in various states—there were then no national newspapers—and, while in general misleading, gave many readers a justified confidence that some progress was being made.

The constitution: a minority document

Charles Beard

At the close of this long and arid survey—partaking of the nature of catalogue—it seems worth while to bring together the important conclusions for political science which the data presented appear to warrant.

The movement for the Constitution of the United States was originated and carried through principally by four groups of personalty interests which had been adversely affected under the Articles of Confederation: money, public securities, manufactures, and trade and shipping.

The first firm steps toward the formation of the Constitution were taken by a small and active group of men immediately interested through their personal possessions in the outcome of their labors.

No popular vote was taken directly or indirectly on the proposition to call the Convention which drafted the Constitution.

A large propertyless mass was, under the prevailing suffrage qualifications, excluded at the outset from participation (through representatives) in the work of framing the Constitution.

The members of the Philadelphia Convention which drafted the Constitution were, with a few exceptions, immediately, directly, and personally interested in, and derived economic advantages from, the establishment of the new system.

The Constitution was essentially an economic document based upon the concept that the fundamental private rights of property are anterior to government and morally beyond the reach of popular majorities.

The major portion of the members of the Convention are on record as recognizing the claim of property to a special and defensive position in the Constitution.

In the ratification of the Constitution, about three-fourths of the adult males failed to vote on the question, having abstained from the elections at which delegates to the state conventions were chosen, either on account of their indifference or their disfranchisement by property qualifications.

The Constitution was ratified by a vote of probably not more than one-sixth of the adult males.

It is questionable whether a majority of the voters participating in the elections for the state conventions in New York, Massachusetts, New Hampshire, Virginia, and South Carolina, actually approved the ratification of the Constitution.

The leaders who supported the Constitution in the ratifying conventions represented the same economic groups as the members of the Philadelphia Convention; and in a large number of instances they were also directly and personally interested in the outcome of their efforts.

In the ratification, it became manifest that the line of cleavage for and against the Constitution was between substantial personalty interests on the one hand and the small farming and debtor interests on the other.

The Constitution was not created by "the whole people" as the jurists have said; neither was it created by "the states" as Southern nullifiers long contended; but it was the work of a consolidated group whose interests knew no state boundaries and were truly national in their scope.

A constitution
for all
the people

Robert E. Brown

      At the end of Chapter XI Beard summarized his findings in fourteen paragraphs under the heading of "Conclusions." Actually, these fourteen conclusions merely add up to the two halves of the Beard thesis. One half, that the Constitution originated with and was carried through by personalty interests—money, public securities, manufactures, and commerce—is to be found in paragraphs two, three, six, seven, eight, twelve, thirteen, and fourteen. The other half—that the Constitution was put over undemocratically in an undemocratic society—is expressed in paragraphs four, five, nine, ten, eleven, and fourteen. The lumping of these conclusions under two general headings makes it easier for the reader to see the broad outlines of the Beard thesis.

Before we examine these two major divisions of the thesis, however, some comment is relevant on the implications contained in the first paragraph. In it Beard characterized his book as a long and arid survey, something in the nature of a catalogue. Whether this characterization was designed to give his book the appearance of a coldly objective study based on the facts we do not know. If so, nothing could be further from reality. As reviewers pointed out in 1913, and as subsequent developments have demonstrated, the book is anything but an arid catalogue of facts. Its pages are replete with interpretation, sometimes stated, sometimes implied. Our task has been to examine Beard's evidence to see whether it justifies the interpretation which Beard gave it. We have tried to discover whether he used the historical method properly in arriving at his thesis.

If historical method means the gathering of data from primary sources, the critical evaluation of the evidence thus gathered, and the drawing of conclusions consistent with this evidence, then we must conclude that Beard has done great violation to such method in this book. He admitted that the evidence had not been collected which, given the proper use of historical method, should have precluded the writing of the book. Yet he nevertheless proceeded on the assumption that a valid interpretation could be built on secondary writings whose authors had likewise failed to collect the evidence. If we accept Beard's own maxim, "no evidence, no history," and his own admission that the data had never been collected, the answer to whether he used historical method properly is self-evident.

Neither was Beard critical of the evidence which he did use. He was accused in 1913, and one might still suspect him, of using only that evidence which appeared to support his thesis. The amount of realty in the country compared with the personalty, the vote in New York, and the omission of the part of *The Federalist* No. 10 which did not fit his thesis are only a few examples of the uncritical use of evidence to be found in the book. Sometimes he accepted secondary accounts at face value without checking them with the sources; at other times he allowed unfounded rumors and traditions to color his work.

Finally, the conclusions which he drew were not justified even by the kind of evidence which he used. If we accepted his evidence strictly at face value, it would still not add up to the fact that the Constitution was put over undemocratically in an undemocratic society by personalty. The citing of property qualifications does not prove that a mass of men were disfranchised. And if we accept his figures on property holdings, either we do not know what most of the delegates had in realty and personalty, or we know that realty outnumbered personalty three to one (eighteen to six). Simply showing that a man held public securities is not sufficient to prove that he acted only in terms of his public securities. If we ignore Beard's own generalizations and accept only his evidence, we would have to conclude that most of the property in the country in 1787 was real estate, that real property was widely distributed in rural areas, which included most of the country, and that even the men who were directly concerned with the Constitution, and especially Washington, were large holders of realty.

Perhaps we can never be completely objective in history, but certainly we can be more objective than Beard was in this book. Naturally the historian must always be aware of the biases, the subjectivity, the pitfalls that confront him, but this does not mean that he should not make an effort to overcome these obstacles. Whether Beard had his thesis before he had his evidence, as some have said, is a question that each reader must answer for himself. Certain it is that the evidence does not justify the thesis.

So instead of the Beard interpretation that the Constitution was put over undemocratically in an undemocratic society by personal property, the following fourteen paragraphs are offered as a possible interpretation of the Constitution and as suggestions for future research on that document.

1. The movement for the Constitution was originated and carried through by men who had long been important in both economic and political affairs in their respective states. Some of them owned personalty, more of them owned realty, and if their property was adversely affected by conditions under the Articles of Confederation, so also was the property of the bulk of the people in the country, middle-class farmers as well as town artisans.

2. The movement for the Constitution, like most important movements, was undoubtedly started by a small group of men. They were probably interested personally in the outcome of their labors, but the benefits which they expected were not confined to personal property or, for that matter, strictly to things economic. And if their own interests would be enhanced by a new government, similar interests of other men, whether agricultural or commercial, would also be enhanced.

3. Naturally there was no popular vote on the calling of the convention which drafted the Constitution. Election of delegates by state legislatures was the constitutional method under the Articles of Confederation, and had been the method long established in this country. Delegates to the Albany Congress, the Stamp Act Congress, the First Continental Congress, the Second Continental Congress, and subsequent congresses under the Articles were all elected by state legislatures, not by the people. Even the Articles of Confederation had been sanctioned by state legislatures, not by popular vote. This is not to say that the Constitutional Convention should not have been elected directly by the people, but only that such a procedure would have been unusual at the time. Some of the opponents of the Constitution later stressed, without avail, the fact that the Convention had not been directly elected. But at the time the Convention met, the people in general seemed to be about as much concerned over the fact that they had not elected the delegates as the people of this

country are now concerned over the fact that they do not elect our delegates to the United Nations.

4. Present evidence seems to indicate that there were no "propertyless masses" who were excluded from the suffrage at the time. Most men were middle-class farmers who owned realty and were qualified voters, and, as the men in the Convention said, mechanics had always voted in the cities. Until credible evidence proves otherwise, we can assume that state legislatures were fairly representative at the time. We cannot condone the fact that a few men were probably disfranchised by prevailing property qualifications, but it makes a great deal of difference to an interpretation of the Constitution whether the disfranchised comprised ninety-five per cent of the adult men or only five per cent. Figures which give percentages of voters in terms of the entire population are misleading, since less than twenty per cent of the people were adult men. And finally, the voting qualifications favored realty, not personalty.

5. If the members of the Convention were directly interested in the outcome of their work and expected to derive benefits from the establishment of the new system, so also did most of the people of the country. We have many statements to the effect that the people in general expected substantial benefits from the labors of the Convention.

6. The Constitution was not just an economic document, although economic factors were undoubtedly important. Since most of the people were middle-class and had private property, practically everybody was interested in the protection of property. A constitution which did not protect property would have been rejected without any question, for the American people had fought the Revolution for the preservation of life, liberty, and property. Many people believed that the Constitution did not go far enough to protect property, and they wrote these views into the amendments to the Constitution. But property was not the only concern of those who wrote and ratified the Constitution, and we would be doing a grave injustice to the political sagacity of the Founding Fathers if we assumed that property or personal gain was their only motive.

7. Naturally the delegates recognized that the protection of property was important under government, but they also recognized that personal rights were equally important. In fact, persons and property were usually bracketed together as the chief objects of government protection.

8. If three-fourths of the adult males failed to vote on the election of delegates to ratifying conventions, this fact signified indifference, not disfranchisement. We must not confuse those who could *not* vote with those who *could* vote but failed to exercise their right. Many men at the time bewailed the fact that only a small portion of the voters ever exercised their prerogative. But this in itself should stand as evidence that the conflict over the Constitution was not very bitter, for if these people had felt strongly one way or the other, more of them would have voted.

Even if we deny the evidence which I have presented and insist that American society was undemocratic in 1787, we must still accept the fact that the men who wrote the Constitution believed that they were writing it for a democratic society. They did not hide behind an iron curtain of secrecy and devise the kind of conservative government that they wanted without regard to the views and interests of "the people." More than anything else, they were aware that "the people" would have to ratify what they proposed, and that therefore any government which would be acceptable to the people must of necessity incorporate much of what was customary at the time. The men at Philadelphia were practical politicians, not political theorists. They recognized the multitude of different ideas and interests that had to be reconciled and compromised before a constitution would be acceptable. They were far too practical, and represented far too many clashing interests themselves, to fashion a government weighted in favor of personalty or to believe that the people would adopt such a government.

9. If the Constitution was ratified by a vote of only one-sixth of the adult men, that again demonstrates indifference and not disfranchisement. Of the one-fourth of the adult males who voted, nearly two-thirds favored the Constitution. Present evidence does not permit us to say what the popular vote was except as it was measured by the votes of the ratifying conventions.

10. Until we know what the popular vote was, we cannot say that it is questionable whether a majority of the voters in several states favored the Constitution. Too many delegates were sent uninstructed. Neither can we count the towns which did not send delegates on the side of those opposed to the Constitution. Both items would signify indifference rather than sharp conflict over ratification.

11. The ratifying conventions were elected for the specific purpose of adopting or rejecting the Constitution. The people in general had anywhere from several weeks to several months to decide the question. If they did not like the new government, or if they did not know whether they liked it, they could have voted *no* and there would have been no Constitution. Naturally the leaders in the ratifying conventions represented the same interests as the members of the Constitutional Convention—mainly realty and some personalty. But they also represented their constituents in these same interests, especially realty.

12. If the conflict over ratification had been between substantial personalty interests on the one hand and small farmers and debtors on the other, there would not have been a constitution. The small farmers comprised such an overwhelming percentage of the voters that they could have rejected the new government without any trouble. Farmers and debtors are not synonymous terms and should not be confused as such.

A town-by-town or county-by-county record of the vote would show clearly how the farmers voted.

13. The Constitution was created about as much by the whole people as any government could be which embraced a large area and depended on representation rather than on direct participation. It was also created in part by the states, for as the *Records* show, there was strong state sentiment at the time which had to be appeased by compromise. And it was created by compromising a whole host of interests throughout the country, without which compromises it could never have been adopted.

14. If the intellectual historians are correct, we cannot explain the Constitution without considering the psychological factors also. Men are motivated by what they believe as well as by what they have. Sometimes their actions can be explained on the basis of what they hope to have or hope that their children will have. Madison understood this fact when he said that the universal hope of acquiring property tended to dispose people to look favorably upon property. It is even possible that some men support a given economic system when they themselves have nothing to gain by it. So we would want to know what the people in 1787 thought of their class status. Did workers and small farmers believe that they were lower-class, or did they, as many workers do now, consider themselves middle-class? Were the common people trying to eliminate the Washingtons, Adamses, Hamiltons, and Pinckneys, or were they trying to join them?

As did Beard's fourteen conclusions, these fourteen suggestions really add up to two major propositions: the Constitution was adopted in a society which was fundamentally democratic, not undemocratic; and it was adopted by a people who were primarily middle-class property owners, especially farmers who owned realty, not just by the owners of personalty. At present these points seem to be justified by the evidence, but if better evidence in the future disproves or modifies them, we must accept that evidence and change our interpretation accordingly.

After this critical analysis, we should at least not begin future research on this period of American history with the illusion that the Beard thesis of the Constitution is valid. If historians insist on accepting the Beard thesis in spite of this analysis, however, they must do so with the full knowledge that their acceptance is founded on "an act of faith," not an analysis of historical method, and that they are indulging in a "noble dream," not history.

The founding
fathers:
realists

Richard Hofstadter

WHEREVER *the real power in a government lies, there is the danger of oppression. In our Government the real power lies in the majority of the community.* ... JAMES MADISON

POWER *naturally grows . . . because human passions are insatiable. But that power alone can grow which already is too great; that which is unchecked; that which has no equal power to control it.* JOHN ADAMS

Long ago Horace White observed that the Constitution of the United States "is based upon the philosophy of Hobbes and the religion of Calvin. It assumes that the natural state of mankind is a state of war, and that the carnal mind is at enmity with God." Of course the Constitution was founded more upon experience than any such abstract theory; but it was also an event in the intellectual history of Western civilization. The men who drew up the Constitution in Philadelphia during the summer of 1787 had a vivid Calvinistic sense of human evil and damnation and believed with Hobbes that men are selfish and contentious. They were men of affairs, merchants, lawyers, planter-businessmen, speculators, investors. Having seen human nature on display in the market place, the courtroom, the legislative chamber, and in every secret path and alleyway where wealth and power are courted, they felt they knew it in all its frailty. To them a human being was an atom of self-interest. They did not believe in man, but they did believe in the power of a good political constitution to control him.

This may be an abstract notion to ascribe to practical men, but it follows the language that the Fathers themselves used. General Knox, for example, wrote in disgust to Washington after the Shays Rebellion that Americans were, after all, "men—actual men possessing all the turbulent passions belonging to that animal." Throughout the secret discussions at the Constitutional Convention it was clear that this distrust of man was first and foremost a distrust of the common man and democratic rule. As the Revolution took away the restraining hand of the British government, old colonial grievances of farmers, debtors, and squatters against merchants, investors, and large landholders had flared up anew; the lower orders took advantage of new democratic constitutions in several states, and the possessing classes were frightened. The members of the Constitutional Convention were concerned to create a government that could not only regulate commerce and pay its debts but also prevent currency inflation and stay laws, and check such uprisings as the Shays Rebellion.

Cribbing and confining the popular spirit that had been at large since 1776 were essential to the purposes of the new Constitution. Edmund Randolph, saying to the Convention that the evils from which the country suffered originated in "the turbulence and follies of democracy," and that the great danger lay in "the democratic parts of our constitutions"; Elbridge Gerry, speaking of democracy as "the worst of all political evils"; Roger Sherman, hoping that "the people . . . have as little to do as may be about the government"; William Livingston, saying that "the people have ever been and ever will be unfit to retain the exercise of power in their own hands"; George Washington, the presiding officer, urging the delegates not to produce a document of which they themselves could not approve simply in order to "please the people"; Hamilton, charging that the "turbulent and changing" masses "seldom judge or determine right" and advising a permanent governmental body to "check the imprudence of democracy"; the wealthy young planter Charles Pinckney, proposing that no one be president who was not worth at least one hundred thousand dollars—all these were quite representative of the spirit in which the problems of government were treated.

Democratic ideas are most likely to take root among discontented and oppressed classes, rising middle classes, or perhaps some sections of an old, alienated, and partially disinherited aristocracy, but they do not appeal to a privileged class that is still amplifying its privileges. With a half-dozen exceptions at the most, the men of the Philadelphia Convention were sons of men who had considerable position and wealth, and as a group they had advanced well beyond their fathers. Only one of them, William Few of Georgia, could be said in any sense to represent the yeoman farmer class which constituted the overwhelming majority of the free population. In the late eighteenth century "the better kind of people" found themselves set off from the mass by a hundred visible, tangible, and audible distinctions of dress, speech, manners, and education. There was a continuous lineage of upper-class contempt, from pre-Revolutionary Tories like Peggy Hutchinson, the Governor's daughter, who wrote one day: "The dirty mob was all about me as I drove into town," to a Federalist like Hamilton, who candidly disdained the people. Mass unrest was often received in the spirit of young Gouverneur Morris: "The mob begin to think and reason. Poor reptiles! . . . They bask in the sun, and ere noon they will bite, depend upon it. The gentry begin to fear this." Nowhere in America or Europe—not even among the great liberated thinkers of the Enlightenment—did democratic ideas appear respectable to the cultivated classes. Whether the Fathers looked to the cynically illuminated intellectuals of contemporary Europe or to their own Christian heritage of the idea of original sin, they found quick confirmation of the notion that man is an unregenerate rebel who has to be controlled.

And yet there was another side to the picture. The Fathers were intellectual heirs of seventeenth-century English republicanism with its opposition to arbitrary rule and faith in popular sovereignty. If they feared the advance of democracy, they also had misgivings about turning to the extreme right. Having recently experienced a bitter revolutionary struggle with an external power beyond their control, they were in no mood to follow Hobbes to his conclusion that any kind of government must be accepted in order to avert the anarchy and terror of a state of nature. They were uneasily aware that both military dictatorship and a return to monarchy were being seriously discussed in some quarters—the former chiefly among unpaid and discontented army officers, the latter in rich and fashionable Northern circles. John Jay, familiar with sentiment among New York's mercantile aristocracy, wrote to Washington, June 27, 1786, that he feared that "the better kind of people (by which I mean the people who are orderly and industrious, who are content with their situations, and not uneasy in their circumstances) will be led, by the insecurity of property, the loss of confidence in their rulers, and the want of public faith and rectitude, to consider the charms of liberty as imaginary and delusive." Such men, he thought, might be prepared for "almost any change that may promise them quiet and security." Washington, who had already repudiated a suggestion that he become a military dictator, agreed, remarking that "we are apt to run from one extreme to the other."

Unwilling to turn their backs upon republicanism, the Fathers also wished to avoid violating the prejudices of the people. "Notwithstanding the oppression and injustice experienced among us from democracy," said George Mason, "the genius of the people is in favor of it, and the genius of the people must be consulted." Mason admitted "that we had been too democratic," but feared that "we should incautiously run into the opposite extreme." James Madison, who has quite rightfully been called the philosopher of the Constitution, told the delegates: "It seems indispensable that the mass of citizens should not be without a voice in making the laws which they are to obey, and in choosing the magistrates who are to administer them." James Wilson, the outstanding jurist of the age, later appointed to the Supreme Court by Washington, said again and again that the ultimate power of government must of necessity reside in the people. This the Fathers commonly accepted, for if government did not proceed from the people, from what other source could it legitimately come? To adopt any other premise not only would be inconsistent with everything they had said against British rule in the past but would open the gates to an extreme concentration of power in the future. Hamilton saw the sharp distinction in the Convention when he said that "the members most tenacious of republicanism were as loud as any in declaiming the vices of democracy." There was no better expression of the dilemma of a man who has no faith in the people but insists that government be based upon them than that of Jeremy Belknap, a New England clergyman, who wrote to a friend: "Let it stand as a principle that government originates from the people; but let the people be taught . . . that they are not able to govern themselves."

II

If the masses were turbulent and unregenerate, and yet if government must be founded upon their suffrage and consent, what could a Constitution-maker do? One thing that the Fathers did not propose to do, because they thought it impossible, was to change the nature of man to conform with a more ideal system. They were inordinately confident that they knew what man always had been and what he always would be. The eighteenth-century mind had great faith in universals. Its method, as Carl Becker has said, was "to go up and down the field of history looking for man in general, the universal man, stripped of the accidents of time and place." Madison declared that the causes of political differences and of the formation of factions were "sown in the nature of man" and could never be eradicated. "It is universally acknowledged," David Hume had written, "that there is a great uniformity among the actions of men, in all nations and ages, and that human nature remains still the same, in its principles and operations. The same motives always produce the same actions. The same events always follow from the same causes."

Since man was an unchangeable creature of self-interest, it would not do to leave anything to his capacity for restraint. It was too much to expect that vice could be checked by virtue; the Fathers relied instead upon checking vice with vice. Madison once objected during the Convention that Gouverneur Morris was "forever inculcating the utter political depravity of men and the necessity of opposing one vice and interest to another vice and interest." And yet Madison himself in the *Federalist* number 51 later set forth an excellent statement of the same thesis:

Ambition must be made to counteract ambition. . . . It may be a reflection on human nature that such devices should be necessary to control the abuses of government. But what is government itself, but the greatest of all reflections on human nature? If men were angels, no government would be necessary. . . . In framing a government which is to be administered by men over men, the great difficulty lies in this: you must first enable the government to control the governed; and in the next place oblige it to control itself.

Political economists of the laissez-faire school were saying that private vices could be public benefits, that an economically beneficent result would be providentially or "naturally" achieved if self-interest were left free from state interference and allowed to pursue its ends. But the Fathers were not so optimistic about politics. If, in a state that lacked constitutional balance, one class or one interest gained control, they believed, it would surely plunder all other interests. The Fathers, of course, were especially fearful that the poor would plunder the rich, but most of them would probably have admitted that the rich, unrestrained, would also plunder the poor. Even Gouverneur Morris, who stood as close to the extreme aristocratic position as candor and intelligence would allow, told the Convention: "Wealth tends to corrupt the mind and to nourish its love of power, and to stimulate it to oppression. History proves this to be the spirit of the opulent."

What the Fathers wanted was known as "balanced government," an idea at least as old as Aristotle and Polybius. This ancient conception had won new sanction in the eighteenth century, which was dominated intellectually by the scientific work of Newton, and in which mechanical metaphors sprang as naturally to men's minds as did biological metaphors in the Darwinian atmosphere of the late nineteenth century. Men had found a rational order in the universe and they hoped that it could be transferred to politics, or, as John Adams put it, that governments could be "erected on the simple principles of nature." Madison spoke in the most precise Newtonian language when he said that such a "natural" government must be so constructed "that its several constituent parts may, by their mutual relations, be the means of keeping each other in their proper places." A properly designed state, the Fathers believed, would check interest with interest, class with class, faction with faction, and one branch of government with another in a harmonious system of mutual frustration.

In practical form, therefore, the quest of the Fathers reduced primarily to a search for constitutional devices that would force various interests to check and control one another. Among those who favored the federal Constitution three such devices were distinguished.

The first of these was the advantage of a federated government in maintaining order against popular uprisings or majority rule. In a single state a faction might arise and take complete control by force; but if the states were bound in a federation, the central government could step in and prevent it. Hamilton quoted Montesquieu: "Should a popular insurrection happen in one of the confederate states, the others are able to quell it." Further, as Madison argued in the *Federalist* number 10, a majority would be the most dangerous of all factions that might arise, for the majority would be the most capable of gaining complete ascendancy. If the political society were very extensive, however, and embraced a large number and variety of local interests, the citizens who shared a common majority interest "must be rendered by their number and local situation, unable to concert and carry into effect their schemes of oppression." The chief propertied interests would then be safer from "a rage for paper money, for an abolition of debts, for an equal division of property, or for any other improper or wicked project."

The second advantage of good constitutional government resided in the mechanism of representation itself. In a small direct democracy the unstable passions of the people would dominate lawmaking; but a representative government, as Madison said, would "refine and enlarge the public views by passing them through the medium of a chosen body of citizens." Representatives chosen by the people were wiser and more deliberate than the people themselves in mass assemblage. Hamilton frankly anticipated a kind of syndical paternalism in which the wealthy and dominant members of every trade or industry would represent the others in politics. Merchants, for example, were "the natural representatives" of their employees and of the mechanics and artisans they dealt with. Hamilton expected that Congress, "with too few exceptions to have any influence on the spirit of the government, will be composed of landholders, merchants, and men of the learned professions."

The third advantage of the government the Fathers were designing was pointed out most elaborately by John Adams in the first volume of his *Defence of the Constitutions of Government of the United States of America*, which reached Philadelphia while the Convention was in session and was cited with approval by several delegates. Adams believed that the aristocracy and the democracy must be made to neutralize each other. Each element should be given its own house of the legislature, and over both houses there should be set a capable, strong, and impartial executive armed with the veto power. This split assembly would contain within itself an organic check and would be capable of self-control under the governance of the executive. The whole system was to be capped by an independent judiciary. The inevitable tendency of the rich and the poor to plunder each other would be kept in hand.

III

It is ironical that the Constitution, which Americans venerate so deeply, is based upon a political theory that at one crucial point stands in direct antithesis to the main stream of American democratic faith. Modern American folklore assumes that democracy and liberty are all but identical, and when democratic writers take the trouble to make the distinction, they usually assume that democracy is necessary to liberty. But the Founding Fathers thought that the liberty with which they were most concerned was menaced by democracy. In their minds liberty was linked not to democracy but to property.

What did the Fathers mean by liberty? What did Jay mean when he spoke of "the charms of liberty"? Or Madison when he declared that to destroy liberty in order to destroy factions would be a remedy worse than the disease? Certainly the men who met at Philadelphia were not interested in extending liberty to those classes in America, the Negro slaves and the indentured servants, who were most in need of it, for slavery was recognized in the organic structure of the Constitution and indentured servitude was no concern of the Convention. Nor was the regard of the delegates for civil liberties any too tender. It was the opponents of the Constitution who were most active in demanding such vital liberties as freedom of religion, freedom of speech and press, jury trial, due process, and protection from "unreasonable searches and seizures." These guarantees had to be incorporated in the first ten amendments because the Convention neglected to put them in the original document. Turning to economic issues, it was not freedom of trade in the modern sense that the Fathers were striving for. Although they did not believe in impeding trade unnecessarily, they felt that failure to regulate it was one of the central weaknesses of the Articles of Confederation, and they stood closer to the mercantilists than to Adam Smith. Again, liberty to them did not mean free access to the nation's unappropriated wealth. At least fourteen of them were land speculators. They did not believe in the right of the squatter to occupy unused land, but rather in the right of the absentee owner or speculator to pre-empt it.

The liberties that the constitutionalists hoped to gain were chiefly negative. They wanted freedom from fiscal uncertainty and irregularities in the currency, from trade wars among the states, from economic discrimination by more powerful foreign governments, from attacks on the creditor class or on property, from popular insurrection. They aimed to create a government that would act as an honest broker among a variety of propertied interests, giving them all protection from their common enemies and preventing any one of them from becoming too powerful. The Convention was a fraternity of types of absentee ownership. All property should be permitted to have its proportionate voice in government. Individual property interests might have to be sacrificed at times, but only for the community of propertied interests. Freedom for property would result in liberty for men—perhaps not for all men, but at least for all worthy men. Because men have different faculties and abilities, the Fathers believed, they acquire different amounts of property. To protect property is only to protect men in the exercise of their natural faculties. Among the many liberties, therefore, freedom to hold and dispose property is paramount. Democracy, unchecked rule by the masses, is sure to bring arbitrary redistribution of property, destroying the very essence of liberty.

The Fathers' conception of democracy, shaped by their practical experience with the aggressive dirt farmers in the American states and the urban mobs of the Revolutionary period, was supplemented by their reading in history and political science. Fear of what Madison called "the superior force of an interested and overbearing majority" was the dominant emotion aroused by their study of historical examples. The chief examples of republics were among the city-states of antiquity, medieval Europe, and early modern times. Now, the history of these republics—a history, as Hamilton said, "of perpetual vibration between the extremes of tyranny and anarchy"—was alarming. Further, most of the men who had overthrown the liberties of republics had "begun their career by paying an obsequious court to the people; commencing demagogues and ending tyrants."

All the constitutional devices that the Fathers praised in their writings were attempts to guarantee the future of the United States against the "turbulent" political cycles of previous republics. By "democracy," they meant a system of government which directly expressed the will of the majority of the people, usually through such an assemblage of the people as was possible in the small area of the city-state.

A cardinal tenet in the faith of the men who made the Constitution was the belief that democracy can never be more than a transitional stage in government, that it always evolves into either a tyranny (the rule of the rich demagogue who has patronized the mob) or an aristocracy (the original leaders of the democratic elements). "Remember," wrote the dogmatic John Adams in one of his letters to John Taylor of Caroline, "democracy never lasts long. It soon wastes, exhausts, and murders itself. There never was a democracy yet that did not commit suicide." Again:

If you give more than a share in the sovereignty to the democrats, that is, if you give them the command or preponderance in the . . . legislature, they will vote all property out of the hands of you aristocrats, and if they let you escape with your lives, it will be more humanity, consideration, and generosity than any triumphant democracy ever displayed since the creation. And what will follow? The aristocracy among the democrats will take your places, and treat their fellows as severely and sternly as you have treated them.

Government, thought the Fathers, is based on property. Men who have no property lack the necessary stake in an orderly society to make stable or reliable citizens. Dread of the propertyless masses of the towns was all but universal. George Washington, Gouverneur Morris, John Dickinson, and James Madison spoke of their anxieties about the urban working class that might arise some time in the future—"men without property and principle," as Dickinson described them—and even the democratic Jefferson shared this prejudice. Madison, stating the problem, came close to anticipating the modern threats to conservative republicanism from both communism and fascism:

In future times, a great majority of the people will not only be without landed but any other sort of property. These will either combine, under the influence of their common situation—in which case the rights of property and the public liberty will not be secure in their hands—or, what is more probable, they will become the tools of opulence and ambition, in which case there will be equal danger on another side.

What encouraged the Fathers about their own era, however, was the broad dispersion of landed property. The small land-owning farmers had been troublesome in recent years, but there was a general conviction that under a properly made Constitution a *modus vivendi* could be worked out with them. The possession of moderate plots of property presumably gave them a sufficient stake in society to be safe and responsible citizens under the restraints of balanced government. Influence in government would be proportionate to property: merchants and great landholders would be dominant, but small property-owners would have an independent and far from negligible voice. It was "politic as well as just," said Madison, "that the interests and rights of every class should be duly represented and understood in the public councils," and John Adams declared that there could be "no free government without a democratical branch in the constitution."

The farming element already satisfied the property requirements for suffrage in most of the states, and the Fathers generally had no quarrel with their enfranchisement. But when they spoke of the necessity of founding government upon the consent of "the people," it was only these small property-holders that they had in mind. For example, the famous Virginia Bill of Rights, written by George Mason, explicitly defined those eligible for suffrage as all men "having sufficient evidence of permanent common interest with and attachment to the community"—which meant, in brief, sufficient property.

However, the original intention of the Fathers to admit the yeoman into an important but sharply limited partnership in affairs of state could not be perfectly realized. At the time the Constitution was made, Southern planters and Northern merchants were setting their differences aside in order to meet common dangers—from radicals within and more powerful nations without. After the Constitution was adopted, conflict between the ruling classes broke out anew, especially after powerful planters were offended by the favoritism of Hamilton's policies to Northern commercial interests. The planters turned to the farmers to form an agrarian alliance, and for more than half a century this powerful coalition embraced the bulk of the articulate interests of the country. As time went on, therefore, the main stream of American political conviction deviated more and more from the antidemocratic position of the Constitution-makers. Yet, curiously, their general satisfaction with the Constitution together with their growing nationalism made Americans deeply reverent of the founding generation, with the result that as it grew stronger, this deviation was increasingly overlooked.

There is common agreement among modern critics that the debates over the Constitution were carried on at an intellectual level that is rare in politics, and that the Constitution itself is one of the world's masterpieces of practical statecraft. On other grounds there has been controversy. At the very beginning contemporary opponents of the Constitution foresaw an apocalyptic destruction of local government and popular institutions, while conservative Europeans of the old regime thought the young American Republic was a dangerous leftist experiment. Modern critical scholarship, which reached a high point in Charles A. Beard's *An Economic Interpretation of the Constitution of the United States,* started a new turn in the debate. The antagonism, long latent, between the philosophy of the Constitution and the philosophy of American democracy again came into the open. Professor Beard's work appeared in 1913 at the peak of the Progressive era, when the muckraking fever was still high; some readers tended to conclude from his findings that the Fathers were selfish reactionaries who do not deserve their high place in American esteem. Still more recently, other writers, inverting this logic, have used Beard's facts to praise the Fathers for their opposition to "democracy" and as an argument for returning again to the idea of a "republic."

In fact, the Fathers' image of themselves as moderate republicans standing between political extremes was quite accurate. They were impelled by class motives more than pietistic writers like to admit, but they were also controlled, as Professor Beard himself has recently emphasized, by a statesmanlike sense of moderation and a scrupulously republican philosophy. Any attempt, however, to tear their ideas out of the eighteenth-century context is sure to make them seem starkly reactionary. Consider, for example, the favorite maxim of John Jay: "The people who own the country ought to govern it." To the Fathers this was simply a swift axiomatic statement of the stake-in-society theory of political rights, a moderate conservative position under eighteenth-century conditions of property distribution in America. Under modern property relations this maxim demands a drastic restriction of the base of political power. A large portion of the modern middle class—and it is the strength of this class upon which balanced government depends—is propertyless; and the urban proletariat, which the Fathers so greatly feared, is almost one half the population. Further, the separation of ownership from control that has come with the corporation deprives Jay's maxim of twentieth-century meaning even for many propertied people. The six hundred thousand stockholders of the American Telephone & Telegraph Company not only do not acquire political power by virtue of their stock-ownership, but they do not even acquire economic power: they cannot control their own company.

From a humanistic standpoint there is a serious dilemma in the philosophy of the Fathers, which derives from their conception of man. They thought man was a creature of rapacious self-interest, and yet they wanted him to be free—free, in essence, to contend, to engage in an umpired strife, to use property to get property. They accepted the mercantile image of life as an eternal battleground, and assumed the Hobbesian war of each against all; they did not propose to put an end to this war, but merely to stabilize it and make it less murderous. They had no hope and they offered none for any ultimate organic change in the way men conduct themselves. The result was that while they thought self-interest the most dangerous and unbrookable quality of man, they necessarily underwrote it in trying to control it. They succeeded in both respects: under the competitive capitalism of the nineteenth century America continued to be an arena for various grasping and contending interests, and the federal government continued to provide a stable and acceptable medium within which they could contend; further, it usually showed the wholesome bias on behalf of property which the Fathers expected. But no man who is as well abreast of modern science as the Fathers were of eighteenth-century science believes any longer in unchanging human nature. Modern humanistic thinkers who seek for a means by which society may transcend eternal conflict and rigid adherence to property rights as its integrating principles can expect no answer in the philosophy of balanced government as it was set down by the Constitution-makers of 1787.

The founding
fathers:
Stanley Elkins and Eric McKitrick   activists

The Anti-Federalists . . . were transfixed by the specter of power. It was not the power of the aristocracy that they feared, but power of any kind, democratic or otherwise, that they could not control for themselves. Their chief concern was to keep governments as limited

Reprinted with permission from *Political Science Quarterly*, Vol. LXXVI, No. 2, pp. 200–216.

and as closely tied to local interests as possible. Their minds could not embrace the concept of a national interest which they themselves might share and which could transcend their own parochial concerns. Republican government that went beyond the compass of state boundaries was something they could not imagine. Thus the chief difference between Federalists and Anti-Federalists had little to do with "democracy" (George Clinton and Patrick Henry were no more willing than Gouverneur Morris to trust the innate virtue of the people), but rather in the Federalists' conviction that there was such a thing as national interest and that a government could be established to care for it which was fully in keeping with republican principles. To the Federalists this was not only possible but absolutely necessary, if the nation was to avoid a future of political impotence, internal discord, and in the end foreign intervention. So far so good. But still, exactly how did such convictions get themselves generated?

Merrill Jensen has argued that the Federalists, by and large, were reluctant revolutionaries who had feared the consequences of a break with England and had joined the Revolution only when it was clear that independence was inevitable. The argument is plausible; few of the men most prominent later on as Federalists had been quite so hot for revolution in the very beginning as Patrick Henry and Samuel Adams. But this may not be altogether fair; Adams and Henry were already veteran political campaigners at the outbreak of hostilities, while the most vigorous of the future Federalists were still mere youngsters. The argument, indeed, could be turned entirely around: the source of Federalist, or nationalist, energy was not any "distaste" for the Revolution on these men's part, but rather their profound and growing involvement in it.

Much depends here on the way one pictures the Revolution. In the beginning it simply consisted of a number of state revolts loosely directed by the Continental Congress; and for many men, absorbed in their effort to preserve the independence of their own states, it never progressed much beyond that stage even in the face of invasion. But the Revolution had another aspect, one which developed with time and left a deep imprint on those connected with it, and this was its character as a continental war effort. If there is any one feature that most unites the future leading supporters of the Constitution, it was their close engagement with this continental aspect of the Revolution. A remarkably large number of these someday Federalists were in the Continental Army, served as diplomats or key administrative officers of the Confederation government, or, as members of Congress, played leading roles on those committees primarily responsible for the conduct of the war.

Merrill Jensen has compiled two lists, with nine names in each, of the men whom he considers to have been the leading spirits of the Federalists and Anti-Federalists respectively. It would be well to have a good look at this sample. The Federalists—Jensen calls them "nationalists" —were Robert Morris, John Jay, James Wilson, Alexander Hamilton, Henry Knox, James Duane, George Washington, James Madison, and Gouverneur Morris. Washington, Knox, and Hamilton were deeply involved in Continental military affairs; Robert Morris was Superintendent of Finance; Jay was president of the Continental Congress and minister plenipotentiary to Spain (he would later be appointed Secretary for Foreign Affairs); Wilson, Duane, and Gouverneur Morris were members of Congress, all three being active members of the war committees. The Anti-Federalist group presents a very different picture. It consisted of Samuel Adams, Patrick Henry, Richard Henry Lee, George Clinton, James Warren, Samuel Bryan, George Bryan, George Mason, and Elbridge Gerry. Only three of these—Gerry, Lee, and Adams—served in Congress, and the latter two fought consistently against any effort to give Congress executive powers. Their constant pre-occupation was state sovereignty rather than national efficiency. Henry and Clinton were active war governors, concerned primarily with state rather than national problems, while Warren, Mason, and the two Bryans were essentially state politicians.

The age difference between these two groups is especially striking. The Federalists were on the average ten to twelve years younger than the Anti-Federalists. At the outbreak of the Revolution George Washington, at 44, was the oldest of the lot; six were under 35 and four were in their twenties. Of the Anti-Federalists, only three were under 40 in 1776, and one of these, Samuel Bryan, the son of George Bryan, was a boy of 16.

This age differential takes on a special significance when it is related to the career profiles of the men concerned. Nearly half of the Federalist group—Gouverneur Morris, Madison, Hamilton, and Knox—quite literally saw their careers launched in the Revolution. The remaining five —Washington, Jay, Duane, Wilson, and Robert Morris—though established in public affairs beforehand, became nationally known after 1776 and the wide public recognition which they subsequently achieved came first and foremost through their identification with the continental war effort. All of them had been united in an experience, and had formed commitments, which dissolved provincial boundaries; they had come to full public maturity in a setting which enabled ambition, public service, leadership, and self-fulfillment to be conceived, for each in his way, with a grandeur of scope unknown to any previous generation. The careers of the Anti-Federalists, on the other hand, were not only state-centered but—aside from those of Clinton, Gerry, and the young Bryan —rested heavily on events that preceded rather than followed 1776.

As exemplars of nationalist energy, two names in Professor Jensen's sample that come most readily to mind are those of Madison and Hamilton. The story of each shows a wonderfully pure line of consistency. James Madison, of an influential Virginia family but with no apparent career plans prior to 1774, assumed his first public rôle as a member of the Orange County Revolutionary Committee, of which his father was chairman. As a delegate from Orange County he went to the Virginia convention in 1776 and served on the committee that drafted Virginia's new constitution and bill of rights. He served in the Virginia Assembly in 1776 and 1777 but failed of re-election partly because he refused to treat his constituents to whisky. (He obviously did not have the right talents for a state politician.) In recognition of Madison's services, however, the Assembly elected him to the Governor's Council, where he served from 1778 to 1780. Patrick Henry was then Governor; the two men did not get on well and in time became bitter political enemies. At this period Madison's primary concern was with supplying and equipping the Continental Army, a concern not shared to his satisfaction by enough of his colleagues. It was then, too, that he had his first experience with finance and the problems of paper money. He was elected to the Continental Congress in 1780, and as a member of the Southern Committee was constantly preoccupied with the military operations of Nathanael Greene. The inefficiency and impotence of Congress pained him unbearably. The Virginia Assembly took a strong stand against federal taxation which Madison ignored, joining Hamilton in the unsuccessful effort to persuade the states to accept the impost of 1783. From the day he entered politics up to that time, the energies of James Madison were involved in continental rather than state problems—problems of supply, enlistment, and finance—and at every point his chief difficulties came from state parochialism, selfishness, and lack of imagination. His nationalism was hardly accidental.

The career line of Alexander Hamilton, *mutatis mutandis*, is functionally interchangeable with that of James Madison. Ambitious, full of ability, but a young man of no family and no money, Hamilton arrived in New York from the provinces at the age of 17 and in only two years would be catapulted into a brilliant career by the Revolution. At 19 he became a highly effective pamphleteer while still a student at King's College, was captain of an artillery company at 21, serving with distinction in the New York and New Jersey campaigns, and in 1777 was invited to join Washington's staff as a lieutenant-colonel. He was quickly accepted by as brilliant and aristocratic a set of youths as could be found in the country. As a staff officer he became all too familiar with the endless difficulties of keeping the Continental Army in the field from 1777 to 1780. With his marriage to Elizabeth Schuyler in 1780 he was delightedly welcomed into one of New York's leading families, and his sage advice to his father-in-law and Robert Morris on matters of finance and paper money won him the reputation of a financial expert with men who knew an expert when they saw one. He had an independent command at York-town. He became Treasury representative in New York in 1781, was elected to Congress in 1782, and worked closely with Madison in the fruitless and discouraging effort to create a national revenue in the face of state particularism. In the summer of 1783 he quit in despair and went back to New York. Never once throughout all this period had Alexander Hamilton been involved in purely state affairs. His career had been a continental one, and as long as the state-centered George Clinton remained a power in New York, it was clear that this was the only kind that could have any real meaning for him. As with James Madison, Hamilton's nationalism was fully consistent with all the experience he had ever had in public life, experience whose sole meaning had been derived from the Revolution. The experience of the others—for instance that of John Jay and Henry Knox—had had much the same quality; Knox had moved from his bookstore to the command of Washington's artillery in little more than a year, while Jay's public career began with the agitation just prior to the Revolution and was a story of steady advancement in continental affairs from that time forward.

The logic of these careers, then, was in large measure tied to a chronology which did not apply in the same way to all the men in public life during the two decades of the 1770's and 1780's. A significant proportion of relative newcomers, with prospects initially modest, happened to have their careers opened up at a particular time and in such a way that their very public personalities came to be staked upon the national quality of the experience which had formed them. In a number of outstanding cases energy, initiative, talent, and ambition had combined with a conception of affairs which had grown immense in scope and promise by the close of the Revolution. There is every reason to think that a contraction of this scope, in the years that immediately followed, operated as a powerful challenge.

The stages through which the constitutional movement proceeded in the 1780's add up to a fascinating story in political management, marked by no little élan and dash. That movement, viewed in the light of the Federalist leaders' commitment to the Revolution, raises some nice points as to who were the "conservatives" and who were the "radicals." The spirit of unity generated by the struggle for independence had, in the eyes of those most closely involved in coördinating the effort, lapsed; provincial factions were reverting to the old provincial ways. The impulse to arrest disorder and to revive the flame of revolutionary unity may be pictured in "conservative" terms, but this becomes quite awkward when we look for terms with which to picture the other impulse, so different in nature: the urge to rest, to drift, to turn back the clock.

Various writers have said that the activities of the Federalists during this period had in them a clear element of the conspiratorial. Insofar as this refers to a strong line of political strategy, it correctly locates a key element in the movement. Yet without a growing base of popular dissatisfaction with the status quo, the Federalists could have skulked and plotted forever without accomplishing anything. We now know, thanks to recent scholarship, that numerous elements of the public were only too ripe for change. But the work of organizing such a sentiment was quite another matter; it took an immense effort of will just to get it off the ground. Though it would be wrong to think of the Constitution as something that had to be carried in the face of deep and basic popular opposition, it certainly required a series of brilliant maneuvers to escape the deadening clutch of particularism and inertia. An Anti-Federalist "no" could register on exactly the same plane as a Federalist "yes" while requiring a fraction of the energy. It was for this reason that the Federalists, even though they cannot be said to have circumvented the popular will, did have to use techniques which in their sustained drive, tactical mobility, and risk-taking smacked more than a little of the revolutionary.

By 1781, nearly five years of intimate experience with the war effort had already convinced such men as Washington, Madison, Hamilton, Duane, and Wilson that something had to be done to strengthen the Continental government, at least to the point of providing it with an independent income. The ratification of the Articles of Confederation early in the year (before Yorktown) seemed to offer a new chance, and several promising steps were taken at that time. Congress organized executive departments of war, foreign affairs, and finance to replace unwieldy and inefficient committees; Robert Morris was appointed Superintendent of Finance; and a 5 per cent impost was passed which Congress urged the states to accept.

By the fall of 1782, however, the surge for increased efficiency had lost the greater part of its momentum. Virginia had changed its mind about accepting the impost, Rhode Island having been flatly opposed all along, and it became apparent that as soon as the treaty with England (then being completed) was ratified, the sense of common purpose which the war had created would be drained of its urgency. At this point Hamilton and the Morrises, desperate for a solution, would have been quite willing to use the discontent of an unpaid army as a threat to coerce the states out of their obstructionism, had not Washington refused to lend himself to any such scheme. Madison and Hamilton thereupon joined forces in Congress to work out a revenue bill whose subsidiary benefits would be sufficiently diffuse to gain it general support among the states. But in the end the best that could be managed was a new plan for a 5 per cent impost, the revenues of which would be collected by state-appointed officials. Once more an appeal, drafted by

Madison, was sent to the states urging them to accept the new impost, and Washington wrote a circular in support of it. The effort was in vain. The army, given one month's pay in cash and three in certificates, reluctantly dispersed, and the Confederation government, with no sanctions of coercion and no assured revenues, now reached a new level of impotence. In June, 1783, Alexander Hamilton, preparing to leave Congress to go back to private life, wrote in discouragement and humiliation to Nathanael Greene:

There is so little disposition either in or out of Congress to give solidity to our national system that there is no motive to a man to lose his time in the public service, who has no other view than to promote its welfare. Experience must convince us that our present establishments are Utopian before we shall be ready to part with them for better.

Whether or not the years between 1783 and 1786 should be viewed as a "critical period" depends very much on whose angle they are viewed from. Although it was a time of economic depression, the depressed conditions were not felt in all areas of economic life with the same force, nor were they nearly as damaging in some localities as in others; the interdependence of economic enterprise was not then what it would become later on, and a depression in Massachusetts did not necessarily imply one in Virginia, or even in New York. Moreover, there were definite signs of improvement by 1786. Nor can it necessarily be said that government on the state level lacked vitality. Most of the states were addressing their problems with energy and decision. There were problems everywhere, of course, many of them very grave, and in some cases (those of New Jersey and Connecticut in particular) solutions seemed almost beyond the individual state's resources. Yet it would be wrong, as Merrill Jensen points out, to assume that no solutions were possible within the framework which then existed. It is especially important to remember that when most people thought of "the government" they were not thinking of Congress at all, but of their own state legislature. For them, therefore, it was by no means self-evident that the period through which they were living was one of drift and governmental impotence.

But through the eyes of men who had come to view the states collectively as a "country" and to think in continental terms, things looked altogether different. From their viewpoint the Confederation was fast approaching the point of ruin. Fewer and fewer states were meeting their requisition payments, and Congress could not even pay its bills. The states refused to accept any impost which they themselves could not control, and even if all the rest accepted, the continued refusal of New York (which was not likely to change) would render any impost all but valueless. Local fears and jealousies blocked all efforts to establish uniform regulation of commerce, even though some such regulation seemed indispensable. A number of the states, New York in particular, openly ignored the peace treaty with England and passed discriminatory legislation against former Loyalists; consequently England, using as a pretext Congress' inability to enforce the treaty, refused to surrender the northwest posts. Morale in Congress was very low as members complained that lack of a quorum prevented them most of the time from transacting any business; even when a quorum was present, a few negative votes could block important legislation indefinitely. Any significant change, or any substantial increase in the power of Congress, required unanimous approval by the states, and as things then stood this had become very remote. Finally, major states such as New York and Virginia were simply paying less and less attention to Congress. The danger was not so much that of a split with the Confederation— Congress lacked the strength that would make any such "split" seem very urgent—but rather a policy of neglect that would just allow Congress to wither away from inactivity.

These were the conditions that set the stage for a fresh effort—the Annapolis Convention of 1786—to strengthen the continental government. The year before, Madison had arranged a conference between Maryland and Virginia for the regulation of commerce on the Potomac, and its success had led John Tyler and Madison to propose a measure in the Virginia Assembly that would give Congress power to regulate commerce throughout the Confederation. Though nothing came of it, a plan was devised in its place whereby the several states would be invited to take part in a convention to be held at Annapolis in September, 1786, for the purpose of discussing commercial problems. The snapping-point came when delegates from only five states appeared. The rest either distrusted one another's intentions (the northeastern states doubted the southerners' interest in commerce) or else suspected a trick to strengthen the Confederation government at their expense. It was apparent that no serious action could be taken at that time. But the dozen delegates who did come (Hamilton and Madison being in their forefront) were by definition those most concerned over the state of the national government, and they soon concluded that their only hope of saving it lay in some audacious plenary gesture. It was at this meeting, amid the mortification of still another failure, that they planned the Philadelphia Convention.

The revolutionary character of this move—though some writers have correctly perceived it—has been obscured both by the stateliness of historical retrospection and by certain legal peculiarities which allowed the proceeding to appear a good deal less subversive than it actually was. The "report" of the Annapolis meeting was actually a call, drafted by Hamilton and carefully edited by Madison, for delegates of all the states to meet in convention at Philadelphia the following May for the purpose of revising the Articles of Confederation. Congress itself transmitted the call, and in so doing was in effect being brought to by-pass its own constituted limits. On the one hand, any effort to change the government within the rules laid down by the Articles would have required a unanimous approval which could never be obtained. But on the other hand, the very helplessness which the several states had imposed upon the central government meant in practice that the states were sovereign and could do anything they pleased with it. It was precisely this that the nationalists now prepared to exploit: this legal paradox had hithertho prevented the growth of strong loyalty to the existing Confederation and could presently allow that same Confederation, through the action of the states, to be undermined in the deceptive odor of legitimacy. Thus the Beardian school of constitutional thought, for all its errors of economic analysis and its transposing of ideological semantics, has called attention to one element—the element of subversion—that is actually entitled to some consideration.

But if the movement had its plotters, balance requires us to add that the "plot" now had a considerable measure of potential support, and that the authority against which the plot was aimed had become little more than a husk. Up to this time every nationalist move, including the Annapolis Convention, had been easily blocked. But things were now happening in such a way as to tip the balance and to offer the nationalists for the first time a better-than-even chance of success. There had been a marked improvement in business, but shippers in Boston, New York, and Philadelphia were still in serious trouble. Retaliatory measures against Great Britain through state legislation had proved ineffective and useless; there was danger, at the same time, that local manufacturing interests might be successful in pushing through high state tariffs. In the second place, New York's refusal to reconsider a national impost, except on terms that would have removed its effectiveness, cut the ground from under the moderates who had argued that, given only a little time, everything could be worked out. This did not leave much alternative to a major revision of the national government. Then there were Rhode Island's difficulties with inflationary paper money. Although that state's financial schemes actually made a certain amount of sense, they provided the nationalists with wonderful propaganda and helped to create an image of parochial irresponsibility.

The most decisive event of all was Shays' Rebellion in the fall and winter of 1786–1787. It was this uprising of hard-pressed rural debtors in western Massachusetts that frightened moderate people everywhere and convinced them of the need for drastic remedies against what looked like anarchy. The important thing was not so much the facts of the case as the impression which it created outside Massachusetts. The Shaysites had no intention of destroying legitimate government or of redistributing property, but the fact that large numbers of people could very well imagine them doing such things added a note of crisis which was all to the Federalists' advantage. Even the level-headed Washington was disturbed, and his apprehensions were played upon quite knowingly by Madison, Hamilton, and Knox in persuading him to attend the Philadelphia Convention. Actually the Federalists and the Shaysites had been driven to action by much the same conditions; in Massachusetts their concern with the depressed state of trade and the tax burden placed them for all practical purposes on the same side, and there they remained from first to last.

Once the balance had been tipped in enough states, to the point of a working consensus on the desirability of change, a second principle came into effect. Unless a state were absolutely opposed—as in the extreme case of Rhode Island—to any change in the Articles of Confederation, it was difficult to ignore the approaching Philadelphia Convention as had been done with the Annapolis Convention: the occasion was taking on too much importance. There was thus the danger, for such a state, of seeing significant decisions made without having its interests consulted. New York, with strong Anti-Federalist biases but also with a strong nationalist undercurrent, was not quite willing to boycott the convention. Governor Clinton's solution was to send as delegates two rigid state particularists, John Yates and Robert Lansing, along with the nationalist Hamilton, to make sure that Hamilton would not accomplish anything.

We have already seen that nineteenth-century habits of thought created a ponderous array of stereotypes around the historic Philadelphia conclave of 1787. Twentieth-century thought and scholarship, on the other hand, had the task of breaking free from them, and to have done so is a noteworthy achievement. And yet one must return to the point that stereotypes themselves require some form of explanation. The legend of a transcendent effort of statesmanship, issuing forth in a miraculously perfect instrument of government, emerges again and again despite all efforts either to conjure it out of existence or to give it some sort of rational linkage with mortal affairs. Why should the legend be so extraordinarily durable, and was there anything so special about the circumstances that set it on its way so unerringly and so soon?

The circumstances *were,* in fact, special; given a set of delegates of well over average ability, the Philadelphia meeting provides a really classic study in the sociology of intellect. Divine accident, though in some measure present in men's doings always, is not required as a part of this particular equation. The key conditions were all present in a pattern that virtually guaranteed for the meeting an optimum of effectiveness. A sufficient number of states were represented so that the delegates could, without strain, realistically picture themselves as thinking, acting, and making decisions in the name of the entire nation. They themselves, moreover, represented interests throughout the country that were diverse enough, and they had enough personal prestige at home, that they could act in the assurance of having their decisions treated at least with respectful attention. There had also been at work a remarkably effective process of self-selection, as to both men and states. Rhode Island ignored the convention, and as a result its position was not even considered there. There were leading state particularists such as Patrick Henry and Richard Henry Lee who were elected as delegates but refused to serve. The Anti-Federalist position, indeed, was hardly represented at all, and the few men who did represent it had surprisingly little to say. Yates and Lansing simply left before the convention was over. Thus a group already predisposed in a national direction could proceed unhampered by the friction of basic opposition in its midst. This made it possible for the delegates to "try on" various alternatives without having to remain accountable for everything they said. At the same time, being relieved from all outside pressures meant that the only way a man could expect to make a real difference in the convention's deliberations was to reach, through main persuasion, other men of considerable ability and experience. Participants and audience were therefore one, and this in itself imposed standards of debate which were quite exacting. In such a setting the best minds in the convention were accorded an authority which they would not have had in political debates aimed at an indiscriminate public.

Thus the elements of secrecy, the general inclination for a national government, and the process whereby the delegates came to terms with their colleagues—appreciating their requirements and adjusting to their interests—all combined to produce a growing esprit de corps. As initial agreements were worked out, it became exceedingly difficult for the Philadelphia delegates not to grow more and more committed to the product of their joint efforts. Indeed, this was in all likelihood the key mechanism, more important than any other in explaining not only the peculiar genius of the main compromises but also the general fitness of the document as a whole. That is, a group of two or more intelligent men who are subject to no cross-pressures and whose principal commitment is to the success of an idea, are perfectly capable—as in our scientific communities of today—of performing what appear to be prodigies of intellect. Moving, as it were, in the same direction with a specific purpose, they can function at maximum efficiency. It was this that the historians of the nineteenth century did in their way see, and celebrated with sweeping rhetorical flourishes, when they took for granted that if an occasion of this sort could not call forth the highest level of statesmanship available, then it was impossible to imagine another that could.

Once the Philadelphia Convention had been allowed to meet and the delegates had managed, after more than three months of work, to hammer out a document that the great majority of them could sign, the political position of the Federalists changed dramatically. Despite the major battles still impending, for practical purposes they now had the initiative. The principal weapon of the Anti-Federalists—inertia—had greatly declined in effectiveness, for with the new program in motion it was no longer enough simply to argue that a new federal government was unnecessary. They would have to take positive steps in blocking it; they would have to arouse the people and convince them that the Constitution represented a positive danger.

Moreover, the Federalists had set the terms of ratification in such a way as to give the maximum advantage to energy and purpose; the key choices, this time, had been so arranged that they would fall right. Only nine states had to ratify before the Constitution would go into effect. Not only would this rule out the possibility of one or two states holding up the entire effort, but it meant that the Confederation would be automatically destroyed as an alternative before the difficult battles in New York and Virginia had to be faced. (By then, Patrick Henry in Virginia would have nothing but a vague alliance with North Carolina to offer as a counter-choice.) Besides, there was good reason to believe that at least four or five states, and possibly as many as seven, could be counted as safe, which meant that serious fighting in the first phase would be limited to two or three states. And finally, conditions were so set that the "snowball" principle would at each successive point favor the Federalists.

As for the actual process of acceptance, ratification would be done through state conventions elected for the purpose. Not only would this circumvent the vested interests of the legislatures and the ruling coteries that frequented the state capitals, but it gave the Federalists two separate chances to make their case—once to the people and once to the conventions. If the elected delegates were not initially disposed to do the desired thing, there was still a chance, after the convention met, of persuading them. Due partly to the hampering factor of transportation and distance, delegates had to have considerable leeway of choice and what amounted to quasi-plenipotentiary powers. Thus there could be no such thing as a fully "instructed" delegation, and members might meanwhile remain susceptible to argument and conversion. The convention device, moreover, enabled the Federalists to run as delegates men who would not normally take part in state politics.

The revolutionary verve and ardor of the Federalists, their resources of will and energy, their willingness to scheme tirelessly, campaign everywhere, and sweat and agonize over every vote meant in effect that despite all the hairbreadth squeezes and rigors of the struggle, the Anti-Federalists would lose every crucial test. There was, to be sure, an Anti-Federalist effort. But with no program, no really viable commitments, and little purposeful organization, the Anti-Federalists somehow always managed to move too late and with too little. They would sit and watch their great stronghold, New York, being snatched away from them despite a two-to-one Anti-Federalists majority in a convention presided over by their own chief, George Clinton. To them, the New York Federalists must have seemed possessed of the devil. The Federalists' convention men included Alexander Hamilton, James Duane, John Jay, and Robert Livingston—who knew, as did everyone else, that the new government was doomed unless Virginia and New York joined it. They insisted on debating the Constitution section by section instead of as a whole, which meant that they could out-argue the Anti-Federalists on every substantive issue and meanwhile delay the vote until New Hampshire and Virginia had had a chance to ratify. (Madison and Hamilton had a horse relay system in readiness to rush the Virginia news northward as quickly as possible.) By the time the New York convention was ready to act, ten others had ratified, and at the final moment Hamilton and his allies spread the chilling rumor that New York City was about to secede from the state. The Anti-Federalists, who had had enough, directed a chosen number of their delegates to cross over, and solemnly capitulated.

In the end, of course, everyone "crossed over." The speed with which this occurred once the continental revolutionists had made their point, and the ease with which the Constitution so soon became an object of universal veneration, still stands as one of the minor marvels of American history. But the document did contain certain implications, of a quasi-philosophical nature, that make the reasons for this ready consensus not so very difficult to find. It established a national government whose basic outlines were sufficiently congenial to the underlying commitments of the whole culture—republicanism and capitalism—that the likelihood of its being the subject of a true ideological clash was never very real. That the Constitution should mount guard over the rights of property—"realty," "personalty," or any other kind—was questioned by nobody. There had certainly been a struggle, a long and exhausting one, but we should not be deceived as to its nature. It was not fought on economic grounds; it was not a matter of ideology; it was not, in the fullest and most fundamental sense, even a struggle between nationalism and localism. The key struggle was between inertia and energy; with inertia overcome, everything changed.

There were, of course, lingering objections and misgivings; many of the problems involved had been genuinely puzzling and difficult; and there remained doubters who had to be converted. But then the perfect bridge whereby all could become Federalists within a year was the addition of a Bill of Rights. After the French Revolution, anti-constitutionalism in France would be a burning issue for generations; in America, an anti-constitutional party was undreamed of after 1789. With the Bill of Rights, the remaining opponents of the new system could say that, ever watchful of tyranny, they had now got what they wanted. Moreover, the Young Men of the Revolution might at last imagine, after a dozen years of anxiety, that *their* Revolution had been a success.

SUGGESTIONS FOR FURTHER READING

Those interested in exploring the controversy over the constitution further should begin by reading Charles Beard, *An Economic Interpretation of the Constitution* (New York, 1913); only the conclusions are reprinted in this volume. In many ways the best of the books that attack Beard is Forrest McDonald, *We The People: The Economic Origins of the Constitution* (Chicago, 1958). Basing his conclusions on a great deal of research, McDonald tries to show that Beard was wrong in many particulars and that he grossly over-simplified the story. Merrill Jensen, however, in *The New Nation: A History of the United States During the Confederation, 1781–89* (New York, 1950) and Jackson T. Main in *The Anti-Federalists: Critics of the Constitution* (Chapel Hill, 1961) follow Beard in seeing real economic conflict in the period and in the idea that the constitution was a repudiation of the Articles of Confederation and of the Revolution. That the constitution is still controversial can be seen by reading Jackson T. Main's review of *We The People* and McDonald's reply in *William and Mary Quarterly*, XVII (January, 1960), 86–102. For a brief general account of the Confederation and the Constitution period see, Edmund S. Morgan, *The Birth of the Republic, 1763–1789* (Chicago, 1956), a book that plays down the importance of conflict in the period.

V

JEFFERSONIAN ★
AND ★
JACKSONIAN ★
DEMOCRACY ★

    The ratification and general acceptance of the Constitution did not eliminate all disagreements in the new nation. Indeed, strong differences of opinion arose within George Washington's cabinet, differences which soon spread to the Congress and, through the public press, to the country at large. The economic program proposed by Washington's strong-willed secretary of the treasury, Alexander Hamilton, was soon opposed by the secretary of state, Thomas Jefferson. In less than a decade after the inauguration of the first administration under the new Constitution disagreements had led to the formation of the nation's first organized political parties. The election of 1800 was clearly a party battle, and Jefferson's newly organized Republican party emerged victorious.

    Certainly this was a time of sharp debate and furious party struggle. Yet how significant were the differences which divided the country? In his old age, looking back on the event, Thomas Jefferson called his first election "the revolution of 1800," obviously an assessment which implied vast differences separating him from his opponents. Yet in his first inaugural address, Jefferson minimized the importance of the party conflict from which the country had just emerged. "We are all Republicans, we are all Federalists," he said.

    Because Jefferson himself entertained two seemingly

contradictory evaluations of his victory, later historians have been able to agree with him and still disagree among themselves. For some, Jefferson's victory was indeed a revolution; his administration is said to have ushered in a period of agrarian democracy; his victory signalled the defeat of an aristocratic moneyed power. Others argue that Jefferson changed little of the inheritance from the Federalists he had defeated; in truth, they maintain, Jefferson continued the Federalist program.

The Federalist party never recovered from the defeat administered by the Jeffersonians. Perhaps the reason for this was the completeness of the "revolution" of 1800; on the other hand, perhaps the Federalists disappeared because the Republicans had absorbed their program. Yet if almost everyone in the years following the administration of Thomas Jefferson called himself a Jeffersonian, this did not mean that disagreements disappeared. Conflict between parties gave way to strife within the party. The efforts of influential leaders to win a following in the Party led to factions and factions soon developed into new parties. The leader of one such party, calling itself the Democracy, was Andrew Jackson of Tennessee. Elected in 1828, Jackson claimed to be the people's choice and not the candidate of King Caucus. His opponents charged that Jackson was a tyrant, dubbed him "King Andrew I," and organized the Whig party to oppose the Democrats.

How significant were the disagreements which divided Democrats from Whigs? For some scholars the differences were profound, reflecting class conflict between the rich and the poor, the aristocrats and the democrats. For other scholars, the differences were largely rhetorical, mere political bickering against the background of an essentially equalitarian society.

Varying interpretations of Jeffersonian and Jacksonian democracy may be seen in the following selections. Vernon Parrington pictures Jefferson as the philosopher of agrarian democracy. Jefferson feared the development of cities and of urban "mobs" and believed the future of the country should be in the hands of the yeoman farmers. He had faith in the ability of the common man to rule himself and favored decentralized government. As such, Jeffersonianism was the antithesis of Hamiltonianism. Clearly to Parrington, conflict is the central theme of this period. Morton Borden sees a much different Jefferson.

Writing primarily about Jefferson the president, Borden finds him to be a compromiser, a man who on the most important issues was not in any fundamental disagreement with his opponents. Indeed, to Borden, the genius of Jefferson was that he was able to achieve an American consensus.

Arthur Schlesinger, Jr. describes Jacksonian democracy as a part of "that enduring struggle between the business community and the rest of society." There is no doubt in Schlesinger's mind that there was real and important conflict in the Age of Jackson. Bray Hammond does not agree; he decides that there was little dividing the Jacksonians from their opponents. Rather than an ideological struggle between business and the rest of society, the Age of Jackson was marked by a wild scramble of "expectant capitalists" for a place in the economic sun.

The British historian, Marcus Cunliffe, surveys the entire period and seeks to discover an emerging American character. In so doing he finds an American consensus amidst party and sectional differences.

The separation of Americans into different parties and factions matched by sharp and often abusive exchanges among leaders in the newspapers of the day leaves no doubt of differences among Americans during the Age of Jefferson and Jackson. But how significant were these diferences? Did they arise from basic economic and social cleavages in American society and reflect fundamental class conflict based on real ideological differences? Or did they reflect only minor disagreements within a general context of fundamental agreement or consensus?

Vernon L. Parrington

The years following the great defeat were disastrous to the party of agrarian democracy. Under the brilliant leadership of Hamilton the Federalists went forward confidently, gaining daily a firmer grip on the machinery of government, and establishing their principles in far-reaching legislative enactments. Their appeal to the wealthy classes, to those who made themselves audible above the clamor, was electrical. Hamilton was the hero of the hour, and the effusive approval that augmented with every added profit to the money brokers, seemed to indicate that the country was enthusiastically behind the Federalist policy. To what despondency the democrats were reduced is revealed in Maclay's *Journal*, with its caustic comment on political measures and motives. But the tide was already at the turn. The ideas let loose by the French Revolution were running swiftly through America, awakening a militant spirit in the democracy. Antagonism to the aristocratic arrogance of Federalism, and disgust at its coercive measures, were mounting fast. If that inchoate discontent were organized and directed by a skillful leader, it might prove strong enough to thrust the Hamiltonian party from power. To that work Thomas Jefferson devoted himself with immense tact and untiring patience. A master of political strategy, he spun his webs far and wide, quietly awaiting the time when the bumbling Federalist bees should range too carelessly in search of their honey. Accepted at once as the leader of agrarian America, he was to prove in the course of a long life the most original and native of the political leaders of the time.

Despite the mass of comment that has gathered about Jefferson, the full reach and significance of his political philosophy remains too little understood. Uncritical praise and censure have obscured or distorted his purpose, and allied his principles with narrow and temporary ends. Detraction will not let him alone. The hostility of his enemies, as a recent biographer has remarked, has frequently taken "the peculiar form of editing his works or writing his life." For this distortion there is, perhaps, more than usual excuse. Certainly Jefferson is the most elusive of our great political leaders. Apparently inconsistent, changing his program with the changing times, he seemed to his enemies devoid of principle, a shallow demagogue who incited the mob in order to dupe the people. One of the most bitterly hated and greatly loved men in the day when love and hate were intense, he was the spokesman of the new order at a time of transition from a dependent monarchical state, to an independent republican state. Back of the figure of Jefferson, with his aristocratic head set on a plebeian frame, was the philosophy of a new age and a new people—an age and a people not yet come to the consistency of maturity, but feeling a way through experiment to solid achievement. Far more completely than any other American of his generation he embodied the idealisms of the great revolution—its faith in human nature, its economic individualism, its conviction that here in America, through the instrumentality of political democracy, the lot of the common man should somehow be made better.

From the distinguished group of contemporary political thinkers Jefferson emerges as the preëminent intellectual, widely read, familiar with ideas, at home in the field of speculation, a critical observer of men and manners. All his life he was a student, and his devotion to his books, running often to fifteen hours a day, recalls the heroic zeal of Puritan scholars. He was trained in the law, but he was too much the intellectual, too curious about all sorts of things, to remain a lawyer. For such a man the appeal of political speculation was irresistible, and early in life he began a wide reading in the political classics that far outweighed Coke and Blackstone in creative influence on his mind. He was equally at home with the English liberals of the seventeenth century and the French liberals of the eighteenth; and if he came eventually to set the French school above the English, it was because he found in the back-to-nature philosophy, with its corollary of an agrarian economics and its emphasis on social well-being, a philosophy more consonant with Virginian experience and his own temperament than Locke's philosophy of property. But he was very far from being a narrow French partisan, as has been often charged; rather he judged old-world theory in the light of its applicability to existing American conditions, and restrained his love of speculation by immediate practical considerations. The man of affairs kept a watchful eye on the philosopher in his study.

In the major doctrines of his political philosophy Jefferson was an amalgam of English and French liberalisms, supplemented by the conscious influence of the American frontier. That fusion early took place in his mind. The first bill that he introduced into the Virginia Assembly, at the age of twenty-six, was a bill to permit slave-owners to manumit their slaves; and his first published pamphlet, issued in 1774, rejected the legal reasoning of John Dickinson and Daniel Dulaney—supporting the parliamentary right to impose external taxation—and took its stand on the doctrine of natural right to local self-government and freedom of trade. When two years later he drafted the Declaration of Independence the fusion was complete. The strong influence of French humanitarianism is revealed in the passage on slavery that was stricken out on the floor of Congress, and more significantly in the change in the familiar phrasing of the several natural rights. Samuel Adams and other followers of Locke had been content with the classical enumeration of life, liberty, and property; but in Jefferson's hands the English doctrine was given a revolutionary shift. The substitution of "pursuit of happiness" for "property" marks a complete break with the Whiggish doctrine of property rights that Locke had bequeathed to the English middle class, and the substitution of a broader sociological conception; and it was this substitution that gave to the document the note of idealism which was to make its appeal so perennially human and vital. The words were far more than a political gesture to draw popular support; they were an embodiment of Jefferson's deepest convictions, and his total life thenceforward was given over to the work of providing such political machinery for America as should guarantee for all the enjoyment of those inalienable rights. If the fact that he set the pursuit of happiness above abstract property rights is to be taken as proof that Jefferson was an impractical French theorist, the critic may take what comfort he can from his deduction.

That Jefferson was an idealist was singularly fortunate for America; there was need of idealism to leaven the materialistic realism of the times. It was a critical period and he came at the turn of a long running tide. He watched the beginnings of the political shift in America from isolated colonial commonwealths to a unitary sovereign state; and his wide reading and close observation had convinced him that the impending change was fraught with momentous issues for the common man. He had meditated much on the social results of the slow oscillations in western civilization between social decentralization and centralization, with their contrasting political and economic structures; and he understood how the movement from simplicity to complexity—from freedom to regimentation—creates a psychology and an institutionalism that conducts straight to the leviathan state, controlled by a ruling caste, serving the demands of exploitation, heedless of the well-being of the regimented mass. This great lesson in social drifts he brought home to America. There had been created here the psychology and institutions of a decentralized society, with a corresponding exaltation of the individual and the breakdown of caste. In the broad spaces of America the old-world coercive state had dwindled to a mere police arrangement for parochial duties; the free citizen refused to be regimented; the several communities insisted on managing their affairs by their own agents. Such was the natural consequence of free economics; but with the turning of the tide would not the drift towards centralization nullify the results of earlier American experience and repeat here the unhappy history of European peoples?

To the philosophic mind of Jefferson, such a question was not academic, but urgent and vital. He had been bred in that older world, he believed passionately in the excellence of its virtues, and his political and social philosophy was determined by that experience. He sprang from a society deep-rooted in an agrarian economy, and he wished to preserve that society. Born on the Virginia frontier, he had never seen a hamlet so large as twenty houses before his eighteenth year; his neighbors and associates were capable and vigorous frontier democrats, who managed the affairs of local government with the same homespun skill that went to their farming. "It is not difficult," remarks an acute critic, "to see how the great principle of Jefferson's life—absolute faith in democracy—came to him. He was the product of the first West in American history; he grew up with men who ruled their country well, who fought the Indians valiantly. . . . Jefferson loved his backwoods neighbors, and he, in turn, was loved by them." This early conviction of the excellence of a freehold order was confirmed by later experience; wide observation and much travel convinced him that no other people was so favored by circumstance as the American, or so vigorously self-reliant. That such well-being resulted from a plastic economics, he regarded as self-evident; and from this economic freedom came political freedom. In his European travels he saw everywhere want and wretchedness dwelling in the shadow of the aristocratic state, and he could not dissociate the two. Political tyranny was the outward and visible sign of greater tyrannies that ran down to the very roots of society; the leviathan state was the convenient instrument through which those tyrannies took their heavy toll of the common well-being. America was a land of free men; it was exploited neither by an aristocracy nor a plutocracy. Surely there could be no greater or nobler ambition for an American than to assist in preserving his country from the misery that must attend a change from the present happy condition of democratic industry, to the serfdom of the European wage-taker and peasant.

To a mind imbued with such conceptions the appeal of the Physiocratic theory of social economics would be irresistible. The ground was prepared for the sowing of the seeds of the liberal French thought. With its emphasis laid upon agriculture, its doctrine of the *produit net*, its principle of *laissez faire*, and its social concern, the Physiocratic theory accorded exactly with his familiar experience, and it must have seemed to Jefferson that it was little other than a deduction from the open facts of American life. He had read much in the works of the Physiocratic group, and was intimately acquainted with DuPont de Nemours; and the major principles of the school sank deep into his mind and creatively determined his thinking, with the result that Jeffersonian democracy as it spread through Virginia and west along the frontier assumed a pronounced Physiocratic bias. The sharp struggle between Jefferson and Hamilton must be reckoned, in part at least, a conflict between the rival principles of Quesnay and Adam Smith, between an agrarian and a capitalistic economy. Much as Jefferson feared the ambitions of an aristocracy, he feared quite as much the creation of a proletariat. As he looked into the future he saw great cities rising to breed their Roman mobs, duped and exploited by demagogues, the convenient tools of autocracy; and counting the cost in social well-being, he set his face like flint against the rising capitalism. A free yeomanry he regarded as the backbone of every great people, the producers of the real wealth, the guardians of manly independence; and the number of factory workers measured for him the extent of social disease. It is this Physiocratic conception that explains his bitter hostility to protective tariffs, national banks, funding manipulations, the machinery of credit, and all the agencies of capitalism which Hamilton was skillfully erecting in America. Not to have hated such things Jefferson must first have emptied his mind of the teachings of experience and the lessons of the social philosophers.

In the *Notes on Virginia* there is a well-known passage that amplifies his favorite thesis that a sound American economy was an agrarian economy:

The political economists of Europe have established it as a principle, that every State should endeavor to manufacture for itself; and this principle, like many others, we transfer to America. . . . But we have an immensity of land courting the industry of the husbandman. Is it best then that all our citizens should be employed in its improvement, or that one half should be called off from that to exercise manufactures and handicraft arts for the other? Those who labor in the earth are the chosen people of God, if ever he had a chosen people, whose breasts he has made his peculiar deposit for substantial and genuine virtue. It is the focus in which he keeps alive that sacred fire, which otherwise might escape from the face of the earth. Corruption of morals in the mass of cultivators is a phenomenon of which no age nor nation has furnished an example. It is the mark set on those, who not looking up to heaven, to their own soil and industry, as does the husbandman, for their subsistence, depend for it on casualties and caprice of customers. Dependence begets subservience and venality, suffocates the germ of virtue, and prepares fit tools for the designs of ambition. . . . Generally speaking the proportion which the aggregate of the other classes of citizens bears in any state to that of its husbandmen, is the proportion of its unsound to its healthy parts, and is a good enough barometer whereby to measure its degree of corruption. While we have land to labor then, let us never wish to see our citizens occupied at a work-bench, or twirling a distaff . . . for the general operations of manufacture, let our work-shops remain in Europe. It is better to carry provisions and materials to work-men there, than bring them to the provisions and materials, and with them their manners and principles. . . . The mobs of great cities add just so much to the support of pure government, as sores do to the strength of the human body. It is the manners and spirit of a people which preserve a republic in vigor. A degeneracy in these is a canker which soon eats to the heart of its laws and constitution.

Such was his attitude in 1782, an attitude identical with Franklin's. Thirty-four years later he had modified his views of industrialism. The bitter experience of the Napoleonic wars, with the hardships and losses visited upon neutral shipping, had convinced him of the need of domestic manufactures, and he was then deeply interested in improved machinery, new methods, original ventures. "We must now place the manufacturer by the side of the agriculturist," he conceded, or remain in economic dependence. But how much further the country should be industrialized, whether it "shall be proposed to go beyond our own supply" to compete in foreign markets, was not yet clear to him; the problem remained still to be determined whether "the *surplus* labor" would be "most beneficially employed in the culture of the earth, or in the fabrications of art." In such commentary Jefferson failed to measure the thrust of economic determinism that drives every people to go through with the industrial revolution, once it is begun; but if we recall the primary principle of his political philosophy, that the "care of human life and happiness, and not their destruction, is the first and only legitimate object of good government," we may perhaps judge what would have been his attitude towards a centralized industrialism. He would have judged its desirability, not by the balance sheet of corporate business, but by the social ledger. As a social economist he could not think in terms of the economic man, nor simplify human beings to labor commodity, nor reduce the social tie to the cash nexus. It is inconceivable that he should have shared Hamilton's satisfaction at the contemplation of women and children—and many of the latter "of tender age"—wasting away in the mills; he was too social-minded for that, too much an idealist, too human in short. Though necessity might force him away from a simple agrarian economy, it does not follow that he would become partisan to a centralizing industrialism, with control vested in banking credit.

It is a common charge that Jefferson was consumed with suspicion, and it is set down against him as the mark of a mean and ungenerous nature. That in later years he was suspicious of fair spoken advocates and plausible programs was as true of Jefferson as of Sam Adams; he had learned like the Boston democrat the virtue of the saying, *felix qui cautus,* and with so much at stake he would practice caution. He feared many things, for he was acutely aware of the incapacity of the heedless majority to defend itself against an able and instructed minority. As a child of an aristocratic age he fell into the mistake of visualizing that minority in the guise of a landed gentry, rather than in the guise of plutocracy; but in his quick fear of a minority he had all history as counselor. When he took his seat in Washington's cabinet his suspicions of the Hamiltonian program were quickly aroused. He believed that a monarchy was aimed at, and if that proved unattainable, then a highly centralized state designed to hold in check the democratic tendencies. His line of reasoning may be summarized thus: In consequence of the republican enthusiasm of the early years of the Revolution, democratic reorganization of the several state governments had been successfully achieved. Very great progress towards democracy had been made. Certain legislative acts of agrarian assemblies were now being turned against democracy, to invalidate it as a working system of government. But if agrarian majorities had used their power to enact laws beneficial to their interests, they were only applying a lesson learned from long experience with aristocratic legislatures. Such acts were no serious indictment of the democratic principle, and to make partisan use of them to justify curtailing the powers of the majority, was a betrayal of popular rights. And this, Jefferson believed, was the deliberate purpose of the Federalist leaders. Unable to stem the popular tide in the several commonwealths, the wealthy minority had devised a plan to superimpose upon the sovereign commonwealths a centralized federal government, so hedged about as to lie beyond the reach of local majorities, and hence able to override and nullify the democratic will. Once safely established, this federal government would gather fresh powers into its hands, until there emerged a rigorous machine, modeled after the British system, and as little regardful of the common interests. If this were not the Federalist purpose, why all the praise of the British system as the ripe product of experience, exactly adapted to the political genius of the English race?

In the matter of appeal to past experience, which provided the staple of Federalist argument, Jefferson discovered fresh grounds of fear. The past he looked upon as evil, and the record of experience was a tale of injustice and bitter wrong. He would not have America follow the trodden paths, for whither they led he knew too well. He would countenance no entangling alliances with old-world upper-class systems of statecraft, for such systems would reproduce in America the evils it should be the chief business of America to prevent. There must be erected here no counterpart of the European state; there must be no king, no aristocracy, no plutocracy; but a new democratic organization of government, in which the welfare of the whole people should be the sole concern.

When I left Congress in '76 [he wrote as an old man] it was in the persuasion that our whole code must be revised, adapted to our republican form of government, and now that we had no negatives of Councils, Governors and Kings to restrain us from doing right, that it should be corrected in all its parts with a single eye to reason and the good of those for whose government it was planned.

Not past experience but present need should instruct America in drawing the plans of a new system of government and a new code of law. In

analyzing the evils of European systems Jefferson came to certain conclusions that dominated all his later thinking, and that may be phrased
thus: The political state tends inevitably to self-aggrandizement, the
logical outcome of which is a political leviathan, too big and too complex
for popular control. With sovereign powers vested in the hands of governmental agents, those agents lie under a constant temptation to corruption and tyranny, and in the end they align the powers of the state on
the side of the most ambitious and capable. The greater the power of
government, the ampler its revenues, the more energetic its administration, the more dangerous it may become to the rights of men; for where
the prize is greatest, men struggle most ruthlessly, and what prize could
be greater than the privilege of exploiting society in the name of the
state? History knows no objective more tempting to the will to power,
than the control of the absolute state. A government adequately social-
ized, intent solely upon furthering the common well-being, Jefferson
would have been unanxious about. But such governments existed only in
the dreams of Sir Thomas More and the Utopians; he could discover
none such either in the past or present. Everywhere strong governments
were little more than efficient tax-machines to support armies and provide subsidies and places for the minority. Against such forces of corruption the people struggle in vain.

If such was the common testimony of old-world experience—and no
man who knew the inner workings of government there would deny
it—what reason was there to expect that like causes would work unlike
results in America? To what purpose was the talk of strong government
encouraged amongst the holders of the public debt? To what end had
lobbyists for the funding bill invaded the floor of Congress? It was idle to
expect in America a nullification of the law, that where power sits
within, corruption waits without. The love of power is universal. Most
men are potential autocrats, the strong and capable may become actual
autocrats. No man is good enough, no group of men, to be trusted with
unrestrained powers—in America any more than in Europe. A centralized government in control of the tax-machine, and secure from popular
restraint, would undo the results of the Revolutionary War. The movement to consolidate power, Jefferson asserted, was "but Toryism in disguise." "The generalizing and concentrating all cares and powers into
one body . . . has destroyed the liberty and the rights of men in every
government which has ever existed under the sun."

Our country is too large to have all its affairs directed by a single government. Public servants at such a distance, and from under the eye of their constituents, must, from the circumstance of distance, be unable to administer and
overlook all the details necessary for the good government of the citizens; and
the same circumstance, by rendering detection impossible to their constituents,
will invite the public agents to corruption, plunder and waste.

The practice of local home rule had grown up in America in response to native conditions; it had resulted from democratic needs; and Jefferson was too thoroughly American, too instinctively democratic, to overlook the significance of local sovereignties in a democratic philosophy From the sharp contrast between American and European practice he deduced a cardinal principle, namely, that good government springs from a common interest in public affairs, and that such common interest is possible only when the field of activities is circumscribed. Set government apart from the people, or above them, and public interest is lost in a sense of futility. The danger of an encroaching tyranny by a superimposed sovereignty, is made easy by the public lethargy in respect to distant and unfamiliar things, and establishes itself through the psychology of custom. Jefferson was never greatly concerned about stable government; he was very much more concerned about responsive government—that it should faithfully serve the majority will. He made no god of the political state. He had no conventional reverence for established law and order; he inquired rather what sort of law and order he was asked to accept, was it just or unjust. Changing conditions make ancient good uncouth, and established institutions tend to fall into dry-rot, or to become tyrannical. Men are more important than constitutions, and the public well-being is more sacred than statutes. An occasional revolution, he commented grimly apropos of the hue and cry over Shays's Rebellion, is salutary; if it does not come of itself it might well be brought about. Progress in government results from experiment; and it is easier and safer to experiment on a small scale than on a great. Inertia increases with size, and the more consolidated the government, the more unyielding it becomes. The longest delayed revolutions are the gravest.

In asserting the principle of the majority will, Jefferson like other democratic thinkers of the time, found himself countered by the argument of abstract justice. Vehement denunciation had greeted Paine's doctrine that what a nation chooses to do, it has a right to do. There can be no rights, it was confidently asserted, superior to the right. The people may legislate, but it remains to determine the validity of statutes in the light of justice; that which is unjust is *ipso facto* null and void. It was Coke's doctrine of judicial review, set up in America after its repudiation in England, and Jefferson's hostility to it was bitter. As an intellectual he had none of the lawyer's complacency with legal principles, or conceit of the law's sufficiency; and as a democrat he would not yield sovereignty into the hands of the judiciary. He had no veneration for the Common Law of England: it had grown up by slow accretions during centuries of absolutism; how should it be expected to answer the needs of a freer age? It must be purged of outworn elements, imbued with democratic sympathies. The Revolution had been fought in defense of rights that are broader and more human than legal principles; and to hand over those rights to be interpreted away by lawyers, seemed to him moonstruck madness. It was the law of Blackstone rather than of Coke that he feared most—that "elegant" canonization of the malign influences of Tory reaction, and that was so cried up by the smatterers and "ephemeral insects of the law" in America; whereas Coke "was as good a Whig as ever wrote":

Blackstone and Hume have made tories of all England, and are making tories of those young Americans whose native feelings of independence do not place them above the wily sophistries of a Hume or a Blackstone. These two books, and especially the former [Blackstone], have done more towards the suppression of the liberties of man, than all the million of men in arms of Bonaparte, and the millions of human lives with the sacrifice of which he will stand loaded before the judgment seat of his Maker.

As Jefferson grew older his fear of judicial encroachment on the popular will became acute, but it shifted from distrust of the Common Law to concern over the Supreme Court. A strong and outspoken hatred of the Federal judiciary runs through all his later writings, and he lost no opportunity to popularize the thesis—"It is a misnomer to call a government republican, in which a branch of the supreme power is independent of the nation."

The great object of my fear is the Federal Judiciary. That body, like gravity, ever acting, with noiseless foot, and unalarming advance, gaining ground step by step, and holding what it gains, is engulfing insidiously the special governments into the jaws of that which feeds them.

It is a very dangerous doctrine to consider the judges as the ultimate arbiters of all constitutional questions. It is one which would place us under the despotism of an oligarchy. . . . The Constitution has erected no such single tribunal, knowing that to whatever hands confided, with the corruptions of time and party, its members would become despots.

As Jefferson watched Chief Justice John Marshall gathering all things within the purview of the Federal judiciary, preparing future strongholds by the skillful use of *obiter dicta*, legislating by means of judicial interpretation, nullifying the will of the majority, and with the power of repeal made nugatory by the complexity of the process, he saw clearly what the outcome would be. Surely that was no democracy where judge-made laws were enforced by bench warrants, and where the sovereign power lay beyond the immediate reach of the popular will. The government that he desired would not rest on the legal fiction of an abstract justice above statutes and constitutions, whereof a group of judicial gentlemen were the repositories and guardians. It would be like Paine's, "a plain thing, and fitted to the capacity of many heads"; for "where the law of the majority ceases to be acknowledged, there government ends; the law of the strongest takes its place."

Granted the truth of Jefferson's premises that power tends to contract to the hands of a few, and that all government of the few is vicious, then

democracy is the only form of government under which an approxima-
tion to justice can be realized. A class will serve class interests. Government by an aristocracy is government in the interest of the aristocracy.
For the staple argument of the Federalists, that gentlemen of principle
and property alone may be intrusted with affairs of state, Jefferson had
a quiet contempt. "I have never observed men's honesty to increase with
their riches," he remarked. On the contrary, he regarded the "better sort
of people" as a chief hindrance to the spread of social justice. The past
had been evil because the past had been exploited by gentlemen of principle and property. They had kept government away from the people,
and with their secret councils and secret diplomacy they had plundered
the taxpayers and drenched nations in blood. Their selfish rivalries
everywhere exacted a heavy toll of society and left behind a trail of poverty and wretchedness. The future would be better in the degree that
mastery passed into common hands.

From the conclusions of his democratic premise he did not shrink. If
it were indeed true that the people were beasts, then the democratic government of the future would be a bestial government—and even that
might be better than the old arrangement of masters and slaves. But the
American people whom Jefferson trusted were very far from beasts; he
was convinced that they were honest and well-meaning; and if government were brought close to them, kept responsive to their will, a new and
beneficent chapter in human history would open. The populistic laws
passed by the legislatures of Rhode Island and New Hampshire, about
which such an uproar was raised by fearful creditors, and which were
urged as an argument against popular government, gave him no concern. He understood the ways of propaganda, and he never accepted
judgment of the American people from the mouths of their enemies. The
cure for the evils of democracy, he believed, was more democracy. The
whole are far less likely to be unjust than the few; and if sovereignty
does not rest in the majority will, where shall it lodge?

Hume, the great apostle of toryism, says "the Commons established a principle, which is noble in itself, and seems specious [i.e. pleasing], but is belied
by all history and experience, *that the people are the origin of all just power.*"
And where else will this degenerate son of science, this traitor to his fellow
men, find the origin of *just* power, if not in the majority of the society? Will it
be in the minority? Or in the individual of that minority?

The America of Jefferson's day was a simple world, with a simple
domestic economy. More than ninety per cent were plain country folk,
farmers and villagers, largely freeholders, managing their local affairs
in the traditional way. There were no great extremes of poverty and
wealth, no closely organized class groups. With its sharp restrictions on
suffrage and the prestige accorded the gentry, it was still far from a political democracy; but it was hastening towards a more democratic order.

Remote from the cesspools of European diplomacy, and not yet acquainted with imperialism, it had no need for a leviathan state. Economic conditions sanctioned a *laissez-faire* government, simple and unambitious. In such a world the well-known words of Jefferson's first inaugural address, justified themselves to all who did not seek to use the state for personal advantage.

A wise and frugal government, which shall restrain men from injuring one another, which shall leave them otherwise free to regulate their own pursuits of industry and improvement, and shall not take from the mouth of labor the bread it has earned. This is the sum of good government, and this is necessary to close the circle of our felicities.

In one significant direction he would extend the scope of government—the encouragement of education. An intelligent people is necessary to a democracy; free schools are a sign of a free society. Tyranny thrives on ignorance and superstition, and every exploiting group fears popular education. Free himself in thought and action, believing in the unshackled commerce of ideas, hating all censorships, Jefferson accounted the founding of the University of Virginia his largest contribution to the well-being of his native commonwealth.

To all who profess faith in the democratic ideal Jefferson is a perennial inspiration. A free soul, he loved freedom enough to deny it to none; an idealist, he believed that the welfare of the whole, and not the prosperity of any group, is the single end of government. He was our first great leader to erect a political philosophy native to the economics and experience of America, as he was the first to break consciously with the past. His life was dedicated to the service of freedom, and later generations may well recall his words, "I have sworn upon the altar of God eternal hostility against every form of tyranny over the mind of man." Europe made Jefferson wholly American. From his studies in France he came to see that where men enjoy free access to the sources of subsistence, government is likely to be simple and honest, and society free and content; but where a policy of preëmption has run its course, the function of government is seduced from its social purpose to perpetuate the inequalities which spring from the progressive monopolization of natural resources, with augmenting corruption and injustice. To preserve government in America from such degradation, to keep the natural resources open to all, were the prime desire and object of his life. That such an effort was foredoomed to failure, in presence of imperious forces that shape society beyond the capacity of political means to change or prevent, cannot detract from the nobility of his ideal, or the inspiration of his life. Among the greater thinkers of the constitutional period Jefferson remains by far the most vital and suggestive, the one to whom later generations may return most hopefully.

Morton Borden

For twelve years the Constitution worked, after a fashion. From its inception the new document had been subjected to severe trials and divisive strains. A rebellion in Pennsylvania, a naval war with France, a demand for states' rights from Virginia and Kentucky, and various Western schemes of disunion—all had been surmounted. Had it not been for the great prestige of George Washington and the practical moderation of John Adams, America's second attempt at a federal union might have failed like the first. Partisan passions had run high in the 1790's, and any single factor on which men disagreed—Hamilton's financial plans or the French Revolution or the Sedition Act—might easily have caused a stoppage of the nation's political machinery.

The two-party system emerged during this decade, and on each important issue public opinion seemed to oscillate between Federalist and Democratic-Republican. Perhaps this was to be expected of a young nation politically adolescent. Year by year Americans were becoming more politically alert and active; if there was little room for middle ground between these two factions, yet opinions were hardly fixed and irrevocable. The culmination of partisan controversy and the test of respective strengths took place in the monumental election of 1800.

Jefferson was feared, honestly feared, by almost all Federalists. Were he to win the election, so they predicted, all the hard constructive gains of those twelve years would be dissipated Power would be returned to the individual states; commerce would suffer; judicial power would be lessened; and the wonderful financial system of Hamilton would be dismantled and destroyed. Jefferson was an atheist, and he would attack the churches. Jefferson was a hypocrite, an aristocrat posing as democrat, appealing to the baser motives of human beings in order to obtain votes. Jefferson was a revolutionary, a Francophile and, after ruining the Army and Navy under the guise of economy measures, might very well involve the nation in a war with England. In short, it was doubtful if the Constitution could continue its successful course under such a president.

In like manner the Republicans feared another Federalist victory. To be sure, John Adams had split with Hamilton and had earned the enmity of the Essex Junto. But would he not continue Hamilton's "moneyed system"? Did not Adams share the guilt of every Federalist for the despicable Alien and Sedition Acts? Was it not true that "His Rotundity" so admired the British system that he was really a monarchist at heart? Republicans were not engaging in idle chatter, nor were they speaking solely for effect, when they predicted many dire consequences if Adams were elected. A typical rumor had Adams uniting "his house to that of his majesty of Britain" and "the bridegroom was to be king of America."

Throughout the country popular interest in the election was intense, an intensity sustained over months of balloting. When the Republicans carried New York City, Alexander Hamilton seriously suggested that the results be voided. And when the breach between Adams and Hamilton became public knowledge, Republicans nodded knowingly and quoted the maxim: "When thieves fall out, honest men come by their own."

The Federalists were narrowly defeated. But the decision was complicated by a result which many had predicted: a tied electoral vote between the two Republican candidates, Aaron Burr and Thomas Jefferson. (Indeed, the Twelfth Amendment was adopted in 1804 to avoid any such recurrence.) A choice between the two would be made by the House of Representatives. At this moment, February, 1801, the Constitution seemed on the verge of collapse. Federalist members of the lower house united in support of Burr; Republicans were just as adamant for Jefferson. After thirty-five ballots, neither side had yet obtained the necessary majority. The issue seemed hopelessly deadlocked. What would happen on March 4, inauguration day?

One representative from Maryland, sick with a high fever, was literally carried into Congress on a stretcher to maintain the tied vote of his state. The Republican governor of Pennsylvania, Thomas McKean, threatened to march on Washington with troops if the Federalists persisted in thwarting the will of the people. Hamilton was powerless; his advice that Jefferson was the lesser evil went unheeded. So great was their hatred of the Virginian that most Federalists in Congress would have opposed him regardless of the consequences. After all, they reasoned, Jefferson would dismantle the Federal government anyway. In the end, however, patriotism and common sense prevailed. For the choice was no longer Jefferson or Burr, but Jefferson or no president at all. A few Federalists, led by James A. Bayard of Delaware, could not accept the logic of their party, and threw the election to Jefferson.

What a shock it was, then, to read Jefferson's carefully chosen words in his inaugural address:

But every difference of opinion is not a difference of principle. We have called by different names brethren of the same principle. We are all republicans—we are all federalists. If there be any among us who would wish to dissolve this Union or to change its republican form, let them stand undisturbed as monuments of the safety with which error of opinion may be tolerated where reason is left free to combat it. I know, indeed, that some honest men fear that a republican government cannot be strong; that this government is not strong enough. But would the honest patriot, in the full tide of successful experiment, abandon a government which has so far kept us free and firm, on the theoretic and visionary fear that this government, the world's best hope, may by possibility want energy to preserve itself? I trust not. I believe this, on the contrary, the strongest government on earth. I believe it is the only one where every man, at the call of the laws, would fly to the standard of the law, and would meet invasions of the public order as his own personal concern. Sometimes it is said that man cannot be trusted with the government of himself. Can he, then, be trusted with the government of others? Or have we found angels in the form of kings to govern him? Let history answer this question.

The words were greeted with applause—and confusion. It was obvious that Jefferson wanted to salve the wounds of bitter factionalism. While many Federalists remained distrustful and some even regarded it as hypocritical, most men approved the tone of their new president's message.

But what did Jefferson mean? Were there no economic principles at stake in his conflicts with Hamilton? Were there no political and constitutional principles implicit in the polar views of the respective parties? And, in the last analysis, did not these differences reflect a fundamental philosophical quarrel over the nature of human beings? Was not the election of 1800 indeed a revolution? If not, then what is the meaning of Jeffersonianism?

For two terms Jefferson tried, as best he could, to apply the standards of his inaugural address. Naturally, the Alien and Sedition Acts were allowed to lapse. The new secretary of the treasury, Albert Gallatin, was instructed to devise an easily understood program to erase the public debt gradually. Internal taxes were either abolished or reduced. Frugality and economy were emphasized to an extreme. Elegant and costly social functions were replaced by simple and informal receptions. The expense of maintaining ambassadors at the courts of Portugal, Holland, and Prussia was erased by withdrawing these missions. The Army and Navy were pared down to skeleton size. To be sure, Jefferson had to reverse himself on the matter of patronage for subordinate Government posts. Originally he planned to keep these replacements to a minimum, certainly not to permit an individual's partisan opinions to be a basis for dismissal unless the man manifestly used his office for partisan purposes. This position was politically untenable, according to Jefferson's lieutenants, and they pressed him to accept a moderate number of removals. Indeed, Jefferson's handling of patronage is symbolic of what Hamilton once called his "ineradicable duplicity."

The Federalist leaders cried out in anguish at every one of these policy changes. The lowering of the nation's military strength would increase the danger of invasion. It was a rather risky gamble to assume that peace could be maintained while European war was an almost constant factor, and the United States was the major neutral carrier. The abolition of the excises, especially on distilled spirits, would force the Government to rely on tariffs, an unpredictable source of revenue depending on the wind and waves. It was charged that several foreign ambassadors were offended by Jefferson's rather affected and ultrademocratic social simplicity. Most important, the ultimate payment of the public debt would reduce national power.

This time, however, the people did not respond to the Federalist lament of impending anarchy. After all, commerce prospered throughout most of Jefferson's administration. Somehow the churches remained standing. No blood baths took place. The Bank of the United States still operated. Peace was maintained. Certainly, some Federalist judges were under attack, but the judicial power passed through this ordeal to emerge unscathed and even enhanced. Every economic indicator—urban growth, westward expansion, agricultural production, the construction of canals, turnpikes and bridges—continued to rise, undisturbed by the political bickering in Washington.

At first the Federalists were confident that they would regain power. Alexander Hamilton's elaborate scheme for an organization to espouse Christianity and the Constitution, as the "principal engine" to restore Federalist power, was rejected out of hand. He was told that "our adversaries will soon demonstrate to the world the soundness of our doctrines and the imbecility and folly of their own." But hope changed to despair as the people no longer responded; no "vibration of opinion" took place as in the 1790's. Federalism was the party of the past, an antiquated and dying philosophy. "I will fatten my pigs, and prune my trees; nor will I any longer . . . trouble to govern this country," wrote Fisher Ames: "You federalists are only lookers-on." Jefferson swept the election of 1804, capturing every state except Connecticut and Delaware from the Federalist candidate, Charles C. Pinckney. "Federalism is dead," wrote Jefferson a few years later, "without even the hope of a day of resurrection. The quondam leaders indeed retain their rancour and principles; but their followers are amalgamated with us in sentiment, if not in name."

It is the fashion of some historians to explain the Federalist demise and Republican ascendancy in terms of a great change in Jefferson. A radical natural law philosopher when he fought as minority leader, he became a first-rate utilitarian politician as president. The Virginian became an American. Revolutionary theory was cast aside when Jefferson faced the prosaic problem of having to run the country. He began to adopt some of the techniques and policies of the Federalists. Indeed, it is often observed that Jefferson "outfederalized the Federalists."

There is much to be said for this view. After all, less than three months after he assumed the presidency, Jefferson dispatched a naval squadron to the Mediterranean on a warlike mission, without asking the permission of Congress. Two members of his Cabinet, Levi Lincoln and Albert Gallatin, thought the action unconstitutional, and so advised the President. Almost from the moment of its birth the young nation had paid tribute, as did every European power, rather than risk a war with the Barbary pirates. But Jefferson could not abide such bribery. No constitutional scruples could delay for a moment his determination to force the issue. Later, Congress declared war, and in four years Barbary power was shattered. The United States under Jefferson accomplished an object that England, France, Spain, Portugal, and Holland had desired for more than a century—unfettered commerce in the Mediterranean. Here, then, in this episode, is a totally different Jefferson—not an exponent of states' rights and strict interpretation of the Constitution, but an American nationalist of the first order.

Perhaps the most frequently cited example of Jefferson's chameleon quality, however, was on the question of whether the United States should or should not purchase the Louisiana Territory from France. On this question the fundamental issue was squarely before Jefferson, and a choice could not be avoided. The purchase would more than double the size of the United States. Yet the Constitution did not specifically provide for such acquisition of foreign territory. Further, the treaty provided that this area would eventually be formed into states, full partners in the Union. Again, the Constitution did not specifically cover such incorporation. A broad interpretation of Article IV, Section III, however, might permit United States' ratification of the treaty. Should theory be sacrificed and an empire gained? Or were the means as important as the ends?

Broad or loose construction of the Constitution was the key to the growth of Federal power. Federalists had argued in this vein to justify most of their legislation in the 1790's. To Jefferson, individual liberty and governmental power were on opposite ends of a see-saw, which the Federalists had thrown off balance. He believed that government, especially the central government, must be restricted within rather narrow and essential limits. Only by continually and rigidly applying strict construction to the Constitution could this tendency to overweening power be controlled and individual liberty be safeguarded. As early as 1777, Jefferson, then governor of Virginia, had warned that constitutions must be explicit, "so as to exclude all possible doubt; . . . [lest] at some future day . . . power[s] should be assumed."

On the other hand, the purchase of Louisiana would fulfill a dream and solve a host of problems. Jefferson envisioned an American empire covering "the whole northern, if not the southern continent, with a people speaking the same language, governed in similar forms, and by similar laws." The purchase would be a giant step in the direction of democracy's inevitable growth. "Is it not better," asked Jefferson, "that the opposite bank of the Mississippi should be settled by our own brethren and children, than by strangers of another family?"

Of more immediate interest, Westerners would be able to ship their goods down the Mississippi without fear that New Orleans might be closed. Indian attacks undoubtedly would taper off without the Spanish to instigate them. Uppermost in Jefferson's mind, however, was the freedom from England that the purchase would assure. He did not fear Spanish ownership. A feeble, second-rate nation like Spain on the frontier offered little threat to America's future security. The continued possession of Louisiana by an imperialistic France led by the formidable Napoleon, however, might force the United States into an alliance with England. At first Jefferson thought a constitutional amendment specifically permitting the purchase might solve the dilemma. But Napoleon showed signs of wavering. The treaty had to be confirmed immediately, with no indication of constitutional doubt. Jefferson asked the Republican leaders in the Senate to ratify it "with as little debate as possible, and particularly so far as respects the constitutional difficulty."

In still other ways Jefferson's presidency was marked by Federalist policies which encouraged the growth of central power. Internal improvements loomed large in Jefferson's mind. While many turnpikes and canals were financed by private and state capital, he realized that Federal support would be necessary, especially in the western part of the nation. With the use of Federal money obtained from the sale of public lands, and (later) aided by direct congressional appropriations, the groundwork for the famous Cumberland road was established during Jefferson's administration. He enthusiastically supported Gallatin's plan to spend twenty million dollars of Federal funds on a network of national roads and canals. Other more pressing problems intervened, however, and it was left to later administrations to finance these local and interstate programs. If Hamilton had pressed for internal improvements in the 1790's (he suggested them in the *Report on Manufactures*), Jefferson probably would have raised constitutional objections.

Finally, is not Jefferson's change of tack further reflected in the political history of that era? Over the span of a few years it seemed as if each party had somehow reversed directions. In 1798–99 Jefferson and Madison penned the Virginia and Kentucky Resolutions as an answer to the Federalists' infamous Alien and Sedition Acts. In 1808–9 more radical but comparable rumblings of dissatisfaction emanated from some New England Federalists over Jefferson's Embargo Act. For the embargo, says one of Jefferson's biographers, was "the most arbitrary, inquisitorial, and confiscatory measure formulated in American legislation up to the period of the Civil War." Further, both parties splintered during Jefferson's administration. Many moderate Federalists, like John Quincy Adams, found themselves in closer harmony with Administration policy than with Essex Junto beliefs. And Jefferson's actions alienated old comrades, like John Randolph, Jr., whose supporters were called the Tertium Quids. It is interesting to note that there is no historical consensus of why, when, how, or what precipitated the break between Randolph and Jefferson. Randolph is always referred to as brilliant but erratic; and whatever immediate reason is alleged, the cause somehow has to do with Randolph's personality and Jefferson's betrayal of the true doctrines.

It is part of Jefferson's greatness that he could inspire a myth and project an image. But one must not confuse myth and reality, shadow and substance. Thomas Jefferson as he was, and Thomas Jefferson as people perceived him, are quite different. While both concepts of course, are of equal value in understanding our past, it is always the historian's task to make the distinction. Too often, in Jefferson's case, this has not been done. Too often the biographers have described the myth—have taken at face value the popular view of Jefferson and his enemies, contained in the vitriolic newspaper articles and pamphlets, the passionate debates and fiery speeches of that period—and missed or misconstrued the reality.

This is understandable. Even the principals inevitably became involved and helped to propagate the exaggerated images of the 1790's and thus misunderstood one another's aims and motives. Jefferson, according to his grandson, never considered Federalist fulminations "as abusing him; they had never known him. They had created an imaginary being clothed with odious attributes, to whom they gave his name; and it was against that creature of their imaginations they had levelled their anathemas." John Adams, reminiscing in a letter to Jefferson, wrote: "Both parties have excited artificial terrors and if I were summoned as a witness to say upon oath, which party had excited . . . the most terror, and which had really felt the most, I could not give a more sincere answer, than in the vulgar style 'Put them in a bag and shake them, and then see which comes out first.' "

On March 4, 1801, following a decade of verbal violence, many Americans were surprised to hear that "We are all republicans—we are all federalists." Some historians act as if they, too, are surprised. These historians then describe Jefferson's administration as if some great change took place in his thinking, and conclude that he "outfederalized the Federalists." This is a specious view, predicated on an ultraradical Jefferson of the 1790's in constant debate with an ultraconservative

Hamilton. Certainly Jefferson as president had to change. Certainly at times he had to modify, compromise, and amend his previous views. To conclude, however, that he outfederalized the Federalists is to miss the enormous consistency of Jefferson's beliefs and practices.

Jefferson was ever a national patriot second to none, not even to Hamilton. He always conceived of the United States as a unique experiment, destined for greatness so long as a sharp line isolated American civilization from European infection. Thus he strongly advised our youth to receive their education at home rather than in European schools, lest they absorb ideas and traits he considered "alarming to me as an American." From "Notes on Virginia" to his advice at the time of Monroe's doctrine, Jefferson thought of America first. It matters not that Hamilton was the better prophet; Jefferson was the better American. The French minister Adet once reported: "Although Jefferson is the friend of liberty . . . although he is an admirer of the efforts we have made to cast off our shackles . . . Jefferson, I say, is an American, and as such, he cannot sincerely be our friend. An American is the born enemy of all the peoples of Europe."

Jefferson's nature was always more practical than theoretical, more common-sensical than philosophical. Certainly the essence of his Declaration of Independence is a Lockean justification of revolution; but, said Jefferson, "It was . . . an expression of the American mind," meant "to place before mankind the common sense of the subject." Jefferson always preferred precision to "metaphysical subtleties." The Kentucky and Virginia Resolutions can be understood only as a specific rebuttal of the Sedition Act. "I can never fear that things will go far wrong," wrote Jefferson, "where common sense has fair play."

One must also remember that Hamilton's power lessened considerably in the last four years of Federalist rule. He had a strong coterie of admirers, but the vast body of Federalists sided with John Adams. Despite all Hamilton did to insure Adams' defeat, and despite the split in Federalist ranks, the fact that Jefferson's victory in 1801 was won by a narrow margin indicated Federalist approval of Adams' actions. Certainly the people at that time—Jefferson and Adams included—regarded 1801 as the year of revolution. But if historians must have a revolution, perhaps Adams' split with the Hamiltonians is a better date. "The mid-position which Adams desired to achieve," writes Manning Dauer, "was adopted, in the main, by Jefferson and his successors."

To be sure, the two men disagreed on many matters of basic importance. Jefferson placed his faith in the free election of a virtuous and talented natural aristocracy; Adams did not. Within the constitutional balance, Jefferson emphasized the power of the lower house; Adams would give greater weight to the executive and judiciary. Jefferson, as a general rule, favored a strict interpretation of the Constitution; Adams did not

fear broad construction. Both believed that human beings enjoyed inalienable rights, but only Jefferson had faith in man's perfectability.
Jefferson could say, "I like a little rebellion now and then. It is like a
storm in the atmosphere"; Adams had grown more conservative since
1776. Jefferson always defended and befriended Thomas Paine; Adams
found Edmund Burke's position on the French Revolution more palat-
able.

Yet, the sages of Quincy and Monticello were both moderate and practical men. Despite the obvious and basic contrasts, both Adams and Jefferson stood side by side on certain essentials: to avoid war, to quiet
factionalism, to preserve republican government. Their warm friendship, renewed from 1812 to 1826 in a remarkable and masterful correspondence, was based on frankness, honesty, and respect. "About facts,"
Jefferson wrote, "you and I cannot differ, because truth is our mutual
guide; And if any opinions you may express should be different from
mine, I shall receive them with the liberality and indulgence which I ask
for my own." Jefferson and Adams represent, respectively, the quint-
essence of the very best in American liberalism and conservatism. Their
indestructible link, then, was "a keen sense of national consciousness," a
realization that America's destiny was unique. This is the meaning of
Jefferson's words: "We are all republicans—we are all federalists."

Jacksonian democracy vs. the business community

Arthur M. Schlesinger, Jr.

The Jacksonian revolution rested on premises which the struggles
of the thirties hammered together into a kind of practical social philosophy. The outline of this way of thinking about society was clear. It was
stated and restated, . . . on every level of political discourse from presidential messages to stump speeches, from newspaper editorials to private
letters. It provided the intellectual background without which the party
battles of the day cannot be understood.

I

The Jacksonians believed that there was a deep-rooted conflict in
society between the "producing" and "non-producing" classes—the farm-

ers and laborers, on the one hand, and the business community on the other. The business community was considered to hold high cards in this conflict through its network of banks and corporations, its control of education and the press, above all, its power over the state: it was therefore able to strip the working classes of the fruits of their labor. "Those who produce all wealth," said Amos Kendall, "are themselves left poor. They see principalities extending and palaces built around them, without being aware that the entire expense is a tax upon themselves."

If they wished to preserve their liberty, the producing classes would have to unite against the movement "to make the rich richer and the potent more powerful." Constitutional prescriptions and political promises afforded no sure protection. "We have heretofore been too disregardful of the fact," observed William M. Gouge, "that social order is quite as dependent on the laws which regulate the distribution of wealth, as on political organization." The program now was to resist every attempt to concentrate wealth and power further in a single class. Since free elections do not annihilate the opposition, the fight would be unceasing. "The struggle for power," said C. C. Cambreleng, "is as eternal as the division of society. A defeat cannot destroy the boundary which perpetually separates the democracy from the aristocracy."

The specific problem was to control the power of the capitalistic groups, mainly Eastern, for the benefit of the noncapitalist groups, farmers and laboring men, East, West and South. The basic Jacksonian ideas came naturally enough from the East, which best understood the nature of business power and reacted most sharply against it. The legend that Jacksonian democracy was the explosion of the frontier, lifting into the government some violent men filled with rustic prejudices against big business, does not explain the facts, which were somewhat more complex. Jacksonian democracy was rather a second American phase of that enduring struggle between the business community and the rest of society which is the guarantee of freedom in a liberal capitalist state.

Like any social philosophy, Jacksonian democracy drew on several intellectual traditions. Basically, it was a revival of Jeffersonianism, but the Jeffersonian inheritance was strengthened by the infusion of fresh influences; notably the antimonopolistic tradition, formulated primarily by Adam Smith and expounded in America by Gouge, Legett, Sedgwick, Cambreleng; and the pro-labor tradition, formulated primarily by William Cobbett and expounded by G. H. Evans, Ely Moore, John Ferral.

II

The inspiration of Jeffersonianism was so all-pervading and fundamental for its every aspect that Jacksonian democracy can be properly regarded as a somewhat more hard-headed and determined version of Jeffersonian democracy. But it is easy to understate the differences. Jefferson himself, though widely revered and quoted, had no personal influence on any of the leading Jacksonians save perhaps Van Buren. Madison and Monroe were accorded still more vague and perfunctory homage. The radical Jeffersonians, Taylor, Randolph and Macon, who had regarded the reign of Virginia as almost an era of betrayal, were much more vivid in the minds of the Jacksonians.

Yet even Taylor's contributions to the later period have been exaggerated. His great work, the *Inquiry into the Principles and Policy of the Government of the United States*, published in 1814 just before the Madisonian surrender, had no significant contemporary vogue except among the faithful; and its difficult style, baffling organization and interminable length prevented it ever from gaining wide currency. By Jackson's presidency it was long out of print. In 1835 it was reported unobtainable in New York and to be procured only "with great difficulty" in Virginia. There is little trace of its peculiar terminology in the Jacksonian literature.

While the *Inquiry* properly endured as the most brilliant discussion of the foundations of democracy, many of its details were in fact obsolete by 1830. It was oriented to an important degree around the use of the national debt as the mechanism of aristocracy; in Jackson's day the debt had been extinguished but the aristocracy remained. Moreover, Taylor's arguments against executive power, against the party system and for a revivified militia had lost their point for the Jacksonians. George Bancroft voiced a widely felt need when he called, in 1834, for a general work on American society. "Where doubts arise upon any point relating to the business of government," one radical wrote in response, "no dependence can be placed upon any treatise that has yet appeared which professes to discuss this subject. You must draw upon your own resources, you must think,—and think alone."

The obsolescence of Taylor was caused by the enormous change in the face of America. The period of conservative supremacy from 1816 to 1828 had irrevocably destroyed the agricultural paradise, and the Jacksonians were accommodating the insights of Jefferson to the new concrete situations. This process of readjustment involved a moderately thorough overhauling of favorite Jeffersonian doctrines.

The central Jefferson hope had been a nation of small freeholders, each acquiring thereby so much moral probity, economic security and political independence as to render unnecessary any invasion of the rights or liberties of others. The basis of such a society, as Jefferson clearly recognized, was agriculture and handicraft. What was the status of the Jeffersonian hope now that it was clear that, at best, agriculture must share the future with industry and finance?

Orestes A. Brownson exhausted one possibility in his essay on "The

Laboring Classes." He reaffirmed the Jeffersonian demand: "we ask that every man become an independent proprietor, possessing enough of the goods of this world, to be able by his own moderate industry to provide for the wants of his body." But what, in practice, would this mean? As Brownson acknowledged years later, his plan would have "broken up the whole modern commercial system, prostrated the great industries, . . . and thrown the mass of the people back on the land to get their living by agricultural and mechanical pursuits." Merely to state its consequences was to prove its futility. The dominion of the small freeholder was at an end.

The new industrialism had to be accepted: banks, mills, factories, industrial capital, industrial labor. These were all distasteful realities for orthodox Jeffersonians, and, not least, the propertyless workers. "The mobs of great cities," Jefferson had said, "add just so much to the support of pure government, as sores do to the strength of the human body." The very ferocity of his images expressed the violence of his feelings. "When we get piled upon one another in large cities, as in Europe," he told Madison, "we shall become corrupt as in Europe, and go to eating one another as they do there." It was a universal sentiment among his followers. "No man should live," Nathaniel Macon used to say, "where he can hear his neighbour's dog bark."

Yet the plain political necessity of winning the labor vote obliged a change of mood. Slowly, with some embarrassment, the Jeffersonian preferences for the common man were enlarged to take in the city workers. In 1833 the *New York Evening Post,* declaring that, if anywhere, a large city of mixed population would display the evils of universal suffrage, asked if this had been the case in New York and answered: No. Amasa Walker set out the same year to prove that "great cities are not *necessarily,* as the proverb says, 'great sores,'" and looked forward cheerily to the day when they would be "great fountains of healthful moral influence, sending forth streams that shall fertilize and bless the land." The elder Theodore Sedgwick added that the cause of the bad reputation of cities was economic: "it is the sleeping in garrets and cellars; the living in holes and dens; in dirty, unpaved, unlighted streets, without the accommodations of wells, cisterns, baths, and other means of cleanliness and health"—clear up this situation, and cities will be all right.

Jackson himself never betrayed any of Jefferson's revulsion to industrialism. He was, for example, deeply interested by the mills of Lowell in 1833, and his inquiries respecting hours, wages and production showed, observers reported, "that the subject of domestic manufactures had previously engaged his attentive observation." His presidential allusions to the "producing classes" always included the workingmen of the cities. . . .

III

In several respects, then, the Jacksonians revised the Jeffersonian faith for America. They moderated that side of Jeffersonianism which talked of agricultural virtue, independent proprietors, "natural" property, abolition of industrialism, and expanded immensely that side which talked of economic equality, the laboring classes, human rights and the control of industrialism. This readjustment enabled the Jacksonians to attack economic problems which had baffled and defeated the Jeffersonians. It made for a greater realism, and was accompanied by a general toughening of the basic Jeffersonian conceptions. While the loss of "property" was serious, both symbolically and intellectually, this notion had been for most Jeffersonians somewhat submerged next to the romantic image of the free and virtuous cultivator; and the Jacksonians grew much more insistent about theories of capitalist alienation. Where, for the Jeffersonians, the tensions of class conflict tended to dissolve in vague generalizations about the democracy and the aristocracy, many Jacksonians would have agreed with A. H. Wood's remark, "It is in vain to talk of Aristocracy and Democracy—these terms are too variable and indeterminate to convey adequate ideas of the present opposing interests; the division is between the rich and the poor—the warfare is between them."

This greater realism was due, in the main, to the passage of time. The fears of Jefferson were now actualities. One handled fears by exorcism, but actualities by adjustment. For the Jeffersonians mistrust of banks and corporations was chiefly a matter of theory; for the Jacksonians it was a matter of experience. The contrast between the scintillating metaphors of John Taylor and the sober detail of William M. Gouge expressed the difference. Jefferson rejected the Industrial Revolution and sought to perpetuate the smiling society which preceded it (at least, so the philosopher; facts compelled the President toward a different policy), while Jackson, accepting industrialism as an ineradicable and even useful part of the economic landscape, sought rather to control it. Jeffersonian democracy looked wistfully back toward a past slipping further every minute into the mists of memory, while Jacksonian democracy came straightforwardly to grips with a rough and unlovely present.

The interlude saw also the gradual unfolding of certain consequences of the democratic dogma which had not been so clear to the previous generation. Though theoretically aware of the relation between political and economic power, the Jeffersonians had been occupied, chiefly, with establishing political equality. This was their mission, and they had little time to grapple with the economic questions.

But the very assertion of political equality raised inevitably the whole range of problems involved in property and class conflict. How could political equality mean anything without relative economic equality among the classes of the country? This question engaged the Jacksonians. As Orestes A. Brownson said, "A Loco-foco is a Jeffersonian Democrat, who having realized political equality, passed through one phase of the revolution, now passes on to another, and attempts the realization of social equality, so that the actual condition of men in society shall be in harmony with their acknowledged rights as citizens." This gap between Jeffersonian and Jacksonian democracy enabled men like John Quincy Adams, Henry Clay, Joseph Story and many others, who had been honest Jeffersonians, to balk at the economic extremities to which Jackson proposed to lead them.

The Jacksonians thus opened irrevocably the economic question, which the Jeffersonians had only touched halfheartedly. Yet, while they clarified these economic implications of democracy, the Jacksonians were no more successful than their predecessors in resolving certain political ambiguities. Of these, two were outstanding—the problem of the virtue of majorities, and the problem of the evil of government. . . .

IV

The radical democrats had a definite conception of their relation to history. From the Jeffersonian analysis, fortified by the insights of Adam Smith and Cobbett, they sketched out an interpretation of modern times which gave meaning and status to the Jacksonian struggles.

Power, said the Jacksonians, goes with property. In the Middle Ages the feudal nobility held power in society through its monopoly of land under feudal tenure. The overthrow of feudalism, with the rise of new forms of property, marked the first step in the long march toward freedom. The struggle was carried on by the rising business community— "commercial, or business capital, against landed capital; merchants, traders, manufacturers, artizans, against the owners of the soil, the great landed nobility." It lasted from the close of the twelfth century to the Whig Revolution of 1688 in Britain.

The aristocracy of capital thus destroyed the aristocracy of land. The business classes here performed their vital role in the drama of liberty. The victory over feudalism, as the *Democratic Review* put it, "opened the way for the entrance of the democratic principle into the Government." But the business community gained from this exploit an undeserved reputation as the champion of liberty. Its real motive had been to establish itself in power, not to free mankind; to found government on property, not on the equal rights of the people. "I know perfectly well what I am saying," cried George Bancroft, "and I assert expressly, and challenge contradiction, that in all the history of the world there is not to be found an instance of a commercial community establishing rules for self-government upon democratic principles." "It is a mistake to suppose commerce favorable to liberty," added Fenimore Cooper. "Its tendency is to a monied aristocracy." "Instead of setting man free," said Amos Kendall, it has "only increased the number of his masters."

The next great blow for liberty was the American Revolution, "effected not in favor of men in classes; . . . but in favor of men." But the work of Hamilton halted the march of democracy. "He established the money power," wrote Van Buren, "upon precisely the same foundations upon which it had been raised in England." The subsequent history of the United States was the struggle to overthrow the Hamiltonian policy and fulfill the ideals of the Revolution.

What of the future? The Jacksonians were sublimely confident: history was on their side. "It is now for the yeomanry and the mechanics to march at the head of civilization," said Bancroft. "The merchants and the lawyers, that is, the moneyed interest broke up feudalism. The day for the multitude has now dawned." "All classes, each in turn, have possessed the government," exclaimed Brownson; "and the time has come for all predominance of class to end; for Man, the People to rule."

This was not simply a national movement. It was a movement of all people, everywhere, against their masters, and the Jacksonians watched with keen interest the stirrings of revolt abroad. Jackson and his cabinet joined in the celebrations in Washington which followed the Revolution of 1830 in France; and Van Buren, as Secretary of State, ordered the new government informed that the American people were "universally and enthusiastically in favor of that change, and of the principle upon which it was effected." (The Whigs, on the other hand, in spite of Clay's support of national revolutions in Greece and South America, remained significantly lukewarm.) Lamennais, the eloquent voice of French popular aspirations, was read in Jacksonian circles. The *Paroles d'un Croyant* influenced Orestes A. Brownson, and in 1839 *Le Livre du Peuple* was published in Boston under the title of *The People's Own Book*, translated by Nathaniel Greene, postmaster of Boston, brother of Charles Gordon Greene of the *Post* and intimate of David Henshaw.

Democrats followed with similar enthusiasm the progress of the Reform Bill in England, while the Whigs sympathized with the Tories. The Chartist uprisings at the end of the decade were greeted with delight by the Democratic press. British reformers returned this interest. Not only Cobbett and Savage Landor but the veteran radical Jeremy Bentham observed Jackson's administration with approval. Bentham, a friend of John Quincy Adams, had been disappointed at the triumph in 1828 of this military hero; but early in 1830, as he huddled by his hissing steam radiator, he heard read aloud Jackson's first message to Congress. The old man was highly pleased to discover greater agreement with the new President than with the old. Later he wrote that lengthy and cryptic memorandum entitled *Anti-Senatica*, intended to aid Jackson in the problems of his administration.

Jacksonians everywhere had this faith in the international significance of their fight. For this reason, as well as from a desire to capture their votes, Democratic leaders made special appeals to newly naturalized citizens. Where many Whigs tended to oppose immigration and demand sanctions against it, Democrats welcomed the newcomers with open arms and attacked the nativist agitation. The United States must remain a refuge from tyranny. "The capitalist class," said Samuel J. Tilden, "has banded together all over the world and organized the *modern dynasty of associated wealth,* which maintains an unquestioned ascendency over most of the civilized portions of our race." America was the proving-ground of democracy, and it was the mission of American Democrats to exhibit to the world the glories of government by the people. They were on the spearhead of history. They would not be denied. "With the friends of freedom throughout the world," declared Theophilus Fisk, "let us be co-workers." "The People of the World," cried Fanny Wright, "have but one Cause."

The jacksonians: expectant capitalists

Bray Hammond

During the half century that ended with General Jackson's election, America underwent changes perhaps the most radical and sweeping it has ever undergone in so short a time. It passed the climacteric separating a modern industrial economy from an older one of handicraft; it passed from colonial weakness through bare independence to actual power and from an unjostled rural culture to the complexities of populousness, sectionalism, urban slums, mechanized industry, and monetary credit. Men who had spent their childhood in a thin line of seaboard colonies, close even in their little cities to the edge of the westward continental wilderness, spent their late years in a tamed and wealthy land spread already to the Missouri and about to extend beyond it. They lived to ride on railways and steamships, to use the products of steam-driven machinery, to dwell in metropolitan centers, and to feel within

Reprinted from *Banks and Politics in America from the Revolution to the Civil War* by Bray Hammond. Copyright © 1957 by Princeton University Press. Reprinted by permission of Princeton University Press.

their grasp and the grasp of their sons more potential and accessible wealth than had ever before excited the enterprise of man.

An outstanding factor in the changes that came about was the flow of immigration from Europe. Between 1790 and 1840 the population grew from 4,000,000 to 17,000,000. In the latter year an average of 230 immigrants entered the country daily. Ten years later it was over 1,000 daily. The area of settlement and exploitation expanded swiftly under the pressure of this movement. While General Jackson was President the federal union came to include twice as many states as it had begun with and held territory that recently had belonged to Spain and France. It was shortly to add regions in the South and West taken from Mexico and regions in the Northwest that Great Britain claimed. Its expansion seemed irresistible.

The changes in social outlook were profound. Steam was generating conceptions of life, liberty, and the pursuit of happiness that were quite alien to Thomas Jefferson's; and the newcomers pushing into the country from Europe had more impatient economic motives than their 18th-century predecessors. People were led as they had not been before by visions of money-making. Liberty became transformed into *laisser faire*. A violent, aggressive, economic individualism became established. The democracy became greedy, intolerant, imperialistic, and lawless. It opened economic advantages to those who had not previously had them; yet it allowed wealth to be concentrated in new hands only somewhat more numerous than before, less responsible, and less disciplined. There were unenterprising and unpropertied thousands who missed entirely the economic opportunities with which America was thick. There was poverty in the eastern cities and poverty on the frontier. Those who failed to hold their own in the struggle were set down as unfit.

Wealth was won and lost, lost and won. Patient accumulation was contemned. People believed it was not what they saved but what they made that counted. Jay Cooke, one of America's future millionaires, who was scarcely born poor on a farm but primitively at least, in a frontier settlement, was already on his way to fortune in a private banking firm before the age of twenty and writing home about his work with enthusiasm. This was in the winter of 1839–1840. "My bosses are making money fast," he said. "This business is always good, and those who follow it in time become rich. . . . Among our customers are men of every age and every position in society, from the hoary miser to the dashing buck who lives upon his thousands. Through all grades I see the same all-pervading, all-engrossing anxiety to grow rich." Something of the same sort, to be sure, was taking place in western Europe and especially in Great Britain. Half the people and most of the money for America's transformation came from there. But though industrial and technological revolution occurred also in the Old World, in the New, where vast resources awaited exploitation, it produced a dazzling, democratic expansion experienced nowhere else. The situation was such that the rallying cry, *"Laissez nous faire!"* expressed the views of Americans perfectly, when translated.

Socially, the Jacksonian revolution signified that a nation of democrats was tired of being governed, however well, by gentlemen from Virginia and Massachusetts. As Professor Sumner observed, what seems to have enchanted people with General Jackson when he became a candidate for President was not any principles or policies he advocated but his breaches of decorum, real or alleged. Economically, the revolution signified that a nation of potential money-makers could not abide traditionary, conservative limitations on business enterprise, particularly by capitalists in Philadelphia. The Jacksonian revolution was a consequence of the Industrial Revolution and of a farm-born people's realization that now anyone in America could get rich and through his own efforts, if he had a fair chance. A conception of earned wealth arose which rendered the self-made man as superior morally to the hereditary well-to-do as the agrarian had been. It was like the conception which led Theodoric the Great to boast that he held Italy solely by right of conquest and without the shadow of legal, that is, hereditary right. The humbly born and rugged individualists who were gaining fortunes by their own toil and sweat, or wits, were still simple Americans, Jeffersonian, anti-monopolistic, anti-governmental, but fraught with the spirit of enterprise and fired with a sense of what soon would be called manifest destiny. They envied the social and economic advantages of the established urban capitalists, mercantile and financial; and they fought these aristocrats with far more zeal and ingenuity than the agrarians ever had. They resented the federal Bank's interference with expansion of the monetary supply. They found it bestriding the path of enterprise, and with Apollyon's brag but Christian's better luck they were resolved to spill its soul. They democratized business under a great show of agrarian idealism and made the age of Jackson a festival of *laisser faire* prelusive to the age of Grant and the robber barons.

In their attack on the Bank of the United States, the Jacksonians still employed the vocabulary of their agrarian backgrounds. The phraseology of idealism was adapted to money-making, the creed of an earlier generation becoming the cant of its successor. Their terms of abuse were "oppression," "tyranny," "monied power," "aristocracy," "wealth," "privilege," "monopoly"; their terms of praise were "the humble," "the poor," "the simple," "the honest and industrious." Though their cause was a sophisticated one of enterpriser against capitalist, of banker against regulation, and of Wall Street against Chestnut, the language was the same as if they were all back on the farm. Neither the President, nor his advisers, nor their followers saw any discrepancy between the concept of freedom in an age of agrarianism and the concept of freedom in one of enterprise. Only the poets and philosophers were really aware that a discrepancy existed and though troubled by it their vision was far from clear. Notwithstanding their language, therefore, the Jacksonians' destruction of the Bank of the United States was in no sense a blow at capitalism or property or the "money power." It was a blow at an older set of capitalists by a newer, more numerous set. It was incident to the democratization of business, the diffusion of enterprise among the mass of people, and the transfer of economic primacy from an old and conservative merchant class to a newer, more aggressive, and more numerous body of business men and speculators of all sorts.

The Jacksonians were unconventional and skillful in politics. In their assault on the Bank they united five important elements, which, incongruities notwithstanding, comprised an effective combination. These were Wall Street's jealousy of Chestnut Street, the business man's dislike of the federal Bank's restraint upon bank credit, the politician's resentment at the Bank's interference with states' rights, popular identification of the Bank with the aristocracy of business, and the direction of agrarian antipathy away from banks in general to the federal Bank in particular. Destruction of the Bank ended federal regulation of bank credit and shifted the money center of the country from Chestnut Street to Wall Street. It left the poor agrarian as poor as he had been before and it left the money power possessed of more and more power than ever.

By the term "Jacksonian" I mean not merely the President's Democratic supporters, whom he still called Republican, but in particular his closest advisers and sharers in responsibility. These included most of his "Kitchen Cabinet," some of his official Cabinet, and a number of others. Those most responsible for the destruction of the Bank, without whose urgency and help it might not have been undertaken or achieved, were all either business men or closely concerned with the business world. Named in the approximate order of their appearance, they were Duff Green, Samuel Ingham, Isaac Hill, Martin Van Buren, Amos Kendall, Francis Preston Blair, Churchill C. Cambreleng, Roger B. Taney, and David Henshaw—all but Taney being or becoming men of wealth. They did not include Major William B. Lewis, a Tennessee planter, one of the General's oldest friends and the only one of his intimates not openly hostile to the Bank. Others of importance were Thomas Hart Benton, James K. Polk, Levi Woodbury, Benjamin F. Butler, Jacob Barker, Reuben M. Whitney, William Gouge, and James A. Hamilton.

*   *   *

With the business interests and objectives of the Jacksonians I have no quarrel save for the cant which made the conflict over the Bank of the United States appear to be one of idealism against lucre and of human rights against property rights. The Jacksonians were no less drawn by lucre than the so-called conservatives, but rather more. They had no greater concern for human rights than the people who had what they were trying to get. The millionaires created by the so-called Jacksonian revolution of "agrarians" against "capitalists"—of the democracy against the money-power—were richer than those they dispossessed, they were more numerous, they were quite as ruthless; and *laisser faire*, after destroying the monopolies and vested rights the Jacksonians decried, produced far greater ones. There was nothing sacred about the federal Bank. The defense of it is simply that it was very useful and if not perfect it could have been improved, had its enemies felt any interest in improving it. The Jacksonians paid no heed to its merits but canted virtuously about the rich and the poor, hydras, and other irrelevancies. This was good politics. But it cannot conceal the envy and acquisitiveness that were their real motives. What the Jacksonians decided on, they directed their propaganda toward, and got. What they went for, they fetched, like Amos Kendall. An unusual number of them were not only business men but journalists, and gained both profit and influence through the press—notably Duff Green, Amos Kendall, Francis Preston Blair, Isaac Hill, and David Henshaw. They told the world it was governed too much. They vied with their great contemporary James Gordon Bennett in a glib and vigorous style. The Washington *Globe*, the organ of the administration, was attractively printed on good paper, every active Jacksonian had to take it, and, its contents aside, even the best people could feel satisfied to have it lying on the parlor table. It relied otherwise on unashamed, repetitious adulation of Andrew Jackson and defamation of his enemies. It presented matters in black and white, Bank and President, hydra and hero. "Many a time," Amos Kendall is made to say in John Pendleton Kennedy's satire, *Quod-libet,* "have I riveted by diligent hammering, a politic and necessary fabrication upon the credulity of the people—so fast that no art of my adversary could tear it away to make room for the truth. Therefore, I say to you and our democratic friends—hammer without ceasing."

Andrew Jackson himself had been lawyer, legislator, jurist, merchant, and land speculator, but principally planter and soldier. His origin was humble and agrarian. He was a self-made man. He belonged to an aristocracy of a frontier sort peculiar to the Southwest of his day—landed, proud, individualistic, slave-owning, and more bound by the cruder conventions than the politer ones. Cock-fighting, betting, horse-racing, and the punctilio of the duel seem to have satisfied its cultural needs. It was without the education and discipline of the older aristocracies of the sea-board. It possessed more of the aristocrat's assertive and obnoxious vices than his gentler, liberal virtues and stood on property and pretension rather than birth and breeding. In a quarrel General Jackson would resort to the field of honor if his enemy were a "gentleman" but merely beat him with a stick on sight if he were not. Such distinctions seem to have been lost on Albert Gallatin, an aristocrat of a different water, in whose fastidious judgment President Jackson was "a pugnacious animal."

Yet the distinction and courtesy of the General's manners took by surprise those who knew him first as President; he was by then unwell, grieving over the death of his wife, and softened besides by what age will sometimes do to men. He was not now the brawler in taverns and at racetracks. "I was agreeably disappointed and pleased," wrote William Lyon Mackenzie of Upper Canada in 1829—a man of considerable violence himself in word and deed—"to find in General Jackson great gentleness and benevolence of manner, accompanied by that good natured affability of address which will enable persons who wait upon him to feel at ease in his presence. . . ." When he chose, however, the General still could storm outrageously enough. He could simulate bursts of passion that terrified strangers, who shrank from having the President of the United States burst a blood vessel on their account, even though they were not fond of him. But his tongue seldom slipped. No one profited from blunders of his. What mistakes he made arose from a child-like trust in his friends and not from carelessness with his adversaries.

He was exceptionally susceptible to the flattery and suggestion of his friends. This did not impair his maintaining a forceful, determined leadership. He listened to his advisers individually and chose his plan of action himself. His native views were agrarian and Jeffersonian, though of Jefferson himself he could entertain very low opinions, and no one—not Alexander Hamilton himself—ever went further from the constitutional principles of Jefferson than Jackson did in his nullification proclamation of December 1832. With him, moreover, as with other self-made men of his time, agrarian and Jeffersonian views faded into *laisser faire*. He was a rugged individualist in all directions. He was no friend to the shiftless and indigent who got into debt and then could not get out. He paid his own debts, no matter how hard he found it to do so, and he expected others to pay theirs.

"Andrew Jackson was on the side of the capitalists," writes Mr Marquis James of his earlier career. "His first case in Nashville in 1788 had landed him as champion of the creditors against the debtors. Jackson desired wealth." He had been opposed to western relief measures taken on behalf of debtors in the ten years preceding his election to the Presidency. They were wicked, pernicious, profligate, and unconstitutional. Opinions like this put him logically on the side of the Bank of the United States, which was the pivotal creditor, and opposed him to the banks made of paper, such as the Bank of the Commonwealth of Kentucky, over which his kitchen adviser, Francis Preston Blair, had presided. But solecisms embarrassed the General very little. On the frontier more than elsewhere, the modification of an agrarian economy into an industrial and financial one was such, in William Lyon Mackenzie's words, as to "make speculation as extensive as life, and transform a Jeffersonian democracy into a nation of gamesters and our land into one great gaming house where all are forced to play, while but few can understand the game." General Jackson's prejudices were stronger than his convictions, and he was himself among the least consistent and stable of the Jacksonians. "Not only was Jackson not a consistent politician," says Professor Thomas P. Abernethy, "he was not even a real leader of democracy. He had no part whatever in the promotion of the liberal movement which was progressing in his own state. . . . He was a self-made man . . . he always believed in making the public serve the ends of the politician. Democracy was good talk with which to win the favor of the people and thereby accomplish ulterior objectives. Jackson never really championed the cause of the people; he only invited them to champion his. He was not consciously hypocritical in this. It was merely the usual way of doing business in these primitive and ingenuous times." Of his election to the Presidency Professor Richard Hofstadter writes that it was not "a mandate for economic reform; no financial changes, no crusades against the national Bank, were promised. . . . Up to the time of his inauguration Jackson had contributed neither a thought nor a deed to the democratic movement, and he was elected without a platform."

What counts is that Jackson was popular. He was a picturesque folk character, and it does his memory an injustice to make him out a statesman. "All the remodelling and recoloring of Andrew Jackson," says Professor Abernethy, "has not created a character half so fascinating as he was in reality." To the dissatisfied, whether through distress or ambition, Andrew Jackson offered a distinct and attractive change from the old school of leaders the country had had—and not the least by his want of real ideas. He became the champion of the common man, even though the latter might be no longer either frontiersman or farmer but speculator, capitalist, or entrepreneur of a new, democratic sort, who in every village and township was beginning to profit by the Industrial Revolution, the growth of population, and the expanding supply of bank credit. This new common man was manufacturer, banker, builder, carrier, and promoter. He belonged to the "active and enterprising," in the luminous contrast put by Churchill C. Cambreleng, as against the "wealthier classes." And his conflict was not the traditionary one between the static rich and the static poor but a dynamic, revolutionary one between those who were already rich and those who sought to become rich.

General Jackson was an excellent leader in the revolt of enterprise

against the regulation of credit by the federal Bank. Though the inferior
of his associates in knowledge, he was extraordinarily effective in combat. And as a popular leader he combined the simple agrarian principles
of political economy absorbed at his mother's knee with the most up-to-
date doctrine of *laisser faire*. Along with several of the best constitutional
authorities of his day—but not Mr Taney —General Jackson believed
that the notes issued by state banks were unconstitutional. In 1820 he
wrote to his friend Major Lewis: "You know my opinion as to the banks,
that is, that the constitution of our state as well as the Constitution of
the United States prohibited the establishment of banks in any state.
Sir, the tenth section of the first article of the federal Constitution is
positive and explicit, and when you read the debates in the convention
you will find it was introduced to prevent a state legislature from passing
such bills." Seventeen years later, in 1837, he wrote to Senator Benton:
"My position now is and has ever been since I have been able to form an
opinion on this subject that Congress has no power to charter a Bank and
that the states are prohibited from issuing bills of credit or granting a
charter by which such bills can be issued by any corporation or order."
Yet in effect he did as much as could be done to augment the issue of
state bank notes and was proud of what he did. Most statesmen would
feel some embarrassment in such a performance.

The Jacksonians were anything but rash. Once decided that they
should fight the Bank rather than wed with it, they developed their attack patiently, experimentally, shrewdly, probing the aristocratic victim
and teasing public interest into action. The President himself took no unnecessary chances, but those he had to take he took without fear. He was
a man of "sagacious temerity," in the words of one of his contemporaries.
His attack on the Bank was like his careful slaying of Charles Dickinson
in a duel thirty years before. His opponent had been formidable—much
younger than he and an expert marksman, which he himself was not.
Each was to have one shot. Jackson and his second had gone over the
prospects carefully and decided it would be best to wait for Dickinson to
fire first. For though Jackson would probably be hit, "he counted on the
resource of his will to sustain him until he could aim deliberately and
shoot to kill, if it were the last act of his life." So he awaited his adversary's fire and, as he had expected, he was hit. But his coat, buttoned
loosely over his breast, as was his wont, had presented a deceptive sil-
houette, and the ball had missed his heart. He concealed his hurt and
concentrated on his helpless enemy, whose life he now could take. "He
stood glowering at him for an instant, and then his long pistol arm came
slowly to a horizontal position." He aimed carefully and pulled the trig-
ger. But the hammer stopped at half-cock. The seconds consulted while
the principals stood, and Jackson was allowed to try again. Once more

he took deliberate aim, his victim waiting in evident horror, and fired. Dickinson fell, mortally hurt. "I should have hit him," Jackson asserted later, "if he had shot me through the brain." The same mystical will power, the same canny and studious appraisal of probabilities and of relative advantages and disadvantages, weighed in the conflict with the Bank. The President tantalized the frank and impatient Mr Biddle, he waited for him to make the appropriate mistakes, and then with care and effectiveness he struck. His adversaries' weaknesses were no less at his command than his own skill. . . .

Despite the fact of a strong and determined rebellion within the business world against the Bank of the United States, the fiction that the attack on the Bank was on behalf of agrarians against capitalists, of humanity against property, of the poor against the rich, and of "the people" against "the money power," has persisted. There was, to be sure, an extremely respectable minority comprising the more conservative and thoughtful men of business, Mr Gallatin, for example, and Nathan Appleton, who defended the Bank till near the end, but it will scarcely do to say that they represented the business world while C. C. Cambreleng, David Henshaw, and Reuben Whitney did not.

It is obvious that New York, besides gaining most from a successful attack on the Bank, risked the least; for it did not need, as the South and West did, the capital brought in by the Bank's branches. The West's aversion for the federal Bank was like the nationalistic resentment in a 20th-century under-developed economy which wants and needs imported capital but growls at the "imperialism" of the country that is expected to provide it. The western enemies of the Bank were moved by complex psychological and political considerations—including past distress and present dependence—while its New York enemies were moved, much more simply, by covetousness and rivalry. This was the decisive new ingredient provided in the Jacksonian attack. The agrarian prejudice had been alive since 1791 and most dangerous to the Bank a few years past during its critical days and the distress in the Ohio valley. The state bank opposition was almost as old as the agrarian. And the relative importance of the two varied with the decline of agrarianism and the growth of enterprise. New York, now the center of enterprise, added to the long-lived antagonism a hearty and acute self-interest. That Andrew Jackson proved to be the instrument of her interest was the happy result of Mr Van Buren's skill and devotion.

It goes without saying that Andrew Jackson himself did not understand what was happening. He had started with a vague, agrarian prejudice against banking which on occasion cropped up throughout his life but never led him to deny himself the service of banks or the friendship and support of bankers.* It was no great task for his advisers to arouse this dormant distrust, nourished on what he had read about the South Sea Bubble, and focus it upon the Bank in Philadelphia, a city whence he had suffered years before, at the hands of a bankrupt merchant and speculator, a harsh financial misfortune. Nor was an elaborate plot required to be agreed upon among conspirators. The first harassment of the Bank from the administration group was evidently spontaneous and simply aimed at making the Bank Jacksonian. Some time elapsed before it got under directed control. Even then there is no reason to suppose that the program was not mainly opportunistic. In the early stages the object need have been only to make sure that the charter be not renewed. To this end the General's mind must be fixed against the Bank, and the proper improvement of opportunities could be left to the discretion of those in whose path the opportunities appeared. The adviser who influenced the General most directly or who perhaps left the best record of what he did was Roger B. Taney, though he joined the Jacksonian circle late. He succeeded in filling the General's mind with a vindictiveness that Martin Van Buren or Amos Kendall would probably not have produced. They too would have killed the Bank but with less emotion and less cant. "When a great monied institution," Mr Taney told the General, "attempts to overawe the President in the discharge of his high constitutional duties, it is conclusive evidence that it is conscious of possessing vast political power which it supposes the President can be made to feel." The Taney reasoning is sound, but the premises are misrepresented, and the effect was to fill the President with bitter suspicion of the Bank; though the alleged "attempts to overawe the President"—this was written in June 1832—were the reasonable attempts of Mr Biddle to gain support for the Bank, find out what the scowls and rumblings from Washington signified, and remove the doubts that he thought were troubling the President.

But thanks to the sort of thing Mr Taney kept telling him, the President by now had few doubts such as Mr Biddle imagined. He was merely considering how best to proceed against the Bank. Replacement, he realized, was necessary, and for a long time he was fumbling over unintelligible projects to that end. One of these projects, which may be intelligible to those whose understanding has not been corrupted by some knowledge and experience of the subject, was described to James A. Hamilton, 3 June 1830. The President had in mind "a national bank chartered upon the principles of the checks and balances of our federal government, with a branch in each state, the capital apportioned agree-

* He did not cease transacting personal and family business with the Nashville office of the Bank of the United States, which he presumably dissociated from the main office in Philadelphia. The view was reasonable. Gravitation of the branches toward independence was a perennial source of weakness to the Bank; and eventually they became local banks in fact.

ably to representation and to be attached to and be made subject to supervision of the Secretary of the Treasury." He recalls having shown
Mr Hamilton "my ideas on a bank project, both of deposit (which I
think the only national bank that the government ought to be connected
with) and one of discount and deposit, which from the success of the
State Bank of South Carolina I have no doubt could be wielded profitably
to our government with less demoralizing effects upon our citizens than
the Bank that now exists. But a *national* Bank, entirely *national* Bank
of deposit is all we ought to have: but I repeat a national Bank of discount and deposit may be established upon our revenue and national
faith pledged and carried on by salaried officers, as our revenue is now
collected, with less injury to the morals of our citizens and to the destruction of our liberty than the present hydra of corruption and all the emol-
uments accrue to the nation as part of the revenue." But these rumina-
tions belonged merely to a period of waiting. As soon as a promising
arrangement offered, the President acted. He ordered the federal funds
removed from the Bank and put in the banks of his friends.

Besides contributing mainly, by this course, to a shift of the money
market from Chestnut Street to Wall Street, the General contributed to
the inflation, the speculation, and the various monetary evils which,
with a persistent agrarian bias, he blamed on banks and paper money.
There were plenty of men in his own party, among them better agrarians
than himself, who would have cleared his vision and tried to, but the old
gentleman preferred the sycophantic advisers who stimulated his suspicions and prejudices, blinded him to facts, confused him about the
nature of the federal Bank's usefulness, diverted his attention from the
possibility that it be amended and corrected instead of being destroyed,
and allowed him to declaim the most ignorant but popular clap-trap.

The nation takes shape

Marcus Cunliffe

In summing up the quality of the period 1789–1837 two tempta-
tions should be avoided. One is that of investing it with a false aura of
tranquillity. In some respects, especially up to 1815, it was a time of
prolonged crisis, full of regret and foreboding, hostility and confusion.

From *The Nation Takes Shape: 1789–1837*, by Marcus Cunliffe. Copyright © 1959
by the University of Chicago. Reprinted by permission of the University of Chicago
Press.

The other danger is of assuming that the period constitutes an "era" of its own, separate from what came before and after, instead of being merely a half-century removed from the continuum of American history.

There is nevertheless some point in regarding the period as an entity and in trying to identify its special features. After all, its terminal dates have a certain force. At least 1789 has, as the beginning of the United States under a new Constitution. The working-out of that Constitution, in its various governmental, judicial, political, economic, social, and patriotic implications, is in large part the story of the period. As for 1837, it or its near neighbors in the decade of the 1830's can be argued to mark the inauguration of another era. . . .

. . . Granted that there are some features of the time that disappear subsequently—its homogeneity of population and its pre-industrial economy are two of the chief examples—nevertheless, the American character seems to have been formed in essence within a generation of George Washington's accession to the presidency. How else are we to account for the remarkable freshness, even for the present day, of Alexis de Tocqueville's *Democracy in America,* which was based on a visit to the United States in 1831–32? "National character" is a hazy expression. But for our approximate purposes we may think of it as an assemblage of beliefs and patterns of behavior which are widely recognized, inside and outside the country in question, as being more common among its citizens than among those of other nations. If this clumsy description is acceptable, then we may go on to suggest that Tocqueville's diagnosis of American attitudes to commerce, to social class, to politics, to literature, and a dozen other matters could be applied with surprising relevance to the America of 1870 or even 1950.

One might object that Tocqueville was not really writing about the United States but about the social and political phenomenon of democracy, and that his book is therefore not a guide to American character but a brilliant piece of intellectual prophecy relating to the whole Western world. The criticism cannot be altogether brushed aside. Now and then, in the interests of his thesis, he did overstress the "democratic" ethos of America and the correspondingly "aristocratic" nature of Europe, making the one stand schematically for tomorrow and the other for yesterday. However, the objection can be answered in large part by pointing out that Tocqueville's diary of his American travels—a day-to-day record—embodies the same observations. So, broadly speaking, do the travel narratives of other contemporary European visitors, and so do the commentaries by Americans of the period when they discuss their native qualities. Then, as now, the South was held to be an exception to the prevailing American mood of egalitarian bustle. Then, as now, the more recently settled western areas were praised by some witnesses for their additional informality or "democracy" and criticized by others for their excessive uncouthness. But on the whole, whether favorable or not, the picture drawn by Tocqueville and by lesser men was consistent and is still recognizable. . . .

To observers in the early nineteenth century, then, Americans seem restless, competitive, "go-ahead" (another revealing Americanism coined in Jackson's time), egalitarian, naïve, serious, coarse and importunate yet in some ways prim and moralistic, matter-of-fact and yet imbued with vague, soaring notions of American futurity. This last point was wittily made by Tocqueville, in the comment that the American mind is either concentrated upon the practical and parochial or else diffused in vast and formless reverie, and that in between lies a vacuum. One could go on adding almost indefinitely to the list of American characteristics identified during the period, and nearly all would support the assertion that American "national character" has not altered fundamentally since its early definitions. Similarly, if we glance at the conflicting elements in the picture and at the actual controversies that have separated individual from individual and section from section in American history, there appear to be certain enduring features in the record.

However, . . . it is extremely difficult to analyze American experience in satisfactory terms. Some Europeans and a few disillusioned Americans during the period 1789–1837 gave up the effort or concluded that the effort was not worth making. The United States, they felt, was an unstable experiment, hopelessly divided within itself, lacking in all the necessary safeguards of true nationhood, like some badly designed Mississippi steamboat whirling downriver until the irrevocable collision or explosion shattered her. Even Tocqueville, immeasurably more judicious than most spectators, doubted whether the Union could long hold together—and of course it did not.

By contrast, a number of recent American historians have dwelt upon the essential soundness of their country's early disposition. Seizing like Tocqueville on the absence of feudalism as the basic clue to American national development—on the fact that she was "born in broad daylight," unhampered by the past, dating the origin of her own national epic no farther back than 1776 and therefore able to carry the national legend around with her, so to speak, as a portable heritage—seizing on this truth, these historians have interpreted America's past as an organic affair. American politics were to a considerable degree a matter of *ad hoc* local or sectional bargaining. American ideology was an affair of fine shades, qualifications, ambiguities, contradictions. Perhaps, in such a view, it could be held that Emerson came near to grasping a subtle truth. In his unsystematic, perceptive way he typified the American intellect. He may have touched the heart of American reality with his doctrine of "compensation," according to which dualities are friendly rather than inimical, since they cancel one another out and thus lead to a kind of equilibrium:

> Foolish hands may mix and mar;
> Wise and sure the issues are.
> Round they roll till dark is light.

Some of these newer interpretations are highly sophisticated, so much so that they come full circle and are able to make good use of the old cynical-contemptuous, European view of the United States as a mere shapeless agglomerate. Thus they might fasten upon and extract significance from a casual remark made by the British visitor Mrs. Trollope as she watched a Methodist camp meeting in Ohio. The passage as a whole, from her book *Domestic Manners of the Americans* (1832) is censorious. But she also admits, "I . . . experienced a strange vibration between tragic and comic feeling." In such an *aperçu* a modern commentator might find much food for thought, for it hints at the tantalizing oddity of some sides of American history that could mean little or could mean far more than appears at first glimpse. The revivalist frenzy Mrs. Trollope witnesses is cheap, banal, erotic. Yet it has a pathos, a novelty, a colloquial vigor, a directness of emotion that go deeper than the occasion—like that of a Negro spiritual (the word "spiritual" being both neologist noun and poignant adjective).

Between the sweeping disapproval of a Frances Trollope and the refined insights of a study like R. W. B. Lewis' *The American Adam: Innocence, Tragedy, and Tradition in the Nineteenth Century* (1955) come a quantity of attempts to interpret American history in terms of some bold polarity. In the widest terms of all, the division is seen as that of America versus Europe, which can be taken to imply democracy versus aristocracy, adaptability versus rigidity, innocence versus experience, and so on. Or, in the influential thesis of Frederick Jackson Turner, as West versus East, which represents a not-too-different polarity. Some scholars, for instance, now expound American history within an "Atlantic community," within which in turn there is a boundary between West and East—a boundary that shifts steadily inland across America, so that during part of the nineteenth century the eastern seaboard of the United States is linked economically and culturally with Europe rather than with the trans-Appalachian West.

Or again, there is the familiar polarity of Jefferson versus Hamilton, which can be visualized as a contest between Republicanism and Federalism, or agrarianism and capitalism, or rural life and urbanism, or debtor and creditor, or free trade and the tariff, or Jacksonianism and the "Monster Bank," or state rights and centralization in government, or

—by extension—North and South, which can be again stylized as a division between Massachusetts and Virginia or between freedom and slavery. Present in some interpretations is a theory of class conflict or of sectional controversy as being principally economic in origin.

There is much to be said for these polarities. They have the merit of clarity. They satisfy our ingrained habit of thinking dualistically, in terms of body and soul, god and devil, and so on; we respond readily, for example, to Emerson's idea of an American schism between "the party of the Past and the party of the Future" or to George Bancroft's statement of an immemorial feud between "the capitalist and laborer, the house of Have and the house of Want." They escape the current tendency in historiography to explain away conflicts as mere smoke screens behind which men maneuver and chaffer for "real" benefits.

The arguments epitomized in the string of contests cited above *were* important to those involved in them. Apart from the slavery dispute, perhaps no American controversy was as implacable as some in Europe. They often seem almost pastorally mild after one has looked at the mortal enmities of the Old World during the period. But though in this sense they might be circumscribed quarrels, some of them implied profound differences of viewpoint on how to shape the future. Americans under their new Constitution were gravely conscious that their decisions would be imprinted upon and enlarged in the lives of successive generations. Theirs, they wished to believe, was *tabula rasa*—the clean slate.

But current historiography has nevertheless made some of these polarities seem blurred and dubious; Americans even more than the rest of mankind have been described as likelier to choose "and . . . and" than "either . . . or." . . . Republicanism versus Federalism and Jackson versus the B.U.S. are instances of contests that are by no means clear cut. It is not just that we are uncertain which side is hero and which villain, but that we are not always able to say with confidence which side is which, so confusing and sudden are the shifts in allegiance. Moreover, though some of the polarities seem nearly synonymous and though all are to some extent linked with one another, it is not possible to arrange them meaningfully by parceling them into teams, like this:

America	Europe
West	East
Democracy	Aristocracy
Agrarianism	Capitalism
State Rights	Centralization
South	North

There is a rough correspondence, perhaps, in each of the two groups. But it is so rough as to be almost worthless. Worse than that, it is positively misleading. Overly simple groupings of this kind have led some American historians to attach a spurious dynamism to geography (for such men, one feels, if Bishop Berkeley had never written his celebrated line,"Westward the course of empire," it would have been necessary to invent it. How fitting that the line was stamped on the cover of the first volume of Bancroft's sonorously patriotic history, published in 1834). Others have exaggerated the difference between Europe and the United States, making Europe more tyrannical and obsolescent than it really was and the United States more freedom-loving and progressive than any nation could be under heaven. One can but maintain that Turner's frontier thesis, while "true" and "useful" within limits, suffers from being so simplistic in shape. In his day there were cogent reasons for attempting a synthesis of geography-*cum*-idealism. And in European history, partly because one is dealing with fixed geographical/ethnic areas, partly because of the severity of European controversies and their relation to a well-defined class and occupational structure, it *is* possible to make up quite coherent "teams" of the sort shown above.

For the United States, the thing cannot be done. As some recent neoconservative writings reveal, the teams will not line up properly. What is "South" doing in the left-hand table if "Aristocracy" is in the right-hand column? One cannot construct an American "conservative" or "liberal" genealogy by any straightforward method. The result is full of illegitimacies, adoptions, divorces, remarriages.

If two teams cannot be chosen, is there any other way of representing the issues of American history for the period (which, to reiterate, embodies or foreshadows most of the major problems in American domestic experience)? The word "polarity" suggests a slightly less obvious diagram, by reminding us of a compass. So let us construct a diagram of polarities set out as a kind of compass and using the same twelve labels as before. North, South, East, and West, though standing for states of mind as well as actual geographical areas of the United States, can be left in their conventional places, as if they were compass points.

This is a more plausible representation. If we regard each of the twelve "points" as a concept or a cluster of attitudes, then this diagram suggests better than the two-team listing the complexities of the American situation. In fact, the diagram could be thought of more fitly as a spectrum of continuous and continuously modified color, each "point" shading off into those adjacent. Neighboring attitudes are shown to bear a sympathetic relationship to one another—like that between "centralization" and "capitalism." In fact, so do any four attitudes within a quadrant—say "aristocracy," "South," "state rights," "agrarianism." The polar opposites can be seen as mutually antagonistic. Here is a pictorial representation that avoids some of the oversimplifications we have alluded to.

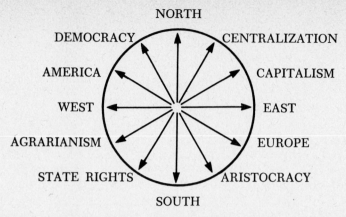

However, the diagram is still not really satisfactory, and no re-shuffling of the points will altogether remedy its weaknesses. One trouble is that it perpetuates the notion that the West is more innately "American" than the East and that the West is almost diametrically opposed to "capitalism." Also, of course, the diagram is static. It does not take into account the fluctuations of American development: the process, for instance, by which North and West were drawn together, instead of West to South, or that by which "state rights" became a southern instead of a New England doctrine.

Like the effort to compile two rival teams, it overlooks a basic truth about America. This is the truth grasped by Tocqueville, though he missed some of the historical factors that underlay it and though he emphasized the Europe-America polarity a little too much: in comparison with at any rate the Europe of his father's day, the United States was an amazingly unformed and unfettered society. What was already formed, thanks to the British heritage and to the happy outcome of the Revolutionary War, was acquisitive, Protestant, libertarian, reasonably law-abiding. The rest was a matter for posterity to determine or, rather, for the Americans themselves to impose upon posterity, since they were free agents to a unique degree.

In this whole context rather than in preoccupation with the frontier, the United States was differentiated from Europe (though, in relation to the European continent, Britain itself was a more open and flexible society).

This is not to contend that America had no problems during the period or that she solved them. She was haunted by colonialism and wracked with dissension at the same time that she grew and thrived and exulted. But the point to stress, if we are searching for interpretations, is this: There are ideological polarities of real import. The nature and mission of the United States, the struggle to make it in a new likeness without reference to the Old World, constituted a vital quest, and the continuing influence of Europe posed a genuine dilemma. The wrangle over the balance between the federal government and the states, while it later lost much of its gravity, was during the period a weighty matter. The mutual hostilities of North and South embraced profound issues of government, political economy, and human nature.

These are all significant, and so are other issues. . . . Moreover, Americans alive between 1789 and 1837 took them seriously. But—and here we reach the crux—though the polarities are more or less fixed, the personnel are not. The arguments stand fast, rooted in permanent considerations of law, order, and society, heavy and dignified (if not, as we have seen, speculative in the sense of academic philosophy). The men who employ the arguments, however, constantly change their own standpoints. They change their minds and their political parties, and the parties likewise reverse names and strategies. In 1815 New England and its "godlike" Daniel Webster adopt the extreme state-rights position, while the South and its spokesman John C. Calhoun breathe the spirit of nationalism. Fifteen years later, Calhoun and the South are sectionalist; Webster and his region stand for the federal Union. Similar examples can be found, not merely in politics, throughout the land and throughout the half-century.

Why? Not because politicians were all rogues or because Americans were all vulgar opportunists. But for two reasons. First, that since the United States was inchoate, there were no permanent sectional, political, economic, religious, or occupational groupings of the kind which are immediately recognizable in Europe and which impart a degree of coherence to European affairs even when these affairs include revolutions or other violent upheavals. American society was not entirely fluid; all sorts of rules and associations affected its operation. But they did not form inviolable taboos and imperatives. American society was tentative. Its rules could be modified; "joiners" could be and were "leavers," moving from one societal institution to another at will, and sometimes abruptly from one polar extreme to the other. Such looseness perhaps encouraged cynicism and corruptness of purpose, as permissive situations tend to. But expediency was not an inherent vice.

The second reason has already been suggested. It is that the range of possible choices was, by European standards, extraordinarily wide. Not merely was the American at liberty to change his occupation, his religious and political affiliations, his home and state; he saw before him all sorts of more solemn alternatives on which he was required by the nature of American democracy to have an opinion. His vote was endlessly solicited, his brain teased by conundrums about internal improvements, interstate commerce, the limits of suffrage, policy on land settlement, new states, tariffs. What he decided might make or mar his country. But how on such complex questions *could* he decide? No wonder that the average American changed his mind or did not bother to have an opinion or voted according to calculations of how his pocket would feel—and heavy financial stakes were frequently involved. Again, he was not being inherently irresponsible.

To recapitulate, the polarities are more or less fixed, the personnel are not. The people choose the position that matches their need or conviction of the moment and will shift to another if pressed. Some verities or some symbols of nationality—the Christian church, the Declaration of Independence, the Constitution, the memory of George Washington—are unchallenged in their broad generality; they are in the possession of virtually all Americans. The rest are a common heritage that may be repudiated or accepted as the situation dictates. The comedy of the situation is not lost upon Americans; one side of their nature, in the eyes of European visitors, is a cliché-ridden pomposity that makes them talk all too often like Supreme Court justices or like Independence Day orators. But the other side is a glorious irreverence; they coin big, nonsensical words like "splendiferous," revel in mock solemnity, delight in puncturing the national self-image, for the disparity between the unchanging pieties of nationhood and the nimble uses to which they are put is rich material for the humorist.

A diagram that sought to convey something of this would be too complicated to depict here. In part, though, it could still be conceived of as a fixed compass card of concept polarities, except that we might remove the four geographical labels—North, South, East, West—from the card and perhaps substitute other polarities. On top of the fixed card we might visualize another, floating dial. The superimposed dial would represent various sectional, political, and occupational groups pivoted loosely above the permanent card, defining positions in relation to it: a dial fluctuating, swayed, so cynical-righteous that Tocqueville shuddered a little at the intellectual slovenliness of America, so unsteady that he foresaw the dismemberment of the Union, so buoyant that he rightly marveled at the fortuitous miracle of American democracy.

Such a device may serve to elucidate much that is characteristic and puzzling in American experience. From George Washington to Andrew Jackson (and since), it is the symbol of a people at once erratic and straightforward, self-conscious and demonstrative, friendly and suspicious, tolerant and bigoted, radical and conservative, confident and nostalgic. "Inconsistencies cannot both be right," says the philosopher Imlac in Samuel Johnson's *Rasselas;* "but, imputed to man, they may both be true." His comment hints that one might enter similar claims on behalf of other peoples. Even so, as the events of the formative half-century from 1789 to 1837 may have made plain, it is no accident that while the American language abounds in such words and expressions as "footloose" and "every which way," many of America's national and state mottoes emphasize unity, sameness, perpetuity. Not all these expressions and mottoes were coined during the period but nearly all were anticipated then.

SUGGESTIONS FOR FURTHER READING

Two provocative interpretative essays on Jefferson and Jackson may be found in Richard Hofstadter, *The American Political Tradition (New York, 1948). Hofstadter plays down the differences between Hamilton and Jefferson and pictures the followers of Jackson as expectant capitalists, rather than as disgruntled farmers and workers seeking more democracy. Claude Bowers in Jefferson and Hamilton: The Struggle for Democracy in America (Boston, 1925) has written the classic interpretation of the Jefferson-Hamilton struggle as a "clear-cut fight between democracy and aristocracy." On the other hand Nathan Schachner in *The Founding Fathers (New York, 1954), is one of several recent historians who is sympathetic to Hamilton. Merrill D. Peterson, *The Jeffersonian Image in the American Mind (New York, 1960) is a fascinating study of the shifting interpretations of Jefferson.

The most controversial recent book on Jacksonian democracy is Arthur Schlesinger, *The Age of Jackson (Boston, 1945), a portion of which is reprinted here. But for a critical analysis see, Bray Hammond's review in Journal of Economic History, VI (May, 1946), 79–84. Hammond and Hofstadter, unlike Schlesinger, see little conflict in the Jackson period. John Ward in *Andrew Jackson: Symbol for an Age (New York, 1955) sees conflict, but Jackson becomes a symbol that provided direction for social advance. Marvin Meyers, on the other hand, in *Jacksonian Persuasion (Stanford, 1957) sees the followers of Jackson trapped by the past, trying desperately to recapture an agrarian dream in an age of expanding industrialism.

VI
AMERICAN ⋆
NEGRO ⋆
SLAVERY ⋆

The first Negroes in the English colonies of North America arrived in 1619; John Rolfe recorded that in that year a Dutch ship "sold" twenty Negroes in Virginia. While there is some dispute about when the institution of slavery was actually established—the early arrivals were probably indentured servants with limited terms of servitude—it is quite clear that by 1660 the Negro had become a slave. Servitude had become permanent and children of slaves according to law themselves became slaves. In the years that followed, slaves increased in numbers and gradually displaced indentured servants as the primary form of labor on Southern plantations.

Declining profits in tobacco culture in the late eighteenth century, combined with the nagging contradiction between human bondage and colonial proclamations of liberty and human rights, led many Americans to foresee an early end to slavery. These expectations dissolved, however, with the discovery of a new staple crop in the South—cotton. Moreover, Eli Whitney's invention of the cotton gin in 1793 made commercial cotton growing economically feasible and suddenly Southern planters found a new and profitable use for their slaves.

In the North, slavery gradually disappeared, but in the South the number of slaves grew rapidly as planters and farmers moved west carving plantations and farms out of the wilderness. By 1860 the nation had some four million slaves, most of them living in the cotton-growing areas. Slavery had become the South's "peculiar institution."

The existence of slavery produced a number of contradictions in American society. Many felt that the holding of human beings as property offended their religious scruples and their democratic inclinations, and often such people became militant abolitionists. Others were sure that slavery was a menace to free labor everywhere and they fought the extension of slavery into new territories. Some charged that servile labor held back economic development and consigned the South to poverty.

But perhaps the most potent of the contradictions was that between the slave and his owner. The slave was restricted in his movements, forced to work for little more than subsistence, subject to corporal punishment, and had little or no legal redress for grievances. It might be expected that such conditions in the midst of an essentially democratic society would have induced longings for freedom as well as resentments which bring on servile insurrections. Slaves who escaped from the South often wrote of their experiences in slavery in just such terms; and the elaborate precautions Southerners took to prevent revolt reflected their concern.

Yet there was another side to the question. Even as they spoke of the dangers of slave revolts, Southerners argued that the slaves were happy in their condition. On the one hand, it was explained, slaves were better treated than abolitionists and antislavery proponents charged; indeed, Negro slaves were far better off than the white "wage slaves" of the North. On the other hand, defenders of slavery noted, the Negro was incapable of understanding and appreciating freedom. The Negro was said to be inferior to the white man and had to be forced to work under direction in order to survive.

Thus debate on the Negro's response to slavery is as old as the peculiar institution itself. Historians investigating the problem have often found themselves as sharply divided as were contemporaries. If some emphasize the slave's opposition to his status, others point to the slave's docile acceptance of his lot. Some historians have emphasized race, while others find racial charac-

teristics irrelevant. Some point to the terror and repression in the slave South, while others argue that the slaveowners were generally kind to their chattels either because of an overriding paternalism or simply because they were anxious to protect a valuable investment.

A part of the debate may be seen in the following selections. Kenneth Stampp finds the slave restive under his bondage, seeking always to lessen its restraints, willing to chance punishment in order to escape, and at times even attempting outright rebellion. Implicit in his approach to the Negro in the selection given here is a point of view which he expresses explicitly in the preface to the book from which the selection is taken: "I have assumed that the slaves were merely ordinary human beings, that innately Negroes *are,* after all, only white men with black skins, nothing more, nothing less."

Stanley M. Elkins and Eugene D. Genovese do not accept this assumption nor do they accept Stampp's emphasis on conflict between slave and master. Elkins finds a peculiar Negro personality arising in the South, a personality necessary for survival in a closed social system which offered no protection for the slave. Genovese insists that the weakness of the slave's opposition to his condition stemmed from a lack of ideology, unity, and tradition; his argument rests on essentially political rather than psychological grounds.

Evaluation of this debate requires that two different sets of questions be asked. One must first assess the degree of resistance on the part of slaves. Did the slaves take every opportunity to break the chains of their bondage? Or did most of them remain docile? How significant were slave insurrections such as Nat Turner's rebellion? Such questions attempt to evaluate concrete manifestations of conflict within the slave society.

Another set of questions may help to explain the more subtle workings of Southern society. How did the experience of slavery affect the Negro himself? Did severe repression and intimidation so mold the slave's personality or political outlook that it prevented him from exhibiting overt signs of his opposition? Did such conditions actually create slaves willing to accept their position? Or did they produce resentments, frustrations, and a will to resist which, when occasions arose, led to conflict and rebellion?

A troublesome property

Kenneth M. Stampp

Slaves apparently thought of the South's peculiar institution chiefly as a system of labor extortion. Of course they felt its impact in other ways —in their social status, their legal status, and their private lives—but they felt it most acutely in their lack of control over their own time and labor. If discontented with bondage, they could be expected to direct their protests principally against the master's claim to their work. Whether the majority were satisfied with their lot, whether they willingly obeyed the master's commands, has long been a controversial question.

It may be a little presumptuous of one who has never been a slave to pretend to know how slaves felt; yet defenders of slavery did not hesitate to assert that most of them were quite content with servitude. Bondsmen generally were cheerful and acquiescent—so the argument went—because they were treated with kindness and relieved of all responsibilities; having known no other condition, they unthinkingly accepted bondage as their natural status. "They find themselves first existing in this state," observed a Northerner who had resided in Mississippi, "and pass through life without questioning the justice of their allotment, which, if they think at all, they suppose a natural one."[1] Presumably they acquiesced, too, because of innate racial traits, because of the "genius of African temperament," the Negro being "instinctively . . . contented" and "quick to respond to the stimulus of joy, quick to forget his grief." Except in rare instances when he was cruelly treated, his "peaceful frame of mind was not greatly disturbed by the mere condition of slavery."[2]

Though sometimes asserted with such assurance, it was never proved that the great majority of bondsmen had no concept of freedom and were therefore contented. It was always based upon inference. Most masters believed they understood their slaves, and most slaves apparently made no attempt to discourage this belief. Instead, they said the things they thought their masters wanted to hear, and they conformed with the rituals that signified their subservience. Rare, no doubt, was the master who never heard any of his humble, smiling bondsmen affirm their loyalty and contentment. When visitors in the South asked a slave whether he wished to

1. [Ingraham], *South-West*, II, p. 201.

2. Francis P. Gaines, *The Southern Plantation: A Study in the Development and the Accuracy of a Tradition* (New York, 1924), p. 244.

258

be free, he usually replied: "No, massa, me no want to be free, have good massa, take care of me when I sick, never 'buse nigger; no, me no want to be free."[3]

This was dubious evidence, as some slaveholders knew and others learned. (They would have acknowledged the validity of an affirmation later to be made by a post-bellum South Carolinian: "the white man does not know the Negro so well as he thinks he does."[4]) A Virginia master believed that slaves had their faculties "sharpened by constant exercise" and that their perceptions were "extremely fine and acute." An overseer decided that a man who "put his confidence in a Negro . . . was simply a Damned Fool." A Georgia planter concluded: "So deceitful is the Negro that as far as my own experience extends I could never in a single instance decipher his character. . . . We planters could never get at the truth."[5] When advertising for runaways, masters repeatedly confirmed these opinions by describing them as being "very artful," as acting and conversing in a way "calculated to deceive almost any one," and (most frequently) as possessing a "pretty glib and plausible tongue." Yet proslavery writers swallowed whole the assurances of contentment which these glib-tongued "scoundrels" gave them.

Since there are few reliable records of what went on in the minds of slaves, one can only infer their thoughts and feelings from their behavior, that of their masters, and the logic of their situation. That they had no understanding of freedom, and therefore accepted bondage as their natural condition, is hard to believe. They had only to observe their masters and the other free men about them to obtain a very distinct idea of the meaning and advantages of freedom. All knew that some Negroes had been emancipated: they knew that freedom was a *possible* condition for any of them. They "continually have before their eyes, persons of the same color, many of whom they have known in slavery . . . freed from the control of masters, working where they please, going whither they please, and expending their money how they please." So declared a group of Charleston whites who petitioned the legislature to expel all free persons of color from South Carolina.[6]

Untutored slaves seldom speculated about freedom as an abstraction. They naturally focused their interest upon such immediate and practical benefits as escaping severe discipline and getting increased compensation for less labor. An ex-slave explained simply what freedom meant to her: "I am now my own mistress, and need not work when I am sick. I can do my own thinkings, without having any to think for me,—to tell me when

3. Ethan A. Andrews, *Slavery and the Domestic Slave Trade in the United States* (Boston, 1836), pp. 97–99.

4. Mason Crum, *Gullah: Negro Life in the Carolina Sea Islands* (Durham, 1940), p. 80.

5. Abdy, *Journal*, II, pp. 216–17; Manigault Ms. Plantation Records, summary of plantation events, May 1863–May 1864; entry for March 22, 1867.

6. Phillips (ed.), *Plantation and Frontier*, II, pp. 108–11.

to come, what to do, and to sell me when they get ready."[7] Though she may never have heard of the doctrine of natural rights, her concept of freedom surely embraced more than its incidental aspects.

If slaves had some understanding of the pragmatic benefits of freedom, no doubt most of them desired to enjoy these benefits. Some, perhaps the majority, had no more than a vague, unarticulated yearning for escape from burdens and restraints. They submitted, but submission did not necessarily mean enjoyment or even contentment. And some slaves felt more than a vague longing, felt a sharp pang and saw a clear objective. They struggled toward it against imposing obstacles, expressing their discontent through positive action.

Were these, the actively discontented, to be found only among slaves exposed to great physical cruelty? Apparently not. Slaves of gentle masters might seek freedom as eagerly as those of cruel ones. Frederick Douglass, the most famous refugee from slavery, testified: "Beat and cuff your slave, keep him hungry and spiritless, and he will follow the chain of his master like a dog; but feed and clothe him well,—work him moderately— surround him with physical comfort,—and dreams of freedom intrude. Give him a *bad* master, and he aspires to a *good* master; give him a good master, and he wishes to become his *own* master."[8] Here was a problem confronting conscientious slaveholders. One confessed that slaveownership subjected "the man of care and feeling to more dilemmas than perhaps any other vocation he could follow. . . . To moralize and induce the slave to assimilate with the master and his interest, has been and is the great desideratum aimed at; but I am sorry to say I have long since despondent in the completion of this task."[9] Another slaveholder who vaguely affirmed that his bondsmen were "as contented as their nature will permit" was in reality agreeing with what a white man once bluntly stated before the Louisiana Supreme Court: The desire for freedom "exists in the bosom of *every* slave—whether the recent captive, or him to whom bondage has become a habit."[10]

Slaves showed great eagerness to get some—if they could not get all— of the advantages of freedom. They liked to hire their own time, or to work in tobacco factories, or for the Tredegar Iron Company, because they were then under less restraint than in the fields, and they had greater opportunities to earn money for themselves. They seized the chance to make their condition approximate that of freedmen.

But they were not satisfied with a mere loosening of the bonds. Former slaves affirmed that one had to "know the *heart* of the poor slave—learn

7. Drew, *The Refugee,* p. 177.
8. Douglass, *My Bondage,* pp. 263–64.
9. *Southern Agriculturist,* III (1830), p. 238.
10. Ebenezer Pettigrew to Mrs. Mary Shepard, September 22, 1847, Pettigrew Family Papers; Catterall (ed.), *Judicial Cases,* III, p. 568.

his secret thoughts—thoughts he dare not utter in the hearing of the white man," to understand this. "A man who has been in slavery knows, and no one else can know, the yearnings to be free, and the fear of making the attempt." While he was still in bondage Douglass wondered how white people knew that God had made black people to be slaves. "Did they go up in the sky and learn it? or, did He come down and tell them so?"[11] A slave on a Louisiana sugar plantation assured Olmsted that slaves did desire freedom, that they talked about it among themselves, and that they speculated about what they would do if they were emancipated. When a traveler in Georgia told a slave he understood his people did not wish to be free, "His only answer was a short, contemptuous laugh."[12]

If slaves yielded to authority most of the time, they did so because they usually saw no other practical choice. Yet few went through life without expressing discontent somehow, some time. Even the most passive slaves, usually before they reached middle age, flared up in protests now and then. The majority, as they grew older, lost hope and spirit. Some, however, never quite gave in, never stopped fighting back in one way or another. The "bad character" of this "insolent," "surly," and "unruly" sort made them a liability to those who owned them, for a slave's value was measured by his disposition as much as by his strength and skills. Such rebels seldom won legal freedom, yet they never quite admitted they were slaves.

Slave resistance, whether bold and persistent or mild and sporadic, created for all slaveholders a serious problem of discipline. As authors or as readers they saw the problem discussed in numberless essays with such titles as "The Management of Negroes," essays which filled the pages of southern agricultural periodicals. Many masters had reason to agree with the owner of a hundred slaves who complained that he possessed "just 100 troubles," or with the North Carolina planter who said that slaves were "a troublesome property."[13]

The record of slave resistance forms a chapter in the story of the endless struggle to give dignity to human life. Though the history of southern bondage reveals that men *can* be enslaved under certain conditions, it also demonstrates that their love of freedom is hard to crush. The subtle expressions of this spirit, no less than the daring thrusts for liberty, comprise one of the richest gifts the slaves have left to posterity. In making themselves "troublesome property," they provide reassuring evidence that slaves seldom wear their shackles lightly.

The record of the minority who waged ceaseless and open warfare

11. Northup, *Twelve Years a Slave*, pp. 206–207; Drew, *The Refugee*, pp. 43, 115; Douglass, *My Bondage*, pp. 89–91.

12. Olmsted, *Seaboard*, pp. 679–80; James Stirling, *Letters from the Slave States* (London, 1857), p. 201.

13. Gustavus A. Henry to his wife, November 25, 1849, Henry Papers; William S. Pettigrew to James C. Johnston, January 6, 1947 (copy), Pettigrew Family Papers.

against their bondage makes an inspiring chapter, also, in the history of Americans of African descent. True, these rebels were exceptional men, but the historian of any group properly devotes much attention to those members who did extraordinary things, men in whose lives the problems of their age found focus, men who voiced the feelings and aspirations of the more timid and less articulate masses. As the American Revolution produced folk heroes, so also did southern slavery—heroes who, in both cases, gave much for the cause of human freedom. . . .

According to Dr. Cartwright, there was a . . . disease peculiar to Negroes which he called *Drapetomania*: "the disease causing negroes to run away." Cartwright believed that it was a "disease of the mind" and that with "proper medical advice" it could be cured. The first symptom was a "sulky and dissatisfied" attitude. To forestall the full onset of the disease, the cause of discontent must be determined and removed. If there were no ascertainable cause, then "whipping the devil out of them" was the proper "preventive measure against absconding."[14]

Though Cartwright's dissertations on Negro diseases are mere curiosities of medical history, the problem he dealt with was a real and urgent one to nearly every slaveholder. Olmsted met few planters, large or small, who were not more or less troubled by runaways. A Mississippian realized that his record was most unusual when he wrote in his diary: "Harry ran away; *the first* negro that ever ran from me." Another slaveholder betrayed his concern when he avowed that he would "rather a negro would do anything Else than runaway."[15]

The number of runaways was not large enough to threaten the survival of the peculiar institution, because slaveholders took precautions to prevent the problem from growing to such proportions. But their measures were never entirely successful, as the advertisements for fugitives in southern newspapers made abundantly clear. Actually, the problem was much greater than these newspapers suggested, because many owners did not advertise for their absconding property. (When an owner did advertise, he usually waited until his slave had been missing for several weeks.) In any case, fugitive slaves were numbered in the thousands every year. It was an important form of protest against bondage.

Who were the runaways? They were generally young slaves, most of them under thirty, but occasionally masters searched for fugitives who were more than sixty years old. The majority of them were males, though female runaways were by no means uncommon. It is not true that most of them were mulattoes or of predominantly white ancestry. While this group was well represented among the fugitives, they were outnumbered

14. *De Bow's Review*, XII (1851), pp. 331–33.
15. Olmsted, *Back Country*, p. 476; Newstead Plantation Diary, entry for June 7, 1860; Davis (ed.), *Diary of Bennet H. Barrow*, p. 165.

by slaves who were described as "black" or of seemingly "pure" African ancestry. Domestics and skilled artisans—the ones who supposedly had the most intimate ties with the master class—ran away as well as common field-hands. . . .

"His look is impudent and insolent, and he holds himself straight and walks well." So a Louisiana master described James, a runaway slave.[16] There were always bondsmen like James. In 1669, a Virginia statute referred to "the obstinacy of many of them"; in 1802, a South Carolina judge declared that they were "in general a headstrong, stubborn race of people"; and in 1859, a committee of a South Carolina agricultural society complained of the "insolence of disposition to which, as a race, they are remarkably liable." An overseer on a Louisiana plantation wrote nervously about the many "outrageous acts" recently committed by slaves in his locality and insisted that he scarcely had time to eat and sleep: "The truth is no man can begin to attend to Such a business with any Set of negroes, without the Strictest vigilance on his part."[17] It was the minority of slaves whom his discipline could not humble (the "insolent," "surly," and "unruly" ones) that worried this overseer—and slaveholders generally. These were the slaves whose discontent drove them to drastic measures.

Legally the offenses of the rebels ranged from petty misdemeanors to capital crimes, and they were punished accordingly. The master class looked upon any offense as more reprehensible (and therefore subject to more severe penalties) when committed by a slave than when committed by a free white. But how can one determine the proper ethical standards for identifying undesirable or even criminal behavior among slaves? How distinguish a "good" from a "bad" slave? Was the "good" slave the one who was courteous and loyal to his master, and who did his work faithfully and cheerfully? Was the "bad" slave the one who would not submit to his master, and who defiantly fought back? What were the limits, if any, to which a man deprived of his freedom could properly go in resisting bondage? How accountable was a slave to a legal code which gave him more penalties than protection and was itself a bulwark of slavery? This much at least can be said: many slaves rejected the answers which their masters gave to questions such as these. The slaves did not thereby repudiate law and morality: rather, they formulated legal and moral codes of their own.

The white man's laws against theft, for example, were not supported by the slave's code. In demonstrating the "absence of moral principle" among bondsmen, one master observed: "To steal and not to be detected is a merit among them." Let a master turn his back, wrote another, and

16. New Orleans *Picayune,* November 4, 1851.
17. Hurd, *Law of Freedom and Bondage,* I, p. 232; Catterall (ed.), *Judicial Cases,* II, pp. 281–82; *De Bow's Review,* XXVI (1859), p. 107, Moore Rawls to Lewis Thompson, May 9, 1858, Lewis Thompson Papers.

some "cunning fellow" would appropriate part of his goods. No slave would betray another, for an informer was held "in greater detestation than the most notorious thief."[18]

If slaveholders are to be believed, petty theft was an almost universal "vice"; slaves would take anything that was not under lock and key. Field-hands killed hogs and robbed the corn crib. House servants helped themselves to wines, whiskey, jewelry, trinkets, and whatever else was lying about. Fugitives sometimes gained from their master unwilling help in financing the journey to freedom, the advertisements often indicating that they absconded with money, clothing, and a horse or mule. Thefts were not necessarily confined to the master's goods: any white man might be considered fair game.

Some bondsmen engaged in theft on more than a casual and petty basis. They made a business of it and thus sought to obtain comforts and luxuries which were usually denied them. A South Carolina master learned his house servants had been regularly looting his wine cellar and that one of them was involved in an elaborate "system of roguery." A planter in North Carolina found that three of his slaves had "for some months been carrying on a robbery" of meat and lard, the leader being "a young carpenter, remarkable for smartness . . . and no less worthy for his lamentable deficiency in common honesty."[19]

If the stolen goods were not consumed directly, they were traded to whites or to free Negroes. This illegal trade caused masters endless trouble, for slaves were always willing to exchange plantation products for tobacco, liquor, or small sums of money. Southern courts were kept busy handling the resulting prosecutions. One slaveholder discovered that his bondsmen had long been engaged in an extensive trade in corn. "Strict vigilance," he concluded, was necessary "to prevent them from theft; particularly when dishonesty is inherent, as is probably the case with some of them."[20] Dishonesty, as the master understood the term, indeed seemed to be a common if not an inherent trait of southern slaves.

The slaves, however, had a somewhat different definition of dishonesty in their own code, to which they were reasonably faithful. For appropriating their master's goods they might be punished and denounced by him, but they were not likely to be disgraced among their associates in the slave quarters, who made a distinction between "stealing" and "taking." Appropriating things from the master meant simply taking part of his property for the benefit of another part or, as Frederick Douglass phrased it, "taking his meat out of one tub, and putting it in another." Thus a

18. Harrison, *Gospel Among the Slaves*, p. 103; *Farmers' Register*, V (1837), p. 302.
19. Hammond Diary, entry for October 16, 1835; William S. Pettigrew to (James C. Johnston), October 3, 1850, Pettigrew Family Papers.
20. William S. Pettigrew to J. Johnston Pettigrew, March 9, 1840, Pettigrew Family Papers; Catterall (ed.), *Judicial Cases, passim*.

female domestic who had been scolded for the theft of some trinkets was reported to have replied: "Law, mam, don't say I's wicked; ole Aunt Ann says it allers right for us poor colored people to 'popiate whatever of de wite folk's blessings de Lord puts in our way." Stealing, on the other hand, meant appropriating something that belonged to another slave, and this was an offense which slaves did not condone.[21]

The prevalence of theft was a clear sign that slaves were discontented, at least with the standard of living imposed upon them. They stole food to increase or enrich their diets or to trade for other coveted commodities. Quite obviously they learned from their masters the pleasures that could be derived from the possession of worldly goods; and when the opportunity presented itself, they "took" what was denied them as slaves.

Next to theft, arson was the most common slave "crime," one which slaveholders dreaded almost constantly. Fire was a favorite means for aggrieved slaves to even the score with their master. Reports emanated periodically from some region or other that there was an "epidemic" of gin-house burnings, or that some bondsman had taken his revenge by burning the slave quarters or other farm buildings. More than one planter thus saw the better part of a year's harvest go up in flames.[22] Southern newspapers and court records are filled with illustrations of this offense, and with evidence of the severe penalties inflicted upon those found guilty of committing it.

Another "crime" was what might be called self-sabotage, a slave deliberately unfitting himself to labor for his master. An Arkansas slave, "at any time to save an hour's work," could "throw his left shoulder out of place." A Kentucky slave made himself unserviceable by downing medicines from his master's dispensary (thus showing a better understanding of the value of these nostrums than his owner). A slave woman was treated as an invalid because of "swellings in her arms"—until it was discovered that she produced this condition by thrusting her arms periodically into a beehive. Yellow Jacob, according to his master's plantation journal, "had a kick from a mule and when nearly well would bruise it and by that means kept from work."[23] Another Negro, after being punished by his owner, retaliated by cutting off his right hand; still another cut off the fingers of one hand to avoid being sold to the Deep South.[24]

A few desperate slaves carried this form of resistance to the extreme of self-destruction. Those freshly imported from Africa and those sold away

21. Douglass, *My Bondage*, pp. 189–91; Austin Steward, *Twenty-Two Years a Slave* (Canandaigua, N.Y., 1856), p. 29; Olmsted, *Seaboard*, pp. 116–17; Sellers, *Slavery in Alabama*, p. 257.

22. Davis (ed.), *Diary of Bennet H. Barrow*, p. 131 n.; Rachel O'Conner to David Weeks, June 16, 1833, Weeks Collection; S. Porcher Gaillard Ms. Plantation Journal, entry for May 9, 1856.

23. Helena (Ark.) *Southern Shield*, July 23, 1853; Buckingham, *Slave States*, I, p. 402; Gaillard Plantation Journal, entry for May 9, 1856.

24. Harriet Martineau, *Society in America* (New York, 1837), II, p. 113; Drew, *The Refugee*, p. 178.

from friends and relatives were especially prone to suicide.[25] London, a slave on a Georgia rice plantation, ran to the river and drowned himself after being threatened with a whipping. His overseer gave orders to leave the corpse untouched "to let the [other] negroes see [that] when a negro takes his own life they will be treated in this manner." A Texas planter bewailed the loss of a slave women who hanged herself after two unsuccessful breaks for freedom: "I had been offered $900.00 for her not two months ago, but damn her . . . I would not have had it happened for twice her value. *The fates pursue me.*"[26]

Some runaways seemed determined to make their recapture as costly as possible and even resisted at the risk of their own lives. One advertisement, typical of many, warned than an escaped slave was a "resolute fellow" who would probably not be taken without a "show of competent force." When, after a day-long chase, three South Carolina fugitives were cornered, they "fought desperately," inflicted numerous wounds upon their pursuers with a barrage of rocks, and "refused to surrender until a force of about forty-five or fifty men arrived."[27] In southern court records there are numerous cases of runaway slaves who killed whites or were themselves killed in their frantic efforts to gain freedom.

In one dramatic case, a Louisiana fugitive was detected working as a free Negro on a Mississippi River flatboat. His pursuers, trailing him with a pack of "Negro dogs," finally found him "standing at bay upon the outer edge of a large raft of drift wood, armed with a club and pistol." He threatened to kill anyone who got near him. "Finding him obstinately determined not to surrender, one of his pursuers shot him. He fell at the third fire, and so determined was he not to be captured, that when an effort was made to rescue him from drowning he made battle with his club, and sunk waving his weapon in angry defiance."[28]

An effort to break up an organized gang of runaways was a dangerous business, because they were often unwilling to surrender without a fight. The fugitives in one well-armed band in Alabama were building a fort at the time they were discovered. Their camp was destroyed after a "smart skirmish" during which three of them were killed.[29] Such encounters did not always end in defeat for the slaves; some runaway bands successfully resisted all attempts at capture and remained at large for years.

Ante-bellum records are replete with acts of violence committed by

25. Phillips (ed.), *Plantation and Frontier*, II, p. 31; Catterall (ed.), *Judicial Cases*, II, pp. 425–26; III, pp. 216–17; Drew, *The Refugee*, p. 178.

26. Phillips (ed.), *Plantation and Frontier*, II, p. 94; John R. Lyons to William W. Renwick, April 4, 1854, William W. Renwick Papers.

27. Petition of William Boyd to South Carolina legislature, November 29, 1858, in South Carolina Slavery Manuscripts Collection.

28. *Feliciana Whig*, quoted in Olmsted, *Back Country*, p. 474.

29. Phillips (ed.), *Plantation and Frontier*, II, pp. 90–91; Bassett, *Plantation Overseer*, pp. 78–79.

individual slaves upon masters, overseers, and other whites. A Texan complained, in 1853, that cases of slaves murdering white men were becoming "painfully frequent." "Within the last year or two many murders have taken place, by negroes upon their owners," reported a Louisiana newspaper. And a Florida editor once wrote: "It is our painful duty to record another instance of the destruction of the life of a white man by a slave."[30]

Many masters owned one or more bondsmen whom they feared as potential murderers. A Georgia planter remembered Jack, his plantation carpenter, "the most notoriously bad character and worst Negro of the place." Jack "was the only Negro ever in our possession who I considered capable of Murdering me, or burning my dwelling at night, or capable of committing any act."[31]

Slaves like Jack could be watched closely; but others appeared to be submissive until suddenly they turned on their masters. Even trusted house servants might give violent expression to long pent up feelings. One "first rate" female domestic, while being punished, abruptly attacked her mistress, "threw her down, and beat her unmercifully on the head and face." A "favorite body servant" of a "humane master who rarely or never punished his slaves" one day became insolent. Unwilling to be disciplined, this slave waylaid his owner, "knocked him down with a whiteoak club, and beat his head to a pumice."[32] Here was another reason why it seemed foolish for a master to put his "confidence in a Negro."

At times these acts of violence appeared to be for "no cause"—that is, they resulted from a slave's "bad disposition" rather than from a particular grievance. But more often they resulted from a clash of personalities, or from some specific incident. For example, a slave who had been promised freedom in his master's will, poisoned his master to hasten the day of liberation. A South Carolina bondsman was killed during a fight with an overseer who had whipped his son. In North Carolina a slave intervened while the overseer was whipping his wife, and in the ensuing battle the overseer met his death.[33]

The most common provocation to violence was the attempt of a master or overseer either to work or to punish slaves severely. An Alabama bondsman confessed killing the overseer because "he was a hard down man on him, and said he was going to be harder." Six Louisiana slaves together killed an overseer and explained in their confession that they found it impossible to satisfy him. Three North Carolina slaves killed their master when they decided that "the old man was too hard on them, and they

30. Austin *Texas State Gazette*, September 3, 1853; Alexandria (La.), *Red River Republican*, April 24, 1852, Pensacola *Gazette*, May 4, 1839.

31. Manigault Plantation Records, entry for March 22, 1867.

32. Rachel O'Conner to A. T. Conrad, May 26, 1836, Weeks Collection; Austin *Texas State Gazette*, September 23, 1854.

33. Martineau, *Society in America*, II, pp. 110–11; Catterall (ed.), *Judicial Cases*, II, pp. 206–207, 434–35.

must get rid of him."[34] During one of these crises an overseer called upon his hands to help him punish an "unmanageable" slave: "not one of them paid the least attention to me but kept on at their work." These encounters did not always lead to death, but few plantations escaped without at least one that might easily have ended in tragedy. "Things move on here in the old Style except that now and then a refractory negro has to be taken care of," was the off-hand comment of a planter.[35]

Sometimes a slave who showed sufficient determination to resist punishment managed to get the best of his owner or overseer. A proud bondsman might vow that, regardless of the consequences, he would permit no one to whip him.[36] An overseer thought twice before precipitating a major crisis with a strong-willed slave; he might even overlook minor infractions of discipline.

But an impasse such as this was decidedly unusual; if it had not been, slavery itself would have stood in jeopardy. Ordinarily these clashes between master and slave were fought out to a final settlement, and thus a thread of violence was woven into the pattern of southern bondage. Violence, indeed, was the method of resistance adopted by the boldest and most discontented slaves. Its usual reward, however, was not liberty but death!

No ante-bellum Southerner could ever forget Nat Turner. The career of this man made an impact upon the people of this section as great as that of John C. Calhoun or Jefferson Davis. Yet Turner was only a slave in Southampton County, Virginia—and during most of his life a rather unimpressive one at that. He was a pious man, a Baptist exhorter by avocation, apparently as humble and docile as a slave was expected to be. There is no evidence that he was underfed, overworked, or treated with special cruelty. If Nat Turner could not be trusted, what slave could? That was what made his sudden deed so frightening.

Somehow Turner came to believe that he had been divinely chosen to deliver his people from bondage, and he persuaded several other slaves to assist him. In due time he saw the sign for which he had waited, and early in the morning of August 22, 1831, he and his followers rose in rebellion. They began by killing the family to whom Turner belonged. As they marched through the Southampton countryside they gained additional recruits, making a total of about seventy. (Others seemed ready to join if the rebels came their way. The slave Jacob, for example, pro-

34. Catterall (ed.), *Judicial Cases*, III, pp. 238–41; Reuben Carnal to Lewis Thompson, June 17, 1855, Lewis Thompson Papers; Hardy Hardison to William S. Pettigrew, February 11, 1858, Pettigrew Family Papers.

35. Taylor, "Negro Slavery in Louisiana," pp. 258–59; Charles L. Pettigrew to William S. Pettigrew, October 9, 1837, Pettigrew Family Papers.

36. Douglass, *My Bondage*, pp. 95, 242–46; Brown, *Narrative*, pp. 17–18.

claimed "that if they came by he would join them and assist in killing all the white people.") Within two days they killed nearly sixty whites. They could have killed more. They left undisturbed at least one poor white family, "because they thought no better of themselves than they did of the negroes." To justify the killings, members of Turner's band declared that they had had enough of punishment, or that they now intended to be as rich as their masters. One rebel demonstrated his new status by walking off in his late owner's shoes and socks.

The Nat Turner rebellion lasted only forty-eight hours. Swiftly mobolizing in overwhelming strength, the whites easily dispersed the rebels. Then followed a massacre during which not only the insurrectionists but scores of innocent bondsmen were slaughtered. Others, charged with "felonously consulting, advising and conspiring . . . to rebel . . . and making insurrection and taking the lives of divers free white persons of this Commonwealth," were tried before a court of oyer and terminer during the months of September and October. Some were executed, others transported. Most of those transported had not actively participated in the rebellion; they had merely expressed sympathy for the rebels.

Nat Turner himself was not captured until October 30, more than two months after the uprising. He was brought to trial on November 5, convicted the same day, and hanged six days later.[37] Thus ended an event which produced in the South something resembling a mass trauma, from which the whites had not recovered three decades later. The danger that other Nat Turners might emerge, that an even more serious insurrection might some day occur, became an enduring concern as long as the peculiar institution survived. Proslavery writers boldly asserted that Southerners did not fear their slaves, that a rebellion of the laboring class was more likely to transpire in the North than in the South; but the fear of rebellion, sometimes vague, sometimes acute, was with them always.

Though it was the most disastrous (for both slaves and masters), Nat Turner's was not the first insurrection. Several earlier conspiracies, which narrowly missed being carried into execution might easily have precipitated rebellions much more extensive than that of Turner.[38] These up-

---

37. Details of the Turner insurrection can be found in contemporary Richmond newspapers, and in the manuscript records of the trials in Southampton County Minute Book, 1830–1835. See also William S. Drewry, *The Southampton Insurrection* (Washington, D. C., 1900); Thomas R. Gray, *The Confessions of Nat Turner* (Baltimore, 1831).

38. Herbert Aptheker, *American Negro Slave Revolts* (New York, 1943) presents evidence of many conspiracies and a few rebellions, each involving ten or more slaves, from the colonial period to the end of the Civil War. See also Joseph C. Carroll, *Slave Insurrections in the United States, 1800–1865* (Boston, 1938); Harvey Wish, "American Slave Insurrections before 1861," *Journal of Negro History*, XXII (1937), pp. 299–320.

risings and conspiracies began as early as the seventeenth century and kept Southerners apprehensive throughout the colonial period. The preamble to the South Carolina statute of 1740 defining the duties of slave patrols stated that many "horrible and barbarous massacres" had been committed or plotted by the slaves who were "generally prone to such cruel practices."[39] On the eve of the American Revolution a Charlestonian wrote about a "disturbance" among the bondsmen who had "mimicked their betters in crying *Liberty*." In 1785, a West Florida slaveholder was dismayed to learn that several of his slaves were involved in an insurrection plot: "Of what avail is kindness and good usage when rewarded by such ingratitude . . . [?]"[40] Such incidents set the pattern for the nineteenth century.

The new century opened with the Gabriel Conspiracy (August, 1800) in Henrico County, Virginia, in which at least a thousand slaves were implicated. The warnings of two bondsmen and a severe storm enabled the whites to forestall a projected march upon Richmond. A decade later some five hundred slaves in St. John the Baptist Parish, Louisiana, armed with cane knives and other crude weapons, advanced toward New Orleans. But the planters and a strong detachment of troops put them to flight. In 1822, Denmark Vesey, a free Negro in Charleston, planned a vast conspiracy which came to nothing after it was given away by a slave. These and other plots were invariably followed by severe reprisals, including the indiscriminate killing of slaves as well as mass executions after regular trials. The heads of sixteen Louisiana rebels were stuck upon poles along the Mississippi River as a grim warning to other slaves. After the Vesey conspiracy, Charlestonians expressed disillusionment with the idea that by generous treatment the slaves "would become more satisfied with their condition and more attached to the whites."[41]

The shock of Nat Turner caused Southerners to take preventive measures, but these never eliminated their apprehension or the actual danger. Hardly a year passed without some kind of alarming disturbance somewhere in the South. When no real conspiracy existed, wild rumors often agitated the whites and at times came close to creating an insurrection panic. The rumors might be entirely unfounded, or they might grow out of some local incident which was magnified by exaggeration. Even the historian cannot always distinguish between the rumors and the facts. Most of the stories seem to have had a foundation in at least a minor disturbance, limited perhaps to a single plantation where the slaves suddenly became insubordinate, or to a whole neighborhood where they showed

39. Hurd, *Law of Freedom and Bondage*, I, p. 308.
40. Henry Laurens to J. Gervais, January 29, 1766, Henry Laurens Ms. Letter Book, 1762–1766, Historical Society of Pennsylvania, Philadelphia (copy in possession of Professor Carl Bridenbaugh); Sellers, *Slavery in Alabama*, pp. 13–14.
41. Aptheker, *American Negro Slave Revolts*, pp. 209–92; Taylor, "Negro Slavery in Louisiana," pp. 268–74; Phillips, *Plantation and Frontier*, II, pp. 103–104.

signs of becoming restive. Whether caused by rumor or fact, the specter of rebellion often troubled the sleep of the master class.

The Turner rebellion itself produced an insurrection panic that swept the entire South. A Richmond editor wondered whether the southern press was trying to give the slaves "false conceptions of their numbers and capacity, by exhibiting the terror and confusion of the whites, and to induce them to think that practicable, which they see is so much feared by their superiors."[42] In eastern North Carolina the panic caused the arrest of scores of slaves and the execution of more than a dozen. A South Carolinian reported that there was "considerable alarm" in his state too and that some slaves were hanged to prevent a rumored uprising.[43] The excitement spread into the Southwest where it was feared that the bondsmen would become "troublesome." A Mississippian, confessing "great apprehension," noted that "within 4 hours march of Natchez" there were "2200 able bodied male slaves." He warned: "It behooves [us] to be vigilent—but silent."[44]

Similar insurrection panics developed from time to time thereafter. In 1835, one of these frightful disturbances centered in Mississippi and Louisiana; before it subsided, numerous bondsmen had been legally or extralegally executed. This panic even spread into Roane County in East Tennessee, though that county contained a very small slave population. There was "a great deal of talk and some dread of the negroes rising at Christmas or new year," reported a local slaveholder. "I can not say that I have had much fear of their rising here, but have thought it right to be careful and watchful. It is a disagreeable state of living to be ever suspicious of those with whom we live."[45] This point was illustrated by a not uncommon incident in a small village on the Eastern Shore of Virginia. One night in 1849, the firing of guns "alarmed the people very much. They at once thought that the Slaves had risen to murder the white people. Many immediately left their houses and fled to the woods. . . . But it was afterwards ascertained that it was a false alarm."[46] This was indeed a "disagreeable state of living"!

The most acute and widespread insurrection panics, after the Turner rebellion, occurred in 1856 and 1860, each of them resulting in part from the rise of the Republican party and the exciting political campaigns. On both occasions alarming stories of huge conspiracies spread through every slave state, stories frequently mentioning "unscrupulous" white men (pre-

42. Richmond *Whig*, quoted in Alexandria (Va.) *Phenix Gazette*, September 6, 1831.
43. Johnson, *Ante-Bellum North Carolina*, pp. 519–20; Rosannah P. Rogers to David S. Rogers, October 29, 1831, Renwick Papers.
44. Nevitt Plantation Journal, entry for October 28, 1831; Stephen Duncan to Thomas Butler, October 4, 1831, Butler Family Papers.
45. William B. Lenoir to Thomas Lenoir, December 27, 1835, Lenoir Family Papers.
46. J. Milton Emerson Ms. Journal, entry for September 29, 1849.

sumably abolitionist emissaries like John Brown) who were "tampering" with the Negroes and encouraging them to rebel. "All at once, in Kentucky, Tennessee, Missouri, Arkansas, Louisiana and Texas, it is discovered that the slaves are meditating schemes of insurrection," proclaimed a Richmond newspaper in a hysterical editorial. "From almost every point in the Southwest, rumors of insurrectionary movements among the negroes come upon us with more or less distinct and authentic detail." In Virginia, as a slaveholder noted, "reports of negro plots" had "induced proper measures of vigilance."[47] A South Carolinian observed privately that there was "a good deal of anxiety," but little was being said about it, "as every one felt it should not be the subject of general talk." In Texas, one of the principal centers of these insurrection panics, vigilance committees were hastily formed to deal with the expected emergency.[48] On these occasions, as on others, there was some substance to the rumors, however much they were exaggerated. In 1856 slave unrest did increase noticeably in certain areas, including Texas, where there was at least one well authenticated conspiracy.[49]

Sometimes rebellions took odd forms. The Seminole War in Florida was in part a slave revolt, for many fugitive Negroes fought alongside the Indian warriors. In 1841, a group of slaves being carried from Virginia to New Orleans on the brig *Creole* rose in rebellion, seized the ship, and sailed it to the Bermudas. In 1848, about seventy-five slaves from Fayette County, Kentucky, led by a white man, made a break for the Ohio River. They waged a brisk battle with their pursuers before they were forced to surrender. More than forty of them were tried for "most wickedly, seditiously, and rebelliously" making a "public insurrection." Three of the slaves were executed, and their white leader was sentenced to twenty years in prison.[50]

One of the last ante-bellum slave conspiracies occurred in October, 1860, in the neighborhood of Plymouth, in eastern North Carolina. It began when a score of slaves met in a swamp to plan an insurrection. Their plan was to persuade several hundred bondsmen to join them in a march on Plymouth; they would kill all the whites they met on the road, burn the town, take money and weapons, and escape by ship through

---

47. Richmond *Enquirer,* December 16, 1856; Edmund Ruffin Ms. Diary, entry for December 25, 1856.
48. Easterby (ed.), *South Carolina Rice Plantation,* p. 136; Austin *Texas State Gazette,* November 15, 22, 29, 1856; Harvey Wish, "The Slave Insurrection Panic of 1856," *Journal of Southern History,* V (1939), pp. 206–22.
49. Aptheker, *American Negro Slave Revolts,* pp. 325–58; Wendell G. Addington, "Slave Insurrections in Texas," *Journal of Negro History,* XXXV (1950), pp. 408–35.
50. Porter, "Florida Slaves and Free Negroes in the Seminole War, 1835–1842," *loc. cit.,* pp. 420–21; Catterall (ed.), *Judicial Cases,* III, pp. 565–67; Coleman, *Slavery Times in Kentucky,* pp. 88–92.

Albemarle Sound. The plot was betrayed by a slave, and once again panic spread throughout the neighborhood. "When I reached Plymouth," wrote a local planter, "the town was in the greatest of commotion, and, as even calm persons thought, with some reason." The country people were "so much excited and alarmed as to vow themselves as ready to slaughter the negroes indiscriminately." This planter believed that during an insurrection panic "the negroes are in much more danger from the non slave holding whites than the whites are from the negroes."[51] He was probably right, though the slaveholders were hardly less inclined, on that account, to be ruthless whenever rumors of rebellion swept through the land.

That there was no slave conspiracy comparable to Denmark Vesey's and no rebellion comparable to Nat Turner's, during the three decades before the Civil War, has been explained in many ways. The explanations, however, do not sufficiently emphasize the impact which the Turner rebellion had on the slaves themselves. The speed with which it was crushed and the massacre that followed were facts soon known, doubtless, to every slave in Virginia and, before long, to almost every slave in the South. Among the Negroes everywhere, news generally spread so far and so fast as to amaze the whites. The Turner story was not likely to encourage slaves to make new attempts to win their freedom by fighting for it. They now realized that they would face a united white community, well armed and quite willing to annihilate as much of the black population as might seem necessary.

In truth, no slave uprising ever had a chance of ultimate success, even though it might have cost the master class heavy casualties. The great majority of the disarmed and outnumbered slaves, knowing the futility of rebellion, refused to join in any of the numerous plots. Most slaves had to express their desire for freedom in less dramatic ways. They rarely went beyond disorganized individual action—which, to be sure, caused their masters no little annoyance. The bondsmen themselves lacked the power to destroy the web of bondage. They would have to have the aid of free men inside or outside the South.

The survival of slavery, then, cannot be explained as due to the contentment of slaves or their failure to comprehend the advantages of freedom. They longed for liberty and resisted bondage as much as any people could have done in their circumstances, but their longing and their resistance were not enough even to render the institution unprofitable to most masters. The masters had power and, as will be seen, they developed an elaborate technique of slave control. Their very preoccupation with this technique was, in itself, a striking refutation of the myth that slavery survived because of the cheerful acquiescence of the slaves.

51. William S. Pettigrew to James C. Johnston, October 25, 1860, Pettigrew Family Papers.

The
Sambo character
and
southern society

Stanley M. Elkins

Why should it be, turning . . . to Latin America, that there one finds no Sambo, no social tradition, that is, in which slaves were defined by virtually complete consensus as children incapable of being trusted with the full privileges of freedom and adulthood? There, the system surely had its brutalities. The slaves arriving there from Africa had also undergone the capture, the sale, the Middle Passage. They too had been uprooted from a prior culture, from a life very different from the one in which they now found themselves. There, however, the system was not closed.

Here again the concentration camp, paradoxically enough, can be instructive. There were in the camps a very small minority of the survivors who had undergone an experience different in crucial ways from that of the others, an experience which protected them from the full impact of the closed system. These people, mainly by virtue of wretched little jobs in the camp administration which offered them a minute measure of privilege, were able to carry on "underground" activities. In a practical sense the actual operations of such "undergrounds" as were possible may seem to us unheroic and limited: stealing blankets; "organizing" a few bandages, a little medicine, from the camp hospital; black market arrangements with a guard for a bit of extra food and protection for oneself and one's comrades; the circulation of news; and other such apparently trifling activities. But for the psychological balance of those involved, such activities were vital; they made possible a fundamentally different adjustment to the camp. To a prisoner so engaged, there were others who mattered, who gave real point to his existence—the SS was no longer the *only* one. Conversely, the role of the child was not the only one he played. He could take initiative; he could give as well as receive protection; he did things which had meaning in adult terms. He had, in short, alternative roles; this was a fact which made such a prisoner's transition from his old life to that of the camp less agonizing and destructive; those very prisoners, moreover, appear to have been the ones who could, upon liberation, resume normal lives most easily. It is, in fact, these people—not those of the ranks—who have described the camps to us.

From Stanley M. Elkins, *Slavery*, pp. 134–139, 211–222. Copyright © 1959 by the University of Chicago. Reprinted by permission of The University of Chicago Press.

It was just such a difference—indeed, a much greater one—that separated the typical slave in Latin America from the typical slave in the United States. Though he too had experienced the Middle Passage, he was entering a society where alternatives were significantly more diverse than those awaiting his kinsman in North America. Concerned in some sense with his status were distinct and at certain points competing institutions. This involved multiple and often competing "significant others." His master was, of course, clearly the chief one—but not the only one. There could, in fact, be a considerable number: the friar who boarded his ship to examine his conscience, the confessor; the priest who made the rounds and who might report irregularities in treatment to the *procurador*; the zealous Jesuit quick to resent a master's intrusion upon such sacred matters as marriage and worship (a resentment of no small consequence to the master); the local magistrate, with his eye on the king's official protector of slaves, who would find himself in trouble were the laws too widely evaded; the king's informer who received one-third of the fines. For the slave the result was a certain latitude; the lines did not all converge on one man; the slave's personality, accordingly, did not have to focus on a single role. He was, true enough, primarily a slave. Yet he might in fact perform multiple roles. He could be a husband and a father (for the American slave these roles had virtually no meaning); open to him also were such activities as artisan, peddler, petty merchant, truck gardener (the law reserved to him the necessary time and a share of the proceeds, but such arrangements were against the law for Sambo); he could be a communicant in the church, a member of a religious fraternity (roles guaranteed by the most powerful institution in Latin America—comparable privileges in the American South depended on a master's pleasure). These roles were all legitimized and protected *outside* the plantation; they offered a diversity of channels for the development of personality. Not only did the individual have multiple roles open to him as a slave, but the very nature of these roles made possible a certain range of aspirations should he some day become free. He could have a fantasy-life not limited to catfish and watermelons; it was within his conception to become a priest, an independent farmer, a successful merchant, a military officer. The slave could actually—to an extent quite unthinkable in the United States—conceive of himself *as a rebel.* Bloody slave revolts, actual wars, took place in Latin America; nothing on this order occurred in the United States.[1] But even without a rebellion, society here had a network of cus-

---

[1]Compared with the countless uprisings of the Brazilian Negroes, the slave revolts in our own country appear rather desperate and futile. Only three emerge as worthy of any note, and their seriousness—even when described by a sympathetic historian like Herbert Aptheker—depends largely on the supposed plans of the rebels rather than on the things they actually did. The best organized of such "revolts," those of Vesey and Gabriel, were easily suppressed, while the most dramatic of them—the Nat Turner Rebellion—was characterized by little more than aimless butchery. The Brazilian revolts, on the other hand, were marked by imagi-

tomary arrangements, rooted in antiquity, which made possible at many points a smooth transition of status from slave to free and which provided much social space for the exfoliation of individual character.

To the typical slave on the ante-bellum plantation in the United States, society of course offered no such alternatives. But that is hardly to say that something of an "underground"—something rather more, indeed, than an underground—could not exist in Southern slave society. And there were those in it who hardly fitted the picture of "Sambo."

The American slave system, compared with that of Latin America, was closed and circumscribed, but, like all social systems, its arrangements were less perfect in practice than they appeared to be in theory. It was possible for significant numbers of slaves, in varying degrees, to escape the full impact of the system and its coercions upon personality. The house servant, the urban mechanic, the slave who arranged his own employment and paid his master a stipulated sum each week, were all figuratively members of the "underground." Even among those working on large plantations, the skilled craftsman or the responsible slave foreman had a measure of independence not shared by his simpler brethren. Even the single slave family owned by a small farmer had a status much closer to that of house servants than to that of a plantation labor gang. For all such people there was a margin of space denied to the majority; the system's authority-structure claimed their bodies but not quite their souls.

Out of such groups an individual as complex and as highly developed as William Johnson, the Natchez barber, might emerge. Johnson's diary reveals a personality that one recognizes instantly as a type—but a type whose values came from a sector of society very different from that which formed Sambo. Johnson is the young man on the make, the ambitious free-enterpriser of American legend. He began life as a slave, was manumitted at the age of eleven, and rose from a poor apprentice barber to

---

nation and a sense of direction, and they often involved large-scale military operations. One is impressed both by their scope and their variety. They range from the legendary Palmares Republic of the seventeenth century (a Negro state organized by escaped slaves and successfully defended for over fifty years), to the bloody revolts of the Moslem Negroes of Bahia which, between 1807 and 1835, five times paralyzed a substantial portion of Brazil. Many such wars were launched from the *quilombos* (fortified villages built deep in the jungles by escaped slaves to defend themselves from recapture); there were also the popular rebellions in which the Negroes of an entire area would take part. One is immediately struck by the heroic stature of the Negro leaders: no allowances of any sort need be made for them; they are impressive from any point of view. Arthur Ramos has described a number of them, including Zambi, a fabulous figure of the Palmares Republic; Luiza Mahin, mother of the Negro poet Luiz Gama and "one of the most outstanding leaders of the 1835 insurrection"; and Manoel Francisco dos Anjos Fereira, whose followers in the *Balaiada* (a movement which drew its name from "Baliao," his own nickname) held the *entire province* of Maranhao for three years. Their brilliance, gallantry, and warlike accomplishments give to their histories an almost legendary quality. On the other hand, one could not begin to think of Nat Turner in such a connection.

become one of the wealthiest and most influential Negroes in ante-bellum Mississippi. He was respected by white and black alike, and counted among his friends some of the leading public men of the state.

It is of great interest to note that although the danger of slave revolts (like Communist conspiracies in our own day) was much overrated by touchy Southerners; the revolts that actually did occur were in no instance planned by plantation laborers but rather by Negroes whose qualities of leadership were developed well outside the full coercions of the plantation authority-system. Gabriel, who led the revolt of 1800, was a blacksmith who lived a few miles outside Richmond. Denmark Vesey, leading spirit of the 1822 plot at Charleston, was a freed Negro artisan who had been born in Africa and served several years aboard a slave-trading vessel; and Nat Turner, the Virginia slave who fomented the massacre of 1831, was a literate preacher of recognized intelligence. Of the plots that have been convincingly substantiated (whether they came to anything or not), the majority originated in urban centers.

For a time during Reconstruction, a Negro elite of sorts did emerge in the South. Many of its members were Northern Negroes, but the Southern ex-slaves who also comprised it seem in general to have emerged from the categories just indicated. Vernon Wharton, writing of Mississippi, says:

A large portion of the minor Negro leaders were preachers, lawyers, or teachers from the free states or from Canada. Their education and their independent attitude gained for them immediate favor and leadership. Of the natives who became their rivals, the majority had been urban slaves, blacksmiths, carpenters, clerks, or waiters in hotels and boarding houses; a few of them had been favored body-servants of affluent whites.

The William Johnsons and Denmark Veseys have been accorded, though belatedly, their due honor. They are, indeed, all too easily identified, thanks to the system that enabled them as individuals to be so conspicuous and so exceptional and, as members of a group, so few. . . .

The decade of the 1830's saw the completion of a consensus throughout Southern society on the subject of slavery that became ever broader and deeper. What the abolitionist blasts of Garrison and the others could then do, and did with peculiar effectiveness, was to bring that consensus to an acute pitch of self-awareness. The "argument," such as it had been, was all but closed. And now, the fact that abolitionists were virtually all Northerners—and that their attacks were so violent and uncompromising— could hardly have been better suited for a general mobilization of sectional patriotism. Indeed, there was nothing in the abolitionist program of immediate emancipation that even made connections with whatever anti-slavery sentiment still persisted in such areas as western Virginia, Tennessee, and North Carolina. All that Garrison and Phillips could do with the people of these places was to repel and alienate them. And so it would be with the most humane and sensitive planter, wherever he might be found; such a man was just as much Garrison's target as was the most brutal slave-beater in Mississippi. Be he ever so ridden with doubts about the morality and justice of slavery, the fanatics of New England seemed to leave him with little choice. What was he to do with *his* guilt? He could do as the abolitionists demanded and get rid of his slaves; he might then, as Birney did, go North and proselytize. He would not have had much company. Or, he might simply discharge his sense of guilt by turning upon his tormentors. With that, he entered a growing phalanx of Southerners, high, low, and middling.

The existence of thoroughgoing consensus in a democratic community appears to create two sorts of conditions for the functioning of intellect. One is sternly coercive, the other, wildly permissive. On the one hand, consensus narrows the alternatives with which thought may deal; on the other, it removes all manner of limits—limits of discrimination, circumspection, and discipline—on the alternatives that remain. The former function is probably better understood than the latter; both, however, were fully at work in the intellectual life of the ante-bellum South.

When Tocqueville wrote out his ideas on the "tyranny of the majority" over matters of thought, he was specifically using America as his model. The "most absolute monarchs in Europe," he declared, "cannot prevent certain opinions hostile to their authority from circulating in secret through their dominions, and even in their courts." But, he continued,

It is not so in America; as long as the majority is still undecided, discussion is carried on; but as soon as its decision is irrevocably pronounced, every one is silent, and the friends as well as the opponents of the measure unite in assenting to its propriety. . . .
The authority of a king is physical, and controls the actions of men without subduing their will. But the majority possesses a power which is physical and moral at the same time, which acts upon the will as much as upon the actions, and represses not only all contest, but all controversy.

It is a process in which "the body is left free, and the soul is enslaved."

Such was the process whereby the young bloods of Virginia in 1831, and any who shared their views, to say nothing of men who may have entertained truly radical ones, were finally silenced. We cannot know for certain that they stopped thinking; most certainly they stopped speaking.

Before considering the other, the permissive, function of democratic consensus, it should be granted that the very effort which went into the proslavery argument did force ante-bellum Southern thinkers to view society in certain ways that were not congenial to the generality of Americans at the time, ways that would doubtless not have been hit upon otherwise. More than one recent writer has discerned the odd affinity between some of these men's social commentaries and those of Karl Marx himself. Insofar as a burgeoning industrial order was conceived as the enemy, the

South did in its way confront that order with its busiest critics. John C. Calhoun, to mention the most eminent of them, worried the subject to death, but "he also set forth," as Richard Hofstadter has said, "a system of social analysis that is worthy of considerable respect." Calhoun was perfectly willing to recognize the exploitative potentialities of industrial capitalism; class revolution was to him quite conceivable—as it was to Marx and other European thinkers—in consequence of what he assumed as capital's tendency to concentrate itself while wearing out its ever expendable supply of "free" labor. The point, for him, was that the irresponsibility of wage employment for the employee was absent under chattel slavery.

A number of other Southerners followed, or paralleled, Calhoun in this line of thinking, and in the course of it produced observations of at least a proto-sociological sort. Especially noteworthy in this respect were such men as George Fitzhugh, Thomas R. Dew, George Frederick Holmes, and Henry Hughes. In all times and in all societies, they argued, were forces that made for authority on one side and subordination on the other. Under feudalism, the principle worked through a kind of "natural" ordering of class and function, of responsibilities and duties; under capitalism, the ordering process is accomplished only through the untrammeled motive of gain, with the exploitation and ultimate starvation of labor as its result. This was the condition toward which the Northern laboring classes were headed—if they were not hopelessly mired in it already—and the Southern arrangement of outright lifetime bondage could thus be seen as the truly humane, rational, and beneficent solution for the subordinated orders. So long as capital *owned* labor, the owner had not only a responsibility for, but a vested interest in, the laborer's well-being. The argument, in such writings as those of Simms, Hammond, and Tucker, envisioned an aristocratic idyl of productive leisure and protected labor; under the "sociologists" and political economists it also brought forth a labor, as opposed to a property, theory of value.

To the extent that the thinker, in order to acquire insights into a society, must stand a little off, or at least see his society in a kind of double vision, to such an extent may it be said that these Southerners were able to see things about American society that to Northerners were more or less invisible. As we have already noted, the Northerner's sense of structure, of authority, of labor and property and institutions, had atrophied to the point of childishness in an expanding universe of individual enterprise, when it came to assessing these things intellectually. The Southerner, being just enough out of phase with the drift of society at large, was anything but ready to take it all uncritically for granted. And yet, as Louis Hartz remarks of Fitzhugh, all around this intellectual heave-to in behalf of slavery lingers the echo of the mad genius. All these perceptions about the nature and conditions of free labor under property-grounded laissez-faire capitalism were well and good. But they were gained not so much through a critical contrast with slavery as through a general agreement to stop thinking about slavery altogether; the failure of any free workers to present themselves for enslavement can serve as one test of how much the analysis may have added to Americans' understanding of themselves. "Everything that the Southerners had said," observes Mr. Hartz, "was superlatively a matter of degree. . . ."

Whether this were true "conservative" thought—or, indeed, "thought" of any kind as it is commonly carried on—may be judged from a glance at a British conservative thinker who was full of sympathy for the slave-holding South and who was the closest British counterpart to the American proslavery writers. Thomas Carlyle, in his own writings, had opposed emancipation in the West Indies and had vigorously attacked the "misguided philanthropists" who held forth at London's Exeter Hall. Carlyle was much praised and widely quoted in the American South, and he himself appeared not unwilling to lend his pen to the Southerners in defense of their institutions. But he had his conditions. *Some* account must be taken of slavery as it now existed, and something had to be done; intellect, without its Exeter Hall, was to him unthinkable. "Give me leave, in my dim light, but in my real sympathy with your affairs," he wrote to his friend Beverley Tucker,

to hint . . . [a] thought I have. It is, that this clamour from your "Exeter Hall" and ours, which few persons can regard with less reverence than I, was nevertheless a thing *necessary.* My notion is, that the relation of the white man to the black is *not* at present a just one, according to the Law of the Eternal; and though "abolition" is by no means the way to remedy it . . . yet, beyond all question, remedied it must be; and peace upon it is not possible till a remedy be found, and begin to be visibly applied. "A servant hired *for life,* instead of by the day or month": I have often wondered that wise and just men in your region (of whom I believe there are many) had not come upon a great many methods, or at least some methods better than those yet in use, of justly enunciating this relation. . . .

This could strike Tucker only as a rather unpleasant digression. He passed Carlyle's letter on to Hammond, remarking, "He has still prejudices growing out of perverted statements which in England pass for truth, but his thoughts and feelings are strongly drawn to the subject." Complexity of such a sort, at this stage, was hardly what Tucker, Hammond, or any Southerner wanted from Carlyle, who was asking them to use intellect in the service of their own problems. And so it was, that in the end all that these men actually took from their British friend was his "real sympathy" with their affairs.

In reality, the contour of this body of thought was governed by the fact that the South was talking no longer to the world, or even to the North, but to itself. It is this fact—the fact of internal consensus and the peculiar lack of true challenge-points at any level of Southern society—that gives the proslavery polemic its special distinction. Consensus, while withdrawing one kind of liberty, conferred in its place another kind which had not previously been there. The mind could now conceive the enemy in any size or shape it chose; specters were utterly free to range, thrive, and proliferate.

Only in such a setting of nightmare does it seem plausible, for example, that one of the most non-intellectual paradoxes should have developed in men's writing and talk regarding the Negro slave and his present and hypothetical behavior. On the one hand, the ideal picture of Southern life was one of contentment, of plantations teeming with faithful and happy black children young and old—helpless, purposeless children incapable of sustained and unsupervised initiative. On the other hand was the picture of doom; the hint of freedom, whispered by designing abolitionists, would galvanize the sleeping monster in every slave, arouse bloody revolts, and bring hordes of black primitives bent on murder and destruction. For the first picture, though it tended to blur alongside the other, there was at least a substantial amount of evidence; for the second, which grew in luridness the longer men stared at it, there was next to none.

A heavy and cramping tension thus exists in most of the formal writings. The spokesmen did not want it supposed for an instant that the South was unable to control its slave population or that the inferior creatures were anything but pleased with their happy condition. But on the other hand, in order that the abolitionist menace might be given reality and concreteness in their own community, the Southerners could only murmur of insurrection as the price of non-vigilance. Any talk of liberation, on whatever terms, would open doors to the unspeakable. "A merrier being does not exist on the face of the globe, than the negro slave of the U. States," wrote Professor Dew, one of the earliest and least troubled of the proslavery essayists. And yet he warned: "Let the wily philanthropist but come and whisper into the ears of such a slave that his situation is degrading and his lot a miserable one . . . and that moment, like the serpent that entered the garden of Eden, he destroys his happiness and his usefulness." Rebuking the emancipationists in the Virginia legislature, Dew wrote of their schemes: "They are admirably calculated to excite plots, murders and insurrections; whether gradual or rapid in their operation, this is the inevitable tendency." William Gilmore Simms insisted in 1837:

Perhaps there is nothing in the world that the people of the South less apprehend, than . . . the insurrection of their negroes. The attempts of this people at this object have been singularly infrequent, and perhaps never would be dreamed of, were their bad passions not appealed to by the abolitionists or their emissaries. They are not a warlike people; are, indeed, rather a timid race. . . .

The irritability mounts. Chancellor William Harper of South Carolina took note, in 1837, of insinuations that his countrymen were "nightly reposing over a mine [of potential revolt], which may at any moment explode," whereupon he himself exploded. He declared that "if any thing is certain in human affairs, it is certain and from the most obvious considerations, that we are more secure in this respect than any civilized and fully peopled society upon the face of the earth." Later in his essay, however, Harper observed gloomily that it was doubtless through "the exertions of the *amis des noirs* in France" that "the horrors of St. Domingo were perpetrated." One of the most lyrical passages in praise of slavery was penned by Governor Hammond of South Carolina:

And our patriarchal scheme of domestic servitude is indeed well calculated to awaken the higher and finer feelings of our nature. It is not wanting in its enthusiasm and its poetry. The relations of the most beloved and honored chief ... are frigid and unfelt compared with those existing between the master and his slaves—who served his father, and rocked his cradle, or have been born into his household, and look forward to serve his children—who have been through life the props of his fortune, and the objects of his care —who have partaken of his griefs, and looked to him for comfort in their own—whose sickness he has so frequently watched over and relieved— whose holidays he has so often made joyous by his bounties and his presence; for whose welfare, when absent, his anxious solicitude never ceases, and whose hearty and affectionate greetings never fail to welcome him home. In this cold, calculating, ambitious world of ours, there are few ties more heartfelt, or of more benignant influence, than those which mutually bind the master and the slave, under our ancient system, handed down from the father of Israel.

And yet in the same essay Hammond, rhetorically addressing the abolitionists, demands: "Allow our slaves to read your writings, stimulating them to cut our throats! Can you believe us to be such unspeakable fools?"

By the 1850's the argument had become mechanical. In Albert Taylor Bledsoe's "Liberty and Slavery," it was only a single step from a peaceful countryside (upon which the author contented himself by simply quoting Hammond) to the hideous specter of Santo Domingo. Emancipation, Bledsoe announced, "would furnish the elements of the most horrible civil war the world has ever witnessed."

As Robespierre caused it to be proclaimed to the free blacks of St. Domingo that they were naturally entitled to all the rights and privileges of citizens; as Mr. Seward proclaimed the same doctrine to the free blacks of New York; so there would be kind benefactors enough to propagate the same sentiments among our colored population. . . . If the object of such agitators were . . . to stir up scenes of strife and blood, it might be easily attained. . . .

Such imaginings took even more fantastic form in the popular mind. Despite the fact that after 1831 no more slave insurrections were seen in the South, it was precisely then that the South became most victimized by its own fears, being "racked at intervals," as Clement Eaton writes, "by dark rumors and imagined plots." These periodic unheavals over suspected revolts—characterized by furious vigilante hunts and wild confusion, all based on mirage—constitute one of the more bizarre chapters in Southern history. Indeed, the very absence of slave uprisings all during this period, and thus their very imaginary character, may have been the real key to their frightfulness. "Negro insurrection," wrote a skeptical resident of Falmouth, Virginia,

is the name for every horror, simply because it is one of which the Southerners know nothing. . . . The present generation has seen nothing of the kind. That is the very reason why there is such a horror and a panic about it: it is a vague, mysterious, and unknown evil.

It was a matter, moreover, not of division but of consensus, consensus in its ultimate stage of democratization; the "black terror" now meant virtually the same thing to everyone.

In trying to explain the mounting passions of the period, more than one writer has declared, with a kind of desperate irritability, that the South's fears were simply "unreal." Though this in itself may not explain much, there is good reason to conclude that the South's horror of insurrection was a product not of real insurrection but, oddly enough, of a united mind. *This*—its own unanimity—was what the South had girded itself and rigged all its alarms to defend. It was now, in short, not so much physical peril that Southerners most feared, but something else; they feared subversion. The fear itself, if not its object, was real enough; Southern newspapers, month after month, teemed with evidence of it. Those old papers thus leave ironic traps for us, even today. We have a monograph on slave revolts, written in scholarly modern times, that can offer nothing but this kind of "evidence"—fear of subversion—for a multitude of "revolts" that never materialized. At the bottom of nearly every imaginary "plot" was an imaginary abolitionist—a "foreign agent" or a domestic fellow traveler.

An elusive attribute of internal danger is that at the moment when a society is most fully committed to resist it, the "danger" itself has for that very reason become least dangerous. Conversely, then, it is hardly a paradox that the farther away the enemy is, the more menacing he seems and the more devilish are the shapes he assumes; and this is because all, not just a few, are hunting him everywhere in their midst. If he is imagined to be lurking under every bed, it is because no one meets him face to face any more in the market place. If he were indeed real and present, some men—the community's intellectuals at least—might try to reason with him. But a democratic people no longer "reasons" with itself when it is all of the same mind. Men will then only warn and exhort each other, that their solidarity may be yet more perfect. The South's intellectuals, after the 1830's, did really little more than this. And when the enemy's reality disappears, when his concreteness recedes, then intellect itself, with nothing more to resist it and give it resonance, merges with the mass and stultifies, and shadows become monsters.

The legacy of slavery

Eugene D. Genovese

American radicals have long been imprisoned by the pernicious notion that the masses are necessarily both good and revolutionary, and by the even more pernicious notion that, if they are not, they should be. The principal task of radical historians therefore has too often been to provide the masses with historical heroes, to make them aware of their glorious tradition of resistance to oppression, and to portray them as having been implacably hostile to the social order in which they have been held. This viewpoint now dominates the black liberation movement, which has been fed for decades by white radical historians who in this one respect have set the ideological pace for their liberal colleagues. It has become virtually sacrilege—or at least white chauvinism—to suggest that slavery was a social system within which whites and blacks lived in harmony as well as antagonism, that there is little evidence of massive, organized opposition to the regime, that the blacks did not establish a revolutionary tradition of much significance, and that our main problem is to discover the reasons for the widespread accommodation and, perhaps more important, the long-term effects both of the accommodation and of that resistance which did occur.

In 1831 Nat Turner led a slave revolt on which has hung most of the legend of armed black resistance to slavery. Of the 250 or so revolts chronicled and analyzed in Herbert Aptheker's *American Negro Slave Revolts*, Turner's has pride of place and was described by Aptheker as a "cataclysm." Yet, when we look closely, this revolt, like the total history of such revolts, recedes in importance and magnitude. As many of Aptheker's critics have pointed out, most of the 250 revolts probably never happened, being the imagination of hysterical or self-serving whites, insignificant plots that never matured, or mere local disturbances of a questionable nature. Of the three major revolts, one, Denmark Vesey's, was crushed before it came to fruition; only Gabriel Prosser's in 1800 and Turner's reached impressive proportions. Even so painstaking and thorough a scholar as Aptheker has been unable to discover firm evidence of a major revolt between 1831 and 1865. As for Turner's, less than one hundred slaves joined. A revolt of this size would rate little more than a

From Eugene D. Genovese, "The Legacy of Slavery and the Roots of Black Nationalism," *Studies on the Left* (1966), Vol. VI, pp. 3–11. Reprinted by permission of *Studies on the Left*.

page or two in a comprehensive work on slave revolts in Brazil. To cite only two outstanding examples, runaway slaves in the Brazilian Northeast organized their own colony, Palmares, and waged a 65-year struggle for autonomy with as many as 20,000 people. During the first four decades of the nineteenth century there were a series of violent and extensive risings in Bahia, culminating in the great Muslim-led holy war of 1835. We need not dwell on Haiti, as the record of Jamaica, Cuba and other countries is also impressive. Even if, as Aptheker suggests, news of many smaller risings was suppressed, the effect would have been to prevent the accumulation of a tradition to encourage and sustain revolt-prone slaves. On balance, we find the absence or extreme weakness of such a tradition.

There were many reasons for this extreme weakness. First, we need to consider the kind of Africans brought here. It has long been falsely assumed that, since slave traders mixed their cargoes, all parts of the hemisphere received similarly mixed bags. But Brazil, for example, received large numbers of Angolans and Congolese, whose military and cultural traditions made them especially difficult to control. Brazil also received a large number of Muslim slaves from Upper Guinea who proved intractable everywhere in the hemisphere. The United States, on the other hand, largely drew its slaves from those portions of Lower Guinea which had a population previously disciplined to servitude and domination. Ironically, these Africans were, in some respects, among the most advanced in technical culture.

Second, the slave trade to the United States came to an end in 1808, although illegal importations continued to trickle in; in contrast, the trade to Cuba and Brazil continued well into the nineteenth century. The presence of large numbers of newly imported Africans can generally be correlated with incidence of revolt. In the United States the great majority of slaves during the antebellum period had been born and raised on Southern plantations. Their ranks received little reinforcement from newly enslaved and aggressive Africans.

Third, a review of the history of Brazil and the Caribbean suggests that an important ingredient in the development of revolts out of local disturbances was the division of the whites into warring factions and the general weakness of the state apparatus. Together with these conditions went the general influence of geography in relation to state power. Where suitable terrain was combined with a weak state, runaway slaves could and did found maroon colonies, which directly fomented revolts and kept alive a tradition of armed resistance. With minor qualifications, these conditions did not exist in the United States.

Fourth, a substantial revolt presupposed the formation of ideology and leadership. In Brazil and the Caribbean two circumstances combined to encourage both: the cultivation of sugar led to the establishment of plantations averaging perhaps 200 slaves or more, and the size of the white population was small. As a result the blacks could keep alive much of their African culture or could develop a syncretized Afro-Brazilian or Afro-Cuba culture, which militated against the loss of identity and which could, under proper conditions, nurture resistance movements. Apart from Islam, non-Christian religious cults, generally of a syncretized type, played a great role in hemispheric slave revolts. In the United States an imposed Protestantism, when effective, generally kept the slaves docile.

Half the slaves in the United States lived on units of twenty or less; most of the others lived on plantations of fifty or less. Although blacks heavily outnumbered whites in large areas of the South, they were, in general, floating in a white sea. The white planters were residents, not absentees; the non-slaveholders were loyal, armed and disciplined; the country immediately beyond the plantation areas was inhabited by armed whites completely hostile to the blacks. Death, not refuge, lay beyond the plantation. For this reason, among others, blacks often looked to their masters to protect them against the depredations and viciousness of the poorer whites. We may therefore understand how, during race riots like that in Atlanta in 1906, blacks reportedly ran to whites—or at least to some whites—for protection.

The residency of the planters and their hegemony across the South gave American slavery its particular quality and especially set it off from Caribbean slavery. Between the Revolutionary War and the War for Southern Independence the treatment of slaves, defined as day-to-day conditions of life (housing, food, rigor of work routine, leisure time, incidence and character of corporal punishment) improved steadily and perceptibly. Although manumission was made increasingly difficult and escape from the system was sealed off, the harsh slave codes were steadily tempered by community sentiment and the interpretations of the state supreme courts. During the late antebellum period steady pressure built up to reform the slave codes in order to protect slave family life and to check glaring abuses of the slave's person. The purpose and effect of this amelioration in practice and at law was not to pave the way to freedom, but to consolidate the system from within and without. Like all liberal reformism it aimed to strengthen the social system.

For the planters these trends formed part of a developing world view within which paternalism became the specific manifestation of class consciousness. Paternalism did not mean kindness or generosity or love, although it embraced some of each; essentially it meant a special notion of duty and responsibility toward one's charges. Arbitrary power, harshness toward disobedience, even sadism, constituted its other side. For our immediate purposes, paternalism and the trend of treatment are especially noteworthy in confronting the slave with a world in which resistance could be quickly, severely and legitimately punished, whereas obedience placed him in a position to benefit from the favor of a master who more often than not had a genuine interest in his welfare. The picture of the docile and infantilized Sambo, drawn and analyzed so brilliantly by Stanley M. Elkins, is one-sided, but he is not far from the mark when he argues that the Southern regime greatly encouraged acceptance of and dependence upon despotic authority. Elkins errs in thinking that the Sambo personality arose only in the United States, for it arose wherever slavery existed. He does not err in thinking that it was especially marked and extensive in the United States, where recourse to armed resistance was minimal and the tradition of paternalism took such firm root.

To say that slaves generally accommodated is not to say that they were so dehumanized as to be incapable of all forms of protest. Historians are quick to claim rebelliousness every time a slave broke a plow or stole a hog, but at least some room might be left for lack of initiative, thoughtlessness, stupidity and venality. Yet, we do know of enough instances of deliberate acts of day-to-day resistance to permit us to speak of a strong undercurrent of dissatisfaction and hostility, the manifestations of which require analysis.

One of the more prominent and irritating habits of recalcitrant slaves was stealing. Plundering the hog pen and the smokehouse was an especially happy pastime. Radical and liberal historians have taken particular delight in insisting that slaves might "steal" from each other but only "took" from their masters. After all, their labor being unpaid, they only took that which was rightfully theirs. I can understand this viewpoint from liberals because I can understand almost anything from liberals; I cannot understand it from Marxists. Since Marxists regard all surplus value as deriving from unpaid labor time, we ought, by the same logic, to be delighted every time a worker commits robbery at his plant. I do not wish to discuss the general problem of ethics in relation to class oppression, but I do insist that the encouragement given by the slave system to thefts had dangerous effects on the slaves themselves. The slaves understood the link between conventional morality and the civilized behavior of the whites; by rejecting that morality they registered a protest, but they simultaneously underscored their own isolation from that standard of civilization. Few masters got upset over slave thefts. They expected their slaves to steal, and by doing so, the slaves accepted their master's image of themselves.

Southern folklore abounds with charming stories of slaves outwitting masters by behaving like black versions of the Good Soldier Schweik. The trouble is that too often the masters enjoyed being outwitted in the same way that a tyrannical father sometimes enjoys being outwitted by a child. Every contortion necessary to the job implied inferiority. It proved the slave a clever fellow; it hardly proved him a man. It gained a few privileges or crumbs but undermined self-respect and confirmed the master's sense of superiority. The postslavery tradition of obsequiousness, indirection and the wearing of a mask before white men has played a similar role in the South ever since.

Arson and the mishandling of tools stand out as more positively rebelliousness acts. As expressions of frustration and resentment they are understandable, and might, in a general context of rebellion, have had considerable social value. As it was, they amounted to individual and essentially nihilistic thrashing about. With luck a few slaves might do enough damage to ruin a planter, in which case he would be forced to sell out and perhaps have to break up slave families and friendships. Advocates of the philosophy of "burn-baby-burn," whether on a Mississippi plantation in the 1850's or in a Northern ghetto in the 1960's, would do well to bear in mind that of necessity it is primarily the blacks who get burned. On occasion a slave took direct action against a particularly unpleasant master or overseer and killed him. For that manly act he would, if lucky, be hanged.

As we review these actions, which by no means exhaust the range, we find the formation of a tradition of recalcitrance but not revolution, action but not politics, dim awareness of oppression but not cumulative, ideological growth. Thus, whereas most slaves came out of slavery with a psychology of dependence conditioned by paternalism, the most active spirits came out having learned little more than that they could get away with individual acts of undirected, misdirected or naively directed violence. What was missing was that sense of group consciousness, collective responsibility and joint political effort which is the essence of a revolutionary tradition.

The formation of class leadership presents another side of this development. Legend has it that house slaves and drivers, by virtue of their special positions, arrayed themselves on the side of the master against the field hands, who as the most oppressed were of course the most revolutionary and pure. Examination of plantation documents casts grave doubts on this legend. Few plantations were big enough to carry a staff of servants large enough to constitute a separate caste. Even then the social life of the plantation proved too enticing for them to maintain total separation. With much of their everyday world conditioned by contacts with field slaves, they could ill-afford to be wholly on the side of the whites. The range of behavior was wide, but there were many instances of identification and sympathy.

The drivers, or slave foremen, present an even clearer case. These men often dominated the everyday life of the plantation. On the whole masters trusted them more than they trusted their white overseers; overseers came and went after a year or two, but drivers usually stayed on in positions of authority for many years. Masters relied on their drivers to tell them if an overseer was too lax or too harsh and if the hands respected him. Rarely did a planter take his overseer's word against that of a trusted driver. Some drivers undoubtedly were themselves severe taskmasters who lorded it over their fellow slaves, but drivers, too, had no social life apart from that of the slave quarters and had to live with the others. In general, they compromised as best they could between the master to whom they had pledged loyalty and to whom they were indebted for special favors, and the slaves who constituted their everyday fellows. Often the driver stood as a protector or interpreter between slave and master or overseer. Drivers and house slaves often, although certainly not always, comprised a leading stratum in the eyes of the blacks as well as in the eyes of the whites.

In the Caribbean these privileged slaves led revolts; in the United States they served as agents of accommodation. Toussaint L'Ouverture was only the most prominent of insurrectionary leaders who had been trained to leadership within the system. The problem in the United States was not that the system did not create such privileged strata, nor that these strata were more docile or less courageous than those in the Caribbean. The problem was that the total environment reduced the possibilities for successful insurrection virtually to zero, and therefore made accommodationists out of the most high-spirited slave leaders. When the mass exodus from the plantations took place during the War for Southern Independence, drivers and house slaves often led their people to the Union lines. Not docility but lack of a tradition of armed resistance conditioned their leadership.

Potential recruitment of insurrectionary leaders was hampered by many other circumstances, of which three are especially noteworthy. For reasons already indicated little anti-Christian religious sentiment could develop. Religion (Islam, voodoo, or Afro-Catholic syncretisms) proved to be an essential ingredient in slave cohesion and organized resistance throughout the hemisphere, but in the United States the enforced prevalence of Protestant Christianity played an opposite role. The second group of potential leaders recruited from all strata were those who had sufficient strength, daring and resourcefulness to flee. The runaways are black folk heroes, with good reason, but they also drained the best elements out of the slave class. In much of Brazil and the Caribbean runaways had nowhere to go except into the back country to form maroon colonies, the existence of which encouraged slave disorder and resistance. Finally, the free blacks and mulattoes in the United States had little opportunity for self-development and rarely could or would provide leadership to slaves. Elsewhere in the hemisphere, where whites were relatively few, these free blacks and mulattoes were needed to fill a wide variety of social and economic functions. Often they prospered as a middle class. In some cases, feelings of racial solidarity or, as in Haiti, the racist stupidity of the whites, led them into partial identification with the cause of black freedom. Thus, with the exception of a rare Nat Turner, black leadership fell to those whose position within the plantation itself encouraged accommodation and negated the possibilities of effective political organization.

The War for Southern Independence brought these tendencies to a head. The staggering truth is that not one full-scale slave revolt broke out during a war in which local white police power had been drastically reduced. In only a few isolated cases did slaves drive off their masters and divide the land among themselves. Many, perhaps most, struck for freedom by fleeing to Union lines at the first opportunity. The attitude of the slaves toward the federals varied, but the great majority welcomed them with an adulation, trust and dependence that suggests the full force of the old paternalism. Many blacks, free and slaves, Northern and Southern, entered the Union Army, where despite humiliating discrimination they gave a creditable account of themselves in action.

For all that, the record of the slaves and ex-slaves during the war constituted a disaster. Having relied previously on the protection and guidance of their masters, they now threw themselves on the mercies of the Union Army. As might be expected, untold thousands died in and out of virtual concentration camps, countless women were raped by Union troops, black soldiers generally found themselves used as menials or cannon fodder. Many decent and selfless white and black abolitionists accompanied the Union Army South and earnestly worked to educate and organize the freedmen; they deserve all the praise and attention historians are now heaping on them. The fact remains that no black movement and only a weak black leadership emerged from the war.

SUGGESTIONS FOR FURTHER READING

There is a mass of contemporary writing on all sides of the question. White Southerners, as the readings have shown, were of two minds on the matter. Sometimes they argued that the Negro was a childlike dependent; at other times they expressed fears of a slave insurrection. A contemporary collection of proslavery arguments by Southerners is E. N. Elliott, ed., Cotton Is King and Pro-Slavery Arguments (Augusta, Ga., 1860). George Fitzhugh found the state of the Negro slave far superior to that of Northern and British wage slaves in his *Cannibals All! Or Slaves Without Masters (Richmond, 1857). The most famous discussion by an ex-slave is Frederick Douglass' autobiography *Life and Times of Frederick Douglass (Hartford, Conn., 1882). A convenient modern collection of contemporary writings is Harvey Wish, ed., *Slavery in the South (New York, 1964).

The first systematic study of slavery by a modern American scholar is Ulrich B. Phillips, *American Negro Slavery (New York, 1918; paperback edition, Baton Rouge, 1966). Kenneth Stampp's work, a portion of which is reprinted above, is in many ways an attempted refutation of Phillips. Where Stampp sees runaways, barn burners, and the like as slaves expressing their opposition to slavery, Phillips viewed these same things simply as criminal acts. Herbert Aptheker's pioneering work *American Negro Slave Revolts* (New York, 1943, 1963) finds discontent and rebellion to be characteristic among slaves. Eugene D. Genovese's article (only a part of which is printed here) along with comments and criticisms by Herbert Aptheker, C. Vann Woodward, and Frank Kofsky and a rebuttal by Genovese may be found in *Studies on the Left,* VI (Nov.–Dec., 1966), 4–65. See also Richard C. Wade, *Slavery in the Cities* (New York, 1964).

Some of the most exciting new work on slavery has been in the area of comparative history. In addition to Elkins see Frank Tannenbaum, *Slave and Citizen: The Negro in the Americas* (New York, 1946). A more recent effort is Herbert Klein, *Slavery in the Americas: A Comparative Study of Cuba and Virginia* (Chicago, 1967).

VII
The ★
Abolitionists ★

The age of Jackson was also an age of reform. If it was a time of optimism, intellectual ferment, and growing nationalism, it was also a time when a large number of men and women discovered that America had many problems. A religious revival (The Second Great Awakening), led by ministers like Charles Grandison Finney, spread across the land, leaving in its wake an army of converts ready to drive sin from the face of the earth. But not all reformers were motivated by religious zeal; some were influenced by a rational belief that men could improve their world. Like most Americans these reformers had faith in progress, and they were confident that they could speed the way toward a perfect social order.

The reform impulse took many forms. Some men founded utopian communities, such as Brook Farm near Boston, in order to experiment with new ways of organizing society. Perhaps these utopians were trying to escape the complicated problems of a country just beginning to be transformed by the revolutions in industry and transportation, but they sincerely believed that they were forerunners of a new order and that the world would follow their lead. Although there were a few eccentrics like Sylvester Graham, who was confident that he could change the world by getting everyone to eat "Graham Crackers," most were sincere men and women who set out to promote peace, to improve education, to secure the more humane treatment of prisoners, to win more opportunities and more rights for women, and to prohibit the use of alcoholic beverages. But the greatest reform of all was the crusade against slavery.

There had been opposition to slavery before the 1830's. The Quakers had been one of the few groups that had consistently opposed slavery in the colonial period, but the Revolution, with its emphasis on the rights of "life, liberty and the pursuit of happiness" for all men, initiated a more general movement which resulted by 1804 in the end of slavery, or provision for its abolition, in all Northern states. Even in the South there were many who favored gradual emancipation or who supported the American Colonization Society (organized, 1817) which projected an eventual solution to the problem by shipping freed slaves to Africa.

The antislavery movement changed dramatically about 1830 with the emergence of a small group of abolitionists led by William Lloyd Garrison, Theodore Weld, and other militant radicals who denounced slavery as a crime and demanded immediate emancipation. They were willing to disrupt the union, to incite riot and even war to get rid of human bondage. The abolitionists, always in the minority, often did not agree among themselves, but they uniformly spoke the language of conflict. "I do not wish to think or speak or write with moderation," Garrison announced, "I will not retreat a single inch, and I will be heard."

The abolitionists were controversial at the time and they have continued to arouse disagreement among historians. Any analysis of them depends in part on an evaluation of the institution of slavery, and the antislavery movement before 1830. If one decides that slavery was not a great evil (or a lesser evil than disrupting the union), or if one believes that the movement toward gradual emancipation was making real progress, then it follows that the abolitionists were unnecessarily severe in their attacks on slavery and slaveholders, that the conflict they aroused was unnecessary. If on the other hand one decides that the system of human bondage was shameful and criminal and that such organizations as the American Colonization Society were really attempts to avoid rather than face the problem, then one has reason to defend the militant and aggressive tactics of the abolitionists.

The following selections raise some important and difficult questions regarding the group of militant agitators who believed in conflict to eradicate evil. In the first selection Louis Ruchames takes the abolitionists at their word and takes them seriously. By detailing how little the antislavery movement had accomplished by 1829, he defends the need for a more militant movement in the 1830's. He describes the conflict, the riots, the mobs, the violence, even the killings which the abolitionists provoked by daring to suggest that slavery should be abolished immediately. "The Abolitionists acted vigorously to awaken the antislavery conscience of America and to convince the North of the imperative necessity of abolishing slavery if the rights of all Americans were to be maintained," he concludes.

Avery Craven, in the next selection, takes a quite different position. He assumes that slavery would have been gradually ended through such organizations as the American Colonization Society and he implies that the institution of human bondage itself was not especially evil. For Craven the abolitionists were maladjusted, misguided fanatics. "The extreme and impractical nature of the Garrison antislavery drive served to attract attention and arouse antagonism rather than to solve the problem," he writes. Craven does not deny that the abolitionists provoked conflict, but to him the conflict seems unnecessary and tragic. David Donald analyzes the leaders of the abolitionist movement, and suggests that the reason they became militant reformers was not so much that slavery was evil, but rather that the abolitionists themselves were "an elite without function," suffering because the industrial revolution had displaced them from their positions of leadership in society. "Basically," Donald concludes, "abolitionism should be considered the anguished protest of an aggrieved class against a world they never made." In a different way than Craven, but with similar results, Donald implies that although there was conflict between the abolitionist and the South, the conflict was essentially the product of the reformers' failure to adjust to changes in their society and had little to do with the evils of slavery.

Martin Duberman, one of several young historians who are reexamining the antislavery movement from the perspectives of the 1960's, views the abolitionists in a broader context and is concerned with why the North did not accept the abolitionists' militant solution. He suggests that any radical attack on social problems tends to compromise the national optimism and, therefore, the majority of Americans find it necessary to label "extreme" any movement which calls for large scale readjustments in society. Duberman also strikes out at those historians who suggest that any individual who protests strongly against social injustice is disturbed or fanatical. Those who fail to protest strongly against an institution as inhuman as slavery are the real "neurotics" he suggests.

What then was the Abolitionist movement? Was it a useless crusade led by fanatics or a displaced elite? Or was it a radical and rational attempt to end a great evil—human slavery? The abolitionists believed in conflict, but why did not most Northerners accept their interpretation of the situation? Was the conflict and the antagonism fostered and encouraged by the abolitionists unnecessary and tragic?

The abolitionists: consecrated radicals

Louis Ruchames

"The character of a city is determined by the character of the men it crowns," once remarked Wendell Phillips, quoting the Greek orator Aeschines. Applying the lesson to modern times, there are few periods in American history that offer as remarkable an opportunity for the molding of American character to the highest standards of humanity as that in which the men and women known as Abolitionists lived and wrought. Devoted to the ideals of brotherhood and equality of opportunity for all men, their consciences seared by the heartlessness of slavery in the South and racial prejudice in the North, they consecrated their lives to the eradication of both evils. Encompassed by both indifference and hostility, sub-

Reprinted by permission of G. P. Putnam's Sons from *The Abolitionists*, pp. 13–23, edited by Louis Ruchames. ℗ 1963 by Louis Ruchames.

jected to social ostracism, economic sanctions and physical violence for daring to condemn institutions and customs which were regarded as vital to the welfare of American society and therefore sacrosanct, they stubbornly and heroically continued their efforts until victory in the war against slavery was achieved.

The nature of the revolution wrought by the Abolitionists may best be assessed by placing ourselves in the year 1829, immediately before the rise of the modern Abolitionist movement. In December of that year, the American Convention for Promoting the Abolition of Slavery and Improving the Condition of the African Race held its twenty-first biennial convention at Washington, D. C., with delegates present from New York, Pennsylvania, Maryland, Washington, D. C., and Alexandria, Virginia. Formed thirty-five years earlier in an attempt to unite the efforts of existing state and local anti-slavery groups, the organization's successes and failures during the intervening years were highlighted in three notable reports to the convention.

In the first, Benjamin Lundy, one of the great anti-slavery pioneers, enumerated its successes. These were an increase in the number of anti-slavery advocates from very few to thousands, some of them "among the most influential characters in the nation"; the complete abolition of slavery in certain states, particularly Rhode Island, Connecticut, New York, New Jersey, Pennsylvania, Ohio, Indiana and Illinois; and the passage of the Missouri Compromise in 1820 which had prohibited the extension of slavery north of 36° 30'.

The failures were detailed in two other reports which noted no visible improvement in the treatment of the slave since 1790, the year of the first census, but rather an alarming increase in the number of slaves from 694,280 to about 2,000,000 and a tripling in the area devoted to slavery from an original 212,000 to nearly 600,000 square miles. Most disturbing, however, one report noted, was the public apathy toward all efforts to help the slave, which "are viewed in the light of encroachment on the established order of society, for so deeply has the system of slavery become rooted in the soil, that even those who are not directly interested in its continuance, are not disposed to aid by their countenance, or afford us assistance in pecuniary manner—and thus our usefulness is checked, and our endeavors to lay before the public the train of evils attendant on a state of slavery are retarded. . . ."

That the anti-slavery movement, in the light of its own statements in 1829, had marched into a cul-de-sac which required heroic efforts on its part to extricate itself, seems evident today. The greatest need was a re-examination of its basic strategy which had been based upon "moderation" and "temperance" in describing the nature of slavery and the responsibility of the slaveholder; the espousal of "gradualism" and colonization of former slaves to areas outside the United States as the most feasible methods of hastening the end of slavery; and an emphasis upon convincing the slaveholder that it was to his economic interest to liberate the slave and utilize free labor instead.

The results of this strategy were the very opposite of what its proponents had intended. The recourse to a very cautious "moderation" in language, and the avoidance of any language likely to antagonize the slaveowner, simply minimized the inherent evils of the institution and the responsibility of the slaveowner for the suffering of the slave and made it more difficult to awaken the public conscience to a recognition of the evil; the appeal to self-interest foundered upon the reality of slavery as a source of wealth to the master and his family; the policy of gradual emancipation provided an excuse for doing nothing immediately and salved the consciences of those who were indisposed to take vigorous action; while colonization, recommended by the American Colonization Society since 1816—and by many who were sincerely interested in helping the slave—actually hindered emancipation and the struggle for equal rights for the Negro. For colonization assumed the inferiority of the Negro and regarded his presence in this country as a danger to white American society and thus reinforced the very arguments which were being used to keep him in slavery and to deprive him, when free, of the rights of a white man.

The resulting situation has been perceptively summarized by Albert Bushnell Hart.

When Jackson became president, in 1829, anti-slavery seemed, after fifty years of effort, to have spent its force. The voice of the churches was no longer heard in protest; the abolitionist societies were dying out; there was hardly an abolitionist militant in the field; the Colonization Society absorbed most of the public interest in the subject, and it was doing nothing to help either the free Negro or the slave; in Congress there was only one anti-slavery man, and his efforts were without avail. It was a gloomy time for the little band of people who believed that slavery was poisonous to the south, hurtful to the north, and dangerous to the Union.

It was at this point that William Lloyd Garrison appeared with a revolutionary philosophy that challenged every basic assumption of the existing anti-slavery societies, and building upon new foundations, created a movement which ultimately brought about the destruction of slavery. Harriet Martineau, the English author, in her little volume entitled *The Martyr Age of the United States*, has called Garrison "the mastermind of the great revolution." He was indeed that and more. Born in 1805 to a mother who was a pious Baptist and a father who deserted his family when the boy was three years old, Garrison early sought to prepare himself for the profession of writing. A newspaper apprentice at thirteen, he later edited newspapers in Newburyport, Boston and Bennington. In 1827, in Boston, he met Benjamin Lundy, a New Jersey Quaker who had been carrying on a one-man crusade against slavery for more than fifteen years. Lundy had formed anti-slavery societies throughout the country, had promoted schemes for Negro colonization in Mexico and Haiti, and had been editing the *Genius of Universal Emancipation* since 1821. Lundy persuaded Garrison to move to Baltimore in the fall of 1829 and join him in editing his newspaper, which then became a weekly. Several months later the partnership was interrupted when Garrison, convicted of libel by a Baltimore jury for excoriating a Massachusetts shipowner who had been transporting slaves for the South, was jailed upon failure to pay the fine of $50 and costs. Upon his release—the fine having been paid by Arthur Tappan, a New York merchant and anti-slavery philanthropist—he made plans to issue his own newspaper, which he realized with the appearance of the *Liberator* in Boston on January 1, 1831. Starting without capital and aided by Isaac Knapp, a printer, Garrison relied for financial support primarily upon Negro contributions and subscriptions, supplemented by those of a few white sympathizers.

The revolutionary nature of Garrison's thought, made manifest in the first pages of the *Liberator*, was summarized years later by Wendell Phillips in his comment that Garrison "undertook to look at the slave question as the Negro looked at it." Identifying himself completely with the slave, Garrison saw and felt slavery in all its terror and misery, refused to accept as valid any excuse for its continuance, and demanded its immediate and total abolition. Identifying himself, too, with the free Negro, he affirmed the latter's right to complete equality of opportunity and condemned the American Colonization Society for viewing the Negro as a danger to American society, to be freed from slavery only if he left the country. Indeed, within a few years after he had begun to expose the pernicious nature of this philosophy, an anti-slavery man who defended the American Colonization Society became a rarity. One aspect of Garrison's philosophy was his refusal to bate one jot or tittle from the deserved condemnation of either slavery or the slaveholder. Viewing slavery as a crime against millions of human beings which contravened the established moral and religious principles of decent humanity, to Garrison the slaveholder was a criminal whose piety as a Christian and respectability as citizen, husband and father, did not palliate in the slightest the horror of his action toward the slave. So accustomed was American society of that day—including many who were honestly anti-slavery—to speak in soft tones of slavery and the slaveholder, that Garrison's language seemed outlandish and violent. Yet what he wrote was never coarse or vulgar, and to the fair-minded observer today, remembering the villainy that had to be described and the indifference to be overcome, it appears appropriate and necessary.

Through the cogency of his arguments and the sincerity and vitality of his writings and speeches, Garrison soon attracted to himself a varied group of friends and associates.

Harriet Martineau once wrote:

There is a remarkable set of people now living and vigorously acting in the world, with a consonance of will and understanding which has perhaps never been witnessed among so large a number of individuals of such diversified powers, habits, opinions, tastes and circumstances. The body comprehends men and women of every shade of color, of every degree of education, of every variety of religious opinion, of every gradation of rank, bound together by no vow, no pledge, no stipulation but of each preserving his individual liberty; and yet they act as if they were of one heart and of one soul. Such union could be secured by no principle of worldly interest; nor, for a term of years, by the most stringent fanaticism. A well-grounded faith, directed towards a noble object, is the only principle which can account for such a spectacle as the world is now waking up to contemplate in the abolitionists of the United States.

Among the first to be deeply influenced were Samuel J. May, of Brooklyn, Connecticut, the only Unitarian minister then in the state; May's brother-in-law Bronson Alcott; and Samuel E. Sewall, May's cousin, a young Boston lawyer who was a descendant of Judge Samuel Sewall of Colonial fame and a member of one of the most prominent families of the Commonwealth. The three had attended a lecture by Garrison in Boston in October 1830 at which Garrison had argued the doctrine of immediate emancipation. They had been deeply impressed, had offered Garrison their cooperation, and had invited him to Bronson Alcott's home where they spent several hours. So great was the impact of that meeting that almost forty years later May still retained much of his original fervor when he wrote: "That night my soul was baptized in his spirit, and ever since I have been a disciple and fellow-laborer of William Lloyd Garrison." May helped in the formation of the American Anti-Slavery Society, served as general agent and secretary of the Massachusetts Anti-Slavery Society, and in the midst of a busy ministerial career devoted to many causes, achieved a notable reputation as a reformer and friend of the slave. Others who joined Garrison's standard were John Greenleaf Whittier, whose poems Garrison was the first to publish in the Newburyport *Herald*, and who became an early and devoted friend, though the two later differed on the question of political action; Ellis Gray Loring, a rising young Boston lawyer of a socially prominent family, who took his place as a leader in the Massachusetts Anti-Slavery Society; Oliver Johnson, born and raised in Vermont, who was first influenced by Garrison's *Journal of the Times*, and who later, in 1831, as editor of the *Christian Soldier*—with an office in the building in which the *Liberator* was published—became his devoted friend, collaborator and the author of his first full-length biography; Arnold Buffum, a Quaker hat manufacturer who became the first president of the New England Anti-Slavery Society, although he later left the Garrison camp for political action with the Liberty Party; and David and Lydia Maria Child, husband and wife, the former a journalist, teacher, lawyer and for a short period a member of the Massachusetts legislature, the latter a popular novelist and publicist whose *An Appeal in Favor of that Class of Americans Called Africans*, published in July 1833, gained many new converts for the anti-slavery movement.

The first organizational result of Garrison's teaching was the formation, after several meetings, of the New England Anti-Slavery Society on

January 6, 1832. Its constitution, adopted on that day, was the first to avow the principle of immediate emancipation. Among the twelve who signed it were Garrison, Johnson, Buffum, Knapp and Joshua Coffin. Although David Child, Sewall and Loring at first objected to the inclusion of the immediate emancipation clause on grounds of expediency and refused to sign, they did so soon after and assumed leading posts in the organization.

Of great significance to the cause was the publication in 1832 of a pamphlet by Garrison entitled "Thoughts on African Colonization," which exposed the pretensions of the American Colonization Society and condemned it out of the writings and speeches of its leaders as an anti-Negro, pro-slavery organization. The pamphlet had a wide impact, influencing such men as Elizur Wright, Jr. and Beriah Green, two professors at Western Reserve College who were later to play a prominent part in the anti-slavery movement, as well as Lewis and Arthur Tappan, the influential businessmen-philanthropists of New York.

Anti-slavery sentiment now increased in different parts of the country and voices were raised in favor of forming a national anti-slavery organization upon the principles of immediate, unconditional emancipation. The publication in 1833 of Whittier's pamphlet, "Justice and Expediency" and of Lydia Maria Child's *Appeal*, further stirred public opinion and gained new converts. So did the persecution of Prudence Crandall by leading public officials of the State of Connecticut for seeking to educate Negro girls in her school in Canterbury, Connecticut. At this time, too, there emerged in New York City a group of anti-slavery men of ability and vision who began to agitate for the formation of anti-slavery societies in New York City and nationally. These included, along with the Tappans, William Goodell, an editor of the *Genius of Temperance* and later of the *Emancipator*, established in 1833; Isaac T. Hopper, a radical Quaker of Philadelphia who had moved to New York, and who had been helping escaped slaves and free Negroes for many years; Joshua Leavitt, editor of the *Evangelist* and subsequently of the *Emancipator*; and William Jay, author and reformer, the son of Chief Justice John Jay. These took the lead in forming a New York anti-slavery society in October 1833.

On October 29, 1833, a month after Garrison's return from England, where he had spent several months securing the support of English Abolitionists for the American anti-slavery movement and their condemnation of the American Colonization Society, a call for a national convention was issued. According to varying estimates, between 50 and 60 delegates, among whom were several Negroes, met in Philadelphia on three days in early December. Beriah Green, then president of Oneida Institute, acted as president, with Lewis Tappan and Whittier as secretaries. Garrison, May and Whittier were chosen to draw up a declaration of principles. Asked by the other two to write a draft, Garrison wrote through the night at the home of his host, Frederick A. Hinton—a Negro Abolitionist of Philadelphia and a delegate to the convention—and completed it by morning. Samuel J. May had this to say about the impact of the declaration upon the delegates: "Never in my life have I seen a deeper impression made by words than was made by that admirable document upon all who were there present . . . We felt that the word had just been uttered which would be mighty, through God, to the pulling down of the strongholds of slavery."

The formation of the national society gave an additional fillip to growing anti-slavery sentiment. From New England to the Mississippi River, anti-slavery organizations mushroomed into being. In 1835, Garrison referred to "our 4 or 500 societies." During that year alone, 328 new societies were formed, 254 of which boasted 27,182 members. By 1838, there were 1,350 societies in the national organization, with a membership of about 250,000. In Massachusetts, in 1837, there were 145 local societies, in New York 274 societies, and in Ohio, the most ardent anti-slavery state in the West, 213.

In 1834, a *cause célèbre* occurred near Cincinnati that proved of immense significance to the anti-slavery movement, especially in the West. The locale was Lane Seminary, which had been founded to prepare young men for the ministry and whose president was the eminent Boston minister, Lyman Beecher. In 1834, as a result of the publication of Garrison's *Thoughts on African Colonization* and the founding of the American Anti-Slavery Society, discussions arose among the students concerning the aims and methods of the anti-slavery enterprise. It was decided to debate two questions: the validity of immediate, unconditional emancipation and the worthwhileness of the American Colonization Society. The upshot was a debate extending over eighteen evenings; the result, the passage of resolutions approving immediate emancipation and condemning the American Colonization Society. Reports of the proceedings were published throughout the country, with ensuing public pressure which impelled the faculty and board of overseers to ban the newly formed student anti-slavery society as well as a previously approved colonization society. Most of the students resigned in protest, and many—including several Southerners—became active Abolitionists and leaders in the American Anti-Slavery Society. Among these were Amos Dresser, who received twenty lashes on his back when found with anti-slavery literature in Tennessee; James A. Thome, son of a Kentucky slaveholder; Henry B. Stanton, who was appointed agent and lecturer for the American Anti-Slavery Society; and most prominent of all, Theodore D. Weld, regarded by the trustees as instigator of the entire episode, of whom Samuel J. May has written that "no one except Garrison and Phillips had done more for the abolition of American slavery." It was partly as a result of the Lane episode, as well as the impact of the formation of the American Anti-Slavery Society, that James G. Birney of Kentucky was led to abandon the American Colonization Society and to participate actively in the anti-slavery movement.

As the Abolitionist movement grew, so did the fears of the friends of slavery and their hatred of the Abolitionists. The outcome included frequent mob riots, beatings and even killings. On October 21, 1835, a Boston mob consisting mostly of "gentlemen of property and influence" broke up a meeting of the Boston Female Anti-Slavery Society, which was to be addressed by George F. Thompson, a well-known English Abolitionist. In the course of the riot, Garrison was almost hanged and was finally saved by being lodged in jail. On the same day, in Utica, a meeting of 600 delegates assembled to form a New York State anti-slavery society was broken up by rioters. It was as a result of this riot that Gerrit Smith, a prominent reformer and philanthropist, joined the American Anti-Slavery Society. Henry B. Stanton is supposed to have been mobbed at least two hundred times, Theodore Weld's speeches were frequently disrupted, and in 1837 Owen Lovejoy, the anti-slavery editor, was slain at Alton, Illinois, while trying to prevent the destruction of his fourth newspaper press. It was at a meeting in Boston, called to memorialize Lovejoy's death, that Wendell Phillips, then twenty-six years old, made an impromptu address and began a career which in anti-slavery importance was second perhaps only to Garrison's.

Until 1837, the history of the anti-slavery movement was one of a continuously growing and united movement despite religious, political and social differences among its members. In that year, however, the first of a number of schisms, which ultimately were to lead to a divided movement, appeared. In Massachusetts, an "Appeal of Clerical Abolitionists on Anti-Slavery Measures," which criticized some of Garrison's tactics, was followed by another statement by the Abolitionists of Andover Theological Seminary which objected to Garrison's language, his attacks upon church ministers who refused to cooperate with the Abolitionists, and his espousal of public lectures by women.

These attacks soon involved several of the New York anti-slavery leaders and others of the national organization who refused to come to Garrison's defense and were therefore, in Garrison's opinion, giving tacit approval to his critics. These included the Tappans, Birney, Elizur Wright, Leavitt and others who did not share Garrison's views on the place of women in the anti-slavery movement, who thought his attacks on the churches ill-considered, his language abusive and his negative attitude toward certain kinds of political action a deterrent to the further development of the anti-slavery movement. The conflict came to a head at the annual convention of the national organization in 1840, when Garrison and his followers elected Abby Kelley to the society's business committee. Thereupon, Lewis Tappan, who had been the society's president, led his followers from the convention and formed the American and Foreign Anti-Slavery Society. The *Emancipator*, the official newspaper of the original organization, had been transferred earlier to the New York Anti-Slavery Society, which was controlled by anti-Garrison forces. In its place, Garrison and his group established the *National Anti-Slavery Standard* under the aegis of the American Anti-Slavery Society. Lydia M. Child soon assumed the duties of editor, was followed by her husband David Lee Child and then by Sydney Gay, who edited the paper with the help of Edmund Quincy and James Russell Lowell.

It may be noted that while the American Anti-Slavery Society carried on with undiminished vigor until after the Civil War, the American and Foreign Anti-Slavery Society, though it held annual meetings and issued some effective pamphlets, gradually dwindled in strength and passed out of existence in the 1850's, while the *Emancipator* stopped publication even earlier. Years later, Lewis Tappan, in the biography of his brother Arthur, implied that, judged by its results, the secession was not as well-advised as it seemed to be at the time. For though the secessionists adopted "such language and such measures as Christians could not reasonably object to, those who had been loudest in their opposition and most offended with what they termed the unchristian spirit of the Abolitionists, kept aloof as well from the American and Foreign Anti-Slavery Society . . ." It seems reasonable to conclude that it was not Garrison's language or his espousal of the rights of women or his attacks upon the churches for their indifference to slavery which brought down upon the Abolitionists the wrath of so many of America's political, economic and religious leaders, but the doctrine of immediate and unconditional emancipation, which was indeed a revolutionary doctrine for its time and represented a threat to what many believed to be the foundation of the existing social and economic order.

The abolitionists: irresponsible fanatics

Avery Craven

Removing motes from a brother's eye is an ancient practice. The urge to make over other individuals and to correct real or fancied evils in society operates with unusual force in certain individuals. This used to be

From Avery Craven, *The Coming of the Civil War*, pp. 117–119, 134–150. Copyright © 1957 by Avery Craven. Reprinted by permission of The University of Chicago Press.

ascribed to a peculiar sensitiveness to wrongdoing—a willingness to sacrifice personal comfort for a larger good. Perpetual reformers, though resented as meddlers by those they disturbed, have been hailed as pioneers and martyrs who have unselfishly helped to usher in new eras and a better world.

The modern psychologist is somewhat skeptical of such explanations. He talks of youthful experiences, maladjustments, inferiority complexes, and repressed desires. He is not so sure about the sources of the reform impulse or the unselfish character of the reformer. The student of social affairs is likewise less inclined to grant unstinted praise to the fanatic and is not certain about the value of the contribution. He views him as a normal product of social phenomena acting on certain types of personality. He sees the triumph of emotion over reason in the extremist's course and sometimes wonders if the developments of history might not have been more sound without him. He talks with less assurance about "progress" in human affairs.

At all events, recent historians have been inclined to reconsider the part played by the abolitionists in the coming of the War Between the States. They have judged the reformer and his efforts to be open fields for new study. The old assumptions that the movements against slavery arose entirely from a disinterested hatred of injustice and that their results were good beyond question can no longer be accepted without reservations. Those who force the settlement of human problems by war can expect only an unsympathetic hearing from the future. Mere desire to do "right" is no defense at the bar of history.

*   *   *   *

Slavery as a reality and slavery as the symbol about which sectional conflict raged for a generation were two different things. The first was a very ancient labor system, drastically adjusted to local American conditions, and one which may have been almost ready to break down of its own weight in one of the last corners left to it on the face of the earth; the second was the creation of inflamed imaginations which endowed the institution with all the ills possible in its theory and assigned to the slaveowner all the qualities and characteristics desirable in a bitter rival. The first was not a major economic factor in Southern life, as the record of free Negroes since the war has amply demonstrated. The second was an emotional influence which left few pages in the nation's history untouched from 1820 to 1860.

In the period before 1820 slavery had been sharply criticized by farseeing men in all parts of the nation. Quaker groups, especially in Pennsylvania, Virginia, and the Carolinas, early and late quietly insisted on its moral weakness. The doctrines of natural rights and individual equality emphasized by the American Revolution increased the opposition, and unprofitableness in periods of depression after independence was won permitted open condemnation. In the Northern states, where slaves were too few to create a race problem and where white families were usually large enough to furnish a labor supply for small-scale effort, slavery was gradually abolished. Even in the South, where the institution was then localized, Washington apologized for it and Jefferson roundly denounced it. Teachers in Southern colleges questioned its economic value and its ethical foundations. Most Southern men spoke of it as an institution which they confidently expected to disappear in due season. They helped to check the slave trade and to keep slavery from the Northwest Territory. Many freed their own slaves; more hoped to do so at a later time.

The much abused American Colonization movement was a sane effort to give practical expression to these sentiments. It recognized the race problem produced by manumission as the one serious difficulty in the way. It proposed to transport out of the country all slaves whom masters might free. That would solve the social problem and encourage further grants of freedom. The assumption, clearly implied, was that all fair men recognized the evil in slavery and that human beings could be relied upon to act justly in regard to it. Cooperation was a better way of getting results than angry attack. . . .

The abolition movement was . . . closely related in origins, leadership, and expression to the peace movement, the temperance crusade, the struggles for women's rights, prison and Sabbath reform, and the improvement of education. It was not unrelated to the efforts to establish communities where social-economic justice and high thinking might prevail. It was part of the drive to unseat aristocrats and re-establish American democracy according to the Declaration of Independence. It was a clear-cut effort to apply Christianity to the American social order.

The anti-slavery effort was at first merely one among many. It rose to dominance only gradually. Fortunate from the beginning in leadership, it was always more fortunate in appeal. Human slavery more obviously violated democratic institutions than any other evil of the day; it was close enough to irritate and to inflame sensitive minds, yet far enough removed that reformers need have few personal relations with those whose interests were affected. It rasped most severely upon the moral senses of a people whose ideas of sin were comprehended largely in terms of self-indulgence and whose religious doctrines laid emphasis on social usefulness as the proper manifestation of salvation. And, what was more important, slavery was now confined to a section whose economic interests, and hence political attitudes, conflicted sharply with those of the Northeast and upper Northwest.

Almost from the beginning of the new anti-slavery movement, two distinct centers of action appeared, each with its distinct and individual approach to the problem. One developed in the industrial areas of New England. Its most important spokesman was William Lloyd Garrison, founder and editor of a Boston abolition paper called the *Liberator*. Garrison at first accepted the old idea that slavery was an *evil* to be pointed out and gradually eradicated by those among whom it existed, but he shifted his position in the early 1830's and denounced slavery as a damning crime to be unremittingly assailed and immediately destroyed. The first issue of his paper announced a program from which he never deviated: "... *I do not wish to think or speak or write with moderation. I will not retreat a single inch, and I will be heard.*" The problem, as Garrison saw it, was one of abstract right and wrong. The Scriptures and the Declaration of Independence had already settled the issue. Slavery could have no legal status in a Christian democracy. If the Constitution recognized it, then the Constitution should be destroyed. Slaveholders were both sinners and criminals. They could lay no claim to immunity from any mode of attack.

The character of this movement and its leadership is strikingly revealed in an incident related by one of Garrison's traveling companions:

As we rode through the [Franconia] Notch after friends Beach and Rogers, we were alarmed at seeing smoke issue from their chaise-top, and we cried out to them that their chaise was afire! We were more than suspicious that it was something worse than that, and that the smoke came out of friend Rogers' mouth. And so it turned out. This was before we reached the Notch tavern. Alighting there to water our beasts, we gave him, all round a faithful admonition. For anti-slavery does not fail to spend its intervals of public service in mutual and searching correction of the faults of it friends. We gave it soundly to friend Rogers—that he, an abolitionist, on his way to an anti-slavery meeting, should desecrate his anti-slavery mouth ... with a stupefying weed. We had halted at the Iron Works tavern to refresh our horses, and while they were eating walked to view the Furnace. As we crossed the little bridge, friend Rogers took out another cigar, as if to light it when we should reach the fire! "Is it any malady you have got, brother Rogers," said we to him "that you smoke that thing, or is it habit and indulgence merely?" "It is nothing but habit," said he gravely; "or I would say, it was nothing else," and he significantly cast the little roll over the railing into the Ammonoosuck.
"A Revolution!" exclaimed Garrison, "a glorious revolution without noise or smoke," and he swung his hat cheerily about his head. It was a pretty incident. ... It was a vice abandoned, a self indulgence denied, and from principle. It was quietly and beautifully done. ... Anti-slavery wants her mouths for other uses than to be flues for besotting tobacco-smoke. They may as well almost be rum-ducts as tobacco-funnels. ... Abolitionists are generally as *crazy* in regard to rum and tobacco as in regard to slavery. Some of them refrain from eating flesh and drinking tea and coffee. Some of them are so bewildered that they want in the way of Christian retaliation ... they are getting to be monomoniacs, as the Reverend Punchard called us, on *every* subject.

The extreme and impractical nature of the Garrison anti-slavery drive served to attract attention and rouse antagonism rather than to solve the problem. It did, however, show how profoundly the conditions of the time had stirred the reform spirit and how wide the door had been opened to the professional reformers—men to whom the question was not so much "how shall we abolish slavery, as how shall we best discharge our duty

. . . to ourselves." Garrison may be taken as typical of the group. His temperament and experiences had combined to set him in most relationships against the accepted order of things. His life would probably have been spent in protesting even if slavery had never existed. From childhood he had waged a bitter fight *against* obstacles and *for* a due recognition of his abilities. A drunken father had abandoned the family to extreme poverty before William was three years old, and the boy, denied all but the rudiments of an education, had first been placed under the care of Deacon Bartlett, and then apprenticed for seven years to one Ephraim Allen to learn the printing trade. His first venture after his apprenticeship was over failed. His second gave him the opportunity to strike back at an unfair world. He became an editor of the *National Philanthropist*, a paper devoted to the suppression of "intemperance and its Kindred vices." This publication served also as a medium through which to attack lotteries, Sabbath-breaking, and war. A new Garrison began to emerge. His personality, given opportunity for expression, asserted itself. Attending a nominating caucus in Boston, he made bold to speak, and, being resented as an upstart, he replied to his critic in a letter to the Boston *Courier*:

> It is true my acquaintance in this city is limited. . . . Let me assure him, however, that if my life be spared, my name shall one day be known to the world—at least to such an extent that common inquiry shall be unnecessary.

To another critic he reiterated this statement, adding these significant words: "I speak in the words of prophecy, not of vainglory—with a strong pulse, a flashing eye, and a glow of the heart. The task may be yours to write my biography."

Anti-slavery efforts entered the Garrison program when Benjamin Lundy, the pioneer abolitionist, invited him to help edit the *Genius of Universal Emancipation* in Baltimore. Hostile treatment there, climaxed by imprisonment for libel, together with the influence of extreme British opinion, changed a moderate attitude which admitted "that immediate and complete emancipation is not desirable . . . no rational man cherishes so wild a vision," into the extreme and uncompromising fanaticism expressed only two years later in the *Liberator*. From that time on Garrison was bothered only by the fact that the English language was inadequate for the expression of his violent opinions. Southerners in Congress were desperados.

> We would sooner trust the honor of the country . . . in the hands of the inmates of our penitentiaries and prisons than in their hands . . . they are the meanest of thieves and the worst of robbers. . . . We do not acknowledge them to be within the pale of Christianity, or republicanism, or humanity!

Hatred of the South had supplanted love for the Negro!

In such an approach as this, there could be no delay, no moderation. Right was right, and wrong was wrong. The Slaveholder could not be spared or given time to learn the evil of his ways. Action immediate and untempered was demanded. Yet this was the same William Lloyd Garrison who, in 1877, replied to Susan B. Anthony's request for aid for Women's Suffrage:

You desire me to send you a letter, to be read at the Washington Convention of the National Woman Suffrage Association, in favor of a petition to Congress, asking that body to submit to the several States a 16th Amendment for the Constitution of the United States, securing suffrage for all, irrespective of sex. On fully considering the subject, I must decline doing so, because such a petition I deem to be quite premature. If its request were complied with by the present Congress—a supposition simply preposterous —the proposed Amendment would be rejected by every State in the Union, and in nearly every instance by such an overwhelming majority as to bring the movement into needless contempt. Even as a matter of "agitation," I do not think it would pay. Look over the whole country, and see in the present state of public sentiment on the question of woman suffrage what a mighty primary work remains to be done in enlightening the masses, who know nothing and care nothing about it, and consequently are not at all prepared to cast their votes for any such thing. . . .

Evidently circumstances alter cases in reform as drastically as in other lines of human endeavor!

The second center of anti-slavery effort was in upper New York and the farther Northwest. Influences from this center included in their sweep, however, much of rural New England and the Middle States and the movement found liberal financial help in New York City. Benjamin Lundy and other Quaker leaders started the crusade, but it did not come to full and wide expression until Theodore Weld, already the ablest temperance orator in the Northwest, set about cultivating the great field prepared for social reform by the Finney revivals.

Weld was, like Garrison, unusual both in abilities and in personal characteristics. He was much given to "anti-meat, -butter, -tea, and -coffee, etc. -ism[s]." He indulged in excessive self-effacement and in extravagant confessions of selfishness, pride, impatience of contradiction, personal recklessness, and "a bad, unlovely temper." Of his pride, "the great besetment of my soul," he wrote:

I am too proud to be ambitious, too proud to seek applause, too proud to tolerate it when lavished upon me, proud as Lucifer that I can and do scorn applause and spurn flattery, and indignantly dash down and shiver to atoms the censer in which others would burn incense to me; too proud to betray emotions, too proud ever for an instant to lose my self possession whatever the peril, too proud to ever move a hair for personal interest, too proud ever to defend my character when assailed or my motives when impeached, too proud ever to wince when the hot iron enters my soul and passes thro it.

He wrote also of his contempt of opponents—"one of the *trade* winds of my nature [which] very often . . . *blows a hurricane*," and he listed by name those "who strangely and stupidly idolize me . . . and yield themselves to my sway in all confidence and love." He boasted of his daring and told of how as a child a tremendous thunderstorm would send him whooping and hallooing through the fields like a wild Indian. He had the Puritan's love of enduring; the saint's "right" to intolerance. He was, in fact, always a revivalist—a man with a mission to perform in the great West—"the battlefield of the World."

The campaign which he launched was but an expansion of the benevolence crusade already a part of the Western revival effort. As W. C. Preston said: "Weld's agents made the anti-slavery cause 'identical with religion,' and urged men, by all they esteem[ed] holy, by all the high and exciting obligations of duty to man and God . . . to join the pious work of purging the sin of slavery from the land." The movement, as it developed, was generally temperate in tone, and tended to function through the existing agencies of religion and politics. Lane Theological Seminary, founded in Cincinnati to train leaders in the Finney tradition, became the center from which Weld worked. Here, in a series of debates, he shaped the doctrine of gradual immediatism which by insisting that *gradual emancipation* begin *at once*, saved the movement from Garrison's extremes; from here he went out to win of group of converts which included James G. Birney, Joshua Giddings, Edwin M. Stanton, Elizur Wright, and Beriah Green; and here he adapted the revival technique to the abolition crusade and prepared the way for his loyal band of Seventy to carry that crusade throughout the whole Northwest.

There was, however, another aspect to the movement in this region—a very hard-headed practical aspect. Its leaders believed in action as well as agitation. And action here meant political action. Western men had a way of viewing evil as something there ought to be a law against. They thought it was the business of government to secure morality as well as prosperity. They were even inclined to regard the absence of prosperity as the result of the existence of evil. Naturally, therefore, in spite of the revival-meeting procedure used to spread the gospel of abolition, action against slavery followed political precedent. This action began with petitions to Congress for such a practical end as the abolition of slavery in the District of Columbia. When Southern resentment of such a measure brought the adoption of gag rule methods, the contest was broadened into a fight on the floors of Congress for the constitutional rights of petition and free speech. This proved to be an excellent way to keep the slavery question before the public and to force slaveholders to reveal their undemocractic attitudes. Petitions arrived in such quantities as to clog the work of Congress. A Washington organization for agitation and lobbying became necessary. Weld himself went to Washington to advise with John Quincy Adams and his fellow workers. Slavery thus again entered national politics, this time by way of the Northwest. Anti-slavery politicians, such as Joshua Giddings and Salmon P. Chase of Ohio, quickly proved the value of the cause as a stepping-stone to public office.

James Birney took the next step. The indifference of old political parties to petitions and abolition demands gave rise to the belief that the slave interest controlled their programs. The conviction that the welfare of other sections was being neglected for the advancement of the South followed logically upon this premise. The slave power, said the abolitionists, had already destroyed the protective system "at the hazard, if not with the intention" of breaking up the manufacturing interests of the free states. The federal government had developed and protected markets for cotton "in all parts of the known world, while it studiously avoided doing anything to procure a market for the free products of the grain-growing Northwest." As a result wheat had been stacked seven successive years in the fields, and none sold. The United States had sent

six expensive embassies to make markets for tobacco. We had one embassy six years to get money for a few slaves wrecked on a British colony; but not one to find a market for the astonishing produce of the great Northwest. We've been thirty years toiling to keep a market for cotton; but not an hour for wheat. If our government was honest; if our statesmen had eyes, they would see that the most important benefit they could render this country would be to find a market for the produce of the Northwest. . . .

Anti-slavery must organize a political party.

The Liberty Party entered the national field in 1840 with James G. Birney as its candidate. It was a protest party. In his acceptance letter, Birney declared that the country was in the hands of the slave power—"the North . . . a conquered province." Its honor, its influence and the real prosperity of the nation had declined in proportion to Southern rule. Tariffs, beneficial to free labor, had been abandoned; monetary affairs had become deranged; commercial opportunities had been neglected. Abolitionists could vote for neither Van Buren nor Harrison.

Having issued this statement, the Liberty Party candidate set out for London to attend the General Anti-Slavery Convention of 1840. He carried with him to the English Anti-Corn Law League a mass of propaganda designed to aid in opening the English markets for the wheat crops of the Old Northwest. His general purpose was to secure the withdrawal of all British restrictions on American wheat and to encourage the growth in India of cotton for English factories. English commercial interests would thus be shifted from the South to the North and slavery in American cotton fields would be rendered unprofitable. Throughout the summer and fall, Birney waged his presidential campaign on British soil. Back home the dejected wheat farmers of the Northwest organized Anti-Corn Law Societies to help influence the course of English politics!

As economic rivalry between North and South increased, the anti-slavery movement gained strength and began to emerge as the dominant reform effort of the period. The motives underlying this development are partly revealed by a letter written by Joshua Leavitt to his friend Joshua Giddings in October, 1841. Leavitt spoke of Giddings' belief that the best

policy for action was to aim "at specific points . . . which you deem beneficial to free labor or rather to the North, as a bank, tariff, etc." and then
declared that his own purpose was to make opposition to slavery the
leading object of public policy. "We must have a leading object," he
continued,

in which we can all harmonize, and to which we shall agree to defer all
other favorite objects. It is vain to think of harmonizing the North in favor
of a restrictive policy or an artificial credit system. . . . There is no object but
slavery that can serve our turn . . . it is the greatest of evils and the prime
cause of other evils. . . .

With the new growth and new importance of the movement, the technique of its propaganda also reached new efficiency. Never before or since
has a cause been urged upon the American people with such consummate
skill and such lasting effects. Every agency possible in that day was
brought into use; even now the predominating opinions of most of the
American people regarding the ante-bellum South and its ways are the
product of that campaign of education.

Indoctrination began with the child's A B C's which were learned from
booklets containing verses like the following:

A is an Abolitionist
A man who wants to free
The wretched slave, and give to all
An equal liberty.

B is a Brother with a skin
Of somewhat darker hue,
But in our Heavenly Father's sight,
He is as dear as you.

C is the Cotton field, to which
This injured brother's driven,
When, as the white man's *slave*, he toils
From early morn till even.

D is the Driver, cold and stern,
Who follows, whip in hand,
To punish those who dare to rest,
Or disobey command.

* * *

I is the Infant, from the arms
Of its fond mother torn,
And at a public auction sold
With horses, cows, and corn.

* * *

Q is the Quarter, where the slave
On coarsest food is fed
And where, with toil and sorrow worn
He seeks his wretched bed.

* * *

W is the Whipping post,
To which the slave is bound,

While on his naked back, the lash
Makes many a bleeding wound.

* * *

Z is a Zealous man, sincere,
Faithful, and just, and true;
An earnest pleader for the slave—
Will you not be so too?

For children able to read, a wider variety of literature was written. One volume in verse urged "little children" to "plead with men, that they buy not slaves again" and called attention to the fact that

They may harken what *you* say,
Though from *us* they turn away.

Another verse suggested that:

Sometimes when from school you walk,
You can with your playmates talk,
Tell them of the slave child's fate,
Motherless and desolate.
And you can refuse to take
Candy, sweetmeat, pie or cake,
Saying "No"—unless 'tis free—
"The slave shall not work for me."

Juvenile story books, with some parts written in verse and printed in large and bold type and the rest written in prose and set in smaller type, were issued with the explanation that the verses were adapted to the capacity of the youngest reader, while the prose was well suited for being read aloud in the family circle. "It is presumed," said the preface, "that [with the prose] our younger friends will claim the assistance of their older brothers and sisters, or appeal to the ready aid of their mamma." Such volumes might contain pictures and stories from *Uncle Tom's Cabin* or they might consist of equally appealing tales of slave children cruelly torn from their parents or tortured by ingenious methods.

For adults the appeal was widened. No approach was neglected. Hymn books offered abolition songs set to familiar tunes. To the strains of "Old Hundred" eager voices invited "ye Yeomen brave" to rescue "the bleeding slave," or, to the "Missionary Hymn," asked them to consider

The frantic mother
Lamenting for her child,
Till falling lashes smother
Her cries of anguish wild!

Almanacs, carrying the usual information about weather and crops, filled their other pages with abolition propaganda. In one of these, readers found the story of Liburn Lewis, who, for a trifling offense, bound his slave, George, to a meat block and then, while all the other slaves looked on, proceeded slowly to chop him to pieces with a broad ax, and to cast the parts into a fire. Local, state, and national societies were organized for more efficient action in petitioning, presenting public speakers, distributing tracts, and publishing anti-slavery periodicals. The American Anti-Slavery Society "in the year 1837-38, published 7,877 bound volumes, 47,256 tracts and pamphlets, 4,100 circulars, and 10,490 prints. Its quarterly *Anti-Slavery Magazine* had an annual circulation of 9,000; the *Slave Friend*, for children, had 131,050; the monthly *Human Rights*, 189,400, and the weekly *Emancipator*, 217,000." From 1854 to 1858 it spent $3281 on a series of tracts discussing every phase of slavery, under such suggestive titles as "Disunion, our Wisdom and our Duty," "Relations of Anti-Slavery to Religion," and "To Mothers in the Free States." Its "several corps of lecturers of the highest ability and worth . . . occupied the field" every year in different states. Its Annual Reports, with their stories of atrocities and their biased discussion of issues, constituted a veritable arsenal from which weapons of attack could be drawn. Like other anti-slavery societies, it maintained an official organ, issued weekly, and held its regular conventions for the generation of greater force.

Where argument and appeal to reason failed, the abolitionists tried entertainment and appeal to emotion. *Uncle Tom's Cabin* was written because its author, "as a woman, as a mother," was "oppressed and broken hearted, with the sorrows & injustice" seen, and "because as a Christian" she "felt the dishonor to Christianity—because as a lover of [her] country, [she] trembled at the coming day of wrath." It became a best seller in the most complete sense. Only the Bible exceeded it in numbers sold and in the thoroughness with which it was read in England and America. Editions were adapted to every pocketbook, and translations carried it throughout the world. Dramatized and put on the stage, it did more to make the theatre respectable in rural America than any other single influence. The fictitious Uncle Tom became the stereotype of all American Negro slaves; Simon Legree became the typical slaveholder. A generation and more formed its ideas of Southern life and labor from the pages of this novel. A romantic South, of planter-gentlemen and poor whites, of chivalry and dissipation, of "sweet but worthless" women, was given an imaginative reality so wide and so gripping that no amount of patient research and sane history writing could alter it. Other novels, such as *Our World: or the Slaveholder's Daughter*, built their plots about the love affairs of Southern planters with their Negro slaves. Jealousies between wives and mistresses, struggles between brothers for the possession of some particularly desirable wench, or the inner conflict of a master over his mulatto bastards, constituted the main appeal in such works. The object was always the same: to reveal the licentious character of Southern men, the unhappy status of Southern homes, and the horrible violation of Negro chastity everywhere existing under slavery.

Reformed slaveholders and escaped slaves were especially valuable in the crusade. Under the warming influence of sympathetic audiences their stories of cruelty and depravity grew apace. Persecution and contempt from old friends increased their zeal. Birney, the Grimké sisters, Frederick Douglass, and many others influenced the movement and were influenced by it in a way comparable only to the relation of reformed drunkards to the temperance cause.

By means of such agencies and methods a well-defined picture of the South and slavery became slowly fixed in Northern minds. The Southern people were divided into two distinct classes—slaveholders and poor whites. The former constituted an aristocracy, living in great white-pillared houses on extended plantations. The latter, ignorant and impotent, made up a rural slum which clung hopelessly to the pine barrens or the worn-out acres on the fringes of the plantations. Planters, who lived by the theft of Negro labor, completely dominated the section. They alone were educated; they alone held office. Non-slaveholders were too poor to "buy an education for themselves and their children," and the planters, not wishing to "endanger their supremacy," refused to establish public schools. Few poor whites could either read or write. They gained their opinions and their principles from "stump speeches and tavern conversations." They were "absolutely in the slaveholder's power." He sent "them to the polls to vote him into office and in so doing to vote down their own rights and interests. . . ." They knew "no more what they [were] about, than so many children or so many Russian serfs. . . ."

Social-economic conditions in the South were described as tumble-down and backward. The slave, lacking the incentive of personal gain, was inefficient. The master, ruined by power, self-indulgence, and laziness, was incapable of sound management. James Birney described the section as one

whose Agriculture is desolation—whose Commerce is mainly confined to a crazy wagon and half fed team of oxen or mules as a means of carrying it on—whose manufacturing "Machinery" is limited to the bones and sinews of reluctant slaves—whose currency is individual notes always to *be* paid (it may be at some broken bank) and mortgages on men and women and children who may run away or die, and on land, which without them is of little value. . . .

Others went so far as to charge the panic of 1837 to Southern profligacy. "The existence of Slavery," resolved the American Anti-Slavery Society in 1840, "is the grand cause of the pecuniary embarrassments of the country; and . . . no real or permanent relief is to be expected . . . until the total abolition of that execrable system." Joshua Leavitt called the slave system "a bottomless gulf of extravagance and thriftlessness." Another explained its "withering and impoverishing effect by the fact that it was the "rule of violence and arbitrary will. . . . It would be quite in character with its theory and practice," he said, "if slave-drivers should refuse to pay their debts and meet the sheriff with dirk and pistol." Leavitt estimated that the South had "taken from the North, within five years, more than $100,000,000, by notes which will never be paid," and quoted an English writer to the effect that "planters are always in debt. The system of society in a slaveholding community is such as to lead to the contraction of debt, which the system itself does not furnish the means of paying. . . ."

Nor did the Southern shortcomings, according to the anti-slavery view, end with things material. Moral weaknesses were even more offensive. Sexual virtue was scarcely known. "The Slave States," wrote an abolitionist, "are Sodoms, and almost every village family is a brothel." Another writer declared that "in the slaveholding settlements of Middle and Southern Mississippi . . . there [was] not a virtuous young man of twenty years of age." "To send a lad to a male academy in Mississippi," he said, "is moral murder." An anti-slavery pamphlet told of "a million and a half of slave women, some of them without even the tinge of African blood . . . given up a lawful prey to the unbridled lusts of their masters." Another widely circulated tract described a slave market in which one dealer "devoted himself exclusively to the sale of young mulatto women." The author pictured the sale of "the most beautiful woman I ever saw," without "*a single trace of the African about her features*" and with "a pair of eyes that pierced one through and through" to "one of the most lecherous-looking old brutes" that he had ever seen. The narrative closed with the shrieking appeal: "God shield the helpless victim of that bad man's power—it may be, ere now, that bad man's lust!" The conclusion was inescapable. Slavery and unrestrained sexual indulgence at Negro expense were inseparable.

In such a section and in the hands of such men, abolitionists assumed that slavery realized its most vicious possibilities. Anti-slavery men early set themselves to the task of collecting stories of cruelty. These were passed about from one to another, often gaining in ferocity as they travelled. Weld gathered them together in a volume entitled *American Slavery As It Is* and scattered them broadcast over the North. The annual reports of the anti-slavery societies, their tracts and periodicals, also revelled in atrocities, asking no more proof of their absolute truth than the word of a fellow fanatic.

The attempt to picture slavery "as it was," therefore, came to consist almost entirely of a recital of brutalities. Now and then a kind master and seemingly contented slaves were introduced for the purpose of contrast—as a device to deepen shadows. But, as a rule, Southerners, according to these tracts, spent their time in idleness broken only by brutal cock-fights, gander pullings, and horse races so barbarous that "the blood of the tortured animal drips from the lash and flies at every leap from the stroke of the rowel." Slavery was one continual round of abuse. The killing of a slave was a matter of no consequence. Even respectable ladies might cause "several to be *whipped to death*." Brandings, ear cropping, and body-maiming were the rule. David L. Child honestly declared: "From all that I have read and heard upon the subject of whipping done by masters and overseers to slaves . . . I have come to the conclusion that some hundreds of *cart whips* and cowskin instruments, which I am told make the skin fly like feathers, and cut frequently to the bone, are in *perpetual daily motion* in the slave states." John Rankin told of Negroes stripped, hung up and stretched and then "whipped until their bodies [were] covered with blood and mangled flesh," some dying "under the lash, others linger[ing] about for a time, and at length die[ing] of their *wounds*. . . . " The recital was indeed one of *"groans, tears, and blood."*

To abuse was added other great wrongs. Everywhere slaves were overworked, underfed, and insufficiently clothed and sheltered. Family ties were cut without the slightest regard for Negro feelings—infants were torn from the mother's breast, husbands separated from their wives and families. Marriage was unknown among slaves, and the right to worship God generally denied. Strangely enough, little was said of slave-breeding for market. That charge was largely left to the politicians of the next decades and to the historians of a later day.

Two principal assumptions stood out in this anti-slavery indictment of the slaveholder. He was, in the first place, the arch-aristocrat. He was the great enemy of democracy. He was un-American, the oppressor of his fellow men, the exploiter of a weaker brother. Against him could be directed all the complaints and fears engendered by industrial captains and land speculators. He, more than any other aristocrat, threatened to destroy the American democratic dream.

In the second place, he was a flagrant sinner. His self-indulgence was unmatched. His licentious conduct with Negro women, his intemperance in the use of intoxicating liquors, his mad dueling, and his passion for war against the weak were enough to mark him as the nation's moral enemy number one! The time for dealing moderately had passed. Immediate reform was imperative.

Thus it was that the slaveholder began to do scapegoat service for all aristocrats and all sinners. To him were transferred resentments and fears born out of local conditions. Because it combined in itself both the moral and the democratic appeal, and because it coincided with sectional rivalry, the abolition movement gradually swallowed up all other reforms. The South became the great object of all efforts to remake American society. Against early indifference and later persecution, a handful of deadly-in-earnest men and women slowly built into a section's consciousness the belief in a Slave Power. To the normal strength of sectional ignorance and distrust they added all the force of Calvinistic morality and American democracy and thereby surrounded every Northern interest and contention with holy sanction and reduced all opposition to abject depravity. When the politician, playing his risky game, linked expansion and slavery, Christian common folk by the thousands, with no great personal urge for reforming, accepted the Abolition attitudes toward both the South and slavery. Civil war was then in the making.

The
abolitionists:
a displaced
elite

David Donald

The abolitionist . . . was a special type of antislavery agitator, and his crusade was part of that remarkable American social phenomenon which erupted in the 1830's, "freedom's ferment," the effervescence of kindred humanitarian reform movements—prohibition; prison reform; education for the blind, deaf, dumb; world peace; penny postage; women's rights; and a score of lesser and more eccentric drives.

Historians have been so absorbed in chronicling what these movements did, in allocating praise or blame among squabbling factions in each, and in making moral judgments on the desirability of various reforms that they have paid surprisingly little attention to the movement as a whole. Few serious attempts have been made to explain why humanitarian reform appeared in America when it did, and more specifically why immediate abolitionism, so different in tone, method, and membership from its predecessors and its successor, emerged in the 1830's.

The participants in such movements naturally give no adequate explanation for such a causal problem. According to their voluminous memoirs and autobiographies, they were simply convinced by religion, by reading, by reflection that slavery was evil, and they pledged their lives and their sacred honor to destroy it. Seeing slavery in a Southern state, reading an editorial by William Lloyd Garrison, hearing a sermon by Theodore Dwight Weld—such events precipitated a decision made on the highest of moral and ethical planes. No one who has studied the abolitionist literature can doubt the absolute sincerity of these accounts. Abolitionism was a dangerous creed of devotion, and no fair-minded person can believe that men joined the movement for personal gain or for conscious self-glorification. In all truth, the decision to become an antislavery crusader was a decision of conscience.

But when all this is admitted, there are still fundamental problems. Social evils are always present; vice is always in the saddle while virtue trudges on afoot. Not merely the existence of evil but the recognition of it is the prerequisite for reform. Were there more men of integrity, were there more women of sensitive conscience in the 1830's than in any previous decade? A generation of giants these reformers were indeed, but why was there such a concentration of genius in those ten years from 1830 to 1840? If the individual's decision to join the abolitionist movement was a matter of personality or religion or philosophy, is it not necessary to inquire why so many similar personalities or religions or philosophies appeared in America simultaneously? In short, we need to know why so many Americans in the 1830's were predisposed toward a certain kind of reform movement.

Many students have felt, somewhat vaguely, this need for a social interpretation of reform. Little precise analysis has been attempted, but the general histories of antislavery attribute the abolitionist movement to the Christian tradition, to the spirit of the Declaration of Independence, to the ferment of Jacksonian democracy, or to the growth of romanticism. That some or all of these factors may have relation to abolitionism can be granted, but this helps little. Why did the "spirit of Puritanism," to which one writer attributes the movement, become manifest as militant abolitionism in the 1830's although it had no such effect on the previous generation? Why did the Declaration of Independence find fulfillment in abolition during the sixth decade after its promulgation, and not in the fourth or the third?

In their elaborate studies of the antislavery movement,[1] Gilbert H. Barnes and Dwight L. Dumond have pointed up some of the more immediate reasons for the rise of American abolitionism. Many of the most important antislavery leaders fell under the influence of Charles Grandison Finney, whose revivalism set rural New York and the Western Reserve ablaze with religious fervor and evoked "Wonderful outpourings of the Holy Spirit" throughout the North. Not merely did Finney's invocation of the fear of hell and the promise of heaven rouse sluggish souls to renewed religious zeal, but his emphasis upon good works and pious endeavor as steps toward salvation freed men's minds from the bonds of arid theological controversies One of Finney's most famous converts was Theodore Dwight Weld, the greatest of the Western abolitionists, "eloquent as an angel and powerful as thunder," who recruited a band of seventy antislavery apostles, trained them in Finney's revivalistic techniques, and sent them forth to consolidate the emancipation movement in the North. Their greatest successes were reaped in precisely those communities where Finney's preaching had prepared the soil.

Barnes and Dumond also recognized the importance of British influence upon the American antislavery movement. The connection is clear and easily traced: British antislavery leaders fought for immediate emancipation in the West Indies; reading the tracts of Wilberforce and Clarkson converted William Lloyd Garrison to immediate abolitionism at about the same time that Theodore Weld was won over to the cause by his English friend Charles Stuart; and Weld in turn gained for the movement the support of the Tappan brothers, the wealthy New York merchants and philanthropists who contributed so much in money and time to the antislavery crusade. Thus, abolition had in British precedent a model, in Garrison and Weld leaders, and in the Tappans financial backers.

Historians are deeply indebted to Professors Barnes and Dumond, for the importance of their studies on the antislavery movement is very great. But perhaps they have raised as many questions as they have answered. Both religious revivalism and British antislavery theories had a selective influence in America. Many men heard Finney and Weld, but only certain communities were converted. Hundreds of Americans read Wilberforce, Clarkson, and other British abolitionists, but only the Garrisons and the Welds were convinced. The question remains: Whether they received the idea through the revivalism of Finney or through the publications of British antislavery spokesmen, why were some Americans in the 1830's for the first time moved to advocate immediate abolition? Why was this particular seed bed ready at this precise time?

I believe that the best way to answer this difficult question is to analyze the leadership of the abolitionist movement. There is, unfortunately, no complete list of American abolitionists, and I have had to use a good deal of subjective judgment in drawing up a roster of leading reformers. From the classified indexes of the *Dictionary of American Biography* and the old Appleton's *Cyclopaedia of American Biography* and from important primary and secondary works on the reform generation, I made a list of about two hundred and fifty persons who seemed to be identified with the antislavery cause. This obviously is not a definitive enumeration of all the important abolitionists; had someone else compiled it, other names doubtless would have been included. Nevertheless, even if one or two major spokesmen have accidentally been omitted, this is a good deal more than a representative sampling of antislavery leadership.

After preliminary work I eliminated nearly one hundred of these names. Some proved not to be genuine abolitionists but advocates of colonizing the freed Negroes in Africa; others had only incidental interest or sympathy for emancipation. I ruthlessly excluded those who joined the abolitionists after 1840, because the political antislavery movement clearly poses a different set of causal problems. After this weeding out, I had reluctantly to drop other names because I was unable to secure more than random bits of information about them. Some of Weld's band of seventy agitators, for instance, were so obscure that even Barnes and Dumond were unable to identify them. There remained the names of one hundred and six abolitionists, the hard core of active antislavery leadership in the 1830's.

Most of these abolitionists were born between 1790 and 1810, and when the first number of the *Liberator* was published in 1831, their median age was twenty-nine. Abolitionism was thus a revolt of the young.

My analysis confirms the traditional identification of radical antislavery with New England. Although I made every effort to include Southern and Western leaders, eighty-five per cent of these abolitionists came from Northeastern states, sixty per cent from New England, thirty per cent from Massachusetts alone. Many of the others were descended from New England families. Only four of the leaders were born abroad or were second-generation immigrants.

The ancestors of these abolitionists are in some ways as interesting as the antislavery leaders themselves. In the biographies of their more famous descendants certain standard phrases recur: "of the best New England stock," "of Pilgrim descent," "of a serious, pious household." The parents of the leaders generally belonged to a clearly defined stratum of society. Many were preachers, doctors, or teachers; some were farmers and a few were merchants; but only three were manufacturers (and two of these on a very small scale), none was a banker, and only one was an ordinary day laborer. Virtually all the parents were stanch Federalists.

These families were neither rich nor poor, and it is worth remembering that among neither extreme did abolitionism flourish. The abolitionist could best appeal to "the substantial men" of the community, thought Weld, and not to "the *aristocracy* and fashionable worldliness" that remained aloof from reform. In *The Burned-Over District*, an important analysis of reform drives in western New York, Whitney R. Cross has confirmed Weld's social analysis. In New York, antislavery was strongest in those counties which had once been economically dominant but which by the 1830's, though still prosperous, had relatively fallen behind their more advantageously situated neighbors. As young men the fathers of abolitionists had been leaders of their communities and states; in their old age they were elbowed aside by the merchant prince, the manufacturing tycoon, the corporation lawyer. The bustling democracy of the 1830's passed them by; as the Reverend Ludovicus Weld lamented to his famous son Theodore: "I have . . . felt like a stranger in a strange land."

If the abolitionists were descendants of old and distinguished New England families, it is scarcely surprising to find among them an enthusiasm for higher education. The women in the movement could not, of course, have much formal education, nor could the three Negroes here included, but of the eighty-nine white male leaders, at least fifty-three attended college, university, or theological seminary. In the East, Harvard and Yale were the favored schools; in the West, Oberlin; but in any case the training was usually of the traditional liberal-arts variety.

For an age of chivalry and repression there was an extraordinary proportion of women in the abolitionist movement. Fourteen of these leaders were women who defied the convention that the female's place was at the fireside, not in the forum, and appeared publicly as antislavery apostles. The Grimké sisters of South Carolina were the most famous of these, but most of the antislavery heroines came from New England.

It is difficult to tabulate the religious affiliations of antislavery leaders. Most were troubled by spiritual discontent, and they wandered from one sect to another seeking salvation. It is quite clear, however, that there was a heavy Congregational-Presbyterian and Quaker preponderance. There were many Methodists, some Baptists, but very few Unitarians, Episcopalians, or Catholics. Recent admirable dissertations on the antislavery movement in each of the Western states, prepared at the University of Michigan under Professor Dumond's supervision, confirm the conclusion that, except in Pennsylvania, it is correct to consider humanitarian reform and Congregational-Presbyterianism as causally interrelated.

Only one of these abolitionist leaders seems to have had much connection with the rising industrialism of the 1830's, and only thirteen of the entire group were born in any of the principal cities of the United States. Abolition was distinctly a rural movement, and throughout the crusade many of the antislavery leaders seemed to feel an instinctive antipathy toward the city. Weld urged his following: "Let the great cities *alone;* they must be burned down by *back fires.* The springs to touch in order to move them *lie in the country.*"

In general the abolitionists had little sympathy or understanding for the problems of an urban society. Reformers though they were, they were men of conservative economic views. Living in an age of growing industrialization, of tenement congestion, of sweat-shop oppression, not one of them can properly be identified with the labor movement of the 1830's. Most would agree with Garrison, who denounced labor leaders for trying "to inflame the minds of our working classes against the more opulent, and to persuade men that they are contemned and oppressed by a wealthy aristocracy." After all, Wendell Phillips assured the laborers, the American factory operative could be "neither wronged nor oppressed" so long as he had the ballot. William Ellery Channing, gentle high priest of the Boston area, told dissatisfied miners that moral self-improvement was a more potent weapon than strikes, and he urged that they take advantage of the leisure afforded by unemployment for mental and spiritual self-cultivation. A Massachusetts attempt to limit the hours of factory operatives to ten a day was denounced by Samuel Gridley Howe, veteran of a score of humanitarian wars, as "emasculating the people" because it took from them their free right to choose their conditions of employment.

The suffering of laborers during periodic depressions aroused little sympathy among abolitionists. As Emerson remarked tartly, "Do not tell me . . . of my obligation to put all poor men in good situations. Are they *my* poor? I tell thee, thou foolish philanthropist, that I grudge the dollar, the dime, the cent I give to such men. . . ."

Actually it is clear that abolitionists were not so much hostile to labor as indifferent to it. The factory worker represented an alien and unfamiliar system toward which the antislavery leaders felt no kinship or responsibility. Sons of the old New England of Federalism, farming, and foreign commerce, the reformers did not fit into a society that was beginning to be dominated by a bourgeoisie based on manufacturing and trade. Thoreau's bitter comment, "We do not ride on the railroads; they ride on us," was more than the acid aside of a man whose privacy at Walden had been invaded; it was the reaction of a class whose leadership had been discarded. The bitterest attacks in the journals of Ralph Waldo Emerson, the most pointed denunciations in the sermons of Theodore Parker, the harshest philippics in the orations of Charles Sumner were directed against the "Lords of the Loom," not so much for exploiting their labor as for changing the character and undermining the morality of old New England.

As Lewis Tappan pointed out in a pamphlet suggestively titled *Is It Right to Be Rich?*, reformers did not object to ordinary acquisition of money. It was instead that "eagerness to amass property" which made a man "selfish, unsocial, mean, tyrannical, and but a nominal Christian" that seemed so wrong. It is worth noting that Tappan, in his numerous examples of the vice of excessive accumulation, found this evil stemming from manufacturing and banking, and never from farming or foreign trade—in which last occupation Tappan himself flourished.

Tappan, like Emerson, was trying to uphold the old standards and to protest against the easy morality of the new age. "This invasion of Nature by Trade with its Money, its Credit, its Steam, its Railroads," complained Emerson, "threatens to upset the balance of man, and establish a new universal monarchy more tyrannical than Babylon or Rome." Calmly Emerson welcomed the panic of 1837 as a wholesome lesson to the new monarchs of manufacturing: "I see good in such emphatic and universal calamity. . . ."

Jacksonian democracy, whether considered a labor movement or a triumph of laissez-faire capitalism, obviously had little appeal for the abolitionist conservative. As far as can be determined, only one of these abolitionist leaders was a Jacksonian; nearly all were strong Whigs. William Lloyd Garrison made his first public appearance in Boston to endorse the arch-Whig Harrison Gray Otis; James G. Birney campaigned throughout Alabama to defeat Jackson; Henry B. Stanton wrote editorials for anti-Jackson newspapers. Not merely the leaders but their followers as well seem to have been hostile to Jacksonian democracy, for it is estimated that fifty-nine out of sixty Massachusetts abolitionists belonged to the Whig party.

Jacksonian Democrats recognized the opposition of the abolitionists and accused the leaders of using slavery to distract public attention from more immediate economic problems at home. "The abolitionists of the North have mistaken the color of the American slaves," Theophilus Fisk wrote tartly; "all the real Slaves in the United States have pale faces. . . . I will venture to affirm that there are more slaves in Lowell and Nashua alone than can be found South of the Potomac."

Here, then, is a composite portrait of abolitionist leadership. Descended from old and socially dominant Northeastern families, reared in a faith of aggressive piety and moral endeavor, educated for conservative leadership, these young men and women who reached maturity in the 1830's faced a strange and hostile world. Social and economic leadership was being transferred from the country to the city, from the farmer to the manufacturer, from the preacher to the corporation attorney. Too distinguished a family, too gentle an education, too nice a morality were handicaps in a bustling world of business. Expecting to lead, these young people found no followers. They were an elite without function, a displaced class in American society.

Some—like Daniel Webster—made their terms with the new order and lent their talents and their family names to the greater glorification of the god of trade. But many of the young men were unable to overcome their traditional disdain for the new money-grubbing class that was beginning to rule. In these plebeian days they could not be successful in politics; family tradition and education prohibited idleness; and agitation allowed the only chance for personal and social self-fulfillment.

If the young men were aliens in the new industrial society, the young women felt equally lost. Their mothers had married preachers, doctors, teachers, and had become dominant moral forces in their communities. But in rural New England of the 1830's the westward exodus had thinned the ranks of eligible suitors, and because girls of distinguished family hesitated to work in the cotton mills, more and more turned to school-teaching and nursing and other socially useful but unrewarding spinster tasks. The women, like the men, were ripe for reform.

They did not support radical economic reforms because fundamentally these young men and women had no serious quarrel with the capitalistic system of private ownership and control of property. What they did question, and what they did rue, was the transfer of leadership to the wrong groups in society, and their appeal for reform was a strident call for their own class to re-exert its former social dominance. Some fought for prison reform; some for women's rights; some for world peace; but ultimately most came to make that natural identification between moneyed aristocracy, textile-manufacturing, and Southern slave-grown cotton. An attack on slavery was their best, if quite unconscious, attack upon the new industrial system. As Richard Henry Dana, Jr., avowed: "I am a Free Soiler, because I am . . . of the stock of the old Northern gentry, and have a particular dislike to any subserviency on the part of our people to the slave-holding oligarchy"—and, he might have added, to their Northern manufacturing allies.

With all its dangers and all its sacrifices, membership in a movement like abolitionism offered these young people a chance for a reassertion of their traditional values, an opportunity for association with others of their kind, and a possibility of achieving that self-fulfillment which should traditionally have been theirs as social leaders. Reform gave meaning to the lives of this displaced social elite. "My life, what has it been?" queried one young seeker; "the panting of a soul after eternity—the feeling that there was nothing here to fill the aching void, to provide enjoyment and occupation such as my spirit panted for. The world, what has it been? a howling wilderness. I seem to be just now awakened . . . to a true perception of the end of my being, my duties, my responsibilities, the rich and perpetual pleasures which God has provided for us in the fulfillment of duty to Him and to our fellow creatures. Thanks to the A[nti]. S[lavery]. cause, it first gave an impetus to my palsied intellect. . . ."

Viewed against the backgrounds and common ideas of its leaders, abolitionism appears to have been a double crusade. Seeking freedom for the Negro in the South, these reformers were also attempting a restoration of the traditional values of their class at home. Leadership of humanitarian reform may have been influenced by revivalism or by British precedent, but its true origin lay in the drastic dislocation of Northern society. Basically, abolitionism should be considered the anguished protest of an aggrieved class against a world they never made.

The northern response to slavery

Martin Duberman

The abolitionist movement never became the major channel of Northern antislavery sentiment. It remained in 1860 what it had been in 1830: the small but not still voice of radical reform. An important analytical problem thus arises: why did most Northerners who disapproved of slavery become "nonextensionists" rather than abolitionists? Why did

From Martin Duberman, ed., *The Anti-Slavery Vanguard: New Essays on the Abolitionists,* pp. 395–413. Reprinted by permission of Princeton University Press. Copyright © 1965 by Princeton University Press.

they prefer to attack slavery indirectly, by limiting its spread, rather than directly, by seeking to destroy it wherever it existed?

On a broad level, the answer involves certain traits in the national character. In our society of abundance, prosperity has been the actual condition—or the plausible aspiration—of the majority. Most Americans have been too absorbed in the enjoyment or pursuit of possessions to take much notice of the exactions of the system. Even when inequalities have become too pronounced or too inclusive any longer to be comfortably ignored, efforts at relief have usually been of a partial and half-hearted kind. Any radical attack on social problems would compromise the national optimism; it would suggest fundamental defects, rather than occasional malfunctions. And so the majority has generally found it necessary to label "extreme" any measures which call for large-scale readjustment. No one reasonably contented welcomes extensive dislocation; what seems peculiarly American is the disbelief, under *all* circumstances, in the necessity of such dislocation.

Our traditional recoil from "extremism" can be defended. Complex problems, it might be said, require complex solutions; or, to be more precise, complex problems have no solutions—at best, they can be but partially adjusted. If even this much is to be possible, the approach must be flexible, piecemeal, pragmatic. The clear-cut blueprint for reform, with its utopian demand for total solution, intensifies rather than ameliorates disorder.

There is much to be said for this defense of the American way—in the abstract. The trouble is that the theory of gradualism and the practice of it have not been the same. Too often Americans have used the gradualist argument as a technique of evasion rather than as a tool for change, not as a way of dealing with difficult problems slowly and carefully, but as an excuse for not dealing with them at all. We do not want time for working out our problems—we do not want problems, and we will use the argument of time as a way of not facing them. As a chosen people, we are meant only to have problems which are self-liquidating. All of which is symptomatic of our conviction that history is the story of inevitable progress, that every day in every way we *will* get better and better even though we make no positive efforts toward that end.

Before 1845, the Northern attitude toward slavery rested on this comfortable belief in the benevolence of history. Earlier, during the 1830's, the abolitionists had managed to excite a certain amount of uneasiness about the institution by invoking the authority of the Bible and the Declaration of Independence against it. Alarm spread still further when mobs began to prevent abolitionists from speaking their minds or publishing their opinions, and when the national government interfered with the mails and the right of petition. Was it possible, men began to ask, that the abolitionists were right in contending that slavery, if left alone, would not die out but expand, would become more not less vital to the country's interests? Was it possible that slavery might even end by infecting free institutions themselves?

The apathetic majority was shaken, but not yet profoundly aroused; the groundwork for widespread anti-slavery protest was laid, but its flowering awaited further developments. The real watershed came in 1845, when Texas was annexed to the Union, and war with Mexico followed. The prospect now loomed of a whole series of new slave states. It finally seemed clear that the mere passage of time would not bring a solution; if slavery was ever to be destroyed, more active resistance would be necessary. For the first time large numbers of Northerners prepared to challenge the dogma that slavery was a local matter in which the free states had no concern. A new era of widespread, positive resistance to slavery had opened.

Yet such new resolve as had been found was not channeled into a heightened demand for the abolition of the institution, but only into a demand that its further extension be prevented. By 1845 Northerners may have lost partial, but not total confidence in "Natural Benevolence"; they were now wiser Americans perhaps, but Americans nonetheless. More positive action against slavery, they seemed to be saying, was indeed required, but nothing too positive. Containing the institution would, in the long run, be tantamount to destroying it; a more direct assault was unnecessary. In this sense, the doctrine of nonextension was but a more sophisticated version of the standard faith in "time."

One need not question the sincerity of those who believed that nonextension would ultimately destroy slavery, in order to recognize that such a belief partook of wishful thinking. Even if slavery was contained, there remained large areas in the Southern states into which the institution could still expand; even without further expansion, there was no guarantee that slavery would cease to be profitable; and finally, even should slavery cease to be profitable, there was no certainty that the South, psychologically, would feel able to abandon it. Nonextension, in short, was hardly a fool-proof formula. Yet many Northerners chose to so regard it. And thus the question remains: why did not an aroused antislavery conscience turn to more certain measures and demand more unequivocal action?

To have adopted the path of direct abolition, first of all, might have meant risking individual respectability. The unsavory reputation of those already associated with abolitionism was not likely to encourage converts to it. Still, if that doctrine had been really appealing, the disrepute of its earlier adherents could not alone have kept men from embracing it. Association with the "fanatics" could have been smoothed simply by rehabilitating their reputations; their notoriety, it could have been said, had earlier been exaggerated—it had been the convenient invention of an apathetic majority to justify its own indifference to slavery. When, after

1861, public opinion did finally demand a new image of the abolitionists, it was readily enough produced. The mere reputation of abolitionism, therefore, would not have been sufficient to repel men from joining its ranks. Hostility to the movement had to be grounded in a deeper source—fear of the doctrine of "immediatism" itself.

Immediatism challenged the Northern hierarchy of values. To many, a direct assault on slavery meant a direct assault on private property and the Union as well. Fear for these values clearly inhibited antislavery fervor (though possibly a reverse trend operated as well—concern for property and Union may have been stressed in order to justify the convenience of "going slow" on slavery).

As devout Lockians, Americans did believe that the sanctity of private property constituted the essential cornerstone for all other liberties. If property could not be protected in a nation, neither could life nor liberty. And the Constitution, so many felt, had upheld the legitimacy of holding property in men. True, the Constitution had not mentioned slavery by name, and had not overtly declared in its favor, but in giving the institution certain indirect guarantees (the three-fifths clause; noninterference for twenty-one years with the slave trade; the fugitive slave proviso), the Constitution had seemed to sanction it. At any rate no one could be sure. The intentions of the Founding Fathers remained uncertain, and one of the standing debates of the ante-bellum generation was whether the Constitution had been meant by them to be a pro- or an antislavery document. Since the issue was unresolved, Northerners remained uneasy, uncertain how far they could go in attacking slavery without at the same time attacking property.

Fear for property rights was underscored by fear for the Union. The South had many times warned that if her rights and interests were not heeded, she would leave the Union and form a separate confederation. The tocsin had been sounded with enough regularity so that to some it had begun to sound like hollow bluster. But there was always the chance that if the South felt sufficiently provoked she might yet carry out the threat.

It is difficult today fully to appreciate the horror with which most Northerners regarded the potential breakup of the Union. The mystical qualities which surrounded "Union" were no less real for being in part irrational. Lincoln struck a deep chord for his generation when he spoke of the Union as the "last best hope of earth"; that the American experiment was thought the "best" hope may have been arrogant, a hope at all, naïve, but such it was to the average American, convinced of his own superiority and the possibility of the world learning by example. Today, more concerned with survival than improvement, we are bemused (when we are not cynical) about "standing examples for mankind," and having seen the ghastly deeds done in the name of patriotism, we are impatient at signs of national fervor. But 100 years ago, the world saw less danger in

nationalism, and Americans, enamored with their own extraordinary success story, were especially prone to look on love of country as one of the
noblest of human sentiments. Even those Southerners who had ceased
to love the Union had not ceased to love the idea of nationhood; they
merely wished to transfer allegiance to a more worthy object.

Those who wanted to preserve the old Union acted from a variety of
motives: the Lincolns, who seem primarily to have valued its spiritual
potential, were joined by those more concerned with maintaining its power
potential; the Union was symbol of man's quest for a benevolent society
—and for dominion. But if Northerners valued their government for differing reasons, they generally agreed on the necessity for preserving it.
Even so, their devotion to the Union had its oscillations. In 1861 Lincoln
and his party, in rejecting the Crittenden Compromise, seemed willing to
jeopardize Union rather than risk the further expansion of slavery (perhaps because they never believed secession would really follow, though this
complacency, in turn, might only have been a way of convincing themselves that a strong antislavery stand would not necessarily destroy the
Union). After war broke out the value stress once more shifted: Lincoln's
party now loudly insisted that the war was indeed being fought to preserve
the Union, not to free the slaves. Thus did the coexisting values of Union
and antislavery tear the Northern mind and confuse its allegiance.

The tension was compounded by the North's ambivalent attitude toward
the Negro. The Northern majority, unlike most of the abolitionists, did
not believe in the equality of races. The Bible (and the new science of
anthropology) seemed to suggest that the Negro had been a separate, inferior creation meant for a position of servitude. Where there was doubt
on the doctrine of racial equality, its advocacy by the distrusted abolitionists helped to settle the matter in the negative.

It was possible, of course, to disbelieve in Negro equality, and yet dis-
approve of Negro slavery. Negroes were obviously men, even if an inferior sort, and as men they could not in conscience (the Christian-
Democratic version) be denied the right to control their own souls and
bodies. But if anti-Negro and antislavery sentiments were not actually
incompatible, they were not mutually supportive either. Doubt of the
Negro's capacity for citizenship continually blunted the edge of anti-
slavery fervor. If God had intended the Negro for some subordinate role
in society, perhaps a kind of benevolent slavery was, after all, the most
suitable arrangement; so long as there was uncertainty, it might be better
to await the slow unfolding of His intentions in His good time.

And so the average Northerner, even after he came actively to disap-
prove of slavery, continued to be hamstrung in his opposition to it by the
competitive pull of other values. Should prime consideration be given to
freeing the slaves, even though in the process the rights of property and the
preservation of the Union were threatened? Should the future of the

superior race be endangered in order to improve the lot of a people seemingly marked by Nature for a degraded station? Ideally, the North would
have liked to satisfy its conscience about slavery and at the same time preserve the rest of its value system intact—to free the Negro and yet do so
without threatening property rights or dislocating the Union. This struggle
to achieve the best of all possible worlds runs like a forlorn hope throughout the ante-bellum period—the sad, almost plaintive quest by the American Adam for the perfect world he considered his birthright.

The formula of nonextension did seem, for a time, the perfect device
for balancing these multiple needs. Nonextension would put slavery in
the course of ultimate extinction without producing excessive dislocation;
since slavery would not be attacked directly, nor its existence immediately
threatened, the South would not be unduly fearful for her property rights,
the Union would not be needlessly jeopardized, and a mass of free Negroes
would not be precipitously thrust upon an unprepared public. Nonextension, in short, seemed a panacea, a formula which promised in time to do
everything while for the present risking nothing. But like all panaceas, it
ignored certain hard realities: would containment really lead to the extinction of slavery? would the South accept even a gradual dissolution of her
peculiar institution? would it be right to sacrifice two or three more generations of Negroes in the name of uncertain future possibilities? Alas for
the American Adam, so soon to be expelled from Eden.

The abolitionists, unlike most Northerners, were not willing to rely on
future intangibles. Though often called impractical romantics, they were
in some ways the most tough-minded of Americans. They had no easy
faith in the benevolent workings of time or in the inevitable triumphs of
gradualism. If change was to come, they argued, it would be the result
of man's effort to produce it; patience and inactivity had never yet helped
the world's ills. Persistently, sometimes harshly, the abolitionists denounced delay and those who advocated it; they were tired, they said, of
men using the councils of moderation to perpetuate injustice.

In their own day, and ever since, the abolitionists have faced a hostile
majority; their policies have been ridiculed, their personalities reviled. Yet
ridicule, like its opposite, adoration, is usually not the result of analysis
but a substitute for it. Historians have for so long been absorbed in de-
nouncing the abolitionists, that they have had scant energy left over for
understanding them. The result is that we still know surprisingly little
about the movement, and certainly not enough to warrant the general
assumptions so long current in the historical profession.

Historians have assumed that the abolitionists were unified in their
advocacy of certain broad policies—immediate emancipation, without
compensation—and also unified in refusing to spell out details for implementing these policies. To some extent this traditional view is warranted.
The abolitionists did agree almost unanimously (Gerrit Smith was one of

the few exceptions) that slaveholders must not be compensated. One does not pay a man, they argued, for ceasing to commit a sin. Besides, the slaveholder had already been paid many times over in labor for which he had never given wages. Defensible though this position may have been in logic or morals, the abolitionists should perhaps have realized that public opinion would never support the confiscation of property, and should have modified their stand accordingly. But they saw themselves as prophets, not politicians; they were concerned with what was "right," not with what was possible, though they hoped that if men were once made aware of the right, they would find some practical way of implementing it.

The abolitionists were far less united on the doctrine of immediate emancipation—at least in the 1830's, before Southern intransigence and British experience in the West Indies, convinced almost all of them that gradualism was hopeless. But during the 1830's, there was a considerable spectrum of opinion as to when and how to emancipate the slave. Contrary to common myth, some of the abolitionists did advocate a period of prior education and training before the granting of full freedom. Men like Weld, Birney, and the Tappans, stressing the debasing experience of slavery, insisted only that gradual emancipation be immediately begun, not that emancipation itself be at once achieved. This range of opinion has never been fully appreciated. It has been convenient, then and now, to believe that all abolitionists always advocated instantaneous freedom, for it thus became possible to denounce any call for emancipation as "patently impractical."

By 1840, however, most abolitionists had become immediatists, and that position, "practical" or not, did have a compelling moral urgency. Men learned how to be free, the immediatists argued, only by being free; slavery, no matter how attenuated, was by its very nature incapable of preparing men for those independent decisions necessary to adult responsibility. Besides, they insisted, the Negro, though perhaps debased by slavery, was no more incapacitated for citizenship than were many poor whites, whose rights no one seriously suggested curtailing.

The immediatist position was not free of contradiction. If slavery had been as horrendous as the abolitionists claimed, it was logical to expect that its victims would bear deep personality scars—greater than any disabilities borne by a poor white, no matter how degraded his position. Either slavery had not been this deadly, or, if it had, those recently freed from its toils could not be expected to move at once into the responsibilities of freedom. This contradiction was apparent to some immediatists, but there was reason for refusing to resolve it. Ordinarily, they said, a system of apprenticeship might be desirable, but if conditions to emancipation were once established, they could be used as a standing rationale for postponement; the Negro could be kept in a condition of semislavery by the self-perpetuating argument that he was not yet ready for his freedom.

Moreover, any intermediary stage before full freedom would require the spelling out of precise "plans," and these would give the enemies of emancipation an opportunity to pick away at the impracticality of this or that detail. They would have an excuse for disavowing the broader policy under the guise of disagreeing with the specific means for achieving it. Better to concentrate on the larger issue and force men to take sides on that alone, the abolitionists argued, than to give them a chance to hide their opposition behind some supposed disapproval of detail. Wendell Phillips, for one, saw the abolitionists' role as exclusively that of agitating the broader question. Their primary job, Phillips insisted, was to arouse the country's conscience rather than to spell out to it precise plans and formulas. *After* that conscience had been aroused, it would be time to talk of specific proposals; let the moral urgency of the problem be recognized, let the country be brought to a determination to rid itself of slavery, and ways and means to accomplish that purpose would be readily enough found.

No tactical position could really have saved the abolitionists from the denunciation of those hostile to their basic goal. If the abolitionists spelled out a program for emancipation, their enemies would have a chance to pick at details; if they did not spell out a program, they could then be accused of vagueness and impracticality. Hostility can always find its own justification.

A second mode of attack on the abolitionists has centered on their personalities rather than their policies. The stereotype which long had currency sees the abolitionist as a disturbed fanatic, a man self-righteous and self-deceived, motivated not by concern for the Negro, as he may have believed, but by an unconscious drive to gratify certain needs of his own. Seeking to discharge either individual anxieties or those frustations which came from membership in a "displaced élite," his antislavery protest was, in any case, a mere disguise for personal anguish.

A broad assumption underlies this analysis which has never been made explicit—namely, that strong protest by an individual against social injustice is ipso facto proof of his disturbance. Injustice itself, in this view, is apparently never sufficient to arouse unusual ire in "normal" men, for normal men, so goes the canon, are always cautious, discreet, circumspect. Those who hold to this model of human behavior seem rarely to suspect that it may tell us more about their hierarchy of values than about the reform impulse it pretends to describe. Argued in another context, the inadequacies of the stereotype become more apparent: if normal people do not protest "excessively" against injustice, then we should be forced to condemn as neurotic all those who protested with passion against the Nazi persecution of the Jews.

Some of the abolitionists, it is true, *were* palpable neurotics, men who were not comfortable within themselves and therefore not comfortable with others, men whose "reality-testing" was poor, whose life styles were pronouncedly compulsive, whose relationships were unusual compounds of demand and phantasy. Such neurotics *were* in the abolitionist movement—the Parker Pillsburys, Stephen Fosters, Abby Folsoms. Yet even here we must be cautious, for our diagnostic accuracy can be blurred if the life style under evaluation is sharply different from our own. Many of the traits of the abolitionists which today "put us off" were not peculiar to them, but rather to their age—the declamatory style, the abstraction and idealization of issues, the tone of righteous certainty, the religious context of argumentation. Thus the evangelical rhetoric of the movement, with its thunderous emphasis on sin and retribution, can sound downright "queer" (and thus "neurotic") to the 20th century skeptic, though in its day common enough to abolitionists and nonabolitionists alike.

Then, too, even when dealing with the "obvious" neurotics, we must be careful in the link we establish between their pathology and their protest activity. It is one thing to demonstrate an individual's "disturbance" and quite another then to explain all of his behavior in terms of it. Let us suppose, for example, that Mr. Jones is a reformer; he is also demonstrably "insecure." It does not necessarily follow that he is a reformer *because* he is insecure. The two may seem logically related (that is, if one's mind automatically links "protest" with "neurosis"), but we all know that many things can be logical without being true.

Even if we establish the neurotic behavior of certain members of a group, we have not, thereby, established the neurotic behavior of *all* members of that group. The tendency to leap from the particular to the general is always tempting, but because we have caught one benighted monsignor with a boy scout does not mean we have conclusively proved that all priests are pederasts. Some members of every group are disturbed; put the local police force, the Medal of Honor winners, or the faculty of a university under the Freudian microscope, and the number of cases of "palpable disturbance" would probably be disconcertingly high. But what *precisely* does their disturbance tell us about the common activities of the group to which they belong—let alone about the activities of the disturbed individuals themselves?

Actually, behavioral patterns for many abolitionists do *not* seem notably eccentric. Men like Birney, Weld, Lowell, Quincy—abolitionists all— formed good relationships, saw themselves in perspective, played and worked with zest and spontaneity, developed their talents, were aware of worlds beyond their own private horizons. They all had their tics and their traumas—as who does not—but the evidence of health is abundant and predominant. Yet most historians have preferred to ignore such men when discussing the abolitionist movement. And the reason, I believe, is that such men conform less well than do the Garrisons to the assumption that those who become deeply involved in social protest are necessarily those who are deeply disturbed.

To evaluate this assumption further, some effort must be made to understand current findings in the theory of human motivation. This is difficult terrain for the historian, not made more inviting by the sharp disagreements which exist among psychologists themselves (though these disagreements do help to make us aware of the complexities involved). Recent motivational research, though not conclusive, throws some useful new perspectives on "reformers."

A reaction has currently set in among psychologists against the older behaviorist model of human conduct. The behaviorists told us that men's actions were determined by the nature of the stimulus exerted upon them, and that their actions always pointed towards the goal of "tension reduction." There was little room in behaviorist theory for freedom of choice, for rationality, or for complex motives involving abstract ideas as well as instinctive drives.

Without denying the tension-reducing motives of certain kinds of human behavior, a number of psychologists are now insisting on making room for another order of motivation, involving more than the mere "restoration of equilibrium." Mature people, they believe—that is, those who have a realistic sense of self—*can* act with deliberation and *can* exercise control over their actions. This new view presumes an active intellect, an intellect capable of interpreting sensory data in a purposive way. The power of reflection, of self-objectification, makes possible a dynamic as opposed to a merely instinctive life. Men, in short, need not be wholly driven by habit and reflex; they need not be mere automatons who respond in predictable ways to given stimuli. Rather, they can be reasoning organisms capable of decision and choice. Among the rational choices mature men may make is to commit themselves to a certain set of ethical values. They are not necessarily forced to such a commitment by personal or social tensions (of which they are usually unaware), but may come to that commitment deliberately, after reflective consideration.

The new psychology goes even one step further. It suggests that the very definition of maturity may be the ability to commit oneself to abstract ideals, to get beyond the selfish, egocentric world of children. This does not mean that every man who reaches outward does so from mature motives; external involvement may also be a way of acting out sick phantasies. The point is only that "commitment" need not be a sympton of personality disturbance. It is just as likely to be a sympton of maturity and health.

It does not follow, of course, that all abolitionists protested against slavery out of mature motives; some may have been, indeed were, "childish neurotics." But if we agree that slavery was a fearful injustice, and if motivational theory now suggests that injustice will bring forth protest from mature men, it seems reasonable to conclude that at least some of those who protested strongly against slavery must have done so from "healthy" motives.

The hostile critic will say that the abolitionists protested *too* strongly to have been maturely motivated. But when is a protest *too* strong? For a defender of the status quo, the answer (though never stated in these terms) would be: when it succeeds. For those not dedicated to the current status, the answer is likely to be: a protest is too strong when it is out of all proportion to the injustice it indicts. Could any verbal protest have been too strong against holding fellow human beings as property? From a moral point of view, certainly not, though from a practical point of view, perhaps. That is, the abolitionist protest might have been *too* strong if it somehow jeopardized the very goal it sought to achieve—the destruction of human slavery. But no one has yet shown this to have been the case.

At any rate, current findings in motivational theory suggest that at the very least we must cease dealing in blanket indictments, in simple-minded categorizing and elementary stereotyping. Such exercises may satisfy our present-day hostility to "reformers," but they do not satisfy the complex demands of historical truth. We need an awareness of the wide variety of human beings who became involved in the abolitionist movement, and an awareness of the complexity of human motivation sufficient to save us from summing up men and movements in two or three unexamined adjectives.

Surely there is now evidence enough to suggest that commitment and concern need not be aberrations; they may represent the profoundest elements of our humanity. Surely there are grounds for believing that those who protested strongly against slavery were not all misguided fanatics or frustrated neurotics—though by so believing it becomes easier to ignore the injustice against which they protested. Perhaps it is time to ask whether the abolitionists, in insisting that slavery be ended, were indeed those men of their generation furthest removed from reality, or whether that description should be reserved for those Northerners who remained indifferent to the institution, and those Southerners who defended it as a "positive good." From the point of view of these men, the abolitionists were indeed mad, but it is time we questioned the sanity of the point of view.

Those Northerners who were not indifferent to slavery—a large number after 1845—were nonetheless prone to view the abolitionist protest as "excessive," for it threatened the cherished values of private property and Union. The average Northerner may have found slavery disturbing, but convinced as he was that the Negro was an inferior, he did not find slavery monstrous. Certainly he did not think it an evil sufficiently profound to risk, by "precipitous action," the nation's present wealth or its future power. The abolitionists were willing to risk both. They thought it tragic that men should weigh human lives in the *same* scale as material possessions and abstractions of government. It is no less tragic that we continue to do so.

SUGGESTIONS FOR FURTHER READING

Louis Filler, *The Crusade Against Slavery* (New York, 1960), is a balanced account which takes the abolitionists seriously and makes connections between the movement and the other reforms of the period. Gilbert H. Barnes, *The Antislavery Impulse, 1830–1844* (New York, 1933), emphasizes the importance of religious revivalism, and especially the leadership of Theodore Weld for the movement. Dwight L. Dumond, *Anti-Slavery Origins of the Civil War in the United States* (Ann Arbor, 1939), is a sympathetic account which stresses the moral basis for the crusade against slavery. Richard O. Curry, *The Abolitionists: Reformers or Fanatics* (New York, 1965), is a convenient collection of essays. William H. and Jane H. Pease, *The Anti-Slavery Agreement* (New York, 1965) and Louis Ruchames, *The Abolitionists: A Collection of Their Writings* (New York, 1963), are collections of documents.

Avery Craven's position is shared by a number of other historians of the period including William B. Hesseltine, *The South in American History* (New York, 1936). For a criticism of Donald's method see Robert A. Skotheim, "A Note on Historical Method: David Donald's 'Toward a Reconsideration of Abolitionists,'" *Journal of Southern History*, XXV (Aug., 1959), 356–65. A fascinating group of essays by a new generation of historians is Martin Duberman, ed., *The Antislavery Vanguard: New Essays on the Abolitionists* (Princeton, 1965). Leon F. Litwack, *North of Slavery: The Negro in the Free States, 1790–1860* (Chicago, 1961), examines the role of Negroes in the Anti-slavery movement, and suggests that some of the abolitionists were not free of racial prejudice.

VIII
THE ★
CIVIL ★
WAR ★

Americans have found their Civil War to be more interesting than any other event in their history. Even the Revolution which marked the birth of the republic cannot compete in popularity with the bloody fratricidal conflict of 1861–1865. The popular imagination has been fed by thousands of books and articles, movies and television performances. Commemorative monuments, museums, parks, and cemeteries dot every state which saw battle. No skirmish, however minor, lacks at least one historical marker to remind visitors of the event, and every state which raised troops has its mementos—flags, uniforms, guns, and equipment—which it treasures. And it is only in recent years that anniversary dates were not marked by the appearance of an old veteran, willing to recount his experiences—real and imagined—in the war.

The historian has not been immune to this fascination with our Civil War. He has recounted the battles many times over and has described, defended, and attacked the actions of the important actors (and many not so important) on both sides of the conflict.

Hundreds of thousands of casualties and millions of dollars in destroyed property are ample evidence that the Civil War marked a sharp conflict in American history. But, how significant were the differences which led to war between North and South in 1861? In October, 1858 William H. Seward, a prominent New York Republican leader, declared that the struggle over slavery which divided North and South was "an irrepressible conflict." Ear-

337

lier that same year an Illinois Republican politician, Abraham Lincoln, had enunciated similar beliefs: "A house divided against itself cannot stand. I believe this government cannot endure permanently, half-slave and half-free."

Taking their lead from such statements some historians have argued that the Civil War revealed deep and abiding differences in American society. So significant were the disagreements between North and South that compromise became impossible. The gulf which separated the sections had become so wide that a bridge of consensus could not be built and conflict in the form of organized warfare was inevitable. Moreover, the defeat and subjugation of the South, many of these scholars argue, marked a fundamental turning point in American history. The victory of the Northern troops led to the victory of the Northern point of view; compromise, which had been impossible, now had become unnecessary.

Other historians dispute this interpretation. The nation had lived with slavery for many generations, they argue, and when disputes arose between the sections they had repeatedly been resolved through compromise. While Lincoln made it clear he did not like slavery, he also made it clear that he would not interfere with it in the South. War was not inevitable; on the contrary it could have been prevented. That it was not prevented was not the result of fundamental differences between North and South, but rather the result of what one historian has called the failures of a "blundering generation."

The three selections which follow give very different evaluations of the significance of the Civil War. For Charles and Mary Beard the Civil War was a struggle for political power waged by representatives of two economic systems. The War was an "irrepressible conflict" between the industrial North and the agricultural South; the prize for which they contended was political domination of the nation. When the North won on the battlefields, the industrialists won in Congress. The domination of the country by the agricultural interests was at an end and as such the Civil War, the Beards conclude, was "a Second American Revolution."

Both Avery Craven and Daniel J. Boorstin strongly dispute this interpretation. Craven argues that war became inevitable only after blind emotionalism based on prejudice and ignorance had fettered the minds of the people of both sections. What were minor differences which could have been settled became moral absolutes which could no longer be amicably resolved. Boorstin is struck by what he considers to be an essential "continuity" of American thought through the period of the Civil War. He finds both sides more alike than different in their arguments about institutions and politics.

It would seem that the American people would turn to war as a way to settle their differences only after every other means of settlement had proved ineffective. Can we say, then, that the Civil War arose because the differences between North and South were so great and so fundamental that compromise became impossible? If so, the Civil War, however tragic, was inevitable and was only a continuation on the battlefield of a basic conflict which divided the sections. On the other hand, few modern social scientists would deny the existence of irrational sources of human behavior. Can such sources explain the Civil War? Did war come because Americans ignored the roads to compromise and accommodation, roads available to them and utilized by them many times before 1861? If so, the war was a double tragedy and could have been avoided had the participants acted more wisely.

The
second
american
revolution

Charles and Mary Beard

Had the economic systems of the North and the South remained static or changed slowly without effecting immense dislocations in the social structure, the balance of power might have been maintained indefinitely by repeating the compensatory tactics of 1787, 1820, 1833, and 1850; keeping in this manner the inherent antagonisms within the bounds of diplomacy. But nothing was stable in the economy of the United States or in the moral sentiments associated with its diversities.

Within each section of the country, the necessities of the productive system were generating portentous results. The periphery of the industrial vortex of the Northeast was daily enlarging, agriculture in the Northwest was being steadily supplemented by manufacturing, and the area of virgin soil open to exploitation by planters was diminishing with rhythmic regularity—shifting with mechanical precision the weights which statesmen had to adjust in their efforts to maintain the equilibrium of peace. Within each of the three sections also occurred an increasing intensity of social concentration as railways, the telegraph, and the press made travel and communication cheap and almost instantaneous, facilitating the centripetal process that was drawing people of similar economic status and parallel opinions into cooperative activities. Finally the intellectual energies released by accumulating wealth and growing leisure—stimulated by the expansion of the reading public and the literary market—developed with deepened accuracy the word-patterns of the current social persuasions, contributing with galvanic effect to the consolidation of identical groupings.

As the years passed, the planting leaders of Jefferson's agricultural party insisted with mounting fervor that the opposition, first of the Whigs and then of the Republicans, was at bottom an association of interests formed for the purpose of plundering productive management and labor on the land. And with steadfast insistence they declared that in the insatiable greed of their political foes lay the source of the dissensions which were tearing the country asunder.

Reprinted with permission of The Macmillan Company from *The Rise of American Civilization*, Vol. II by Charles A. and Mary R. Beard. Copyright 1927 by The Macmillan Company.

"There is not a pursuit in which man is engaged (agriculture excepted)," exclaimed Reuben Davis of Mississippi in 1860, "which is not demanding legislative aid to enable it to enlarge its profits and all at the expense of the primary pursuit of man—agriculture. . . . Those interests, having a common purpose of plunder, have united and combined to use the government as the instrument of their operation and have thus virtually converted it into a consolidated empire. Now this combined host of interests stands arrayed against the agricultural states; and this is the reason of the conflict which like an earthquake is shaking our political fabric to its foundation." The furor over slavery is a mere subterfuge to cover other purposes. "Relentless avarice stands firm with its iron heel upon the Constitution." This creature, "incorporated avarice," has chained "the agricultural states to the northern rock" and lives like a vulture upon their prosperity. It is the effort of Prometheus to burst his manacles that provokes the assault on slavery. "These states struggle like a giant," continued Davis, "and alarm these incorporated interests, lest they may break the chain that binds them to usurpation; and therefore they are making this fierce onslaught upon the slave property of the southern states."

The fact that free-soil advocates waged war only on slavery in the territories was to Jefferson Davis conclusive proof of an underlying conspiracy against agriculture. He professed more respect for the abolitionist than for the freesoiler. The former, he said, is dominated by an honest conviction that slavery is wrong everywhere and that all men ought to be free; the latter does not assail slavery in the states—he merely wishes to abolish it in the territories that are in due course to be admitted to the Union.

With challenging directness, Davis turned upon his opponents in the Senate and charged them with using slavery as a blind to delude the unwary: "What do you propose, gentlemen of the Free-Soil party? Do you propose to better the condition of the slave? Not at all. What then do you propose? You say you are opposed to the expansion of slavery. . . . Is the slave to be benefited by it? Not at all. It is not humanity that influences you in the position which you now occupy before the country. . . . It is that you may have an opportunity of cheating us that you want to limit slave territory within circumscribed bounds. It is that you may have a majority in the Congress of the United States and convert the Government into an engine of northern aggrandizement. It is that your section may grow in power and prosperity upon treasures unjustly taken from the South, like the vampire bloated and gorged with the blood which it has secretly sucked from its victim. . . . You desire to weaken the political power of the southern states; and why? Because you want, by an unjust system of legislation, to promote the industry of the New England states, at the expense of the people of the South and their industry."

Such in the mind of Jefferson Davis, fated to be president of the Confederacy, was the real purpose of the party which sought to prohibit slavery in the territories; that party did not declare slavery to be a moral disease calling for the severe remedy of the surgeon; it merely sought to keep bondage out of the new states as they came into the Union—with one fundamental aim in view, namely, to gain political ascendancy in the government of the United States and fasten upon the country an economic policy that meant the exploitation of the South for the benefit of northern capitalism.

But the planters were after all fighting against the census returns, as the phrase of the day ran current. The amazing growth of northern industries, the rapid extension of railways, the swift expansion of foreign trade to the ends of the earth, the attachment of the farming regions of the West to the centers of manufacture and finance through transportation and credit, the destruction of state consciousness by migration, the alien invasion, the erection of new commonwealths in the Valley of Democracy, the nationalistic drive of interstate commerce, the increase of population in the North, and the southward pressure of the capitalistic glacier all conspired to assure the ultimate triumph of what the orators were fond of calling "the free labor system." This was a dynamic thrust far too powerful for planters operating in a limited territory with incompetent labor on soil of diminishing fertility. Those who swept forward with it, exulting in the approaching triumph of machine industry, warned the planters of their ultimate subjection.

To statesmen of the invincible forces recorded in the census returns, the planting opposition was a huge, compact, and self-conscious economic association bent upon political objects—the possession of the government of the United States, the protection of its interests against adverse legislation, dominion over the territories, and enforcement of the national fugitive slave law throughout the length and breadth of the land. No phrase was more often on the lips of northern statesmen than "the slave power." The pages of the Congressional Globe bristled with references to "the slave system" and its influence over the government of the country. But it was left for William H. Seward of New York to describe it with a fullness of familiar knowledge that made his characterization a classic.

Seward knew from experience that a political party was no mere platonic society engaged in discussing abstractions. "A party," he said, "is in one sense a joint stock association, in which those who contribute most direct the action and management of the concern. The slaveholders contributing in an overwhelming proportion to the capital strength of the Democratic party, they necessarily dictate and prescribe its policy. The inevitable caucus system enables them to do this with a show of fairness and justice." This class of slaveholders, consisting of only three hundred and forty-seven thousand persons, Seward went on to say, was spread from the banks of the Delaware to the banks of the Rio Grande; it possessed nearly all the real estate in that section, owned more than three million other "persons" who were denied all civil and political rights, and inhibited "freedom of speech, freedom of press, freedom of the ballot box, freedom of education, freedom of literature, and freedom of popular assemblies. . . . The slaveholding class has become the governing power in each of the slaveholding states and it practically chooses thirty of the sixty-two members of the Senate, ninety of the two hundred and thirty-three members of the House of Representatives, and one hundred and five of the two hundred and ninety-five electors of the President and Vice-President of the United States."

Becoming still more concrete, Seward accused the President of being "a confessed apologist of the slave-property class." Examining the composition of the Senate, he found the slave-owning group in possession of all the important committees. Peering into the House of Representatives he discovered no impregnable bulwark of freedom there. Nor did respect for judicial ermine compel him to spare the Supreme Court. With irony he exclaimed: "How fitting does the proclamation of its opening close with the invocation: 'God save the United States and this honorable court'. . . . The court consists of a chief justice and eight associate justices. Of these five were called from slave states and four from free states. The opinions and bias of each of them were carefully considered by the President and Senate when he was appointed. Not one of them was found wanting in soundness of politics, according to the slaveholder's exposition of the Constitution, and those who were called from the free states were even more distinguished in that respect than their brethren from the slaveholding states."

Seward then analyzed the civil service of the national government and could descry not a single person among the thousands employed in the post office, the treasury, and other great departments who was "false to the slaveholding interest." Under the spoils system, the dominion of the slavocracy extended into all branches of the federal administration. "The customs-houses and the public lands pour forth two golden streams—one into the elections to procure votes for the slaveholding class; and the other into the treasury to be enjoyed by those whom it shall see fit to reward with places in the public service." Even in the North, religion, learning, and the press were under the spell of this masterful class, frightened lest they incur its wrath.

Having described the gigantic operating structure of the slavocracy, Seward drew with equal power a picture of the opposing system founded on "free labor." He surveyed the course of economy in the North—the growth of industry, the spread of railways, the swelling tide of European immigration, and the westward roll of free farmers—rounding out the country, knitting it together, bringing "these antagonistic systems" continually into closer contact. Then he uttered those fateful words which startled conservative citizens from Maine to California—words of prophecy which proved to be brutally true—"the irrepressible conflict."

This inexorable clash, he said, was not "accidental, unnecessary, the work of interested or fanatical agitators and therefore ephemeral." No. "It is an irrepressible conflict between opposing and enduring forces." The hopes of those who sought peace by appealing to slave owners to reform themselves were as chaff in a storm. "How long and with what success have you waited already for that reformation? Did any property class ever so reform itself? Did the patricians in old Rome, the noblesse or clergy in France? The landholders in Ireland? The landed aristocracy in England? Does the slaveholding class even seek to beguile you with such a hope? Has it not become rapacious, arrogant, defiant?" All attempts at compromise were "vain and ephemeral." There was accordingly but one supreme task before the people of the United States—the task of confounding and overthrowing "by one decisive blow the betrayers of the Constitution and freedom forever." In uttering this indictment, this prophecy soon to be fulfilled with such appalling accuracy, Seward stepped beyond the bounds of cautious politics and read himself out of the little group of men who were eligible for the Republican nomination in 1860. Frantic efforts to soften his words by explanations and additions could not appease his critics.

Given an irrepressible conflict which could be symbolized in such unmistakable patterns by competent interpreters of opposing factions, a transfer of the issues from the forum to the field, from the conciliation of diplomacy to the decision of arms was bound to come. Each side obdurately bent upon its designs and convinced of its rectitude, by the fulfillment of its wishes precipitated events and effected distributions of power that culminated finally in the tragedy foretold by Seward. Those Democrats who operated on historic knowledge rather than on prophetic insight, recalling how many times the party of Hamilton had been crushed at elections, remembering how the Whigs had never been able to carry the country on a cleancut Webster-Clay program, and counting upon the continued support of a huge array of farmers and mechanics marshaled behind the planters, imagined apparently that politics—viewed as the science of ballot enumeration—could resolve the problems of power raised by the maintenance of the Union.

And in this opinion they were confirmed by the outcome of the presidential campaign in 1852, when the Whigs, with General Winfield Scott, a hero of the Mexican war, at their head, were thoroughly routed by the Democratic candidate, General Franklin Pierce of New Hampshire. Indeed the verdict of the people was almost savage, for Pierce carried every state but four, receiving 254 out of 296 electoral votes. The Free-Soil party that branded slavery as a crime and called for its prohibition in the territories scarcely made a ripple, polling only 156,000 out of more than three million votes, a figure below the record set in the previous campaign.

With the Whigs beaten and the Free-Soilers evidently a dwindling handful of negligible critics, exultant Democrats took possession of the Executive offices and Congress, inspired by a firm belief that their tenure was secure. Having won an overwhelming victory on a definite tariff for revenue and pro-slavery program, they acted as if the party of Hamilton was for all practical purposes as powerless as the little band of abolitionist agitators. At the succeeding election in 1856 they again swept the country—this time with James Buchanan of Pennsylvania as their candidate. Though his triumph was not as magisterial as that of Pierce it was great enough to warrant a conviction that the supremacy of the Democratic party could not be broken at the polls.

During these eight years of tenure, a series of events occurred under Democratic auspices, which clinched the grasp of the planting interest upon the country and produced a correlative consolidation of the opposition. One line of development indicated an indefinite extension of the slave area; another the positive withdrawal of all government support from industrial and commercial enterprise. The first evidence of the new course came in the year immediately following the inauguration of Pierce. In 1854, Congress defiantly repealed the Missouri Compromise and threw open to slavery the vast section of the Louisiana Purchase which had been closed to it by the covenant adopted more than three decades before. On the instant came a rush of slavery champions from Missouri into Kansas determined to bring it into the southern sphere of influence. Not content with the conquest of the forbidden West, filibustering parties under pro-slavery leaders attempted to seize Cuba and Nicaragua and three American ministers abroad flung out to the world a flaming proclamation, known as the "Ostend Manifesto," which declared that the United States would be justified in wresting Cuba from Spain by force—acts of imperial aggression which even the Democratic administration in Washington felt constrained to repudiate.

Crowning the repeal of the Missouri Compromise came two decisions of the Supreme Court giving sanction to the expansion of slavery in America and assuring high protection for that peculiar institution even in the North. In the Dred Scott case decided in March, 1857, Chief Justice Taney declared in effect that the Missouri Compromise had been void from the beginning and that Congress had no power under the Constitution to prohibit slavery in the territories of the United States anywhere at any time. This legal triumph for the planting interest was followed in 1859 by another decision in which the Supreme Court upheld the fugitive slave law and all the drastic procedure provided for its enforcement. To the frightened abolitionists it seemed that only one more step was needed to make freedom unconstitutional throughout the country.

These extraordinary measures on behalf of slavery were accompanied by others that touched far more vitally economic interests in the North. In 1859, the last of the subsidies for trans-Atlantic steamship companies was ordered discontinued by Congress. In 1857, the tariff was again reduced, betraying an unmistakable drift of the nation toward free trade. In support of this action, the representatives of the South and Southwest were almost unanimous and they gathered into their fold a large number of New England congressmen on condition that no material reductions should be made in duties on cotton goods. On the other hand, the Middle States and the West offered a large majority against tariff reduction so that the division was symptomatic.

Immediately after the new revenue law went into effect an industrial panic burst upon the country, spreading distress among business men and free laborers. While that tempest was running high, the paper money anarchy let loose by the Democrats reached the acme of virulence as the notes of wildcat banks flooded the West and South and financial institutions crashed in every direction, fifty-one failing in Indiana alone within a period of five years. Since all hope of reviving Hamilton's system of finance had been buried, those who believed that a sound currency was essential to national prosperity were driven to the verge of desperation. On top of these economic calamities came Buchanan's veto of the Homestead bill which the impatient agrarians had succeeded in getting through Congress in a compromise form—an act of presidential independence which angered the farmers and mechanics who regarded the national domain as their own inheritance. . . .

The amazing acts of mastery—legislative, executive, judicial—committed by the federal government in the decade between 1850 and 1860 changed the whole political climate of America. They betrayed a growing consolidation in the planting group, its increased dominance in the Democratic party, and an evident determination to realize its economic interests and protect its labor system at all hazards. In a kind of doom, they seemed to mark the final supremacy of the political army which had swept into office with Andrew Jackson. During the thirty-two years between that event and the inauguration of Lincoln, the Democrats controlled the Presidency and the Senate for twenty-four years, the Supreme Court for twenty-six years, and the House of Representatives for twenty-two years. By the end of the period, the old farmer-labor party organized by Jackson had passed under the dominion of the planting interest and the farming wing of the North was confronted with the alternative of surrender or secession.

In this shift of power the Whigs of the South, discovering the tendencies of the popular balloting, moved steadily over into the Democratic camp. Though unavoidable, the transfer was painful; the planting Whigs, being rich and influential, had little affection for the white farmers who rallied around the Jacksonian banner. According to the estimate of a southern newspaper in 1850, the Whigs owned at least three-fourths of all the slaves in the country and it was a matter of common knowledge that leaders among them disliked wildcat banking as much as they hated high duties on the manufactured goods they bought. Indeed to a southern gentleman of the old school the radical agrarianism of Andrew Jackson was probably more odious than the tariff schedules devised by Daniel Webster. It was said that one of them, when asked whether a gentleman could be a Democrat, snapped back the tart reply: "Well, he is not apt to be; but if he is, he is in damned bad company."

But the rich planters were relatively few in numbers and virtue was subject to the law of necessity; the populace had the votes, northern manufacturers were demanding protection, abolitionists were agitating, and in the end all but the most conservative remnant of the southern Whigs had to go over to the party that professed the dangerous doctrines of Jackson. The achievements of the years that lay between 1850 and 1860 seemed to justify the sacrifice.

Though the drift toward the irrepressible conflict was steady and strong, as events revealed, the politics of the decade had the outward semblances of dissolution. The abolitionists and free-soilers, while a mere minority as we have seen, were able to worry the politicians of both parties in the North. Largely deserted by their southern cohorts, the Whigs, whose organization had always been tenuous at best, could discover no way of mustering a majority of votes on the bare economic policies of Hamilton and Webster. Their two victories—in 1840 and 1848— had been dubious and their only hope for a triumph at the polls lay in a combination with other factors. . . .

The signal for a general realignment of factions and parties was given by the passage of the Kansas-Nebraska bill of 1854 repealing the Missouri Compromise. In fact, while that measure was pending in Congress a coalescing movement was to be observed: northern Whigs persuaded that their old party was moribund, Democrats weary of planting dominance, and free-soilers eager to exclude slavery from the territories began to draw together to resist the advance of the planting power. In February of that year, a number of Whigs and Democrats assembled at Ripon, Wisconsin, and resolved that a new party must be formed if the bill passed.

When the expected event occurred, the Ripon insurgents created a fusion committee and chose the name "Republican" as the title of their young political association. In July, a Michigan convention composed of kindred elements demanded the repeal of the Kansas-Nebraska act, the repeal of the fugitive slave law, and the abolition of slavery in the District of Columbia. This convention also agreed to postpone all differences "with regard to political economy or administrative policy" and stay in the field as a "Republican" party until the struggle against slavery extension was finished. All over the country similar meetings were mustered and the local cells of the new national party rose into being. Meanwhile the old Whigs who wanted peace and prosperity were floating about looking for any drifting wreckage that might hold them above the waves. . . .

"The Government has fallen into the hands of the Slave Power completely," wrote Wendell Phillips in 1854. "So far as national politics are concerned, we are beaten—there's no hope. We shall have Cuba in a year or two, Mexico in five, and I should not wonder if efforts were made to revive the slave trade, though perhaps unsuccessfully, as the northern slave states, which live by the export of slaves, would help us in opposing that. Events hurry forward with amazing rapidity; we live fast here. The future seems to unfold a vast slave empire united with Brazil and darkening the whole West. I hope I may be a false prophet, but the sky was never so dark."

Three years later, when the inauguration of Buchanan had turned discouragement into despair, the only strategic stroke that Phillips and his colleagues could invent was to hold an abolition convention in Massachusetts and adopt a solemn slogan calling for the disruption of the Union with the slave states. And the events of the swiftly flowing months that followed, as we have already indicated, merely seemed to confirm the belief of Phillips in the supremacy of the Democratic party led by the indomitable planting interest; events such as the downward revision of the tariff, the withdrawal of the ship subsidies, and the Dred Scott decision opening the territories to slavery.

All the while the conflict was growing more furious. Advocates of protection, taking advantage of the panic which followed the tariff revision, organized a stirring campaign to wean workingmen from their allegiance to a free-trade Democracy. Advocates of a sound currency protested against the depreciated notes and the wildcat banks that spread ruin through all sections of the land. The abolitionists maintained their fusillade, Garrison and Phillips, despite their pessimism, resting neither day nor night. Going beyond the bounds of mere agitation, the slavery faction of Missouri in its grim determination to conquer Kansas for bondage and northern abolitionists in their equally firm resolve to seize it for freedom convulsed the country by bloody deeds and then by bloody reprisals. In a powerful oration, "The Crime against Kansas," done in classical style but bristling with abuse of the slavery party, Charles Sumner threw Congress into a tumult in 1856 and provided a text for the free-soilers laboring to wrest the government from the planting interest. Before the public excitement caused by this speech had died away, the attention of the nation was arrested by a series of debates between Lincoln and Douglas held in Illinois in 1858—debates which set forth in clear and logical form the program for excluding slavery from the territories and the squatter-sovereignty scheme for letting the inhabitants decide the issue for themselves.

Then came the appalling climax in 1859 when John Brown, after a stormy career in Kansas, tried to kindle a servile insurrection in the South. In the spring of that year, Brown attended an anti-slavery convention from which he went away muttering: "These men are all talk; what we need is action—action!" Collecting a few daring comrades he made a raid into Harper's Ferry for the purpose of starting a slave rebellion. Though his efforts failed, though he was quickly executed as a "traitor to Virginia," the act of violence rocked the continent from sea to sea.

In vain did the Republicans try to treat it as the mere work of a fanatic and denounce it as "among the gravest of crimes." In vain did Lincoln attempt to minimize it as an absurd adventure that resulted in nothing noteworthy except the death of Brown. It resounded through the land with the clangor of an alarm bell, aggravating the jangling nerves of a people already excited by fears of a race war and continued disturbances over the seizure of slaves under the fugitive slave act—disorders which sometimes assumed the form of menacing riots.

The turmoil in the country naturally found sharp echoes in the halls of Congress. Buchanan's policy of aiding the slavery party in its efforts to get possession of Kansas and the taunting action of the free-soilers in their determination to save it for liberty, gave abundant occasions for debates that grew more and more acrimonious. Indeed the factions in Congress were now almost at swords' points, passion in argument and gesture becoming the commonplace of the day.

When Senator Sumner made a vehement verbal attack on Senator Butler of South Carolina in 1856, Preston Brooks, a Representative from the same state and a relative of the latter, replied in terms of physical force, catching Sumner unawares and beating his victim senseless with a heavy cane. Though the act was not strictly chivalrous—for Sumner, wedged in between his chair and his desk, could not defend himself—admiring South Carolinians gave Brooks a grand banquet and presented him with a new cane bearing the words: "Use knockdown arguments." On both sides of the Senate chamber all the arts of diplomacy were discarded, and the meanest weapons of personal abuse brought into play. Douglas called Sumner a perjurer who spat forth malignity upon his colleagues. The prim, proud Senator from Massachusetts, conscious of possessing a mellow culture, replied by likening Douglas to a "noisome, squat and nameless animal" that filled the Senate with an offensive odor.

Things were even worse in the lower house. Again and again debate was on the verge of physical combat, for which members equipped themselves with knives and revolvers. A Representative from Pennsylvania and another from North Carolina had to be put under bonds to keep the peace. A general mêlée occurred in the spring of 1860 when Lovejoy, whose brother had been shot by a pro-slavery mob in Illinois, made an unbridled attack on slave owners and Democrats, advanced to their side of the house shaking his fists in a terrible rage, and threw the whole chamber into such a confusion that all the resources of experienced leaders were needed to prevent bloodshed then and there. Without ex- aggeration did Jefferson Davis exclaim that members of Congress were more like the agents of belligerent states than men assembled in the in- terest of common welfare—an utterance that was startlingly accurate— born of prophetic certainty. After a few fleeting days, the irrepressible conflict that had so long been raging was actually to pass from the forum to the battlefield, to that court where the only argument was the sword and where the one answer that admitted of no appeal was death.

Every shocking incident on the one side only consolidated the forces on the other. By 1860 leaders of the planting interest had worked out in great detail their economic and political scheme—their ultimatum to the serried opposition—and embodied it in many official documents. The economic elements were those made familiar to the country through twenty years of agitation: no high protective tariffs, no ship subsidies, no national banking and currency system; in short, none of the measures which business enterprise deemed essential to its progress. The remain- ing problem before the planting interest, namely, how to clinch its grip and prevent a return to the Hamilton-Webster policy as the industrial North rapidly advanced in wealth and population, was faced with the same penchant for definition.

Plans for accomplishing that purpose were mapped out by able spokes- men from the South in a set of Senate resolutions adopted on May 24– 25, 1860: slavery is lawful in all the territories under the Constitution; neither Congress nor a local legislature can abolish it there; the federal government is in duty bound to protect slave owners as well as the hold- ers of other forms of property in the territories; it is a violation of the Constitution for any state or any combination of citizens to intermeddle with the domestic institutions of any other state "on any pretext what- ever, political, moral, or religious, with a view to their disturbance or sub- version"; open or covert attacks on slavery are contrary to the solemn pledges given by the states on entering the Union to protect and defend one another; the inhabitants of a territory on their admission to the Union may decide whether or not they will sanction slavery thereafter; the strict enforcement of the fugitive slave law is required by good faith and the principles of the Constitution.

In brief, the federal government was to do nothing for business enter- prise while the planting interest was to be assured the possession of enough political power to guarantee it against the reënactment of the Hamilton-Webster program. Incidentally the labor system of the planting interest was not to be criticized and all runaway property was to be returned. Anything short of this was, in the view of the planting statesmen, "subversive of the Constitution."

The meaning of the ultimatum was not to be mistaken. It was a demand upon the majority of the people to surrender unconditionally for all time to the minority stockholders under the Constitution. It offered nothing to capitalism but capitulation; to the old Whigs of the South nothing but submission. Finally—and this was its revolutionary phase —it called upon the farmers and mechanics who had formed the bulk of Jacksonian Democracy in the North to acknowledge the absolute sovereignty of the planting interest. Besides driving a wedge into the nation, the conditions laid down by the planters also split the Democratic party itself into two factions.

Soon after the Democratic convention assembled at Charleston in April, 1860, this fundamental division became manifest. The northern wing, while entirely willing to indorse the general economic program of the planters, absolutely refused to guarantee them sovereignty in the party and throughout the country. Rejecting the proposal of the southern members to make slavery obligatory in the territories, it would merely offer to "abide by the decisions of the Supreme Court on all questions of constitutional law." Since the Dred Scott case had opened all the territories to slavery, that tender seemed generous enough but the intransigent representatives of the planting interest would not accept it as adequate. Unable to overcome the majority commanded in the convention by the northern group, they withdrew from the assembly, spurning the pleas of their colleagues not to break up the union of hearts on "a mere theory" and countering all arguments with a declaration of finality: "Go your way and we will go ours."

After balloting for a time on candidates without reaching a decision under the two-thirds rule, the remaining members of the Charleston conference adjourned to meet again at Baltimore. When they reassembled, they nominated Stephen A. Douglas of Illinois, the apostle of "squatter sovereignty," who was ready to open the territories to slavery but not to guarantee the planting interest unconditional supremacy in the Democratic party and the Union. Determined to pursue their separate course to the bitter end, the Charleston seceders adopted the platform rejected by the Douglas faction and chose as their candidate, John C. Breckinridge of Kentucky, an unyielding champion of planting aristocracy and its labor system. The union of farmers and slave owners was thus severed: the Republicans had carried off one large fragment of the northern farmers in 1856; Douglas was now carrying off another.

During the confusion in the Democratic ranks, the Republicans, in high glee over the quarrels of the opposition, held their convention in Chicago—a sectional gathering except for representatives from five slave states. Among its delegates the spirit of opposition to slavery extension, which had inspired the party assembly four years before, was still evident but enthusiasm on that ticklish subject was neutralized by the prudence of the practical politicians who, sniffing victory in the air, had rushed to the new tent. Whigs, whose affections were centered on Hamilton's program rather than on Garrison's scheme of salvation, were to be seen on the floor. Advocates of a high protective tariff and friends of free homesteads for mechanics and farmers now mingled with the ardent opponents of slavery in the territories. With their minds fixed on the substance of things sought for, the partisans of caution were almost able to prevent the convention from indorsing the Declaration of Independence. Still they were in favor of restricting the area of slavery; they had no love for the institution and its spread helped to fasten the grip of the planting interest on the government at Washington. So the Republican convention went on record in favor of liberty for the territories, free homesteads for farmers, a protective tariff, and a Pacific railway. As the platform was read, the cheering became especially loud and prolonged when the homestead and tariff planks were reached. Such at least is the testimony of the stenographic report.

Since this declaration of principles was well fitted to work a union of forces, it was essential that the candidate should not divide them. The protective plank would doubtless line up the good old Whigs of the East but tender consideration had to be shown to the Ohio Valley, original home of Jacksonian Democracy, where national banks, tariffs, and other "abominations" still frightened the wary. Without Ohio, Indiana, and Illinois, the Republican managers could not hope to win and they knew that the lower counties of these states were filled with settlers from the slave belt who had no love for the "money power," abolition, or anything that savored of them. In such circumstances Seward, idol of the Whig wing, was no man to offer that section; he was too radical on the slavery issue and too closely associated with "high finance" in addition. "If you do not nominate Seward, where will you get your money?" was the blunt question put by Seward's loyal supporters at Chicago. The question was pertinent but not fatal.

Given this confluence of problems, a man close to the soil of the West was better suited to the requirements of the hour than a New York lawyer with somewhat fastidious tastes, obviously backed by fat purses. The available candidate was Abraham Lincoln of Illinois. Born in Kentucky, he was of southern origin. A son of poor frontier parents, self-educated, a pioneer who in his youth had labored in field and forest, he appealed to the voters of the backwoods. Still by an uncanny genius for practical affairs, he had forged his way to the front as a shrewd lawyer and politician. In his debates with Douglas he had shown himself able to cope with one of the foremost leaders in the Democratic party. On the tariff, bank, currency, and homestead issues he was sound. A local railway attorney, he was trusted among business men.

On the slavery question Lincoln's attitude was firm but conservative. He disliked slavery and frankly said so; yet he was not an abolitionist and he saw no way in which the institution could be uprooted. On the contrary, he favored enforcing the fugitive slave law and he was not prepared to urge even the abolition of slavery in the District of Columbia. His declaration that a house divided against itself could not stand had been counterbalanced by an assertion that the country would become all free or all slave—a creed which any southern planter could have indorsed. Seward's radical doctrine that there was a "higher law" than the Constitution, dedicating the territories to freedom, received from the Illinois lawyer disapproval, not commendation.

Nevertheless Lincoln was definite and positive in his opinion that slavery should not be permitted in the territories. That was necessary to satisfy the minimum demands of the anti-slavery faction and incidentally it pleased those Whigs of the North who at last realized that no Hamiltonian program could be pushed through Congress if the planting interest secured a supremacy, or indeed held an equal share of power, in the Union. Evidently Lincoln was the man of the hour: his heritage was correct, his principles were sound, his sincerity was unquestioned, and his ability as a speaker commanded the minds and hearts of his auditors. He sent word to his friends at Chicago that, although he did not indorse Seward's higher-law doctrine, he agreed with him on the irrepressible conflict. The next day Lincoln was nominated amid huzzas from ten thousand lusty throats.

A large fraction of Whigs and some fragments of the Know Nothing, or American, party, foreseeing calamity in the existing array of interests, tried to save the day by an appeal to lofty sentiments without any definitions. Assuming the name of Constitutional Unionists and boasting that they represented the "intelligence and respectability of the South" as well as the lovers of the national idea everywhere, they held a convention at Baltimore and nominated John Bell of Tennessee and Edward Everett of Massachusetts for President and Vice-President. In the platform they invited their countrymen to forget all divisions and "support the Constitution of the country, the union of the states, and the enforcement of the laws." It was an overture of old men—men who had known and loved Webster and Clay and who shrank with horror from agitations that threatened to end in bloodshed and revolution—a plea for the maintenance of the status quo against the whims of a swiftly changing world.

A spirited campaign followed the nomination of these four candidates for the presidency on four different platforms. Huge campaign funds were raised and spent. Beside pursuing the usual strategy of education, the Republicans resorted to parades and the other spectacular features that had distinguished the log-cabin crusade of General Harrison's year. Emulating the discretion of the Hero of Tippecanoe, Lincoln maintained a judicious silence at Springfield while his champions waged his battles for him, naturally tempering their orations to the requirements of diverse interests. They were fully conscious, as a Republican paper in Philadelphia put it, that "Frémont had tried running on the slavery issue and lost." So while they laid stress on it in many sections, they widened their appeal.

In the West, a particular emphasis was placed on free homesteads and the Pacific railway. With a keen eye for competent strategy, Carl Schurz carried the campaign into Missouri where he protested with eloquence against the action of the slave power in denying "the laboring man the right to acquire property in the soil by his labor" and made a special plea for the German vote on the ground that the free land was to be opened to aliens who declared their intention of becoming American citizens. Discovering that the homestead question was "the greatest issue in the West," Horace Greeley used it to win votes in the East. Agrarians and labor reformers renewed the slogan: "Vote yourself a farm."

In Pennsylvania and New Jersey, protection for iron and steel was the great subject of discussion. Curtin, the Republican candidate for governor in the former state, said not a word about abolishing slavery in his ratification speech but spoke with feeling on "the vast heavings of the heart of Pennsylvania whose sons are pining for protection to their labor and their dearest interests." Warming to his theme, he exclaimed: "This is a contest involving protection and the rights of labor. . . . If you desire to become vast and great, protect the manufactures of Philadelphia. . . . All hail, liberty! All hail, freedom! freedom to the white man! All hail freedom general as the air we breathe!" In a fashion after Curtin's own heart, the editor of the Philadelphia *American* and *Gazette*, surveying the canvass at the finish, repudiated the idea that "any sectional aspect of the slavery question" was up for decision and declared that the great issues were protection for industry, "economy in the conduct of the government, homesteads for settlers on the public domain, retrenchment and accountability in the public expenditures, appropriation for rivers and harbors, a Pacific railroad, the admission of Kansas, and a radical reform in the government."

With a kindred appreciation of practical matters, Seward bore the standard through the North and West. Fully conversant with the Webster policy of commercial expansion in the Pacific and knowing well the political appeal of Manifest Destiny, he proclaimed the future of the American empire—assuring his auditors that in due time American outposts would be pushed along the northwest coast to the Arctic Ocean, that Canada would be gathered into our glorious Union, that the Latin-American republics reorganized under our benign influence would become parts of this magnificent confederation, that the ancient Aztec metropolis, Mexico City, would eventually become the capital of the United States, and that America and Russia, breaking their old friendship, would come to grips in the Far East—"in regions where civilization first began." All this was involved in the election of Lincoln and the triumph of the Republican party. Webster and Cushing and Perry had not wrought in vain.

The three candidates opposed to Lincoln scored points wherever they could. Douglas took the stump with his usual vigor and declaimed to throngs in nearly every state. Orators of the Breckinridge camp, believing that their extreme views were sound everywhere, invaded the North. Bell's champions spoke with dignity and warmth about the dangers inherent in all unwise departures from the past, about the perils of the sectional quarrel. When at length the ballots were cast and counted, it was found that the foes of slavery agitation had carried the country by an overwhelming majority. Their combined vote was a million ahead of Lincoln's total; the two Democratic factions alone, to say nothing of Bell's six hundred thousand followers, outnumbered the Republican army. But in the division and uproar of the campaign Lincoln, even so, had won the Presidency; he was the choice of a minority—a sectional minority at that—but under the terms of the Constitution, he was entitled to the scepter at Washington.

From what has just been said it must be apparent that the forces which produced the irrepressible conflict were very complex in nature and yet the momentous struggle has been so often reduced by historians to simple terms that a re-examination of the traditional thesis has become one of the tasks of the modern age. On the part of northern writers it was long the fashion to declare that slavery was the cause of the conflict between the states. Such for example was the position taken by James Ford Rhodes and made the starting point of his monumental work.

Assuming for the moment that this assertion is correct in a general sense, it will be easily observed even on a superficial investigation that "slavery" was no simple, isolated phenomenon. In itself it was intricate and it had filaments through the whole body economic. It was a labor system, the basis of planting, and the foundation of the southern aristocracy. That aristocracy, in turn, owing to the nature of its economic operations, resorted to public policies that were opposed to capitalism, sought to dominate the federal government, and, with the help of free farmers also engaged in agriculture, did at last dominate it. In the course of that political conquest, all the plans of commerce and industry for federal protection and subvention were overborne. It took more than a finite eye to discern where slavery as an ethical question left off and economics—the struggle over the distribution of wealth—began.

On the other hand, the early historians of the southern school, chagrined by defeat and compelled to face the adverse judgment of brutal fact, made the "rights of states"—something nobler than economics or the enslavement of Negroes—the issue for which the Confederacy fought and bled. That too like slavery seems simple until subjected to a little scrutiny. What is a state? At bottom it is a majority or perhaps a mere plurality of persons engaged in the quest of something supposed to be beneficial, or at all events not injurious, to the pursuers. And what are rights? Abstract, intangible moral values having neither substance nor form? The party debates over the economic issues of the middle period answer with an emphatic negative. If the southern planters had been content to grant tariffs, bounties, subsidies, and preferences to northern commerce and industry, it is not probable that they would have been molested in their most imperious proclamations of sovereignty.

But their theories and their acts involved interests more ponderable than political rhetoric. They threatened the country with secession first in defying the tariff of abominations and when they did secede thirty years later it was in response to the victory of a tariff and homestead party that proposed nothing more dangerous to slavery itself than the mere exclusion of the institution from the territories. It took more than a finite eye to discern where their opposition to the economic system of Hamilton left off and their affection for the rights of states began. The modern reader tossed about in a contrariety of opinions can only take his bearings by examining a few indubitable realities.

With reference to the popular northern view of the conflict, there stands the stubborn fact that at no time during the long gathering of the storm did Garrison's abolition creed rise to the dignity of a first-rate political issue in the North. Nobody but agitators, beneath the contempt of the towering statesmen of the age, ever dared to advocate it. No great political organization even gave it the most casual indorsement.

When the abolitionists launched the Liberty party in the campaign of 1844 to work for emancipation, as we have noted, the voters answered their plea for "the restoration of equality of political rights among men" in a manner that demonstrated the invincible opposition of the American people. Out of more than two and a half million ballots cast in the election, only sixty-five thousand were recorded in favor of the Liberty candidate. That was America's answer to the call for abolition; and the advocates of that policy never again ventured to appeal to the electorate by presenting candidates on such a radical platform.

No other party organized between that time and the clash of arms attempted to do more than demand the exclusion of slavery from the territories and not until the Democrats by repealing the Missouri Compromise threatened to extend slavery throughout the West did any party poll more than a handful of votes on that issue. It is true that Van Buren on a free-soil platform received nearly three hundred thousand votes in 1848 but that was evidently due to personal influence, because his successor on a similar ticket four years afterward dropped into an insignificant place.

Even the Republican party, in the campaign of 1856, coming hard on the act of defiance which swept away the Missouri compact, won little more than one-third the active voters to the cause of restricting the slavery area. When transformed after four more years into a homestead and high tariff party pledged merely to liberty in the territories, the Republicans polled a million votes fewer than the number cast for the opposing factions and rode into power on account of the divided ranks of the enemy. Such was the nation's reply to the anti-slavery agitation from the beginning of the disturbance until the cannon shot at Sumter opened a revolution.

Moreover not a single responsible statesman of the middle period committed himself to the doctrine of immediate and unconditional abolition to be achieved by independent political action. John Quincy Adams, ousted from the presidency by Jacksonian Democracy but returned to Washington as the Representative of a Massachusetts district in Congress, did declare that it was the duty of every free American to work directly for the abolition of slavery and with uncanny vision foresaw that the knot might be cut with the sword. But Adams was regarded by astute party managers as a foolish and embittered old man and his prophecy as a dangerous delusion.

Practical politicians who felt the iron hand of the planters at Washington—politicians who saw how deeply intertwined with the whole economic order the institution of slavery really was—could discover nothing tangible in immediate and unconditional abolition that appealed to reason or came within the range of common sense. Lincoln was emphatic in assuring the slaveholders that no Republican had ever been detected in any attempt to disturb them. "We must not interfere with the institution of slavery in the states where it exists," he urged, "because the Constitution forbids it and the general welfare does not require us to do so."

Since, therefore, the abolition of slavery never appeared in the platform of any great political party, since the only appeal ever made to the electorate on that issue was scornfully repulsed, since the spokesman of the Republicans emphatically declared that his party never intended to interfere with slavery in the states in any shape or form, it seems reasonable to assume that the institution of slavery was not the fundamental issue during the epoch preceding the bombardment of Fort Sumter.

Nor can it be truthfully said, as southern writers were fond of having

it, that a tender and consistent regard for the rights of states and for a
strict construction of the Constitution was the prime element in the dispute that long divided the country. As a matter of record, from the
foundation of the republic, all factions were for high nationalism or low
provincialism upon occasion according to their desires at the moment,
according to turns in the balance of power. New England nullified federal law when her commerce was affected by the War of 1812 and came
out stanchly for liberty and union, one and inseparable, now and forever,
in 1833 when South Carolina attempted to nullify a tariff act. Not long
afterward, the legislature of Massachusetts, dreading the overweening
strength of the Southwest, protested warmly against the annexation of
Texas and resolved that "such an act of admission would have no binding force whatever on the people of Massachusetts."

Equally willing to bend theory to practical considerations, the party of
the slavocracy argued that the Constitution was to be strictly and narrowly construed whenever tariff and bank measures were up for debate;
but no such piddling concept of the grand document was to be held when
a bill providing for the prompt and efficient return of fugitive slaves was
on the carpet. Less than twenty years after South Carolina prepared to
resist by arms federal officers engaged in collecting customs duties, the
champions of slavery and states' rights greeted with applause a fugitive
slave law which flouted the precious limitations prescribed in the first ten
Amendments to the Constitution—a law which provided for the use of
all the powers of the national government to assist masters in getting
possession of their elusive property—which denied to the alleged slave,
who might perchance be a freeman in spite of his color, the right to have
a jury trial or even to testify in his own behalf. In other words, it was
"constitutional" to employ the engines of the federal authority in catching slaves wherever they might be found in any northern community and
to ignore utterly the elementary safeguards of liberty plainly and specifically imposed on Congress by language that admitted of no double interpretation.

On this very issue of personal liberty, historic positions on states'
rights were again reversed. Following the example of South Carolina on
the tariff, Wisconsin resisted the fugitive slave law as an invasion of her
reserved rights—as a violation of the Constitution. Alarmed by this action, Chief Justice Taney answered the disobedient state in a ringing
judicial decision announcing a high nationalism that would have delighted the heart of John Marshall, informing the recalcitrant Wisconsin
that the Constitution and laws enacted under it were supreme; that the
fugitive slave law was fully authorized by the Constitution; and that the
Supreme Court was the final arbiter in all controversies over the respective powers of the states and the United States. "If such an arbiter had
not been provided in our complicated system of government, internal

tranquility could not have been preserved and if such controversies were left to the arbitrament of physical force, our Government, State and National, would cease to be a government of laws, and revolution by force of arms would take the place of courts of justice and judicial decisions." No nullification here; no right of a state to judge for itself respecting infractions of the Constitution by the federal government; federal law is binding everywhere and the Supreme Court, a branch of the national government, is the final judge.

And in what language did Wisconsin reply? The legislature of the state, in a solemn resolution, declared that the decision of the Supreme Court of the United States in the case in question was in direct conflict with the Constitution. It vowed that the essential principles of the Kentucky doctrine of nullification were sound. Then it closed with the rebel fling: "that the several states . . . being sovereign and independent, have the unquestionable right to judge of its [the Constitution's] infraction and that a positive defiance by those sovereignties of all unauthorized acts done or attempted to be done under color of that instrument is the rightful remedy."

That was in 1859. Within two years, men who had voted for that resolution and cheered its adoption were marching off in martial array to vindicate on southern battlefields the supremacy of the Union and the sovereignty of the nation. By that fateful hour the southern politicians who had applauded Taney's declaration that the Supreme Court was the final arbiter in controversies between the states and the national government had come to the solemn conclusion that the states themselves were the arbiters. Such words and events being facts, there can be but one judgment in the court of history; namely, that major premises respecting the nature of the Constitution and deductions made logically from them with masterly eloquence were minor factors in the grand dispute as compared with the interests, desires, and passions that lay deep in the hearts and minds of the contestants.

Indeed, honorable men who held diametrically opposite views found warrant for each in the Constitution. All parties and all individuals, save the extreme abolitionists, protested in an unbroken chant their devotion to the national covenant and to the principles and memory of the inspired men who framed it. As the Bible was sometimes taken as a guide for theologians traveling in opposite directions, so the Constitution was the beacon that lighted the way of statesmen who differed utterly on the issues of the middle period. . . .

When the modern student examines all the verbal disputes over the nature of the Union—the arguments employed by the parties which operated and opposed the federal government between the adoption of the Constitution and the opening of the Civil War—he can hardly do otherwise than conclude that the linguistic devices used first on one side and then on the other were not derived from inherently necessary concepts concerning the intimate essence of the federal system. The roots of the controversy lay elsewhere—in social groupings founded on differences in climate, soil, industries, and labor systems, in divergent social forces, rather than varying degrees of righteousness and wisdom, or what romantic historians call "the magnetism of great personalities."

In the spring of 1861 the full force of the irrepressible conflict burst upon the hesitant and bewildered nation and for four long years the clash of arms filled the land with its brazen clangor. For four long years the anguish, the calamities, and the shocks of the struggle absorbed the energies of the multitudes, blared in the headlines of the newspapers, and loomed impressively in the minds of the men and women who lived and suffered in that age.

Naturally, therefore, all who wrote of the conflict used the terms of war. In its records, the government of the United States officially referred to the contest as the War of the Rebellion, thus by implication setting the stigma of treason on those who served under the Stars and Bars. Repudiating this brand and taking for his shield the righteousness of legitimacy, one of the leading southern statesmen, Alexander H. Stephens, in his great history of the conflict, called it the War between the States. This, too, no less than the title chosen by the federal government, is open to objections; apart from the large assumptions involved, it is not strictly accurate for, in the border states, the armed struggle was a guerrilla war and in Virginia the domestic strife ended in the separation of several counties, under the aegis of a new state constitution, as West Virginia. More recently a distinguished historian, Edward Channing, entitled a volume dealing with the period The War for Southern Independence—a characterization which, though fairly precise, suffers a little perhaps from abstraction.

As a matter of fact all these symbols are misleading in that they overemphasize the element of military force in the grand denouement. War there was unquestionably, immense, wide-sweeping, indubitable, as Carlyle would say. For years the agony of it hung like a pall over the land. And yet with strange swiftness the cloud was lifted and blown away. Merciful grass spread its green mantle over the cruel scars and the gleaming red splotches sank into the hospitable earth.

It was then that the economist and lawyer, looking more calmly on the scene, discovered that the armed conflict had been only one phase of the cataclysm, a transitory phase; that at bottom the so-called Civil War, or the War between the States, in the light of Roman analogy, was a social war, ending in the unquestioned establishment of a new power in the government, making vast changes in the arrangement of classes, in the accumulation and distribution of wealth, in the course of industrial development, and in the Constitution inherited from the Fathers. Merely by the accidents of climate, soil, and geography was it a sectional struggle. If the planting interest had been scattered evenly throughout the industrial region, had there been a horizontal rather than a perpendicular cleavage, the irrepressible conflict would have been resolved by other methods and accompanied by other logical defense mechanisms.

In any event neither accident nor rhetoric should be allowed to obscure the intrinsic character of that struggle. If the operations by which the middle classes of England broke the power of the king and the aristocracy are to be known collectively as the Puritan Revolution, if the series of acts by which the bourgeois and peasants of France overthrew the king, nobility, and clergy is to be called the French Revolution, then accuracy compels us to characterize by the same term the social cataclysm in which the capitalists, laborers, and farmers of the North and West drove from power in the national government the planting aristocracy of the South. Viewed under the light of universal history, the fighting was a fleeting incident; the social revolution was the essential, portentous outcome.

To be sure the battles and campaigns of the epoch are significant to the military strategist; the tragedy and heroism of the contest furnish inspiration to patriots and romance to the makers of epics. But the core of the vortex lay elsewhere. It was in the flowing substance of things limned by statistical reports on finance, commerce, capital, industry, railways, and agriculture, by provisions of constitutional law, and by the pages of statute books—prosaic muniments which show that the so-called civil war was in reality a Second American Revolution and in a strict sense, the First. . . .

An outburst of emotion

Avery Craven

When Lee surrendered at Appomattox a tall gaunt North Carolinian stolidly stacked arms and fell back into line. He was worn, hungry, and dirty. The insistent Yankees had granted him little time during the past weeks for relaxation. Food had been scarce; the opportunities for cleanliness lacking. He had gone on fighting more from habit than purpose. He had quit because the orders were to that effect. Suddenly, with a sharp realization of what was taking place around him, he turned to his neighbor and drawled: "Damn me if I ever love another country!"

From *An Historian and The Civil War* by Avery Craven. Copyright © 1964 by the University of Chicago. Reprinted by permission of The University of Chicago Press.

In these words the disheartened Tarheel passed judgment on a generation.

Up to 1825 there had been no "United South" nor no "self-conscious North." There were some recognizable differences between these larger sections, in climate, in economic interests, in ideals, and in those intangible things which go to make "a way of life." But these differences were of long standing and were no more acute than those existing between other geographic regions within the nation. With a population ever on the move toward the West or the city, new and old societies constantly found themselves bound together under the same political organization. With highly diversified natural resources, conflicting types of economic endeavor grew up, side by side, to contend for favorable legislation. Social patterns brought into new lands from different sources fought for dominance. The struggle for control in governments, where majorities ruled, forms the central theme in more than one era of the nation's history.

Nor were the sections units. The careful scholar must ever recognize the cleavage between Upper and Lower New England; between the Ohio Valley and the lake region of the Old Northwest; between the mountains and the bluegrass of Kentucky and Tennessee. He must understand the basic differences between the "tidewater districts" and the "upcountry" in the Old South. He must know that before 1860 every issue which later divided North and South had been fought out and reduced to a workable compromise by Southern men struggling against Southern men in Virginia and the Carolinas—the rights of minorities, the distribution of power between local and central governments, the relative values of a single economic effort as against diversification secured by tariffs and other legislative aids, even the problem of free and slave labor!

Differences—economic, social, and political—did not then or afterwards portend an "irrepressible conflict" between North and South, to be settled only by bloodshed. The War Between the States in 1861–1865 did not come simply because one section was agricultural and the other industrial; because one exploited free labor and the other slaves; or because a sectional majority refused to respect the constitutional rights of the minority! The Northwest was as thoroughly agricultural as the South; the Republican party was vigorous in disclaiming abolition tendencies and was willing to leave slavery alone where it was; the minority has never found the constitution of much value in the face of "manifest destinies." The problem of why these sections went to war lies deeper. It is one of emotions, cultivated hostilities, and ultimately of hatred between sections. Bloodshed was "necessary" because men associated their rivals with disliked and dishonorable symbols, and crowned their own interests with moral sanctions. Differences were but the materials with which passions worked. Each side, in the end, fought the other for principles and the glory of God, for the preservation of civilizations, for the maintenance of honor. The conflict was the work of politicians and pious cranks! The peoples knew little of each other as realities. They were both fighting mythical devils.

The steps by which sectional differences were emotionalized are highly involved and often obscure. Of one thing only can we be reasonably certain: The first apprehensions and resentments which stirred the people in each section were the product of purely local conditions. We can understand the national situation only when we have grasped the vital forces at work in each locality. Men react to what they know—they create their symbols from such experiences. But they shed blood for and against abstractions which better carry all the good and all the evils which they imagine possible from their limited experiences. We must begin with everyday affairs in each section.

The general period in American history from 1825 to 1860 was one of vast material growth and expansion. But it was also one in which the wealth and power of the few grew disproportionately to that of the many. Democracy was not functioning properly. *Liberty* was putting an end to *equality*. If some were content, others felt deepest resentments and dreamed of a more perfect society as the political and moral right of an American. It is sometimes difficult to discover whether this claim rested on the Constitution, the Scriptures, or the Declaration of Independence. Perhaps they did not make such unimportant distinctions. But at any rate injustice, lack of material prosperity, loss of equality or failure to achieve American purposes—all became matters of moral significance and evidence of God's plan thwarted. It was on the one hand, a day of pulling down aristocrats, fighting devils, saving democratic institutions, acquiring material things as a natural and moral right; and on the other, of checking harebrained movements which threatened social security, private rights, and private property.

In the Northeast the Industrial Revolution was in full swing. Old commercial centers and fishing villages found themselves overshadowed by a new life which grew up at the fall line. The city became a land of opportunity—the center of a varied and attractive life. Wealth shifted into new hands and new places. Labor became dependent on capital. Dominance in legislative halls passed from farmers, merchants, and fishermen to industrial leaders and the lawyers they sent to do their bidding. Daniel Webster's conversion from free trade to protection was only a larger manifestation of a common phenomenon. The harbor was passing into eclipse.

Along side of these urban changes went an agricultural revolution as significant in effects. For the first time the farmers of this region had expanding markets of their own. Opportunities for specialized crops which could feed both men and machines brought capital into farming, crowded out the less efficient, and often set sheep, as in Old England, "to gobbling up" their farms and villages. Thousands, unwilling or unable to make the required adjustments, turned cityward or toward the New West from which they soon poured floods of agricultural produce to plague those who remained behind. Every decade held a crisis for those who tilled the soils of New England and Upper New York. The abandoned farm became the symbol of permanent decline.

Meanwhile a series of Wests were rising one after the other in the great region which stretched from New York to the Mississippi—"a greater New England," the Ohio Valley, the Old Northwest. Each began as a frontier but hurried on as rapidly as exploitation of natural resources could accomplish the task toward a more perfect and complex society. Their citizens had sacrificed the present for future returns which depended on easy access to rich lands and open ways to profitable markets. Their hopes ever outran their realizations but their faith in the dividends of democracy did not decline. They were American pioneers and they had a right to prosper and would do so if democracy functioned properly. But the Panic of '37 spread wreck and ruin among them; land legislation lagged behind their demands; internal improvements came all too slowly; prices slumped as home markets broke and "overproduction" glutted the few outside markets they had developed. Throughout the "middle period" this was a region of half-realized purposes, of extravagant dreams checked by hard raw realities; of plain men who sought consolation and found emotional outlet in evangelical churches; of earnest souls who, here and there, even talked with God. All things, economic as well as social, were either "right" or "wrong." And too many things in this period were "wrong."

The rural North, therefore, throughout the era, was a region of potential and actual unrest. The "average farmer," for whose welfare the American system had been established, resented bitterly the growing importance of the city and the mounting wealth of those engaged in what he considered "minor pursuits." Securing the support of the lesser folk of the towns, only recently come from nearby farms, he launched his protests in various forms, but all in the name of a faltering democracy. The labor movements of the period, says Commons, were "not so much the modern alignment of wage-earner against employer" as they were the revolts of "the poor against the rich, the worker against the owner." Professor Darling has shown that the "Workingmen's Movement" in Massachusetts was almost exclusively a farmers' effort—"a protest against the 'accumulations' in Bostonian society, the assault of 'country folk' on the 'exclusive privileges' of the wealthy." The bitter New England farmer who declared he would "sooner, infinitely sooner, follow [his] daughters to the grave than see them 'go out to service'" in the kitchens of those "who by successful industry, by good luck, or possibly fraud were in a situation to make hewers of wood and drawers of water of their less fortunate sisters and brethren," was merely expressing a very prevalent attitude.

The Locofoco groups were even more concerned about inequality and privilege. An Upper New York convention in 1836, "appointed by the farmers, mechanics and others friendly in their views," struck at the "Banking System" because it "filled the coffers of the already wealthy and took from the earnings of the poor." It denounced the practices of "the courts of law" for being "aristocratic"; it declared in form consciously modeled after the Declaration of Independence that "the foundations of Republican Government are in the equal rights of every citizen, in his person and property, and in their management." This group talked much of the "aristocracy of wealth" and "the odious distinctions betwixt the rich and the poor." They would restore democracy by public education and by granting to every man his "inalienable right to a share of the bounties of our Common Father"—meaning the public domain.

It should also be noted that the transcendental protest against materialism took point from the new urban-industrial growth; that Brook Farm, Hopedale, and Fruitlands represented a return to rural-agricultural living; that the well-being of common men in a democracy formed a basic argument for temperance, peace, women's rights, and abolition. Both the misfortunes and the hopes of a disgruntled people were moving under the banners of *democracy*.

To this glorification was soon added another. The cause of the oppressed was also the cause of "righteousness." Rural folk, whose one social center was the church and whose great spokesman was the preacher, could hardly have escaped this conclusion. The great revivals which burned through the back country and in which Charles Grandison Finney was the leader, shifted the emphasis in Calvinism from "a painful quest for a safe escape from life" to the transforming of this world into the Kingdom of Heaven. Salvation was no longer the "end of all human desire"; it was but the beginning of *"being useful in the highest degree possible."* Not only was social reform an obligation but social evils had to do with morality; and the purposes of religion, society, and democratic politics were one and the same. "It is a departure, in our representatives and judges, from the laws of nature and laws of the Creator, which has produced the derangement in the affairs of our State," declared the Locofoco convention referred to above. "To a Believer who has rejoiced in the light of Locofocoism, as an outward sign of the inward light of Christianity," was the dedication in F. Byrdsall's history of the movement. The *Democratic Review* echoed this sentiment by insisting that ". . . Democracy is the cause of Humanity. . . . It is essentially involved in Christianity, of which it has been well said that its pervading spirit of democratic equality among men is its highest fact." Gerrit Smith's congregation at Peterboro in December, 1840, re-solved among other things, that:

> Whereas there is, ever amongst professors of religion, a prevailing opinion that it is wrong to preach politics on the Sabbath. *Resolved*, That the correct-ness of this opinion turns wholly on the character of the politics which are preached; for whilst it is clearly wrong to preach anti-Bible or unrighteous politics on the Sabbath or on any other day, nothing can be clearer than that no day is too holy to be used in preaching the politics which are inculcated in the Bible.

Smith himself declared that "No man's religion is better than his poli-tics." He believed that righteous civil governments depended on "the prevalence of [a] Christianity," which kept from office "anti-abolitionists, and land-monopolists and other enemies of human rights." To leave God out of "a moral reformation" was like enacting "the play of Othello" and leaving "out the part of Othello." To him "Civil Government" was "of God." And Jeffersonian Democracy was God's chosen form of civil government.

In the Northwest the sublimation of local resentments in terms of democracy and morality was even more pronounced. The addition of men and ideas from the Northeast played some part in the formation of attitudes but the expression was largely native. Western men began with the naïve assumption voiced by the members of the Missouri assembly that "Our country is peculiarly the asylum of the oppressed, and em-phatically the poor man's home." They were certain that "Every law . . . which opens to the poor man the way to independence . . . not only sub-serves the cause of Humanity but advances and maintains the funda-mental principles of our Government." They believed that "persons . . . disposed to live out of the labors of others" (meaning land speculators) were establishing "a petty aristocracy" which would "choke the tree of Liberty and cause her leaves to wither so that her sons . . . [could] no more recline under her balmy shadows, but . . . [would] be compelled to endure the scorching rays and blasting influences of the slavery making idol of money tyrants." In early days the danger arose from " 'Eastern *millionaires* . . . who like the flies that come upon the borders of Egypt' " caused " 'the land to stink' " but their resentments were vague enough to be lodged in any direction as occasion required. Senator Lewis Cass of Michigan climaxed the argument in favor of settlers by insisting that "we shut our eyes upon the seven hundred per cent., and look to our duty as a Christian people." And a colleague in the House argued that the public lands should go "as God intended, and as good governments and good men desire they should go, into the hands *of the people*." The significant fact was that here were men who believed in the natural right of settlers to lands and who felt that the failure to secure that right con-stituted an infringement on democracy and on God's purposes.

AN OUTBURST OF EMOTION   367

The Jacksonian war against "the money power" in an earlier period was "from this same cloth." It represented far more the deep resentments of a "grasping" people than it did a belief in abstract ideals. The same holds, in a degree, for the so-called "free-soil" movement. Historians have largely overlooked the fact that the "liberty groups" with a single human rights appeal failed to gain any great following in the Northwest —but that when Salmon P. Chase, the Democrat, broadened the platform to one in which homesteads, internal improvements at Federal expense, and home markets by tariffs, were included, the moral indignation against slavery rose to a burning flame. A local convention in Chicago in 1848 resolved that the Wilmot Proviso "is now and ever has been the doctrine of the Whigs of the free States" and added hastily, "the Whig party has ever been the firm, steady, and unchanging friend of harbor and river appropriations." Lincoln himself would keep slavery from the territories because God had intended them "for the homes of free white people." The Wisconsin farmer, whose interest in Negroes was slight, did not further heckle this great Commoner when the assurance was given that the prime purpose behind his program was a 160-acre farm for all interested persons. Thus the halo of democracy and morality, in part borrowed from the abolitionist, was placed upon the brow of all vital Western needs, and its bitterness from unrealized ambitions became a holy sentiment.

The next step in the process was one of transferring the resentment, generated out of local conditions, to the Southern planter, and fashioning him into the great symbol of aristocracy, of immorality, and of disloyalty to the democratic government. It began when the evangelical churches accepted slavery as a sin rather than an evil; it reached its climax in the triumph of a political party, purely sectional and openly hostile on moral grounds to the institutions of another section.

The antislavery movement was, in the beginning, part and parcel of the larger humanitarian impulse which got going in the early nineteenth century and which sought to be rid of injustice and to establish a more wholesome social order. It was closely related to the peace movement, the effort for women's rights, the temperance crusade, prison and Sabbath reforms, the improvement of education, and many other efforts of the kind. It rose to particular dominance only gradually and among certain well-defined groups. It was fortunate in leadership but more fortunate in its appeal. Human slavery more clearly violated democratic institutions than any other evil of the day; it was close enough to be touched now and then, yet far enough removed to give widest scope to the imagination; it violated most completely the moral senses of a people whose ideas of sin were largely in terms of self-indulgence and whose purposes in religious expression were toward the social betterment of the downtrodden; and, what was as important, it constituted the most

talked-of feature in the life of a rival section long contending for control
in a government of majorities. Garrison, who, if living today, could
profitably consult a psychiatrist, early denounced slavery as a crime
and the slaveholder as a criminal. But, of more reaching consequences
were the teachings of Theodore Weld and his type, who as W. C. Preston
said, made "the anti-slavery cause identical with religion" and urged
men "by all the high and exciting obligations of duty of man to God, by
all that can warm the heart and inflame the imagination, to join the
pious work of purging the sin of slavery from the land."

It was but a step from such attitudes to the condemnation of Southern
men for holding slaves or permitting others to hold them. By 1841 Garrison was speaking of "The desperadoes from the South, in Congress"
and declaring that "We would sooner trust the honor of the country . . .
in the hands of the inmates of our penitentiaries and prisons, than in
their hands . . . they are the meanest of thieves and the worst of rob-
bers. . . . We do not acknowledge them to be within the pale of Christianity, of republicanism, of humanity." And then finding his hatred
not entirely spent he lamented the poverty of the English language
which prevented doing full justice to the infamy of the South.

This conception of the slaveholder opened the way for abolition
imaginations to create much needed symbols. In a surprisingly short
time *all* Southerners, except a few "poor whites," were planters, living in
great white-pillared mansions, drinking intemperately, consorting with
female slaves, and selling "down river" their own blood without the
trace of a civilized blush. "A million and a half slave women, some of
them without a tinge of African blood, are given up, a lawful prey to the
unbridled lusts of their masters," declared an antislavery tract. A whole
section of the nation living upon the toil of a downtrodden race. Here
was the aristocrat *par excellence;* the perfection in licentiousness and
self-indulgence! Harriet Beecher Stowe in *Uncle Tom's Cabin* pictured a
way of life which would have done credit to the romancing of a Thomas
Nelson Page; novels, and there were scores of them, like *Our World:
or the Slaveholder's Daughter,* pictured a society of licentiousness which
must have disturbed the dreams of many an abstemious Puritan. The
South had begun to do service for all aristocrats and all sinners in an
era of democracy and morality!

Garrison and his kind, of course, were few; his violence was shared
by only a handful of antislavery men, who in turn formed a very, very
small minority in the North. His attitudes are important only because
they were *extreme,* and by their extremeness reveal in clearest fashion
something of what was gradually to seep into the subconsciousness of a
whole people. One day, only a few decades off, the moral weaknesses of
slaveholding would form a vital part of the understanding of a whole
section and hatred of Southerners be so near the surface that "the shed-

ding of a little blood" would set them savagely at the throats of their neighbors.

The next step in the process was one of directly associating the slave-holding South with the economic and social ills from which men of North and West suffered. The "hard times" of the late 1830's, they said, were due to the fact that Northern capital had been loaned to "prodigal" Southern planters who could not and would not repay. "Slavery," said the report of the American Anti-Slavery Society in 1837, "is the rule of violence and arbitrary will. . . . It would be quite in character both with its theory and practice . . . if the slave-drivers should refuse to pay their debts and meet the sheriff with dirk and pistol." Three years later the Society resolved "That the existence of Slavery is the grand cause of the pecuniary embarrassments of the Country; and that no real permanent relief is to be expected . . . until the total abolition of that execrable system." One writer estimated that within five years the South had taken "more than $100,000,000 by notes which will never be paid."

This period saw also the rise of the idea of a "slave-power" or "slave-ocracy" which had seized control of the Federal government to shape its policies in the interests of slavery. It had already destroyed "the protective system 'at the hazard, if not with the intention' of breaking up the manufacturing interests of the free states." It had developed and protected markets for cotton "in all parts of the known world, while it studiously avoided doing anything to procure a market for the free products of the grain growing Northwest."

The aggressive opposition of Southern leaders to pre-emption and homestead legislation in the period from 1840 to 1860 added to the growing belief that slave interests were hostile to Western development. A typical point of view was that of Senator James M. Mason of Virginia who declared that he had "not yet known . . . a bill so fraught with mischief, and mischief of the most demoralizing tendency, as the homestead bill." *"The Columbus* [Mississippi] *Democrat* insisted that settlers on homesteads would be abolitionists" and declared that it would be "better for us that these territories should remain a waste, a howling wilderness, trod only by red hunters than be so settled." Robert Y. Hayne of South Carolina added insult to injury by implying that a homesteader was a "drone," a man unworthy "of protection in a country where every man goes ahead who has any strength of will, or any firmness, or any character."

Northwestern reaction to such attitudes was sharp and direct. "When did the Senator from Georgia ever vote anything for Iowa or the West?" growled Augustus Caesar Dodge at one who opposed his measures. "I, sir, have inherited my Democracy," said James M. Cavanaugh, member of the House from Minnesota, "have been attached to the Democratic party from my boyhood. . . . But, sir, when I see southern gentlemen come up . . . and refuse . . . to aid my constituents, refuse to place the actual tiller of the soil, the honest, industrious laborer, beyond the grasp and avarice of the speculator, I tell you, sir, I falter and hesitate." The Dubuque (Iowa) *Herald* revealed the emotional extent reached in 1860 in these words: "Last Saturday the old reprobate, who now sits in the Presidential chair at Washington *vetoed the Homestead Bill*. . . . The slave propagandists demanded that the Bill should be vetoed, and their pliant tool was swift to obey them. Let the pimps and hirelings of the old sinner defend this last act of his, if they dare."

Even more bitter was the complaint against Southern opposition to river and harbor improvements. "This harbor question," said the Chicago *Democrat* after Polk's veto of a favorable bill, "is not a political one, but a sectional one. It is one between the North and the South. The iron rod wielded over her [the North] by Southern despots must be broken." Another Chicago paper declared:

The North can and will be no longer hoodwinked. If no measure of protection and improvement of anything North or West are to be suffered by our Southern masters, if we are to be downtrodden and all our cherished interests crushed by them, a signal revolution will eventually ensue. The same spirit and energy that forced emancipation for the whole country from Great Britain will throw off the Southern Yoke. . . . The power to oppress shall not again be entrusted to men who have shown themselves to be slave-holders, but not Americans.

A final charge against the so-called "slaveocracy" was the corruption of the Democratic party. When James K. Polk was elected president in 1844, certain old leaders such as Martin Van Buren, Francis Preston Blair, and Thomas H. Benton were pushed aside. Each in turn blamed John C. Calhoun and the slave interests; each in a different way added to the impression that the party was no longer a fit place for those who followed the immortal Andrew Jackson. The antislavery groups darkened the picture, and Whig and Republican partisans completed it. Distrust thus created ended in a widespread belief that the annexation of Texas, the Mexican War, the Kansas-Nebraska Act, and the Dred Scott Decision were steps in a well-worked out scheme for the extension of slavery and the rule of the slaveholder. Scholars have revealed the falsity of such opinions; yet in the years before the war they served all the purposes of fact, and Seward and Lincoln used them as deliberately as did the recognized demagogues. Even John Wentworth, a staunch Northern Democrat, accused his Southern colleagues of always acting as slaveholders, never as party men. By 1860 Wyndham Robertson, looking back at the recent Republican victory, could say: "The possession of the power of the Federal Government by the Democratic party . . . furnished the pretext . . . to confound the whole slave-holding interest as identical with democracy, and thus to turn and direct opposition, for whatever cause, to the policy and acts of the Democratic party, into opposition to the slave-holding interests."

Thus by 1860 the apprehensions and resentments of the North had deepened as they had been sanctified by democracy and morality. That section, striving as it believed, for things truly American, had fallen short of realization because of opposition from aristocratic and ignoble enemies. The time for being firm had arrived. The right to hate had been achieved. And what was as important the South had been fashioned into the perfect symbol of all they feared and all they despised. The extreme abolition picture of what slaveholders might be had been given legal currency by the bombast of politicians in verbal conflict for place and power and favors. They pictured an aggressive interest, wringing great wealth from unwilling and overworked Negroes, bent on extending its system to the ends of the land. They talked of "a house divided against itself"; of "a higher law" of "the aristocratic lords of slavery." The ends they sought were immediate, but common folk back home, under the sway of unimaginative evangelical clergymen could think only in terms of the eternal verities. In 1854 they created the Republican party which in six short years passed from an expression of the moral indignation of a limited group to the position of carrier of all the material aspirations of a section and the political hopes of most of those not under the Democratic roof. It was the party of homestead legislation—the culmination of America's greatest democratic effort, the fruition of God's purpose, as Senator John P. Hale put it, to have His lands inhabited (and it might be added, a policy made more democratic and more holy by relieving poor settlers from competition with slaveholders). It was the party of internal improvements with Federal aid— a policy now embracing a Pacific Railroad along the central route for the upbuilding of Chicago and St. Louis. Lincoln's railroad support in 1860 rivaled that of Douglas and came from lines better placed for future trends than his. It was the party of protective tariffs—a policy lifted by the logic of William H. Seward into the very cornerstone of democratic society. Free farmers and industrialists at last united for common accomplishment! Satisfactory markets and new prosperity for all, including Pennsylvania and Cameron! Here was a program making the Union worth saving; the experiment in democracy would pay sound dividends.

But this was not all. The great ideals of an evangelistic Calvinistic society had not been sacrificed in the turn toward "respectability." In opposing the extension of slavery, the party skillfully capitalized on all the moral indignation long generating against the institution itself. Its leaders disavowed all the political implications of abolition sentiment yet openly announced their personal abhorrence of slaveholding. They even took profit from the few who went further. Charles Sumner's bitter invectives, aimed "to keep alive that old Puritan hatred of wickedness, which must overthrow slavery," were carefully distributed by the machine throughout the rural North. Seward permitted his "higher law" and "irrepressible conflict" doctrines to become "all things to all men."

And Lincoln's "ultimate extinction" policy was used to satisfy all but the most extreme abolitionists. The Republican "stock in trade" was indeed, as Caleb Cushing said, "the insolent assumption, in some of them, perhaps, the stupid mental delusion, that whatever view they take of the measures of government *is the only moral side of public questions.*"

It was this situation which produced a crisis in the party when Douglas' squatter sovereignty, in practice, yielded only free territory. The danger of slave extension, on which the party was founded, was over. And by 1858 even Republican leaders understood this fact. Some said the party had fulfilled its mission and should join with Stephen A. Douglas in the formation of a new party for wider sectional and national ends. Some talked of a "broad base" by which the Republicans could attack the old Southern Whigs. But Abraham Lincoln, in his "House Divided" speech, prevented himself and his party from being thrust aside by a desperate appeal to old moral foundations. Though *his* own policy and that of "Judge" Douglas gave identical results, the latter was not born of moral conviction. And until the issue was conceived in terms of "the eternal struggle between two principles—right and wrong—throughout the world" the fight must go on. That is why a man who was willing to save the Union at the cost of a bloody civil war, even with slavery untouched, would not save it by a compromise which yielded party principle but which did not sacrifice a single material thing. The party was one with God and the world's great experiment in Democracy.

The Southern side of the story needs only to be suggested. Rural and lacking in means for the easy creation and expression of public opinion, the section was ever peculiarly susceptible to the ideas and oratory of a few leaders. As a result the focal point of consciousness was, in the beginning, generally an abstract and theoretical right which logic deduced from some traditional source. In the ante-bellum period, when farmers, who lived by staple crops, felt the sting of poverty, these spokes·men, under the influence of Old World agrarian thinking, voiced protest in terms of local government versus central government made strong by the power to grant economic favors. Specifically, industry and commerce, largely centering in the North, were, by tariffs and centralization, profiting at the expense of the nation's real producers. Before long Southerners were calculating the millions of dollars tribute paid to this "Lord North" and were talking of being in a state of colonial dependence.

The remedy was found in a strict adherence to the Constitution. Yankee traits could be controlled and Southern rights be preserved by a series of phrases, on the meaning of which not even the framers could agree. The section had begun to chop logic; it was the champion of things as they were,—a conscious minority in a republican system. Yet in its own eyes, the South was the defender of democratic government against the onslaughts of those who would distort sacred institutions in order to promote their own material interests. All that the Revolution had won, all that "the Fathers" had achieved, was involved in the struggle.

When opposition to slavery developed, a new threat of economic loss, now joined with fear of racial conflict and social unrest, was added. When that drive became a moral attack on the whole Southern way of life, the defense broadened in proportion and emotions deepened. The Constitution was not enough against those who would not respect its provisions; the whole South must become unified for political efficiency. The section must have that security which the Constitution guaranteed and an equal right to expand with its institutions *as a matter of principle*. Keen minds set to work to reveal the virtues in slavery and the life it permitted in the South. When they had finished a stratified society, with Negro "mud-sills" at the bottom, alone permitted genuine republican government, escaped the ills of labor and race conflict, gave widest opportunity for ability and culture, and truly forwarded the cause of civilization. The stability and quiet under such a system were contrasted with the restless strife of the North which was developing socialism and threatening the destruction of security in person and in property. The Southern way of life was the way of order and progress.

Here was something else worth fighting to preserve. The old struggle against "King Numbers," which in large part had been won at home, must go on. But the field had broadened and the struggle was against a foe more base and self-seeking. Both the system of republican government and the cause of civilization were bound up in the struggle.

Early efforts at unified defense proved futile because the masses, with cotton and the hopes it gave, could not muster the emotional response to leaders sufficient for action. They neither felt the inferiority suggested by economic dependence nor the compelling force of rights which gave no practical returns. They gladly accepted compromise in 1850, and were surprisingly unmoved throughout the next eight years. Leaders might support the fruitless Kansas-Nebraska Bill, as the Richmond *Enquirer* said, "solely for the reason that it would vindicate the equality and sovereignty of the states." But the masses, to quote one individual, were "not a particle" excited. They knew, as this writer put it, that the struggle was over "a shadow." Their outlook was as yet practical.

But the John Brown raid was another matter. It put reality into the much discussed program of Yankee "money-changers," "peasant farmers," and the "long haired men and short haired women" of the North. The sharpest resentments and deepest fears of which a people were capable broke loose. A race war was impending. And that was a poor man's problem. Albert G. Brown of Mississippi put it this way.

The rich will flee the country. . . . Then the non-slaveholder will begin to see what his real fate is. The Negro will intrude into his preserve . . . insist on being treated as an equal . . . that he shall go to the white man's bed, and the white man his . . . that his son shall marry the white man's daughter, and the white man's daughter his son. In short that they shall live on terms of perfect social equality. The non-slaveholder will, of course, reject the terms. Then will commence a war of races such as has marked the history of San Domingo.

The triumph of the Republican party, sectional and containing, as it did, men as rabid as Sumner and as vague and shifting as Seward and Lincoln, drove the more inflamed Southerners to secession. Lincoln's refusal of compromise and his handling of Fort Sumter forced conservatives to follow. War had become inevitable. Fear and hate had taken charge.

By May, 1861, that staunch lover of the Union, Jonathan Worth, could write from peaceable old Randolph County in North Carolina: "The voice of reason is silenced. Furious passion and thirst for blood consume the air. . . . Nobody is allowed to retain and assert his reason. The cartridge box is preferred to the ballot box. The very women and children are for war."

A little later the New York *Herald* solemnly reported from the battlefield of Bull Run that Southern "fiends in human shape have taken the bayonets and knives of our wounded and dying soldiers and thrust them into their hearts and left them sticking there, and some of the Louisiana Zouaves have severed the heads of our dead from their bodies, and amused themselves by kicking them as footballs."

The old Carolinian at Appomattox was right. It is a serious thing to love a country!

The civil war and the spirit of compromise

Daniel J. Boorstin

As the American Revolution had been a struggle within a long-established colonial framework, so the Civil War was a struggle within a working federal system. The two events were to have analogous consequences in hedging in our political reflection, and in identifying the special institutions of this country with the normal conditions of life on this continent. Whatever theoretical debate went on, with few exceptions, was concerned not with the nature of governments but rather with the nature of this particular government.

That the Civil War was a federal conflict, like the colonial character of our Revolution, seems, perhaps, too obvious to require elaboration. But some of our ablest recent historians have given currency to an emphasis which has tended to obscure, or even to displace, the obvious.

In their brilliant *Rise of American Civilization*, Charles A. and Mary R. Beard christened the Civil War "The Second American Revolution." The phrase and the idea have had wide appeal. It has suited our current attitudes to suspect that the actual subject of debate was not the real cause of the conflict. The battle itself, supposedly, was but a symptom of deeper forces: "the social cataclysm in which the capitalists, laborers, and farmers of the North and West drove from power in the national government the planting aristocracy of the South . . . the social revolution was the essential, portentous outcome." Without denying that such a social revolution was taking place, we can recall that there was another side to the conflict. If we turn our attention from inevitable forces to human debate, we must look primarily at a different aspect of the struggle. This is only appropriate, since we are concerned with the place of theory in our conscious political life.

The name "The Second American Revolution" given by the Beards and their disciples, is misleading. They (and others who find the center of change in economic events) would thus emphasize the *dis*continuity of our history: the Civil War as a hiatus in our development, a gulf between an agricultural-commercial and an industrial society. But to those students who, like me, are impressed by the extraordinary continuity of our history, such an emphasis seems distortion. As we all know, the great economic developments are slow, evolutionary, and sometimes imperceptible; their triumphs are not self-announced in manifestoes. The Industrial Revolution was a matter of centuries, and the kind of revolution to which the Beards refer must also have been a matter of decades.

But *political* history (such events as go by the name of "revolution" and "civil war") has the abruptness of mutation. It is therefore in this area that it would be especially significant to note that what is called a great gulf in our history may not be so great as has been supposed. One of the remarkable characteristics of our Civil War, as contrasted with civil wars of recent European history (excepting possibly the English Civil War), is that ours did *not* significantly interrupt the continuity of our thinking about institutions.

From the point of view of political and constitutional thought, we might do better to call our Civil War "The Second War of Independence." I have already mentioned Guizot's remark that the English Revolution succeeded twice, once in England in the seventeenth century and a second time in America in the eighteenth. We might go further and say that, from the point of view of constitutional law and political theory, the Revolution occurred a third time, namely, in the middle of the nineteenth century. For the relation of the ancient rights of Englishmen to federalism, which was only partly redefined in the course of the American Revolution, was more extensively explored and settled during the Civil War.

That continuity of our political thought which, as we have seen, had been expressed in the legalistic character of the American Revolutionary debate was also expressed later in much of the argument over the Civil War. There is even less evidence here for the pattern which Carl Becker saw in the Revolution. The main current did not seem to rise above the "provincial" level of constitutionalism to the more "cosmopolitan" atmosphere of natural law. Indeed, we find something of the opposite of what Becker remarks as the increasing abstractness of Revolutionary debate. In the South at least, as the crisis proceeded the debate seemed to become more and more legalistic, reaching its climax actually after the war was over. The legal debate never rose to the realm of natural law, not even to the extent found in the American Revolution.

The North and the South each considered that it was fighting primarily for its legal rights under the sacred federal Constitution. A man like Thoreau probably stood only for himself and a few fire-eating abolitionists. On neither side do we hear much of the sort of argument familiar in European civil wars: that the existing federal constitution was bad and ought to be changed, and that was what one should fight for. On the contrary, each side purported to represent the authentic original doctrine, to be *defending* the Constitution.

Calhoun, who was by far the most profound of the southern writers on the subject, shows this peculiarity. His major theoretical work, not published until after his death in 1850, consists of two parts: "A Disquisition on Government" and "A Discourse on the Constitution and Government of the United States." It is on these that his growing reputation as a political philosopher largely depends. These works taken together (as Calhoun intended that they should be) admirably illustrate the point of view I have been describing.

The "Disquisition," an essay of about a hundred pages, though starting from some general principles of psychology and political theory, is primarily a defense of Calhoun's principle of the "concurrent majority" and an exposition of his objections to governments based on the "numerical majority." In a closely reasoned argument, Calhoun points out the dangers of uncontrolled majority rule. The only safeguard, he insists, is a system of constitutionalism which will allow each separate interest a veto on all legislation to which it objects. Such a system, he urges, results in moderation and compromise and still can leave government strong enough to combat enemies from without. He supports his argument by the experience of Rome, Poland, and Great Britain.

"A Discourse on the Constitution and Government of the United States," a work about three times the length of the "Disquisition," is the sequel. In it Calhoun tries to show that "it was the object of the framers of the constitution, in organizing the government, to give to the two elements [the states as units and the voting population], of which it is composed, separate, but concurrent action; and, consequently, a veto on each other, whenever the organization of the department, or the nature of the power would admit: and when this could not be done, so to blend the two, as to make as near an approach to it, in effect, as possible. It is, also, apparent, that the government, regarded apart from the constitution, is the government of the concurrent, and not of the numerical majority" (*Works*, I, 181).

By reference to the proceedings of the Philadelphia convention and of the ratifying conventions, Calhoun demonstrates that, through a happy coincidence, the true and original conception of the federal Constitution was actually nothing but a design for the attainment of his ideal government. The departure from his ideal, the gradual growth of a consolidated national government, and the development of means by which one section could dominate another were all to be explained as departures from the true intent of the Framers.

To the one, or to the other,—to monarchy, or disunion it must come, if not prevented by strenuous and timely efforts. And this brings up the question,—How is it to be prevented? How can these sad alternatives be averted? For this purpose, it is indispensable that the government of the United States should be restored to its federal character. Nothing short of a perfect restoration, as it came from the hands of its framers, can avert them [*Works*, I, 381].

This restoration was to be effected by getting rid of certain perversions which had been introduced after the adoption of the Constitution. Calhoun urges, for example, the repeal of Section 25 of the Judiciary Act of 1789, and of the Act of 1833; "the repeal of all acts by which the money power is carried beyond its constitutional limits"; the confining of the president to those powers expressly conferred on him by the Constitution and by acts of Congress; the return in practice to the original way of electing the president and vice-president.

Such means as these—together with a few reforms like the introduction of a plural executive—would, in Calhoun's phrase, "complete the work of restoration." We are never allowed to forget that what Calhoun aims at is not revolution but *restoration*.

A CONFLICT OF ORTHODOXIES

Here, once again, was a competition between constitutional orthodoxies. As often in American history, a great political conflict was taking the form not of a struggle between essentially different political theories but between differences of constitutional emphasis. There was a striking, if obvious, parallel to the epoch of the Revolution. But the South was now even more conservative than the Revolutionaries had been. It found no reason to issue a Declaration of Independence. The colonists had set themselves up as defenders of the British constitution and contended that it was not they but the parliament who were actually the revolutionaries. So now, champions of the South could—and did— argue that it was not they, but the northerners, who were, properly speaking, the revolutionaries. Each accused the other of seeking to overthrow the established doctrine of the federal Constitution, the ideas of the Founding Fathers.

The Civil War secessionist argument—like that of the Revolution— could be carried on in such a conservative vocabulary because both events were, theoretically speaking, only surface breaches in a firm federal framework. Because of this, they both implied, win or lose, the continued acceptance of the existing structure of local government. Thus in the Civil War southern partisans, like the Americans in the Revolution, could continue to profess loyalty to the theory of the Union. As a New Yorker championing the Southern cause declared in 1860:

> The South views the matter in the spirit of Patrick Henry. "The object is now, indeed, small, but the shadow is large enough to darken all this fair land." They can have no faith in men who profess what they think a great moral principle, and deny that they intend to act upon it. It was the principle of taxation without representation that the colonies resisted, and it is the principle of the "irrepressible conflict," based avowedly on a "higher law," that the South resists. She is now in the position of the Colonies eighty-four years ago, and is adopting the same measures that they adopted. . . . A prompt retreat from this dangerous agitation within the shadow of the Constitution, is the only means of realizing the rich future, which will be the reward only of harmony, good faith, and loyalty to the Constitution [Thomas P. Kettell, *Southern Wealth and Northern Profits* (New York, 1860), p. 5].

On the other side, Lincoln, in nearly every one of his principal speeches, appealed to the authentic Revolutionary tradition. His most succinct statement was, of course, in the familiar opening of the Gettysburg Address, to which I have already referred in another connection. But he rang all the rhetorical changes on this appeal, as, for example, in his speech at Peoria in 1854:

> Our republican robe is soiled and trailed in the dust. Let us repurify it. Let us turn and wash it white in the spirit, if not the blood, of the Revolution. Let us turn slavery from its claims of "moral right" back upon its existing legal rights and its argument of "necessity." Let us return it to the position our fathers gave it, and there let it rest in peace. Let us readopt the Declaration of Independence, and with it the practices and policy which harmonize with it.

Statesmen of the North were perhaps more inclined to appeal to the Declaration of Independence, while those of the South leaned more heavily on the Constitution. But both had in common the assumption that the pretty homogeneous philosophy of the Founding Fathers was what they were being called upon to vindicate. Fitzhugh did, to be sure, characterize the Declaration as "exhuberantly false, and arborescently fallacious." Yet even the Declaration of Independence was by no means generally rejected by southern advocates. Some southerners, for example, Chief Justice Taney in the Dred Scott decision, even argued that their position had been well stated in the Declaration. They adduced historical proof (in my opinion convincing) that the authors of the sacred document had intended that Negroes be excluded from their professions of "equality." Another remarkable feature of the Dred Scott decision for us is the frankness with which it takes a preformation or a static view of the Constitution. Chief Justice Taney seemed to assume that the legal question of Negro status could be resolved by accurate historical definition of the original meaning of the Declaration of Independence and the Constitution, considered together.

Few documents could be more interesting in this connection than one which nowadays is almost never read. For there is probably no more authentic index to the theoretical conservatism of the "rebel" cause than the Constitution of the Confederate States of America. President Jefferson Davis boasted that the document proved the "conservative" temper of the people of the Confederate States. Alexander Stephens, his vice-president, declared that the form of the document showed that "their only leading object was to sustain, uphold, and perpetuate the fundamental principles of the Constitution of the United States." Closely following the original in organization, the Confederate constitution is almost a verbatim copy of the federal Constitution.

Its differences consist mainly in that it incorporates into the body of the document some of the principal amendments to the federal Constitution (the Bill of Rights, for example, being absorbed into Art. I, sec. 9); and it explicitly resolves certain ambiguities (for example, those concerning slavery and the federal principle generally) in the sense which the South believed to have been the original intent of the authors. The Preamble, for example, reads:

> We, the People of the Confederate States, each State acting in its sovereign and independent character, in order to form a permanent Federal Government, establish justice, insure domestic tranquility, and secure the blessings of liberty to ourselves and our posterity—invoking the favor and guidance of Almighty God—do ordain and establish this Constitution for the Confederate States of America.

It is of great significance that in our bloody Civil War the so-called "rebel" side produced, through two of its best minds, treatises on the origin and nature of our Constitution which deserve to stand, alongside *The Federalist* and Adams' *Defence of the Constitutions*, on the small shelf of basic books about the American political system. The first, of course, is Calhoun's "Discourse on the Constitution and Government of the United States" (1851), which I have already described. The second is Alexander H. Stephens' *Constitutional View of the Late War between the States* (1868–70).

We cannot be surprised that the South, weaker in economy and in arms, found an incentive to be stronger in legal debate. But it remains a curiosity of political thought, as well as a pregnant fact of American history, that the principal theoretical defense of the southern position should have been a treatise on the origin of the federal Constitution, produced actually *after* the South had lost the last battle. Stephens' work was dedicated to "All true friends of the Union under the Constitution of the United States, throughout their entire limits, without regard to present or past party associations." The conflict, Stephens emphasized, was not basically over slavery but over two "different and opposing ideas as to the nature of what is known as the General Government. The contest was between those who held it to be strictly Federal in its character, and those who maintained that it was thoroughly National." The work is historical: a documented demonstration that the Constitution was intended to set up a *federal* government.

We can begin to grasp the true proportions of what I have called the continuity of the history of the United States, as contrasted with that of the countries of western Europe, if we try to imagine the leader of a defeated party in any of the recent European civil wars producing a heavy scholarly treatise proving that he had been in the right *strictly from the point of view of constitutional theory.* George Fitzhugh in 1857 and Jefferson Davis in 1881 both earnestly wished for the "strength and perpetuity" of the Union.

In virtually every one of the recent domestic struggles in Europe, the conflict has been so basic that only one side could conceivably have set itself up as the champion of existing legal institutions. The other has proudly stood for a new concept of government, for a new constitution, and another basis of law. Hitler's cynicism toward the German constitution is typical of this frame of mind. Yet in the American Civil War, after hundreds of thousands of lives had been lost, both sides were still thinking on similar constitutional assumptions. An intelligent and realistic critic like Alexander Stephens still after the war considered it possible that his image of the original doctrine (that the Union was a federal and not a national government) might eventually prevail. This hope would have been hardly conceivable, had not both parties to the conflict accepted the same premises of political theory, had they not preserved a common devotion to a hypothetically perfect original theory. This is what I mean by the idea of "preformation."

For the reasons which I have mentioned, the legacy of the Civil War to American thought has been one of sectionalism and constitutional debate rather than of dogmatic nationalism and "return to fundamentals." The tendency of sectionalism has been to reinforce our awareness of variety within our national culture and of the desirability and inevitability of preserving it. The tendency of the continuous constitutional tradition has been to give the defeated cause, the South, a legitimate theoretical position within the federal system.

The South, except in its romantic literature of chivalry and mint juleps, is now no champion of a different concept of life but rather of a different constitutional emphasis. The South remains, as it is desirable that someone should always be, champion of the states'-rights, local-autonomy principle of our federal Constitution. The South can still debate about what it once gave its lives to defend, for it has never lost essential devotion to the constitutional spirit and its pure original image. What Lincoln called "the spirit of concession and compromise, that spirit which has never failed us in past perils, and which may be safely trusted for all the future"—that spirit can survive precisely because the Civil War was poor in political theory. Notwithstanding the abolitionists and people like Garrison who wished to burn the Constitution, the war did not represent a quest for a general redefinition of political values.

Whatever the crimes, the senseless bitterness, that were visited on the South in the era of reconstruction, they were committed in a vindictive or narrowly provincial spirit. The triumph of the national emphasis in the federal structure did not carry with it victory of a nationalist philosophy. In Lincoln's phrase, "the Union"—not any self-conscious national culture—was what was to be preserved. This distinguished him sharply from his contemporaries like Bismarck and Cavour. The remarkable reintegration of the South into our constitutional system is the best evidence of the community of certain assumptions. The Civil War emerged, then, as a struggle over complicated matters, on which everyone knew there had been a long series of compromises, beginning with the Declaration of Independence and the Constitution themselves. Such a controversy could have happened only within the framework of going federal institutions.

Not the least remarkable feature of the Civil War—apart from the fact that it occurred at all—is that it was so unproductive of political theory. This, the bloodiest single civil war of the nineteenth century, was also perhaps the least theoretical. The sectional character of the conflict had tended to make sociology—the description of things as they were—take the place of the uncharted exploration of things as they ought to be. It also prevented the crisis from propagating panaceas. This was another example of the recurrent tendency in American history to identify the "is" with the "ought," to think of values and a theory of society as implicit in facts about society. The era was strikingly lacking in romanticism of the Rousseauistic brand. The romantics of the day were the Thaddeus Stevenses—the bearers of fire and sword.

At the same time, the federal character of the struggle, the fact that it took place within a functioning federal order, confined much of the theoretical discussion within the area of constitutional law, of the search for the true original image of the Constitution. This, too, discouraged American thinkers of the age (excepting a vagrant Thoreau) from making confusion in the market place an excuse for going off into the solitude of the woods to rethink the whole problem of institutions. The sense of "givenness" was reinforced. In this case it meant the empirical tradition, the reliance on constitutionalism, and an unwillingness to remake institutions out of whole cloth.

The continuity of American political thought—which included the American way of *not* philosophizing about politics—was to stay. The mere fact that the nation had survived the ordeal of civil war seemed itself to prove the strength of the thread which bound the present to the past and to confirm the common destiny of the nation.

SUGGESTIONS FOR FURTHER READING

Avery Craven's point of view may be found in greater detail in his *The Coming of the Civil War* (Chicago, 1942) and *The Growth of Southern Nationalism, 1848–1861* (Baton Rouge, 1953). A similar viewpoint is described in an influential article by James G. Randall, "The Blundering Generation," *Mississippi Valley Historical Review*, XXVII (June, 1940).

Charles and Mary Beard's description of the Civil War as a "revolution" is supported by Louis M. Hacker, *The Triumph of American Capitalism* (New York, 1940). Arthur C. Cole finds the Civil War to be *The Irrepressible Conflict, 1850–1865* (New York, 1934), and Robert R. Russell describes some Southern economic grievances in his *Economic Aspects of Southern Sectionalism, 1840–61* (Urbana, Ill., 1924).

David Donald has argued perceptively against both the Craven and the Beard points of view in his "An Excess of Democracy: The American Civil War and the Social Process," Chapter XI of *Lincoln Reconsidered (New York, 1961).

No subject has received more attention than the Civil War; the bibliography is endless. Those wishing to delve into the literature may start with Thomas J. Pressly, *Americans Interpret Their Civil War* (Princeton, 1954). A convenient collection of primary and secondary sources on the war may be found in Edwin C. Rozwenc, ed., *The Causes of the American Civil War* (Boston, 1961).

General Bibliography

Those interested in pursuing the theme of conflict and consensus further should begin with the three giants of American historiography who reshaped the writing of American history in the twentieth century—Charles Beard, Vernon Parrington, and Frederick Jackson Turner. The best approach to Beard is through Charles and Mary Beard, *The Rise of American Civilization* (New York, 1927, 1930), a lively and interesting interpretation of the whole course of American history with an emphasis on class and economic conflict. Parrington's one important book, *Main Currents in American Thought* (New York, 1927, 1930) complements Beard's work and deals with the relationship of literature and ideas to society and social movements. Turner wrote very little but had an immense influence. A convenient introduction to Turner, his critics, and his supporters is George Rogers Taylor, ed., *The Turner Thesis Concerning the Role of the Frontier in America* (Boston, 1956). Turner's essays may be found in *The Frontier in American History* (New York, 1920) and *The Significance of Sections in American History* (New York, 1932). See also his *Rise of the New West, 1819–1829* (New York, 1906).

The best general introduction to the consensus interpretation (which in a sense is an attack on Parrington, Beard, and Turner) can be found in Louis Hartz, *The Liberal Tradition in America* (New York, 1955), and Daniel J. Boorstin, *The Genius of American Politics* (Chicago, 1953). Both men see a uniform and essentially harmonious tradition in American politics that has made debate and disagreement mere shadow boxing. Some of the implications of the rise of the consensus interpretation are explored in two provocative essays: John Higham, "The Cult of the American Consensus," *Commentary*, XXVII (February, 1959), 93–100; J. Rogers Hollingsworth, "Consensus and Continuity in Recent American Historical Writing," *South Atlantic Quarterly*, LXI (Winter, 1962), 40–50. An article which deals with a group of young historians who reject the consensus position is: Irwin Unger, "The 'New Left' and American History: Some Recent Trends in United States Historiography," *American Historical Review*, LXXVII (July, 1967), 1237–1263.

Many of the younger American historians have adopted a consensus approach, but there are still many followers of Beard, Parrington, and Turner. For a discussion of recent trends in American historiography, including the problem dealt with in this book, see John Higham, ed., *The Reconstruction of American History* (New York, 1962). Several discussions on a theme closely related to the problem of conflict and consensus are brought together by John A. Braeman, Robert H. Bremner, and Everett Walters, eds., *Change and Continuity in Twentieth Century America* (Columbus, Ohio, 1965).

0123456789